D0850204

THE WAFFEN-SS AT WAR

HITLER'S PRAETORIANS 1925–1945

THE WAFFEN-SS AT WAR

HITLER'S PRAETORIANS 1925–1945

TIM RIPLEY

ZENITH
PRESS

This edition published in 2004 by Zenith Press,
an imprint of MBI Publishing Company,
Galtier Plaza, Suite 200, 380 Jackson Street,
St. Paul, MN 55101-3885 USA

The information in this book is true and complete to the
best of our knowledge. All recommendations are made
without any guarantee on the part of the author or
Publisher, who also disclaim any liability incurred in
connection with the use of this data or specific details.

We recognize that some words, model names and
designations, for example, mentioned herein are the
property of the trademark holder. We use them for
identification purposes only. This is not an official
publication.

Zenith Press titles are also available at discounts in bulk
quantity for industrial or sales-promotional use. For details
write to Special Sales Manager at Motorbooks
International Wholesalers & Distributors, Galtier Plaza,
Suite 200, 380 Jackson Street, St. Paul,
MN 55101-3885 USA.

ISBN 0-7603-2068-3

Printed in China

Editorial and design:
The Brown Reference Group plc
8 Chapel Place
Rivington Street
London
EC2A 3DQ
UK
www.brownreference.com

Senior Editor: Peter Darman
Editor: John Davison
Proofreader: Alan Marshall
Picture Researcher: Andrew Webb
Designer: Steve Wilson
Production Director: Alastair Gourlay
Index: Indexing Specialists

Dedication

This book is dedicated to the heroes of the Red Army's
XVIII and XXIX Tank Corps, which first engaged II SS
Panzer Corps at Prokhorovka in the titanic tank battle
on 12 July 1943. For the next two years, brave Soviet
tank crews of these two fine units would be in the
vanguard of driving Hitler's Waffen-SS panzer élite
back into the heart of the Third Reich, so freeing
Europe of Nazi tyranny for good.

Acknowledgments

The author would like to thank the following people
for their help during the researching and writing of
this study: Neil Tweedie, of *The Daily Telegraph*, for
his insights into the Nazi mentality gained during his
attendance at the David Irving libel trial; the records
staff at the Imperial War Museum, London, for their
help with research into German World War II records;
the British Army Staff College, Camberley, for allowing me access to numerous German World War II
records in their possession; Steve Dempster for the
vital task of proofreading the text; Peter Darman of
the Brown Reference Group, for giving me the opportunity to fulfil my long-held ambition to write about
the Eastern Front; Mr McApline, my history teacher at
Forres Academy, for beginning my interest in World
War II history; Micky Brooks and Ceri Hobbs for their
hospitality; and Major Hasse Ressenbro of the Danish
Guard Hussar Regiment for helping me to follow in
Joachim Peiper's footsteps in the Ardennes. Finally, my
wonderful wife Amanda, who boosted my morale at
vital moments during the writing of this book.

Contents

Key to Maps

Military Units – Sizes

XXXXX
Army group/front

XXXX
Army

XXX
Corps

XX
Division

X
Brigade

III
Regiment

II
Battalion

Military Units – Types

Infantry

Armoured/panzer

Panzergrenadier

Parachute

Cavalry

National Colours

German

Soviet

United States

British & Commonwealth

Romanian

French

Italian

Polish

Hungarian

General Military Symbols

Minefield

Airfield

Machine guns

Parachute landing

Army Movements

Attack/advance (in national colours)

Retreat (in national colours)

Frontline (in national colours)

Heavy defence line (in national colours)

Defence line (in national colours)

Geographical Symbols

River

Road

Railroad

Urban area

Town

Capital city

Marsh

Trees

Bridge

Mountains

International border

Introduction

The Schutz Staffel (SS) – Protection Squad – was the physical embodiment of National Socialist ideology. In the Nazi state the SS enforced internal security, racist legislation and the organization of conquered territories after 1939. The Waffen-SS (Armed SS) was initially formed to provide Hitler with an ultra-loyal force for internal security. But it eventually became Germany's second army.

At the height of the Nazi Blitzkrieg across Europe in World War II, the Nordic runes of the SS spread terror and fear among the enemies of Adolf Hitler's Germany. From the west coast of France to the Russian steppes, the SS was in the vanguard of Hitler's effort to create a racially "pure" zone, where all other races would be the slaves of the German people. From the early days of Hitler's self-proclaimed "Thousand Year Reich", the SS had a special place in his plans for global conquest. At first it was seen as the guardian of Hitler's rule within Germany, acting as a brutal enforcer against his political opponents. The SS rapidly took control of many police and internal security organizations in Germany in the 1930s. It also had responsibility for ensuring the racial purity of the German people and, bizarrely, boasted an élite corps of genealogists to trace family "blood-lines" to purge those tainted with non-German blood. Once Hitler's rule was secure in Germany, he began to view his élite group of ultra-loyal henchmen as a key instrument to enforce German rule over Europe. SS men were eventually used to hunt down any resistance to German rule in occupied countries, massacre racial minorities and ensure the loyalty to Hitler of other German military units.

As his plans for this "state within a state" were taking shape in the mid-1930s, Hitler also began to envisage the SS as having an élite combat force to ensure no group in Germany could challenge his rule (the SS provided the guards for the concentration camps, where "state enemies" were incarcerated). This force would eventually be known as the Waffen-SS. Hitler devoted increasing resources on what in effect was the Nazi Party's private army. By the start of World War II in 1939, the SS was able to put a division's worth of troops into the field to fight alongside the soldiers of the German Wehrmacht (armed forces).

As the fortunes of war turned against Germany, Hitler began to lose faith in his "defeatist" generals and their demoralized armies. He turned to the Waffen-SS in the hope that it would keep fighting against impossible odds. By the end of the war more than a million men had been recruited into the Waffen-SS, and over a third of them had been killed in action.

In the aftermath of World War II, the SS as a whole was judged to be a criminal organization by the International Military Tribunal at the Nuremberg war crimes trials. All members of the SS were declared to be war criminals who had participated in war crimes, or in the planning of crimes against humanity. This ruling covered all branches of the huge SS organization, including the Waffen-SS, much to the consternation of its veterans. They claimed to be "simple" soldiers, just doing their duty like other soldiers.

Controversy raged during the 1950s and 1960s as Waffen-SS veteran groups fought high-profile legal battles in the newly founded West Germany to overturn the Nuremberg ruling, and win pension rights for their members. The judgement of Nuremberg could not be overturned, but in the ensuing refighting of history, many of the former enemies of the Waffen-SS appeared to question the old black-and-white assessment of Hitler's élite troops.

A UNIQUE FIGHTING FORCE

While their despicable cause and bloody massacres were universally held in contempt, the combat record of the Waffen-SS was recognized as being unsurpassed. It played a key role in many of the German Blitzkrieg victories in Russia in 1941–42, and then fought determined rearguard actions during the final years of Hitler's empire. It was during the years of defeat that the Waffen-SS earned the respect of its opponents, time and again fighting against overwhelming odds. Kharkov, Kursk, Normandy, Arnhem and the Ardennes are synonymous with the Waffen-SS. In these battles and in scores of other actions in the dying days of Hitler's Reich, the Waffen-SS fought tenaciously to inflict heavy losses on their British, Russian and American opponents. Amid the ruins of the Third Reich, the Waffen-SS men left alive were marched into captivity and history. Some faced trials for war crimes; others fled into exile to escape the victors' justice. The vast majority suffered years of captivity before returning to Germany to rebuild their lives.

What kind of men swore their loyalty to Hitler and all he stood for? The early recruits to the SS in the 1920s were largely disillusioned former soldiers and policemen who fell under the Hitler's spell during his early efforts to form the National Socialist German Workers' Party, or Nazi Party. These men acted as bodyguards and drivers to Hitler and other Nazi leaders in the days after the disastrous Beer Hall Putsch, a coup d'etat attempt in Munich in 1923.

After Hitler rose to ultimate power in Germany in 1933, the SS began to attract a very different type of recruit. Ambitious young men from all over Germany saw the SS as a way to secure access to future careers at the centre of their country's government as it appeared to enter an exciting new phase. These men were also attracted to the glamour of the SS, which was at the heart of Nazi propaganda during the 1930s.

As the SS expanded and the Waffen-SS was born, the members of the new force were put through intensive military training to prepare them for the challenges to come when Hitler launched them on the offensive. The intensity of their training and Nazi ideological indoctrination made these men self-confident to the point of arrogance. Nazi propaganda told them that they were "super-human" Germans who were destined to rule over lesser races. Once it began its war of conquest in 1939, the prejudices of the Waffen-SS were reinforced as army after army collapsed in the face of the German Blitzkrieg.

At this early stage of the war, the small Waffen-SS units were led by a group of determined and charismatic officers who moulded them into an élite force. Men like "Sepp" Dietrich, Paul Hausser, Joachim Peiper and Kurt Meyer would win their spurs in these Blitzkrieg battles, and then go on to lead the Waffen-SS in the desperate final battles of the war. These men became infamous as they led the Waffen-SS through battles in France, the Balkans and Russia. Often their leadership was the only thing that held their units together in circumstances that would have forced other units to collapse. They led by example rather than brutal discipline. When the fighting was at its worst, they would be leading from the front, rather than skulking in the safety of a headquarters far to the rear.

MASTERS OF MECHANIZED WARFARE

When the Waffen-SS found itself locked into the bloody war of survival on the Eastern Front from late 1941, Hitler's élite was soon fighting for its life. No mercy was shown by either side. The Waffen-SS now showed that it was more than just a glorified murder squad. Its commanders and soldiers showed they could master the art of mechanized warfare, and scored a number of highly impressive victories in tank battles against overwhelming odds. In these defensive battles, the early arrogance of the Waffen-SS was replaced by grim determination and hard, skilful soldiering. Time and again, Waffen-SS units were defeated in battle but quickly regrouped and struck back when other armies would have given up the fight.

During the Blitzkrieg years, the mass of the Waffen-SS was still inspired by Nazi ideology to win "living space" for the German people. As the war degenerated into a bloody battle of attrition, less idealistic motives came to the fore as the hard-core Waffen-SS officers found themselves being dispatched into battle repeatedly against impossible odds. Casualties took their toll, and the time to recuperate between campaigns became shorter. At this time the loyalty from shared experiences and battles came to the fore, as Waffen-SS men fought increasingly for the sake of their comrades rather than for their Führer. Senior Waffen-SS officers also began to take common cause with their Wehrmacht colleagues and question Hitler's orders to fight to the last man.

Nazi ideology saw non-Aryan races as inferior to Germans and consigned Europe's Slavs and Jews to servitude or extermination. In the conquered countries of Western Europe, Hitler and his SS supremo, Heinrich Himmler, were keen to recruit non-German Aryans to their cause. Puppet pro-Nazi parties were used to help rule in occupied Norway, Denmark, Holland and France. After the invasion of Russia in the summer of 1941, the need for manpower to feed the Eastern Front led Himmler to begin setting up so-called foreign legions in the Waffen-SS. These were manned by opportunists, adventurers and Nazi fellow travellers, who often did not know what they had let themselves in for.

High casualties in battles with the Red Army forced Himmler to look to Eastern Europe to fill the ranks of the Waffen-SS. Germany was running out of manpower, and the number of Western Europeans volunteering to serve in the Waffen-SS was also dwindling. Increasingly, conscripts and unemployed Luftwaffe ground staff and Kriegsmarine sailors were also finding themselves drafted into the Waffen-SS to replace those killed or wounded in battle. They were far from being highly motivated.

At first, so-called Volksdeutsche (ethnic Germans) living outside Germany were called upon to serve their new homeland, but these manpower pools were soon bled dry. In an act of desperation, Himmler then turned to Muslims from Yugoslavia and Albania, Catholic Ukrainians and citizens of the Baltic states to serve in the Waffen-SS, turning Nazi racial theory on its head. The final irony was the recruitment of former Soviet soldiers from German prison camps into the Waffen-SS.

Foreign recruits eventually numbered hundreds of thousands and could, in the final year of the war, be found in the ranks of even the supposedly élite Waffen-SS panzer divisions. The recruits from Western Europe often fought well and were fully integrated with mainstream Waffen-SS units. Eastern volunteer units were less effective, and they were generally relegated to anti-partisan or garrison roles. They developed notorious reputations for massacres and mistreatment of civilians in general. In addition, by using the cover of anti-partisan operations as an excuse, they could continue age-old ethnic feuds.

This book aims to provide an overview of the formation, ideology and campaigns of the Waffen-SS. It will look at the place of the Waffen-SS in the wider SS organization, and its relationship with Hitler and other senior Nazi leaders. The selection and training of the early Waffen-SS units will be examined, as well as their role in the first Blitzkrieg victories in Poland and France. The bloody battles that followed the move eastwards in June 1941 will then be detailed. The key role of the Waffen-SS in the swirling tank battles that determined the course of the war on the Eastern Front is covered in great detail.

Efforts by the Waffen-SS to counter the US and British landings in Normandy and their advance across France in 1944 will then be considered, as will the fate of the Waffen-SS in the final cataclysmic battles in the spring of 1945 as Hitler's Reich collapsed. Finally, the legacy of the Waffen-SS will be assessed, looking at its complicity in Nazi atrocities and its contribution to Germany's defeat.

Part I

Origins

Bodyguards for Hitler

In the 1920s Adolf Hitler, the leader of the right-wing National Socialist German Workers' Party, formed a small bodyguard called the Schutz Staffel (SS) – Protection Squad. Always small and select, the SS became the guardian of a National Socialist Germany following Hitler's accession to power in 1933. Thereafter it grew in both size and power to become a state within a state.

Adolf Hitler, Nazi dictator of Germany (in vehicle), with Reichsführer-SS Heinrich Himmler (left) on the occasion of the Führer's birthday, 20 April 1939. They are viewing a march-past of the *Leibstandarte*.

The personal oath taken by each SS man encapsulated the fact that, from the moment he entered the service of Hitler, he owed his loyalty to the Führer alone and to no one else. How Hitler built up his personal guard from a small team of beer-hall bodyguards into a force of several hundred thousand in the final year of World War II is a remarkable story.

"I swear to you, Adolf Hitler, as Führer and Reich Chancellor, loyalty and bravery. I vow to you and those you have named to command me, obedience unto death. So help me God."

Germany in the aftermath of World War I was gripped by anarchy and political violence. The old political order of the kaiser, Wilhelm II, and the Prussian royal family was replaced by the democratic Weimar Republic. On the streets, ultra-right-wing Freikorps (mainly composed of former officers, demobilized soldiers and fanatical nationalists) battled communists. Polish troops were skirmishing with German militia units on the country's eastern borders, while British, French and American troops occupied the Rhineland. The country's economy

was desperately trying to adjust from war to peace. At the same time, under the terms of the controversial Versailles Treaty, Germany had to pay huge reparations to the countries that had been the "victims" of its "aggression" during the war. Unemployment was rife as hyper-inflation destroyed many companies and demobilized soldiers found they had no jobs to return to. The treaty also forced Germany's military to be reduced to no more than 100,000 professional soldiers, and forbade it from having an air force, tanks, submarines and heavy battleships.

In this climate of chaos, radical political parties proliferated as the German people sought a saviour to give them hope that their country had a future, or at least to provide answers to their problems. In the eyes of many, the new Weimar Republic lacked legitimacy, and was seen as little more than a foreign-imposed government of "traitors". Politics in post-World War I Germany was a brutal and unforgiving business. On the radical fringes it had more in common with urban warfare than rational debate. Every extreme right- and left-wing party seemed to employ a private army of heavily armed ex-soldiers, who were used to break up rivals' meetings or attempt

Members of the Stosstrupp Adolf Hitler, formed in Munich, whose job was to protect the Führer's life. The unit's founder, Julius Schreck, is the man in the centre with a moustache.

to overthrow local governments not to their liking. Such groups included the so-called Stahlhelm (Steel Helmet), a nationalist ex-servicemen's association formed in 1918. On the left, the Red Front Fighters' Association was the army of the communists. The police and the much reduced army, the Reichswehr (Defensive Land Forces), were hard pressed to maintain order, and street battles were common in most major German cities during the early 1920s.

In the southern city of Munich an obscure demobilized Austrian corporal, Adolf Hitler, was rising fast through the ranks of the ultra-right-wing National Socialist German Workers' Party, or Nazi Party. Through the sheer force of his personality, Hitler transformed the party from a ramshackle group of disgruntled ex-soldiers, initially dubbed the Deutsche Arbeiterpartei (German Workers' Party), into a tightly organized force that attracted increasing support not only in Bavaria but in many other German cities (the party had 3000 members in January 1921). Hitler's philosophy appealed

across the political spectrum from out-of-work soldiers to dispossessed small businessmen, disgruntled army officers and government officials whose pensions and savings had been eroded. He preached that Germany had to be great again and that the "collaborators" of the Weimar Republic needed to be overthrown to allow that to happen. Once the shackles of the Versailles Treaty were gone, then Germany and her people would be prosperous and free again, or so Hitler said.

Hitler saw politics as a struggle in which only the fittest would survive. Ultimately, he believed that the struggle had to involve destroying Germany's true enemies, the Jews and Slav communists, who were trying to prevent its people achieving their destiny. In Hitler's world view, the Jews and Slavs had conspired against Germany during World War I, and fermented revolution at home just as the army was about to achieve victory on the battlefield. This was the "stabbed in the back" myth that had a great resonance with the confused and dispirited German public at the time.

In his twisted world, Hitler had no qualms about the methods to be used to achieve supreme power in Germany. In his Darwinian view, street fighting and other forms of political violence were just an extension of the struggle for the German people's survival. Given the desperate conditions in Germany during the early 1920s, it was not surprising that such views attracted support from ordinary people who had little idea of what their future would hold. Hope was a precious commodity in 1920s Germany, and Hitler seemed to offer it.

Bavarian politics of the early 1920s were a particularly violent sub-genre of the German political scene, and revolved around meetings in Munich's famous beer halls. Fuelled by strong beer and fiery rhetoric, bloody street fights between rival groups were common. The Nazi Party was in thick of this maelstrom.

To take the fight to his communist rivals, in 1921 Hitler organized a party militia dubbed the Sturmabteilung (Storm Detachment) or SA, under a former army captain, Ernst Röhm. Soon nicknamed the Brown Shirts because of their distinctive uniforms, the SA stormtroopers were in the thick of riots and other trouble. Hitler also moved to set up a new ultra-loyal paramilitary group that would have the job of protecting him and other senior Nazi leaders. As many SA members were former Freikorps, he needed men who would give him unquestioning loyalty. In March 1923, he set up the Stabswache (Headquarters Guard), which initially consisted of just two men. Within weeks the expanded group was reorganized as the Stosstrupp (Shock Troop) Adolf Hitler. The group's distinctive black uniforms soon became a feature of Nazi Party meetings, and members were always ready to do their master's bidding. At this point Hitler's bodyguards never numbered more than a few dozen men.

By early November 1923, Hitler was convinced that the Weimar Republic was on the verge of collapse, and

A Nazi Party rally in 1931. The figure on the left of centre with the scar on his left cheek is SA chief Ernst Röhm. Standing on his right in the black kepi is Heinrich Himmler.

HEINRICH HIMMLER

Heinrich Himmler was born in 1900 in Landshut, Bavaria. He became involved in nationalist politics early in life, joining the Nazi Party and taking part in the 1923 Beer Hall Putsch. Becoming Reichsführer-SS in 1929 (the same year he became a poultry farmer), he transformed the tiny SS (300 in 1929) into a large organization (52,000 by 1933). When Hitler became chancellor in 1933, Himmler seized control of the police apparatus of the German state and further expanded the role of the SS. The SS absorbed the Gestapo secret police and used it alongside its own intelligence unit, the SD. He also organized the concentration camps, and in turn created the SS-Totenkopfverbände (SS Death's Head Units) to run them. Himmler was, above all, an ambitious bureaucrat who was obsessed with maintaining the racial purity of the German race. To him it was thus logical to organize the Final Solution of the "Jewish problem". His Einsatzgruppen massacred hundreds of thousands of Jews in Russia, and his death camps murdered millions more. Named Minister of the Interior in 1943, and put in charge of the German armies facing the Allies in 1944, he died by committing suicide after capture on 22 May 1945.

he declared that the Nazi Party was to lead a "march on Berlin" to overthrow Germany's government of "Jewish-Marxist traitors". The first stage of the Nazi revolution would take place in Munich, where Hitler and the SA planned to depose the Bavarian state government and win over local army units to their cause. After a rabble-rousing speech in a beer hall from their leader, Hitler's supporters spread out through the city with the intention of seizing key buildings. This resulted in the coup d'etat attempt being dubbed the Beer Hall Putsch. The small Stosstrupp Adolf Hitler was given the task of ransacking the offices of the social-democratic *Munich Post* newspaper, as Hitler and the main column of Nazis headed for the Bavarian War Ministry building. Unfortunately for Hitler, he had misjudged the mood of the country, which was now starting to recover from the post-war chaos. The army soldiers outside the ministry stood their ground and opened fire on the Nazi plotters. Some 16 Nazis were killed in the confusion, and Hitler dislocated his shoulder as he dived for cover. The putsch ended in fiasco. Hitler and several other plotters were arrested.

During the 13 months he spent in Landsberg prison (he was convicted of conspiracy to commit treason and given a five-year sentence), Hitler's bodyguard was disbanded. The period of imprisonment did nothing to dampen Hitler's quest for power; rather, he emerged from jail with a long-term plan to achieve his aims. Germany was now a more prosperous and stable place, so Hitler's apocalyptic vision of future struggles had to be tempered. He now talked about using legal methods to gain power, and tried to portray himself as a "normal" constitutional politician.

Hitler was still convinced that his opponents, both within and outside the Nazi Party, would try to kill him if they had the opportunity. On his release from prison he

moved quickly to re-establish his bodyguard. In April 1925 only eight men were in the group that was soon renamed the Schutz Staffel, or Protection Squad. This title was quickly abbreviated to SS, creating the infamous name and, because of their distinctive black uniforms, they were soon nicknamed the Black Guard or Black Order. Their uniforms were adorned with the letters SS, stylized as distinctive Nordic runes.

For the next four years the SS was a small, élite group of bodyguards that travelled with Hitler wherever he went. They were initially volunteers who did their security work in the evenings or at weekends. Only a small number of the 300 or so SS men were full-time on the Nazi Party payroll. As Hitler moved to establish the Nazi Party as a national body outside of his Bavarian power base, the SS was expanded and small detachments were set up in every major German city to protect local leaders and party meetings. The SS was deliberately kept small so its total loyalty to Hitler could be assured. Already, Hitler was growing suspicious of Röhm and the SA because their "hot-headed" behaviour was threatening his attempts to re-brand the Nazi Party as a "respectable" political force (Röhm saw the SA as the nucleus of a revolutionary army).

In January 1929 Hitler appointed a chicken farmer, Heinrich Himmler, as head of the SS with the brief to build it up as a force to rival the SA. Even though the SS was nominally part of Röhm's force, Himmler was totally loyal to Hitler and threw himself into expanding his new fiefdom. Over the next four years he expanded the SS to some 52,000 men, which not only included bodyguards but also a covert secret intelligence organization called the Sicherheitsdienst (Security Service, or SD). Loyalty to Hitler was at the core of the SS ethos. The expanded SS organization was essentially a shadow internal security apparatus that would help the Nazis gain and keep power in Germany.

Events across the Atlantic soon intervened to change the fortunes of Hitler and his Nazi Party. The Wall Street stock market crash of October and November 1929 rapidly sent ripples of economic crisis around the world. Germany's fragile recovery was stopped in its tracks. Millions were soon unemployed, and the value of Germany's currency went through the floor (there were 1.6 million unemployed in October 1929; by February 1932 this figure had increased to 6.12 million). The Great Depression gave Hitler the chance he was looking for, and again he portrayed himself as Germany's new messiah. From having only 12 seats in the Reichstag, the German parliament, in 1928, the Nazis managed to win 107 seats and six million votes in the 1930 election.

Over the next three years, as Germany's economic crisis worsened, the Nazi Party's vote increased, as did the votes going to the communists. Squeezed from left and right, the centre parties found themselves unable to form governments without the support of either of the political extremes. Governments lasted only a few months, preventing the implementation of the necessary measures to restore the economy. Germany's democracy was locked into a spiral of economic and political decline.

HITLER BECOMES CHANCELLOR

By the middle of 1932, the Nazis were the largest party in the Reichstag. Even though they did not have a majority of seats to allow them to form a government, they held the balance of power and Hitler was now a key power broker. For six months Germany was in political turmoil as the ageing President Paul von Hindenburg tried to form a government that excluded Hitler, despised by the former field marshal because of his lowly Austrian birth.

In January 1933, Hindenburg bowed to the inevitable and appointed Hitler as Germany's chancellor, as leader of a coalition with other right-wing parties representing big business interests. Over the next year, Hitler moved systematically to consolidate his grip on power and eventually appointed himself Germany's Führer (Leader) with unlimited dictatorial powers. The SS played a key role in this move to dictatorship.

Once in control of the levers of political power, Hitler moved to put his loyal lieutenants into key positions of influence. Himmler was made police chief in Munich. The SS was also authorized to act as an official police unit, alongside established state police forces. Crucially, money from the Interior Ministry budget was diverted to pay for it. Now many of the part-time SS men could become full-time employees of the German state. SS units around the country were established on a permanent basis with battalions, or political readiness squads, being set up in every major city for so-called "heavy police tasks". These were, in effect, paramilitary squads which owed their loyalty directly to Hitler, even though they remained nominally under Röhm's control. The SA organization by the end of 1933 had mushroomed to three million men, and Hitler was looking for ways to bring it under his control.

A crucial development was the setting up in Berlin in March 1933 of a new, élite grouping within the SS under the command of one of Hitler's old henchmen from Munich. Josef "Sepp" Dietrich was an old party crony of Hitler, whom he trusted implicitly (he had been appointed commander of Hitler's bodyguard in 1928). The new group was initially only 120 men strong and was dubbed the SS Stabswache Berlin. Its job was to guard Hitler and his official residence in the Reich Chancellery. Two months later it was renamed SS Sonderkommando (Special Commando) Zossen, but this was a short-lived title. In September 1933 it became the SS Leibstandarte Adolf Hitler (SS Bodyguard Regiment Adolf Hitler) and in November that year members of this new "life guard" swore an oath of loyalty unto death to their new Führer. Under the leadership of Dietrich, the Leibstandarte would later rise to be Germany's premier armoured division. However, in its early days the unit would gain infamy for its role in one of Hitler's first extra-legal acts as he moved to establish his dictatorship.

NIGHT OF THE LONG KNIVES

By June 1934 Hitler had outwitted most political opponents, banned all parties except for the Nazis and placed his supporters in key positions in the German Government (Reichstag Fire Decree, February 1933 – civil liberties suspended; Enabling Law, March 1933 – established Hitler's dictatorship; May 1933 – destruction of trade unions and arrest of labour leaders). The SA remained the last bastion of potential opposition to Hitler, and he was soon to neutralize this threat. He had decided to remove the socialist elements from the party.

He carefully concocted a bogus coup plot involving Röhm and other SA leaders. The "plotters" were then ordered to be placed under arrest. The Leibstandarte and SS units provided the force for the operation. Hitler himself led the raid in Munich that caught Röhm and several of his key lieutenants. "Sepp" Dietrich then oversaw their execution in Stadelheim prison by a Leibstandarte firing squad. Röhm was shot by a rising SS star, Theodor Eicke, the inspector of concentration

Right: The SS organization included the concentration camp guards, the so-called "Totenkopfverbände". These are some of the guards at Dachau photographed in May 1933. Such men would later fill the ranks of the *Totenkopf* Division.

Below: Reinhard Heydrich, head of the SD and the very epitome of the Nazi racial ideal: tall, blonde and athletic. At his funeral in June 1942 Hitler called him "the man with the iron heart". This was certainly true, as Heydrich was the organizer of the mass murder of European Jews.

camps, after he refused to commit suicide. In Berlin, other SS units arrested some 150 SA leaders. They were then shot four at a time by a *Leibstandarte* firing squad in Berlin's Lichterfelde barracks.

The total number of people killed in the so-called "Blood Purge" or "Night of the Long Knives" is still unclear, but it probably ran to nearly 200. Most were SA cronies of Röhm, but some were leading political opponents of Hitler, such as General Kurt von Schleicher, the last chancellor of the Weimar Republic. The audacious nature of the killings and the lack of response from Hindenburg confirmed Hitler's place as the supreme political power in Germany. Within weeks the president was dead and Hitler assumed the powers of his office, declaring himself to be the German Führer. He then forced army officers to take an oath of loyalty to himself rather than to the German constitution.

The loyalty of the SS during the Blood Purge was soon rewarded by Hitler removing it from control of the SA. Himmler's SS became an independent organization. During the next two years, Himmler proved himself an archetypal Nazi baron, expanding his organization and personal power. Hitler made great efforts to keep his subordinates squabbling among themselves by setting up rival power structures that ensured they had to come to him to broker disputes. So, even though Himmler was nominally boss of the SS, it was in turn broken up into competing fiefdoms.

The first major reorganization of the SS occurred in March 1935 when Hitler formally announced the setting up of the first armed SS units, although the term Waffen-SS (Waffen means "armed") would not come into widespread usage until early 1940. The description of these units had to be carefully packaged, so as not to upset the army generals who a year earlier had been promised that the Wehrmacht would be Germany's "sole arms bearer" in return for their support during the Blood Purge against the SA. These armed SS units were to be

Like many ex-World War I soldiers, Kurt Daluege was involved in right-wing politics after the war. He joined the Nazi Party's SA and then transferred to the SS.

used for "special internal tasks allotted by the Führer". The SS was described as "a militarized force ready for police action within the Reich boundaries when dissident forces are too strong for the normal security services".

The armed SS was initially termed the SS-Verfügungstruppe or SS-VT. These so-called Special Disposal Troops included all the old heavy police units that were now grouped into three regiments, or standarten. In Berlin an expanded *Leibstandarte* formed the core of one of these new regiments. While the units in Munich became the *Deutschland* Regiment in October 1933, those in Hamburg were formed into the *Germania* Regiment in August 1934. These were the three original regiments of the armed SS that would form the nucleus of the force's armoured divisions during the war years.

Himmler was keen to provide the new SS-VT with the best training and weapons, so he persuaded a number of ambitious army officers to transfer to the new force to provide a core of professional officers. The most famous of these was Paul Hausser, who was appointed the commander of the SS-VT. In 1936 he was given a headquarters staff, dubbed the SS-VT Inspectorate, to coordinate the growth of the military arm of the SS. Hausser was also in charge of the first SS officer cadet, or junker, school at Bad Tölz, which was set up in 1935 to train a new type of SS officer. Bad Tölz and a second Junkerschule at Braunschweig turned out a generation of aggressive officers that would rise to command the SS armoured divisions during World War II.

At the same time as the SS-VT was set up, Himmler also established a rival branch eventually dubbed the SS-Totenkopfverbände (SS-TV), or Death's Head Units. This was the responsibility of the head of the concentration camp guard force, Eicke, who set up the first of these infamous camps at Dachau, outside Munich, in 1933. By early 1938, in addition to a string of prison camps around Germany holding thousands of inmates in poor conditions, the SS-TV mustered three regiments of fully motorized troops equipped with machine guns and other light weapons. The *Oberbayern* Regiment was based at Dachau in Bavaria, the *Brandenberg* Regiment operated from Oranienberg concentration camp outside Berlin, and the *Thüringen* Regiment ran the Buchenwald camp near Weimar. It was intended that they would reinforce the SS-VT troops in times of crisis, but also allowed Himmler and Hitler to play off rival SS officers against

each other. Eicke was a brutal thug who showed no pity towards the inmates of his camps. He indoctrinated his men to believe they were responsible for imprisoning Germany's most dangerous enemies, and instructed them to show no mercy. The most minor infringements of his camp rules were to be dealt with by severe beatings and other forms of torture.

This period also saw Himmler move to spread the tentacles of the SS into every sphere of German life. In June 1936, Hitler designated Himmler as head of the unified German police system, as well as head, or Reichsführer, of the SS and chief of the secret police – the infamous Gehieme Staatspolizei, or Gestapo. In this capacity the SS became responsible for all the apparatus of the Nazi police state. Its members were now the masters of terror in Hitler's Germany. By 1939 all the security police organizations of Hitler's Third Reich were brought under the control of Himmler's loyal henchman, Reinhard Heydrich, via the Reichssicherheitshauptamt (RHSA), or Reich Central Security Office. This included the SD, the Gestapo, the ordinary criminal police

(Kriminalpolizei, or Kripo) and security police (Sicherheitspolizei, or Sipo). Heydrich epitomized the Nazi police state. He was ambitious, ruthless and totally loyal to Hitler.

As well as its armed and security branches, the SS also eventually boasted unusual organizations such as the SS marriage bureau, the Rasse-und Siedlungs-hauptamt (Central Office for Race and Resettlement, or RuSHA), which first had the responsibility of confirming the racial purity of the brides of SS men. There was also the Volksdeutsche Mittelstelle (German Racial Assistance Office, or VOMI), which was charged with protecting the well-being of ethnic Germans living outside the borders of the Reich. These groups then helped in the establishment of the Reichskommissariat für die Festigung des Deutschen Volkstums (Reich Office for the Consolidation of the German Nationhood, or RKFDV), which was nominally responsible for the movement of ethnic Germans back into Reich territory, but was really a cover for the deportation and eventual exter-mination of Jews, Slavs and other groups considered *untermenschen* (sub-humans) by Hitler. It finally spawned the SS Wirtschafts-und Verwaltungshauptamt (Economic and Administrative Central Office, or WVHA), which was in charge of the concentration camp system and the "Final Solution" of the Jewish problem (the lead-ers of these organizations developed bland euphemisms for the mass murder of most of Europe's Jews).

By the end of the 1930s, the SS organization had ballooned to some 200,000 men, of whom the vast majority were in its police, security and concentration camp guard units rather than in the SS-VT. During this period the SS became central to Hitler's "folk myth", with senior figures in the organization being portrayed as Nordic gods in Nazi propaganda. The racial purity of SS recruits was given great prominence, and Hitler tried to build on this as a way to indoctrinate the German people with his theories of racial superiority. The SS also had its own rank system that gave members prestige and power over ordinary mortals in the army, the Nazi Party and in civilian branches of government.

EXPANSION OF THE SS

The growth of the armed SS during the later years of the 1930s was one of slow evolution. Much of the ground work for the development of the armed SS was under-taken in great secrecy to allow the opposition of the army High Command to be by-passed or ignored. Hitler was still unwilling to stage an open confrontation with the army's generals, and preferred to dispose of problematic commanders in a series of "dirty tricks" operations to discredit individuals who opposed him. The early devel-opment of the armed SS were therefore characterized by a series of deals with the army High Command.

THE TOTENKOPFVERBÄNDE

In May 1935, joining the armed SS was classified as mili-tary service and it exempted the SS recruit from being conscripted into the army. At the same time, however, the army retained control of the flow of new manpower into the SS-VT, and during most of the 1930s that effectively limited it to a total of under 10,000 men. The army also retained control of military aspects of SS training, and had the right to inspect SS-VT units. To get round these restric-tions, Himmler allowed the Totenkopfverbände to mushroom into a force of some 25,000 men by 1939. He groomed the concentration camp guards to become almost a "ghost" reserve for the SS-VT, and stretched its role as a force for "special tasks of a police nature" to the limit. Because it had no formal military role, the army could not claim any right to interfere in its affairs. Totenkopf-verbände units were fully motorized, had heavy machine guns and other light weapons. Plans were drawn up so SS police reservists aged over 45 could be quickly mobilized to guard the concentration camps in order to release the Totenkopfverbände motorized regiments for combat duties. While on paper Eicke's private army seemed a powerful and heavily armed force, in reality it did not undertake intense combat training and was nowhere near the quality of the mainstream armed units of the SS-VT. During the invasion of Poland and France, for example, its lack of military skills would become very apparent.

Over the next three years a tug-of-war took place as the army tried to strangle the SS-VT at birth. The effort was to little avail, as the growth of the élite force had the personal backing of Hitler. In 1938 he issued instructions codifying the role of the SS-VT. It was to be a permanent armed force at his disposal and a formation of the Nazi Party "recruited and trained in ideological and political matters by the Reichsführer-SS" in accordance with directives given by Hitler. In case of an emergency, it was to be used by the commander-in-chief of the army within the framework of the army, subject to military law and instruction. Politically, though, the armed SS was to remain part of the Nazi Party, even if in the field army commanders had operational control.

Ultimately, Hitler envisaged the armed SS as being an "armed state police" that was to "enforce the authority of the Reich in the interior of the country". He declared that this "duty can only be carried out by a state police containing within its ranks men of the best German blood and identified unquestionably with the ideology upon

which the Greater German Reich is founded. Only a formation constituted upon these lines will be able to resist subversive influences in times of crisis". Hitler further stated that "in order to ensure that the quality of the men in the Waffen-SS always remains high, the number of units must remain limited ... and should, in general, not exceed five to ten percent of the peacetime strength of the army".

After the setting up of the SS-VT units, a frantic effort began to train the new formations in military skills. While they were already drilled in the use of small arms, they were lacking in expertise in military tactics. Hitler insisted that the new force be fully motorized in line with his view that his élite troops had to have the best equipment available.

To speed up the process of training, each armed SS unit was twinned with a local army unit to allow it to share experience and conduct joint training. Relations between the two organizations were frosty at first, but improved as armed SS and army units participated in joint operations during the reoccupation of the Rhineland in 1936 and the union with Austria in 1938.

German troops reoccupy the Rhineland on 7 March 1936. Hitler remarked afterwards: "If the French had marched into the Rhineland we would have had to withdraw."

The armed SS, however, retained control over the selection of its recruits, their ideological training and their transformation into true Aryan warriors, soldiers who would be the vanguard of National Socialism. Hitler saw his SS troops as Aryan "supermen", who would lead the racial struggle with the *untermenschen*. "To judge morality properly, it must be replaced by two concepts borrowed from zoology: the taming of a beast and the breeding of a species", wrote Hitler. "The SS man must be hard, unemotional, fiercely loyal. The SS man's basic attitude must be that of a fighter for fighting's sake; he must be unquestionably obedient and become emotionally hard; he must have contempt for all 'racial inferiors' and for those who do not belong to the order; he must feel the strongest bonds of comradeship with those who do belong, particularly his fellow soldiers, and he must think nothing impossible."

Waffen-SS recruits receive instruction in Nazi ideology. Such indoctrination ensured that the members of the SS viewed themselves as the vanguard of a National Socialist army.

unthinkable, gentlemen, that anyone should report to his superior, 'I can not arrange this or that' or 'I can not do it with so few people' or 'my battalion is not trained' or 'I feel myself incapable'. Gentleman, that kind of reaction is simply not permitted."

SS TRAINING

To mould these supermen, the armed SS training regime emphasized physical toughness and moral supremacy over all enemies. Even before recruits were allowed to begin training they had to pass rigorous racial and physical selection. Himmler insisted that potential SS soldiers had to be aged between 17 and 22, be at least 1.8m (5.9ft) tall and be of the highest physical fitness. Every SS man had to be of a well-proportioned build, with no disproportion between the lower leg and thigh, or between the legs and body, to allow an exceptional load to be carried on long marches. For many years even recruits with fillings in their teeth were rejected. Recruits also had to display an Aryan appearance, with Himmler saying: "The point is that in his attitude to discipline the man should not behave like an underling, that his gait, his hands, everything should correspond to the ideal which we set ourselves."

The Aryan recruit also had to show no traces of Jewish or other *untermenschen* blood in his ancestry, in the case of ordinary soldiers back to 1800, and to 1750 for officers. Those with "undesirable" blood were refused entry, and if racial impurities came to light during his service an SS man could be summarily dismissed. The future brides of SS men were also subjected to the same level of racial profiling to ensure any offspring were "pure" Aryans.

With the strength of the armed SS limited by the army, these restrictions meant that it was very hard to join the armed force of the Nazi Party. However, such was the mystique built up around the armed SS that every place was over-subscribed, helping to build its image as an élite force. Unlike army conscripts, ordinary enlisted SS men had to serve a minimum of 4 years, noncommissioned officers 12 years and officers 25 years.

Senior armed SS commanders wanted their men to be "supple, adaptable soldiers, athletic of bearing, capable of more than average endurance on the march and in combat", and to be "as much at home on the battlefield as on the athletic field". Recruits were roused from their

Loyalty to Hitler was at the heart of the SS code, with the force having the motto "Loyalty is my Honour". *Leibstandarte* chief Dietrich told new SS recruits: "We ask for and give complete loyalty to the Führer and those he has set above us. To you recruits I say even the smallest wish expressed by one of your noncommissioned officers must be interpreted as an order from the Führer."

"Obedience must be unconditional", said an SS manual. "It corresponds to the conviction that National Socialist ideology must reign supreme ... every SS man, therefore, is prepared to carry out unhesitatingly any order issued by the Führer or a superior, regardless of the sacrifice involved." Himmler considered that his SS men were unstoppable. He told them, "I must repeat – the word 'impossible' must never be heard in the SS. It is

beds at 06:00 hours each morning. They were then subjected to extensive physical training to toughen them up so that eventually they could run 3km (1.86 miles) in 20 minutes wearing full combat kit. Extra physical training was put on the schedule during bad weather to "harden" up the recruits. Later in the morning, recruits underwent training with their weapons on firing ranges. Afternoons were spent doing sports and athletics to help build up recruits' stamina and team spirit. Military skills had a high priority, so drill and parades were a low priority during the training of SS recruits, except for potential *Leibstandarte* men who had to parade in public in Berlin. The final ingredient of SS training was ideological indoctrination to ensure that recruits were fully prepared to be foot soldiers in the coming war for racial supremacy against the *untermenschen*. As training progressed, recruits underwent increasingly sophisticated training, including fire-and-manoeuvre training with live ammunition to teach them how to assault enemy strongpoints using the aggressive "stormtrooper" tactics perfected in the later years of World War I.

While the early armed SS units were predominantly infantry, by the late 1930s the first specialist armoured car, motorcycle, artillery, engineer and communications units started to be formed. The SS began to create its own training schools to turn out these specialist soldiers to a high level of skill. Many of the instructors were former army specialists who had been attracted to the armed SS. Next, the SS formed its own junior noncommissioned officer school at Lauenburg to train its troops to command small groups of men in combat situations. During the war the Waffen-SS established an artillery school at Glau and a panzergrenadier school at Keinschlag.

The SS put great emphasis on the selection and training of its officers. Although the first generation of senior SS men, such as Dietrich and Eicke, were old hands from the Nazi Party's street-fighting days, it was recognized that to turn the armed SS into an élite fighting force a more professional officer corps was needed. The recruitment of professional staff officers, such as Hausser, to

Waffen-SS officer recruits perform drill at the school at Bad Tölz. All potential officers had to serve two years in the ranks before proceeding to officer training.

set up the SS-VT Inspectorate helped improve the quality of the armed SS's higher echelons. There was still, however, a big skills gap at the junior and middle-ranking level. Only SS men who had served two years in the ranks were accepted for officer training. This meant they were already highly trained before they attended either of the Junkerschule at Bad Tölz or Braunschweig.

Potential SS officers were put through an even more rigorous regime, which included far more extensive use of live ammunition in training than for ordinary SS recruits. The results were impressive, the training turned out highly aggressive and self-confident young officers who soon proved themselves in the early Blitzkrieg campaigns of the war. By the end of 1937, the officer training system was running at high gear, turning out 400 officers a year. Before these men could rise through the ranks, the middle- and higher-level command positions in SS units had to be filled by many of the old-guard SS men. This led to accusations that SS officers were not on a par with their Wehrmacht counterparts. Such accusations would continue for many years, until the brutal rigour of combat culled the "dead wood" and allowed the young talent to rise up the ranks.

A key feature of SS officer training was instilling leadership and self-sacrifice. There was none of the social élitism of the army officer corps, which was still dominated by aristocratic families. SS officers were taught to endure the same hardships as their men and to lead by example. There was much talk of the SS being a "brotherhood" in which every member was equal, no matter what his formal rank, and united by shared hardships and loyalty to Hitler. Thus officers and enlisted men often referred to each other by first names. An SS officer was taught to gain his men's trust and respect through demonstrating that he was fitter, a better shot or a superior driver than his men. Once he had proved to them he could do their job, they would respect him as a man and soldier. Then, in the heat of battle, they would follow him come what may.

Within the armed SS there was a unique brand of élitism, which was cultivated by the distinctive character of the early regiments formed during the 1930s. The officers and men of these units often remained together throughout the war. They became close-knit fighting units that learnt their trade together and shared the glory of victory and the privations of defeat. This level of unit cohesion was unsurpassed in the German military during World War II and can account for much of the battlefield success of the Waffen-SS.

The *Leibstandarte* under Dietrich operated largely under its own agenda during the 1930s, even though it was officially part of the SS-VT. Its role as the Führer's bodyguard meant its soldiers spent much of their time in Berlin standing sentry duty outside the Reich Chancellery. They were a law unto themselves because of Dietrich's direct access to the Führer, and this frustrated Hausser's initial attempts to involve the *Leibstandarte* in his efforts to professionalize the armed SS. Hausser was at first only allowed to "attend" *Leibstandarte* parades and had no power to issue regulations or orders to the unit. As the SS-VT became a more professional military organization, the other units started to joke that the *Leibstandarte* were "asphalt soldiers" because all they seemed to do was march up and down in Berlin. These jokes touched a nerve, and Dietrich soon began to draft in more of the new officers from the Junkerschule into his unit, and then began to allow the exchange of company and battalion commanders from other SS units.

JOSEF "SEPP" DIETRICH

Dietrich was born in Bavaria in 1892, and served with the German Army during World War I. Becoming embroiled in right-wing politics after the war (being a member of the Bund Oberland, a paramilitary "Fatherland" organization), he took part in the failed Munich Beer Hall Putsch and joined the Nazi Party in 1928. In June 1932, he was made commander of Hitler's personal bodyguard – the *Leibstandarte* – and in 1934 took a leading role in the purging of the SA. He was awarded the Knight's Cross in 1940 for his actions during the Western Campaign, and Oakleaves were added a year later for action on the Eastern Front. By the war's end, he had won the Swords and Diamonds for the unswerving actions of the forces under his command – he once stated: "Human life matters little to the SS." Ending the war as an SS-Oberstgruppenführer, he surrendered to the Americans, was arrested and charged with complicity in the murder of US POWs in the Ardennes offensive. After serving 10 years of a 25-year sentence, he was released but immediately rearrested for his part in the murder of Ernst Röhm. He served a further 18 months in prison before being released. He died in April 1966 in West Germany.

Above: In the Waffen-SS great emphasis was placed on physical fitness and outdoor activities. Time spent in the field was at the expense of barracks-square drilling.

Right: In the German Army athletics was reduced to spare time; in the Waffen-SS sports were an integral part of the training programme to foster team spirit and fitness levels.

The other units of the SS-VT had their own distinctive traditions and characters, and they all became highly competitive to prove they were better than their rivals. While the *Leibstandarte* were the "aristocrats" of the SS-VT, Hausser's men in the *Germania* and *Deutschland* Regiments liked to boast about their new-found military prowess. There was great rivalry between Dietrich and Hausser. The former stressed his man-management and leadership skills because of his closeness to "his boys"; Hausser liked to portray himself as a skilled tactician and professional staff officer.

The "lowest of the low" in the SS hierarchy were the Totenkopfverbände, who were perceived as little more than over-dressed jail guards by combat-trained SS men. Eicke's guards were always considered outsiders

by the other armed SS men because they had their own training schools and owed their loyalty to the concentration camp boss rather than to Hausser or Dietrich. Even after the *Totenkopf* Division was formally absorbed into the Waffen-SS in 1940, it remained a very different unit, and it was rare for officers from other divisions to serve in its ranks.

If there was great rivalry within the Waffen-SS "brotherhood", it was mild compared with their rivalry with the Wehrmacht. There was a Waffen-SS song that contained the lyrics, "anything the army can do, we can do better". In sports competitions, training exercises and finally on the battlefield, the Waffen-SS tried to outperform their army comrades and show it was fitter and more intelligent. This led to accusations that some SS

Reichsführer-SS Heinrich Himmler during a visit to Dachau concentration camp in May 1936. Such camps housed those whom the Nazi Party demonized: Jews and communists.

officers were foolhardy and wasted their men's lives on operations conceived only out of pride or arrogance. As the Waffen-SS became more battle hardened and experienced in modern combat techniques, such claims became harder to support.

Hitler and his loyal henchman Himmler carefully moulded the armed SS into an élite fighting force in the late 1930s, and the Führer itched to give it a chance to show what it could do. As he manoeuvred Germany towards war, he would soon get his opportunity.

Hitler was determined to break free from the restrictions imposed on Germany by the Versailles Treaty, but he did not want to spark a conflict with his foreign foes until his rearmament programme was beginning to bear fruit. The British and French policy of "appeasement", based on the idea of not provoking Hitler by bowing to the "legitimate" grievances of the German people, only played into Hitler's hands. His first foreign adventure was

launched in March 1936, when German troops were sent to reoccupy the west bank of the Rhine that had been declared a demilitarized zone by Versailles. His general staff warned Hitler that this would provoke a French military response. He told his generals, "if the army is reluctant to lead the way, a suitable spearhead will be provided by the *Leibstandarte*". A company of the élite SS motored down from Berlin and crossed the Rhine ahead of the army troops. The French Army stayed in its barracks, and the *Leibstandarte* men drove into Saarbrucken on Germany's western border to a hero's welcome. Hitler had called the French bluff and got away with it, without even having to fire a shot. In the process the *Leibstandarte* scored a noted coup over its army rivals.

Two years later Hitler was ready to launch his most audacious foreign adventure yet, the seizure of Austria. Austria was the largest independent German-speaking country outside the Reich, and Hitler had long nurtured ambitions to bring it under his control. In the spring of 1938 he set in train a covert operation to seize it, using men of the SD Foreign Intelligence Section under Heydrich's personal direction. He sent his agents to

Vienna to cooperate with local Nazis to generate a crisis. Austria's political leaders tried to deflect Berlin's pressure for their country to be incorporated into Germany by calling a referendum. Hitler was quicker to the draw, and he ordered an invasion before the ballot could be held. Columns of German tanks were sent southwards to Vienna and other Austrian cities. Taking up the rear was a battalion of the *Leibstandarte* that had motored south from Berlin at a few hours' notice. There was no fighting, and the *Leibstandarte* was able to shepherd a grateful Führer into Linz and Vienna, where he was mobbed by happy crowds of Austrians.

While not really being much of a test of the *Leibstandarte*'s fighting skills, the Anschluss, or Union, with Austria proved to be a great test of the organizational and logistical planning skills of senior SS officers. The unit had to move more than 965km (600 miles) in 48 hours as part of a coordinated deployment with army tank divisions. The commander of XVI Army Corps, General Heinz Guderian, reported favourably on the performance of the SS men, which was no small achievement considering that he was the "father of the panzer divisions".

THE SS IN AUSTRIA AND CZECHOSLOVAKIA

The occupation of Austria had an added benefit of increasing the pool of manpower available to the SS. Hausser began to raise a third regiment, *Der Führer*, for his SS-VT in Vienna late in 1938. Eicke was also busy expanding his empire in Austria, forming another Totenkopf regiment, *Ostmark*, under the pretext of guarding the Mauthausen concentration camp that he had established outside Linz.

By the autumn of 1938, Hitler had his sights set on Czechoslovakia, specifically the Sudetenland that contained three million Volksdeutsche (ethnic Germans). Heydrich's covert operatives again stirred up a bogus crisis, involving the ethnic Germans in the Sudetenland. SD agents faked attacks on ethnic German property and planted evidence to blame the Czech Government. Nazi propaganda portrayed the ethnic Germans as the victims of Czech oppression, and Hitler claimed Germany had to go to their rescue. When the British and French Governments refused to back the Czechs, the government in Prague had little option but to cave in to Hitler's demands, and the border regions of its country were

surrendered. Several armed SS and Totenkopf units participated in the invasion. The *Leibstandarte* repeated its undertaking during the Austrian adventure, and acted as a reception party for Hitler when he triumphantly entered Carlsbad in October 1938. The *Germania* and *Deutschland* Regiments also joined in as occupation troops, along with two battalions of Totenkopf soldiers. These later troops were used to assist the SS-controlled Sudeten militia, the Henlein Free Korps, in the rounding up of anti-German civilians. In March 1939, SS police units were at the forefront of the operation to occupy Prague and subjugate the rest of Czechoslovakia. Scores of people were killed as SS squads rounded up opponents of the occupation during the entry of German troops into Prague, which was now declared the capital of the Protectorate of Bohemia and Moravia.

The Czech crisis, however, did generate further moves to boost the strength of the SS because of fears that a general European war was about to break out.

Two members of the *Leibstandarte* outside the Chancellery in Berlin. The *Leibstandarte* maintained a 24-hour guard there, with sentries in full parade dress with fixed bayonets.

SS members carrying "Deutschland Erwache" ("Germany Awake") standards during a pre-war rally. On the eve of World War II Waffen-SS units totalled around 28,000 men.

Hitler passed a decree authorizing service in the Totenkopfverbände to count as military service, and approved it providing combat replacements for units of the SS-VT. Police reservists and SA troopers were also recalled to almost double the SS-VT's strength to some 24,000 men. Members of the SS-VT who were due to complete their service were also diverted to Eicke's force. In the spring of 1939 his men boasted 19,643 carbines and 2269 machine guns.

The other armed SS units were also expanded during this period, with the *Leibstandarte* gaining a fourth infantry battalion, an infantry gun company armed with light 75mm howitzers, an anti-tank company with 37mm cannons, as well as a pioneer platoon of combat engineers and a motorcycle reconnaissance platoon. In the summer of 1939, Hitler's guard force numbered some 3700 men.

Mid-1939 saw Hitler making the final preparations for his next territorial demand, the city of Danzig. The latter had been created a "free city" under the terms of the Treaty of Versailles. In addition, the Polish state had been given a "corridor" of land to the Baltic, which split East Prussia from the rest of Germany.

During this period of tension in Europe, Hitler attended a major exercise by the *Deutschland* Regiment at the Munsterlager training ground. He was so impressed by the simulated assault on a trench position by the SS troops, who made lavish use of live ammunition, that he declared, "only with such soldiers is this sort of thing possible". Within days, Hausser was given the task of forming his SS-VT troops into a combat division, capable of fighting alongside the army during coming campaigns. He was authorized to form the specialist combat units needed to create a division, including an artillery regiment, a motorcycle reconnaissance battalion and a signals or radio communications unit to support the new divisional headquarters. As divisional field commander, Hausser would have less influence over the organizational affairs of the armed SS. Plans were now being developed to expand the combat units of the SS. In late 1940, the term Waffen-SS began to be used as a generic term to represent all SS combat units, although it would be several months until a centralized Waffen-SS command structure would be in place.

Part II

Winning a Reputation

Poland, 1939 – The First Blitzkrieg

The Waffen-SS's part in the 1939 invasion of Poland was small, and did not influence the outcome of the campaign. Nevertheless, the SS units displayed excellent fighting spirit and a knowledge of mechanized warfare, and because they were motorized the army found them useful for rapid deployments. And both Hitler and Himmler were delighted with the performance of the Black Guard.

SS soldiers signal the location of enemy forces to headquarters during the Polish campaign. It was in Poland that SS troops first wore their distinctive disruptive-pattern camouflage smocks.

Hitler's plan for the attack on Poland included many of the features of his moves against Austria and Czechoslovakia. Ultimatums were issued to the Poles to force them to hand over the city of Danzig to Germany. Ethnic Germans in the city caused trouble with the help of Heinrich Himmler. SS men were dispatched to act as a "fifth column" in Danzig even though the city was nominally a neutral or demilitarized zone. During the summer a battalion of the Totenkopfverbände, plus an anti-tank company, were smuggled into the city as "tourists" or as members of SS "sports clubs". Uniforms and weapons were then moved into the city in small boats. Despite heavy security measures, the Polish press was soon full of reports of the movement of arms from Nazi Germany into Danzig. In July the covert SS force was dubbed the SS-Heimwehr *Danzig* and was portrayed as a militia of local Danzig Germans. In reality it was under the direct control of Himmler in Berlin.

The German plan was to defeat the Poles a few weeks before the French and British had time to mobilize and strike from the west. This would be an offensive that the world had not seen before – a Blitzkrieg or lightning war. Hundreds of tanks, dive-bombers and fighter aircraft would spearhead the German offensive, which was intended to paralyze the Polish Army in a matter of days and destroy its fighting ability. Hitler ordered 11 of his new panzer divisions, a total of 3195 tanks, and 4 motorized infantry divisions to lead the assault and open the way for some 40 infantry divisions to mop up the last pockets of Polish resistance. Some 850 bombers and dive-bombers, backed by 40 fighters, would assure the Germans of total air cover. The Polish Army was totally outgunned. It could muster more infantrymen than the Wehrmacht could deploy, but the Poles had only 225 modern tanks and 360 combat aircraft.

Hitler was determined that his SS units would play a prominent role in the coming glorious victory. The reorganization of the SS-VT was not yet complete, so the individual armed SS regiments were assigned to support army divisions and corps on key axes of advance. In East Prussia, the *Deutschland* Regiment was incorporated into an ad hoc panzer division under the army's Major-General Werner Kempf, which was to spearhead the Third Army's offensive from that area. The *Leibstandarte* Regiment and the SS-VT combat engineer battalion was attached to the 17th Infantry Division to lead the assault of the Eighth Army on the Polish Army defending the central city of Lodz. In the south, the *Germania* Regiment was to support VIII Corps' attack on Cracow and Lemberg in the far south of Poland.

Although army commanders were initially reluctant about involving the armed SS units, the fact that they were all motorized meant they would be useful to help maintain the tempo of the advance. The vast majority of the army's infantry divisions marched into battle on foot, and the size of the theatre of war meant motorized units were at a premium. The armed SS regiments were to be used as independent spearhead units to scout ahead of the infantry divisions and exploit any loopholes in the Polish defensive line.

PRELIMINARY MOVES

In the last days of August, Reinhard Heydrich's SD Foreign Intelligence Section played a key role in creating the "justification" for the war. His operatives dressed up in Polish Army uniforms and staged three "incidents" at border posts and a radio station, thus allowing German propaganda to portray the invasion of Poland as a defensive response to hostile provocations. The incidents were scheduled to unfold in the early hours of 1 September, just before the main invasion was to begin.

An even more sinister role was played by three regiments of Eicke's Totenkopfverbände, which were mobilized to follow up behind the army and SS assault troops to eliminate political and racial enemies of the Nazi Party. In total some 18,000 SS men were mobilized to support the invasion of Poland, codenamed Operation White. The SD's special operations went ahead as planned and Hitler had his justification for war. By 04:00 hours on 1 September, the invasion was under way.

Some of the first SS troops in action were from SS-Heimwehr *Danzig*, which launched a dramatic attack on Polish troops at the Danzig Post Office, supported by armoured cars from the Danzig police. The Poles surrendered only when the Danzig Fire Department pumped gas into the building's cellar and ignited it. Another small group of SS men tried to capture a key bridge over the Vistula River, only to be repulsed with the loss of 26 dead. The German battleship *Schleswig Holstein* blasted the Poles around the bridge and the SS force eventually seized the position. Over the next 10 days the SS troops, backed by police, army units and Luftwaffe bombers, mopped up more Polish opposition around the city.

The star of the invasion as far as the armed SS was concerned was the *Leibstandarte*. It began its assault on schedule and proceeded to take apart the Polish frontier defences east of Breslau with great élan. *Leibstandarte*

infantry detachments used the morning mist to cover a river-crossing operation and they overwhelmed lightly manned Polish defensive positions. Follow-up troops then moved forward to clear out Polish rear positions. The Polish troops here were better prepared and they brought up armoured cars to counterattack the SS men, who had to use their 37mm anti-tank guns to repel them. The fighting lasted all day, but soon the *Leibstandarte* gained the upper hand and elements of three Polish divisions and two cavalry brigades were retreating east. In the early afternoon two *Leibstandarte* columns were sent to bypass the Polish resistance and push towards Wieruszow, which was reached by nightfall.

BLOODBATH AT PABIANICE

Despite Polish cavalry attacks during the night, the *Leibstandarte* struck out again the following morning towards a strong Polish defensive line on the Warta River. This was the northern pincer of a move to encircle Polish forces in Lodz. For four days the *Leibstandarte* was locked in a grim battle with Polish troops holding the heavily defended town of Pabianice, which guarded the western approaches to Lodz. Additional reinforcements and civilian volunteers bolstered the line against the *Leibstandarte*, and the battle turned into a bloody struggle to hold a key ridge line outside the town. Polish snipers took a heavy toll on the SS men, who repeatedly tried to break through the defences. To try to counter the concealment tactics of the Poles, the SS men took to wearing camouflage smocks, which would soon become a trademark of the Waffen-SS.

A new plan was needed to break through this strongpoint and so a coordinated assault was ordered for 7 September. Tanks of the 23rd Panzer Regiment were brought in to support the assault which aimed to outflank Pabianice. Almost immediately the German tanks ran into a heavy barrage of well-sighted Polish anti-tank guns. Early model German panzers were not the heavily armoured versions that saw action later in the war, and soon several were hit and destroyed. To provide cover for the withdrawing tanks, and to rescue the crews who had bailed out of their burning panzers, SS infantry were sent into action. They endured withering fire to achieve their mission. German Army artillery observers had gone forward with the *Leibstandarte* and they now began to call down fire on Polish positions. Boosted by this support, the SS assault teams at last penetrated into Pabianice and began to secure the town.

The momentum of the advance was not maintained by army units supporting the SS regiment, and as the afternoon dragged on the *Leibstandarte* men found

BALTIC SEA

Königsberg LITHUANIA

Miles 0 — 150

Km 0 — 240

Danzig

Kaunas

Tczew EAST PRUSSIA

POMERANIA Chelmno

Wilno

Bydgoszcz Minsk

Bialystok

Vistula

Poznan Bug

R U S S I A

Warta Brest Litovsk

Warsaw

G E R M A N Y

Czestochowa

POLAND, 1–5 SEPTEMBER 1939

Widawka

San

Cracow

Lvov

German attacks

ROMANIA

HUNGARY

Between 1 and 5 September, the Germans cleared the Polish corridor, with the Third Army attacking from East Prussia and the Fourth Army from Pomerania. In the south, the German Eight, Tenth and Fourteenth Armies advanced towards Warsaw.

themselves almost cut off in the town. The battle climaxed with a huge human-wave assault by Polish infantry that seemed to involve every one of the town's defenders. SS machine-gun crews and artillery killed hundreds of Poles as they charged forward in a last-gasp effort to drive out the invaders. With the charge defeated, the heart went out of the defence and by nightfall mop-up operations were under way to round up prisoners.

The *Leibstandarte* was now attached to the 4th Panzer Division to help it race eastwards in an attempt to set up a ring of steel around Warsaw. By 8 September the SS regiment had reached the southwestern suburbs of the Polish capital, and was quickly establishing a series of blocking positions to stop the escape of any of its defenders. For two days, parts of three Polish divisions and numerous brigades attempted to batter their way through the *Leibstandarte*'s positions and out of Warsaw. Again, it was German artillery that inflicted most of the slaughter on the Poles as they gathered for their breakout attempts. The SS men were soon exhausted, and the fields around their positions were piled high with the corpses of men and horses.

The Poles now brought forward some of their tank reserves to effect a breakthrough, but the 4th Panzer Division had pre-empted the move and deployed its armoured regiment to counter the Polish threat. The tank duel did not last long because the Polish tanks were totally outclassed by the German panzers. Soon two columns of German panzers were moving forward with a battalion of *Leibstandarte* men following close behind, each one to mop up any pockets of resistance. Two Polish divisions were pushed back along the western bank of the River Vistula, further isolating the Polish capital. Heavy fighting continued for several days as the Germans moved to consolidate their positions west of Warsaw and mop up all remaining pockets of resistance.

To the west, the bypassed Polish Poznan Army was preparing for a last, desperate effort to relieve Warsaw, by turning around its combat divisions and sending them back eastwards towards the capital. Combat engineers from the *Leibstandarte* had just built a bridge across the River Bzura to allow the regiment to attack westwards against the rear of the Poznan Army when its spearheads engaged the SS men.

Polish 7 TP light tanks. Armed with a 37mm gun and a coaxial 7.92mm machine gun, Poland possessed 169 on the eve of World War II. They were no match for the panzers.

Soon the *Leibstandarte* and 4th Panzer Division found themselves outnumbered and outgunned by tens of thousands of fresh Polish troops. Heavy Polish artillery fire smashed the German positions and forced the SS troops and their supporting panzers to pull back. For three days the SS advance battalion and a large chunk of the 4th Panzer Division on the western bank of the Bzura were fighting for their lives. The 35th Panzer Regiment, backed by *Leibstandarte* units, was now launched on a relief operation that hit the flank of the attacking Polish units and eventually opened a corridor to the trapped Germans. At first the German High Command did not realize the significance of the Polish counterattack, but once this mistake was detected it coordinated almost 29 divisions to encircle and then destroy the Poznan Army.

The attack on Bzura was the high tide of Polish resistance. Even as Polish troops battled with the *Leibstandarte* along the banks of the river, Stuka dive-bombers were staging merciless raids on the Poznan Army's command posts, supply lines and artillery positions. It had no air cover and was soon reduced to a mass of individual units fighting their own separate battles. The Poznan Army was doomed from the moment its troops exposed themselves to German airpower.

The *Leibstandarte* men were soon picking their way through a battlefield littered with smashed tanks, trucks, artillery and dead horses. Hitler came to visit them on 25 September outside Warsaw to reward them for their efforts. They had paid a high price for winning their Führer's gratitude, losing some 400 dead and wounded over the previous four weeks. The regiment now moved eastwards to complete the encirclement of the Polish capital. It moved to the northwest of the city and formed part of the southern flank of the German force investing the fortress city of Modlin, on the banks of the Vistula.

As planning for the invasion came together in July 1939, the German Army High Command decided to create a unique unit in preparation for the assault on Poland based around General Kempf's 4th Panzer Brigade. It was a combined army/SS ad hoc panzer division, dubbed at first Panzer Detachment East Prussia and then Panzer Division Kempf. The army's 7th Panzer Regiment provided the armoured power of the force; the *Deutschland* Regiment, the SS-VT's artillery regiment, signals battalion and reconnaissance battalion, along with an army heavy artillery battalion, completed the unit.

East Prussia was separated by the Polish corridor from the rest of Germany, so the SS and panzer units had to be moved by sea, which made them difficult to conceal. A cover story was thus concocted: that the SS troops were part of a new panzer division and would participate as "Wehrmacht representatives" at the Tannenberg (a World War I battle) celebration.

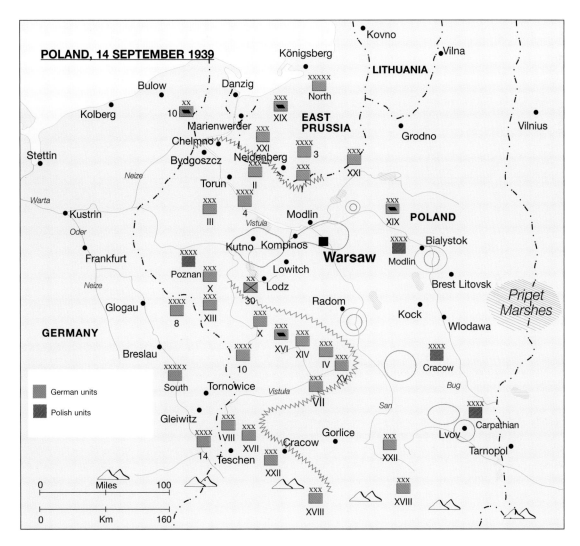

POLAND, 14 SEPTEMBER 1939

German units

Polish units

With so many of the SS-VT's combat units attached to the new force, Paul Hausser accompanied the unit for the duration of its operations in Poland to gather information for the eventual formation of his division. The attack was set for 04:45 hours on 1 September. The *Deutschland* Regiment's task was to force its way through the Mlava Line, an entrenched position fortified with barbed wire, anti-tank obstacles and bunkers and manned by the Polish 20th Infantry Division. After crossing their start lines the SS men moved rapidly forward, meeting little resistance. They soon ran into heavy resistance, however, when they reached the main Mlava Line defences sited along the crest of a hill. They came under a deadly hail of fire from the prepared positions of the defending Poles, and had to abandon the assault. A

Triumph of the Blitzkrieg. The brown circles show fragmented Polish forces, and those brown circles surrounded by a purple ring indicate trapped Polish pockets.

second assault failed just as quickly, prompting General Kempf to order up tank and artillery support for yet another assault during the afternoon.

Only a handful of German tanks could be mustered in time and, after a short artillery strike, the panzers moved forward. As the German tanks came into view of the Polish defenders, Polish artillery opened fire, pinning down the SS infantry and wreaking havoc on the German armour. The Polish anti-tank obstacles, constructed of railway track sections embedded in concrete, channelled

SIG 33

The schwere Infanteriegeschütz 33 (sIG 33) assault gun was designed to provide mechanized infantry with fire support from a self-propelled armoured platform. Produced by the Alkett company, which converted 38 Panzer I chassis, it saw continuous action until around mid-1943. The sIG 33 was a reliable and steady weapon. Its main strengths were its ability to fire a wide range of different ammunition and its impressive range. It suffered, however, from being very heavy for its size, and the crew had to operate from a compartment that was open at the top and back. The sIG 33 formed the heavy infantry gun platoons of Waffen-SS infantry and panzergrenadier regiments.

Type:	heavy infantry gun
Length:	4.67m (15.32ft)
Width:	2.06m (6.75ft)
Height:	2.8m (9.18ft)
Crew:	4
Armament:	1 x 150mm
Range:	140km (87.5 miles)
Speed:	40kmh (25mph)

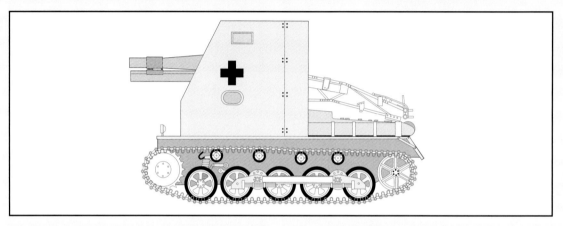

the tanks into killing zones. One by one the tanks were destroyed, forcing the Germans to halt the attack. The SS troops who were caught by the artillery had meanwhile worked their way up the slopes of the hill. When the order to withdraw was given, some of the SS infantry were within 137m (450ft) of their objectives. Even though the 20th Division was able to hold its positions, other Polish units did not fare so well. Eventually the 20th Division was out-flanked and forced to fall back southwards.

After breaking through the Mlava Line, the German Third Army pushed south. Kempf's panzers were in the vanguard of this advance. On 9 September, the Polish line along the River Bug was broken and the battered remnants of the defenders then retreated into a series of fortress cities along the Vistula and Bug rivers, north of Warsaw. The Polish troops included the remnants of the 8th Infantry Division, which struggled to set up defences stretching from Kazun to Nowy Dwor, and included the fortress city of Zacrozym, near Modlin.

Now Warsaw and Modlin were surrounded and the Germans attempted to bring the Polish campaign to a speedy conclusion by unleashing a series of bombings on Warsaw, designed to terrorize its population. The bombings worked, and the Polish Army units in Warsaw surrendered the city on 27 September. This left the

battered and depleted Polish 8th Infantry Division in Modlin holding out to the north. Early on 29 September, the Germans opened with a short bombardment, closely followed by an attack by the *Deutschland* Regiment. Flamethrowing detachments spearheaded the attack by the SS men, and they soon forced a passage into the small town. As the attackers penetrated the defensive lines, the fighting broke down into a series of individual firefights for blocks and buildings. The Polish command ordered the surrender of Polish forces, but in the confusion some units did not receive the order. The fortress garrison was one of those units, and it continued to resist even after the city's surrender. The Germans began a heavy artillery bombardment on Fort No 1, and the last Polish occupants were eventually forced to surrender.

The *Germania* Regiment was assigned to support the Fourteenth Army in the south and was involved in several clashes with the Polish Cracow and Carpathian Armies. The Polish troops were soon in headlong retreat, trying to escape to freedom in Romania before Soviet forces from the east, advancing in cooperation with the Germans under the terms of the non-aggression treaty signed between Stalin and Hitler, cut their escape route.

The Poles put up strong resistance and on 16 September roughly handled the *Germania* Regiment near Przemsyl and Lvov, but by 1 October all organized resistance in Poland had ceased. The country was now in the grip of Nazi terror as Himmler and his SS moved to eradicate all traces of the old Polish Government. Political and community leaders, intellectuals, trade unionists, clergymen and Jews were rounded up by the SS and Gestapo squads that moved into the country in the wake of the Blitzkrieg. Himmler ordered Eicke to form three Einsatzgruppen, or Special Action Squads, from the three Totenkopfverbände regiments mobilized for the campaign. They moved through Polish cities, towns and villages, burning synagogues and arresting and indiscriminately executing any Jews they could catch. Rounding up Jews and locking them inside their synagogues before setting the buildings on fire was a favoured method of murder by the SS Einsatzgruppen. They also arrested and shot Polish civilians, especially intelligentsia, on death lists compiled by the SD, as well as shooting the occupants of any mental hospitals they came across. One Einsatzgruppe murdered 800 people during a two-day period.

SS TERROR

Other SS units were equally quick to join in the pogrom. *Leibstandarte* troops were implicated in several massacres of civilians. They killed scores of local villagers in revenge for the casualties they suffered in the fighting along the Warta River. In the weeks after the Polish defeat, *Leibstandarte* men trawled the areas they occupied, looting property from Jews and staging random killings. The regiment's band machine-gunned more than 50 people in Burzeum who were accused of being "Jewish" criminals. In Danzig the SS-Heimwehr *Danzig* joined in the effort and massacred 33 Polish civilians, while the soldiers of the SS-VT artillery killed 50 Jews when they set their synagogue on fire.

The murderous rampage of the SS through Poland outraged many senior army commanders, who were soon complaining to the High Command in Berlin. Colonel-General Walther von Brauchitsch, the Wehrmacht commander-in-chief, was too timid to raise the SS killings with Hitler personally but did protest to Himmler about the "undisciplined" manner in which the SS troops conducted themselves in Poland. The SS chief promised his men would be more orderly in future, and then quietly arranged with Hitler for a decree to be issued in October 1939 removing the armed SS and SS police units from the legal jurisdiction of the Wehrmacht in occupied territory.

Hitler was enthused by the performance of his SS men, particularly the *Leibstandarte*, and readily acceded to proposals from Himmler in October 1939 for the armed SS to be expanded from one to three combat divisions. The army was instructed to remove its restrictions on recruitment to allow the necessary number of young men to join the armed SS. With German plans for an offensive in the West in the final stages of preparation, Himmler was desperate to form the new units to allow them to share in the glory of the defeat of France.

EXPANSION

The new manpower would not be available until well into 1940. He rapidly moved to turn the "ghost" reserve units of the Totenkopfverbände into combat units. Eicke's four regiments were transformed into the *Totenkopf* Motorized Division, and he was authorized to use his manpower in the concentration camp system to create the artillery, reconnaissance, supply and communications units needed for the new division. The camp system was also ordered to generate the necessary trucks, arms and other equipment needed. A major problem was the supply of artillery (when Eicke's henchmen found a factory in Czechoslovakia full of surplus 150mm artillery, he tried to acquire them for his division by unofficial methods, much to the annoyance of Himmler who was fighting his own battle with the army generals for equipment). This influx of equipment meant Eicke's men had to begin a crash programme of combat training when they were pulled back from Poland during the later months of 1939.

The SS-VT Division was now fully motorized. Its three regiments, *Deutschland*, *Germania* and *Der Führer*, were concentrated at Niedenberg to begin training as a coherent and integrated formation. Each of these regiments was brought back up to strength with three motorized infantry battalions. These battalions were all lavishly equipped with heavy machine guns, mortars and light infantry howitzers. The division was provided with anti-tank, reconnaissance, medical, signals, combat engineer, machine-gun and supply battalions. It was also provided with an artillery regiment with three battalions of 105mm and 150mm howitzers.

The third SS division – the SS *Polizei* (Police) Division – was formed from police reservists. However, it was poorly trained and lacked the trucks to move its troops and supplies or tow its field guns, so could only advance at the rate its soldiers could march.

Hitler's prized *Leibstandarte* was also expanded, gaining more support weapons, motorcycle scout troops and an artillery battalion with 105mm howitzers. The élite SS force was being groomed to act as an independent strike force to allow it to play a key role in the coming invasion of France.

Victory in the West, 1940

After their success in Poland, the units of the Waffen-SS took part in the invasion of the Low Countries and France in May 1940. However, though the Blitzkrieg achieved a stunning breakthrough in the Ardennes, the Western Allies gave the SS units a bloody nose in several small-scale engagements. The SS troops had particular difficulty in overcoming British detachments.

SS soldiers in France in 1940, probably of the SS-Verfügungsdivision. These men are armed with Kar 98K bolt-action rifles, which fired a 7.92mm round and had a magazine capacity of five rounds.

Operation Yellow, the attack on the West, was intended to be a decisive blow that would defeat France in a few weeks. Initially the army High Command proposed to repeat the strategy of the Schlieffen Plan of World War I. This envisaged the bulk of the German Army advancing through Holland and Belgium before trying to outflank Paris from the west. Hitler was unimpressed and turned to a young major-general called Erich von Manstein, who had developed a daring plan to push a tank column through the Belgian Ardennes forest to split open the French and British defences. As a diversion, a strong force would strike into Holland and northern Belgium to draw Allied forces into the Low Countries. Once the panzers had effected a breakthrough, German forces would race to the Channel and defeat the British and French armies piecemeal. The dramatic character of the plan appealed to Hitler, and in the spring of 1940 he overruled his generals and adopted Manstein's scheme.

Fast-moving armoured and motorized units were crucial to the German plan, which relied on surprise and speed to keep the British and French off-balance. Not surprisingly, the motorized units of the armed SS were given a prominent role in the coming campaign. The SS-VT Division and the *Leibstandarte* were assigned spearhead roles for the invasion of Holland. The *Totenkopf* was not considered to be as combat-ready as its counterparts, and was initially assigned only a reserve role, ready to exploit any breakthrough created by the panzers. The *Polizei* Division, however, was relegated to a secondary role reinforcing the troops screening the Maginot Line along the Franco-German border.

Surprise was a key element in the German plans, so the assault force for the attack on Holland was garrisoned far from the border and no obvious preparations were made that would give away the impending attack. The Dutch defence was based on holding a series of key canals and rivers that would prevent any German advance on their main cities far to the west. German plans called for parachute and glider-borne troops to seize key Dutch objectives, particularly strategic road bridges, to allow motorized columns quickly to penetrate Dutch defences. Commando troops from German military intelligence's Brandenburg Regiment also participated in these operations dressed in Dutch uniforms. It was the job of the *Leibstandarte*, the SS-VT and the 9th Panzer Division to take advantage of the opening created by Lieutenant-General Kurt Student's airborne forces to capture the Dutch capital, The Hague, in a lightning advance.

On the issuing of the secret codeword "Danzig" on 9 May 1940, soon after midnight, units of the *Leibstandarte*, followed by the SS-VT Division, were heading northwards from their garrisons in the Ruhr region. Ahead of them thousands of airborne troops were being dropped throughout Holland. On schedule at 05:30 hours, the first *Leibstandarte* troops captured a key bridge at De Poppe to open the way for the 227th Infantry Division to push west towards Amsterdam. The first day's advance was rapid, with the *Leibstandarte* driving more then 217km (135 miles) – most of the Dutch defenders were taken by surprise by the speed of the German move. *Leibstandarte* troops found most of the explosive charges placed under Dutch bridges had not been detonated. In the few cases where bridges were blown, the SS men built improvised bridges from commandeered building materials to allow the advance to continue. On 11 May, the 227th Infantry ordered a full-scale assault on the Ijssel defence line, which was now heavily defended by Dutch troops. The *Leibstandarte* led the main assault over the river, and by nightfall had penetrated 40km (25 miles) behind Dutch lines.

BREAKING THE GREBBE LINE
The main body of the SS-VT attacked to the north of the *Leibstandarte* advance, towards the so-called Grebbe Line that blocked the direct route to Amsterdam from the east. The *Der Führer* Regiment was in the vanguard of this advance, and was soon finding that the Dutch were putting up determined resistance to protect the region they dubbed their "national redoubt", which bristled with machine-gun nests, tank traps and an interlocking network of canals and other water obstacles.

German paratroops in The Hague and Rotterdam were now locked in bitter fighting as Dutch troops battled frantically to stop them capturing a series of strategic bridges over the Rhine and Maas rivers. On the morning of 13 May, the 9th Panzer Division backed by the *Leibstandarte* was ordered to swing south, seize the Moerdijk bridge and then punch a corridor through to the trapped airborne troops. The SS-VT division was to follow up and reinforce the advance once it had extracted itself from the fighting along the Grebbe Line.

The panzer column made good progress. By the evening it was on the outskirts of Rotterdam. The Germans, becoming desperate to break the back of Dutch resistance, issued an ultimatum to the Dutch

commander in the city threatening to level Rotterdam with air raids and artillery barrages unless he surrendered. The Dutch Army agreed to the terms, but the negotiations dragged during the afternoon of 14 May. In the confusion, recall orders to the Luftwaffe bombers failed to get through in time. Some 980 people died in the resulting carnage and 78,000 were made homeless. The Dutch Army command now announced the surrender of all the troops defending the national redoubt.

The *Leibstandarte*'s reconnaissance battalion pushed into the city in the confusion to link up with Student's men. Some Dutch troops had not yet received the surrender orders and fighting continued during the night. In one incident, the SS men mistook a group of German paratroopers for Dutch soldiers and opened fire. Student was among the group and was wounded in the head by the SS fire. The 9th Panzer Division and the *Leibstandarte* now moved to complete the disarming of the Dutch defenders of Rotterdam.

MOPPING UP
The Dutch troops in the south of their country continued to hold out, and the SS-VT Division was sent to mop up all resistance on Walcheren Island. The *Deutschland* Regiment led the attacks through flooded polders and minefields, before capturing the 3.2km (2-mile) causeway to the island with the help of air strikes.

By 18 May, resistance in Holland was over and the German High Command ordered the SS units to swing south to help in the decisive battles in northern France. As the attack on Holland was getting under way, XIX Panzer Corps under Lieutenant-General Heinz Guderian had made its push through the Ardennes in southern Belgium and Luxembourg. His troops met negligible resistance in the poorly defended sector around Sedan, which the Belgian High Command thought was impassable to tanks. The French and British had fallen for the German deception plan: as soon as the fighting broke out in Holland they began moving their best troops northwards to help the Dutch and Belgians. The culmination of these two developments was that the cream of the British and French armies was in danger of being encircled in northern France and Belgium by the German tank thrust that was now heading at breakneck speed for the English Channel. Late in the evening on 20 May, Guderian's panzers captured Abbeville at the mouth of the River Somme, which was only a few miles from the Channel coast. Some 250,000 British and even more French soldiers were now cut off from their main supply bases in central France. The German High Command was determined to exploit its success, and every avail-

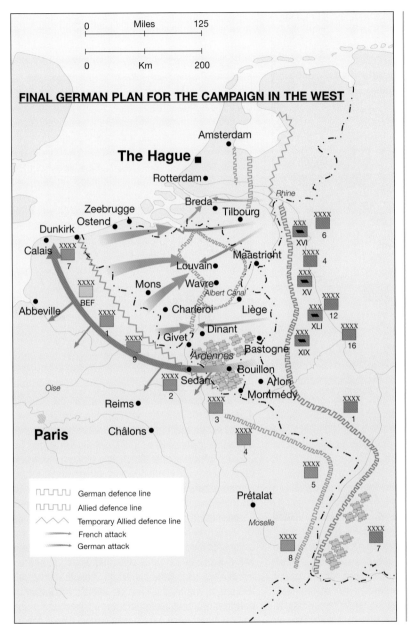

FINAL GERMAN PLAN FOR THE CAMPAIGN IN THE WEST

An armoured strike through the weak centre would be the Germans' main attack, though a secondary effort in northern Belgium and southern Holland was designed to suck British and French forces to the north and away from the centre.

able panzer and motorized unit was dispatched to help Guderian's tanks crews.

Three days earlier, Eicke's *Totenkopf* Division had received orders to move forward from its barracks in the Rhineland to support the panzer advance. Once it crossed the Meuse in southern Belgium, it joined up with Colonel-General Hermann Hoth's XV Panzer Corps that formed the northern wing of the advance to the Channel. This was

spearheaded by a former adjutant of Hitler – the as yet unknown Major-General Erwin Rommel. His 7th Panzer Division was almost a day behind Guderian's spearhead, and on 21 May was only just approaching the town of Arras. The *Totenkopf*'s columns of motorized infantry were following up closely behind Rommel's tanks.

The British and French High Commands had already spotted the danger to their forces, and they prepared a

An SS soldier liaising with an armoured car commander in the West in 1940. Motorized SS units moved fast – the *Leibstandarte* once covered 80km (50 miles) in 6 hours.

The German 37mm anti-tank guns with the 7th Panzer's motorized infantry regiments were brought into action, but their shells bounced off the heavily armoured British tanks, earning the guns the nickname "door knockers" from their crews. Rommel brought up his panzer regiment, but it also found its guns had difficulty penetrating the British armour. The 7th Panzer's columns reeled in confusion as the Matilda tanks pressed on regardless, leaving the British and German infantry in their wake to engage each other.

Two British tank columns pushed through Rommel's troops. One ran into the 7th Panzer's artillery regiment, which turned its 105mm howitzers on them. The division's anti-aircraft battalion was also deployed to the German gun line by Rommel, and eventually the British tanks were halted. It was a desperate battle that involved the German tank general having to rush from gun to gun to encourage his artillery men to keep firing.

To the southwest of Arras, the *Totenkopf* Division ran into the other British tank column. Matildas and armoured cars were soon rampaging over the positions of the SS division's anti-tank battalion. Its 37mm anti-tank guns proved as ineffective as the army's and soon the SS gunners were in full retreat, taking cover with *Totenkopf* infantry in a nearby village. They then tried to return to the battle by forming tank-hunting squads armed with grenades, but their attempts to "stalk" the British tanks were repulsed with heavy losses. For over an hour the situation seemed hopeless as the British armour ranged across the battlefield at will. One SS supply column was badly shot up by the British tanks and its crews fled in confusion, leading Rommel to report gleefully that the whole of the SS division had "panicked".

Like his army counterpart, Eicke threw himself into steadying the morale of his troops, and eventually he deployed the heavy guns of his artillery regiment to drive off the British. The *Totenkopf* Division paid a heavy price for its success, losing 39 dead, 66 wounded and 2 missing during the battle for Arras. The division had been "blooded" in a confused battle, but it had rallied thanks in part to its commander's personal presence.

With their tank attack stalled at Arras, the British began to withdraw north towards Dunkirk. They may have suffered a strategic defeat, but they now set about trying to stall the German advance to allow as many of their troops as possible to escape home across the English Channel.

Rommel's panzers and the *Totenkopf* Division were swung north from Arras to confront the retreating British. Desultory skirmishing characterized the following days' fighting as the SS followed up the British rearguards,

plan to launch simultaneous armoured counterattacks from north and south to open a corridor and re-unite their shattered front. This would turn the table on the Germans and cut off their spearheads. It proved impossible to coordinate the attacks, though, and the French forces from the south never materialized. The British managed to attack using a scratch force built around a tank brigade and the French sent some light mechanized troops to help. The strike force was pitifully small: only 16 Matilda Mark IIs with two-pounder guns and 58 machine-gun-armed Matilda Mark Is, backed by two battalions of British infantry.

The German and British forces had little idea what was happening around them on the morning of 21 May, because both sides were only just arriving on the battlefield after long marches. Rommel's columns were skirting to the south of the town in the early afternoon when the British tanks suddenly started firing on them from the small villages and woods that dotted the landscape.

A Panzer III, probably an Ausf F, in the West in 1940. The fully motorized *Leibstandarte*, Verfügungsdivision and *Totenkopf* worked closely with the panzer divisions.

who struck back on the evening of 22nd with a surprise tank raid that was driven off with loss by Eicke's men.

The British now fought a series of determined rearguard actions to hold defensive lines along key rivers and canals that criss-crossed the industrial landscape of northern France. Eicke's men came up against serious resistance along the La Bassee Canal on the evening of 22 May. The next day the first SS battalion to reach the canal was impetuously ordered to cross it by Eicke before a proper reconnaissance had been conducted. The *Totenkopf* men soon found themselves dangerously exposed in open fields as British artillery and mortar fire rained down on them. To counter this threat and prepare for a second advance, Eicke brought up his own guns and began an artillery duel.

Early on 24 May, Eicke personally led the assault across the canal after his engineers had built an assault bridge. The first wave of troops was soon pinned down by heavy British fire, but Eicke called up reinforcements and he was able to secure a small bridgehead. Just as success seemed in his grasp, orders arrived from higher headquarters ordering him to pull back. Hitler wanted to rest his tired panzer troops for a more deliberate attack on the British bridgehead in a few days. No German

troops were to cross the so-called "canal line". The withdrawal order threw the *Totenkopf* troops into chaos and the British intensified their artillery fire, which eventually resulted in 42 Germans dying, 121 being wounded and 5 going missing.

When Lieutenant-General Erich Hoepner, Eicke's corps commander and immediate army superior officer, arrived later in the evening to inspect the scene, he had a blazing row with Eicke in front of his staff, accusing the SS officer of being a "butcher" who cared nothing for the lives of his men. For two days the *Totenkopf* Division sat licking its wounds in pouring rain as it prepared for the big offensive to finish off the British.

During this pause, the *Leibstandarte* Regiment and the SS-VT Division were racing to catch up with the panzer spearheads. After navigating through the chaotic road network of Belgium and northern France, clogged with German supply columns and civilian refugees, they began moving into the line on 24 May. The *Leibstandarte* joined the 1st Panzer Division close to Dunkirk along the Aa Canal and the SS-VT took up positions farther south, towards the *Totenkopf*. Elements of seven panzer divisions, supported by the SS, were being mustered for the attack. Hitler was now undecided what to do. Hermann Göring assured him that his Luftwaffe could finish off the British in Dunkirk, while the army High Command was pushing for a ground assault to mop up the remaining British troops before they could be lifted off the beaches by the Royal Navy.

The commander of the *Leibstandarte*, Dietrich, had no interest in such debates. As soon as his regiment entered the line opposite the French town of Wormhoudt late on 24 May, he ordered his men to attack. Despite the Führer's stop order, Dietrich was determined to capture a key hill east of the canal that dominated the low-lying countryside around the town.

The regiment's 3rd Battalion was sent across the canal in boats under the cover of artillery fire. The hill was quickly seized and held despite several British counterattacks. Guderian, who was now in command of the *Leibstandarte*'s sector, was equally unhappy at the halt and ordered his panzers to back up the SS success, and Dietrich's men were not thrown off the hill.

For two days Hitler refused to allow his troops to advance, but he relented on the afternoon of 26 May and ordered an all-out offensive. The attack began during the night, backed by heavy artillery fire. Waves of Stuka divebombers appeared over the British lines at first light to begin relentless bombing runs.

Preparations for the *Leibstandarte*'s attack were interrupted by a British spoiling attack by Bren gun carriers, and it was not until 08:20 hours that the SS men were able to move forward along the length of their front. One battalion attacked to the north and another struck to the south of the town, with a third held ready to exploit any breakthrough. The 2nd Battalion, Royal Warwickshire Regiment, proved to be the toughest opponents the *Leibstandarte* had faced to date. All morning the

Above: Soldiers of the *Totenkopf* Division in France (note the death's head collar insignia). The division had the dubious honour of committing the first Waffen-SS atrocity in the West: the massacre of British troops at Le Paradis.

Right: Members of the *Germania* Regiment (note the "2" on the collar patch of the soldier on the left) of the SS-Verfügungsdivision in France in 1940. This regiment was transferred to the *Germania* Division (renamed *Wiking*) in November 1940.

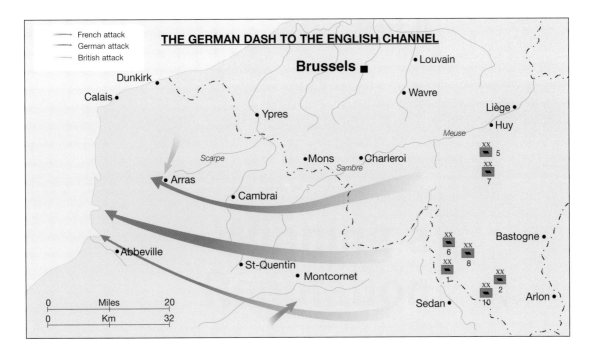

THE GERMAN DASH TO THE ENGLISH CHANNEL

French attack
German attack
British attack

Dunkirk
Calais
Ypres
Brussels
Louvain
Wavre
Liège
Huy
Meuse
Scarpe
Mons • Charleroi
Sambre
Arras
Cambrai
St-Quentin
Montcornet
Sedan
Bastogne
Arlon
Abbeville

0 Miles 20
0 Km 32

outnumbered British defenders of Wormhoudt refused to give ground. British machine-gun and rifle fire swept the open fields around the town, causing heavy losses. Well-aimed anti-tank fire also drove off the handful of German tanks sent by Guderian to support the assault.

All through the morning and into the afternoon the Royal Warwickshires held the SS at bay. When Dietrich decided to find out what was going on, he drove into the middle of a firefight and his staff car was set ablaze. For several hours, Dietrich and his adjutant had to take cover in a ditch as the battle raged around them. Realizing that the SS was in trouble, Guderian ordered the 3rd Panzer Regiment forward. Spotter planes found the British 25-pounder artillery batteries and directed shelling to knock them out. The panzers then swung into action, launching an outflanking attack to the south of the town. They quickly knocked out the handful of British anti-tank guns and then began rolling up the Royal Warwickshire's machine-gun positions. This emboldened the *Leibstandarte* infantry, who now surged forward again. Street fighting raged through the town into the early evening. The intervention of the panzers broke the back of the British defenders, who were now starting to run out of ammunition. A trickle of British soldiers started surrendering, and soon just under 100 were held in a barn by men of Wilhelm Mohnke's 2nd Battalion of the *Leibstandarte*. He ordered the prisoners to be machine-gunned in cold blood.

The "panzer corridor", 13–20 May 1940. Having crossed the Meuse, the German panzer divisions were able to strike for the English Channel, with few Allied units in their way.

A night-time counterattack led by British tanks was beaten off by SS men, who were now in complete control of Wormhoudt. The town was littered with the bodies of dead British and Germans and the burnt-out remains of scores of tanks and military vehicles. In the battle, the Royal Warwickshires had been all but wiped out as a fighting force with hundreds killed and taken prisoner. But the brave regiment had bought a day for the British Expeditionary Force (BEF) to retreat inside its defensive lines outside Dunkirk. The day was particularly frustrating for Dietrich, who after he was rescued by the panzers had to go, still covered in mud from head to toe, and explain himself to Guderian, much to the amusement of the panzer general.

Farther south the SS-VT was coming into the line on 23 May when it was surprised by a column of French tanks and infantry striking south out of the Dunkirk bridgehead at Saint Hillaire. The French tanks swarmed into the positions of the *Der Führer* Regiment, but Hausser's men soon recovered and his tank-hunting teams knocked out 13 tanks and captured 500 prisoners.

After clearing up this problem, later in the day Hausser ordered his troops forward to occupy a section

FLAK 18

The first prototype of the Flak 18 anti-aircraft gun was developed as early as 1928 by Krupp in cooperation with the Swedish Bofors company, but only entered production after Hitler's rise to power in 1933. Mounted on a pivoted cruciform carriage and carried by two single axle trailers, it could be quickly dismounted for action. The Flak 18 had a single-piece barrel, whereas its successors had multi-piece barrels. This 88mm-calibre weapon proved both highly versatile and effective in the anti-tank role. It saw extensive action with most Waffen-SS divisions (the *Leibstandarte* was the first SS unit to receive a heavy flak unit, in 1941), and on every front on which the German armed forces were fighting.

Type:	anti-aircraft/anti-tank gun
Length:	4.93m (16.17ft)
Traverse:	360 degrees
Weight:	3710kg (8180lb)
Elevation:	85 degrees
Rate of fire:	15–20rpm
Calibre:	88mm
Max. ceiling:	10,600m (34,776ft)

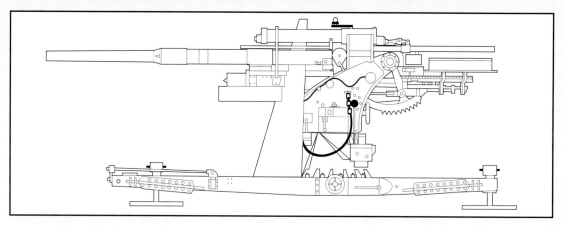

of the La Bassee Canal where they ran into fierce resistance from the British 2nd Division. A strong British counterattack stopped the SS-VT in its tracks, forcing it to reorganize itself before it could attack again.

Like its other SS counterparts, the SS-VT participated in the attack on the British on 26 May, striking north into the Nieppe Wood area against British rearguard units. The fighting against the Queen's Own Royal West Kent Regiment was stiff, and the SS attack did not succeed in destroying the British troops. The SS-VT could not prevent the British escaping into the Dunkirk bridgehead, but the division pressed close on their heels, brushing with the British rearguard at the Lys Canal on 27 May.

In the *Totenkopf* sector, the halt order on the 24th had enraged Eicke but there seemed to be little he could do until the order to attack was given by Hitler. During 25 May, British artillery and mortars were starting to take an increasing toll on the *Totenkopf*, so Eicke ordered a series of raids over the "canal line" by small SS squads to try to put the British guns out of action. On the afternoon of 26 May a night-time assault was ordered to seize a bridgehead over the canal to open the way for the division to strike north to Dunkirk. By 20:30 hours the first SS men were across the canal, and in a few hours had

established a firm foothold. The British, though, launched repeated counterattacks throughout the night.

At dawn the *Totenkopf* Division launched multiple attacks from its small bridgeheads to overwhelm all the British defences in its sector. The sheer weight of numbers in the attack seemed to crush the British defenders from the Royal Scots, Royal Norfolk Regiment and Lancashire Fusiliers. As the morning passed, however, the British defence stiffened and soon the SS attack had broken down into a series of vicious, small actions. As casualties began to mount, Eicke started to struggle to regain control of his troops. By early afternoon the attack had ground to a halt. The divisional command post was in a chaotic state as Eicke tried to come up with a way to get the attack moving again. Amid this crisis, the divisional operations officer collapsed in the headquarters from a haemorrhaging stomach ulcer. A key battalion commander was then killed by a British sniper.

Only a determined attack, pressed home with heavy fire by the division's 2nd Regiment, seemed to restore the situation. The British troops holding the canal broke contact and re-established a new position farther back that was soon reinforced with fresh troops and anti-tank

The grave of a soldier of the *Polizei* Division killed in France. Recruited mainly from the German regular police, the division was not motorized and its artillery was horse-drawn.

guns. It was during this period that 100 soldiers from the Royal Norfolk Regiment surrendered in the village of Le Paradis after they ran out of ammunition. The British had caused the SS unit that captured them several casualties during the battle. In revenge, a *Totenkopf* company commander then ordered the prisoners to be shot as they stood in front of a barn. Miraculously, two British soldiers survived to give evidence against their comrades' murderers.

The *Totenkopf* Division continued to advance during the night of 27/28 May and drove into the new British positions, with heavy resistance forcing it to pull back temporarily. During 28 May, the division launched another large-scale assault to clear out the British position around Estaires. Fatigue and heavy casualties again took their toll, and by the afternoon the attack was stalled. By nightfall, Eicke's men had advanced less than a mile. Overnight, an attack was prepared to punch through the British left flank, but as Eicke's men were gathering in their assembly area before dawn British artillery fire enveloped them, causing chaos and forcing the attack to be called off. By the time Stukas had been called up to silence the guns, the British troops had escaped north. The SS men spent the rest of the day following up the retreating British, to no avail. By nightfall the High Command ordered the pursuit to be taken over by army units. The division had suffered heavily, losing 1140 casualties including some 300 officers. It had also lost scores of vehicles.

Over the next week the German Army closed in on the Dunkirk perimeter, but it was unable to prevent more than 300,000 British, French and Belgian troops escaping. The SS troops were not directly involved in this fighting, but were used to mop up isolated pockets of resistance. The *Totenkopf* linked up with the *Leibstandarte* and pressed on all the way to Boulogne, taking some 6000 prisoners. This time was vital to allow it to regroup and reorganize for the next phase of the campaign.

The German High Command now redirected its panzers south to smash the remaining French units defending Paris along the Somme. The SS units moved to their jump-off positions. The *Leibstandarte* was poised to strike at Soissons, north of Paris. The SS-VT was posted nearby and the *Totenkopf* was positioned to the east.

German troops surged southwards on 5 June and met only minimal resistance from the demoralized French

Army. Columns of *Leibstandarte* troops skirted to the east of Paris and headed towards Vichy in central France. The regiment fought several brief skirmishes with pockets of French troops, but its main problem was finding a route through the roads jammed with German supply columns and refugees. Thousands of French soldiers were captured, and Dietrich also took the opportunity to enhance his art collection from several French chateaux. In one notable incident the élite SS regiment found itself in a brief battle with a detachment of World War I French tanks, which were impervious to its 37mm anti-tank guns. The regiment's 105mm field guns had to be brought up to knock them out.

The SS-VT pushed towards Troyes and fought a stiff action with retreating French troops. Resistance then broke, and soon the SS men were motoring westwards towards Bourdeaux. The *Totenkopf* Division now surged south towards Dijon and Lyon. A few French Moroccan units did put up resistance to Eicke's men, who treated any non-white prisoners with great brutality, executing them on the spot.

By 12 June 1940, German military expertise had effectively destroyed the French will to resist (though there was still enough French strength left to repulse the Italian attacks in the east).

The broken purple line represents the limit of the German advance before the French sued for surrender terms. The solid purple line represents the subsequent demarcation line between German-occupied France in the north and the Vichy regime to the south.

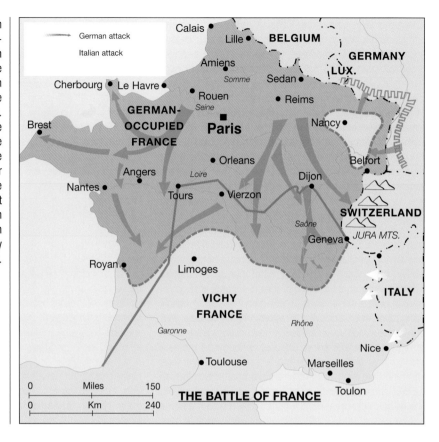

German attack
Italian attack

Calais
Lille
BELGIUM
GERMANY
LUX.
Amiens
Somme
Sedan
Cherbourg • Le Havre
Rouen
Reims
Seine
GERMAN-
OCCUPIED
FRANCE
Brest
Paris
Nancy
Orleans
Belfort
Angers
Loire
Dijon
Nantes
Tours
Vierzon
SWITZERLAND
Saône
JURA MTS.
Geneva
Royan
Limoges
ITALY
VICHY
FRANCE
Garonne
Rhône
Nice
Toulouse
Marseilles
0   Miles   150
0   Km   240
THE BATTLE OF FRANCE
Toulon

By the time the French Government decided to capitulate on 21 June, the three SS units were still racing south. The *Polizei* Division advanced westwards through difficult terrain around Argonne. In the wake of the armistice, the SS units were assigned to garrison duties along the Atlantic coast or the demarcation line with the unoccupied zone run by the new pro-German government that was established in the town of Vichy.

In just under six weeks of combat the SS units had suffered heavy losses, some 270 by the *Leibstandarte*, more than 1500 by the *Totenkopf* and nearly 2000 by the SS-VT. The three units were tested in combat against determined and skilful opponents and generally acquitted themselves well. Their officers could be accused of being overly aggressive and reckless with their men's lives, but they were keen to prove their worth to Hitler, Himmler and the army.

Hitler was delighted with the performance of his élite troops and he showered medals and promotions on his favourites. Dietrich and his *Leibstandarte* came in for special praise from a grateful Führer. Guderian, their commander for much of the invasion of France, was impressed by the speed and élan of the unit. Dietrich went to great lengths to keep secret, even from other members of the SS hierarchy, the role of his men in the massacre of the Royal Warwickshire prisoners, so as not to sour his victory.

Eicke and his *Totenkopf* emerged from the French campaign temporarily out of favour after details of the Le Paradis incident became common knowledge. When General Hoepner ordered an inquiry into the incident, Eicke and his men were initially denied medals for their part in the campaign. But Himmler was not prepared to lose one of his top commanders over what he considered a trivial incident. Eicke kept his job.

Within a few weeks of the French surrender, Hitler set in train a major effort to expand his SS combat units. Although the weaknesses and failures of the armed SS units in France were recognized by the organization's leadership, they were not going to get in the way of the plans to expand the armed SS. After a few weeks preparing for a possible invasion of Britain, the armed SS units in France began readying themselves for a new Blitzkrieg – against Soviet Russia.

Part III

The Ideological Crusade

Expansion, 1940–41

The summer and autumn of 1940 represented a time of furious activity for the officers and men of the Waffen-SS as Himmler brought together the *Leibstandarte*, SS-VT and *Totenkopf*, as well as an assortment of independent regiments and units, under a single chain of command for the first time, much to the resentment of old SS veterans such as "Sepp" Dietrich and Theodor Eicke.

A *Leibstandarte* motorcycle reconnaissance unit on a mountain road in the Peloponnese in Greece. The division's reconnaissance battalion at this time (April 1941) included two motorcycle companies.

Himmler's plans to expand his new army were coming to fruition, and in August 1940 he formally established the Waffen-SS as a branch of his SS organization. The term had been in general usage since late in 1939 to describe armed SS units, but Himmler now created the Kommando der Waffen-SS inside his SS headquarters.

By the summer there were more than 100,000 men in SS combat units, and the system to train, equip and organize them was in desperate need of being streamlined. Crucially, the new organization brought under central control the Totenkopfverbände's byzantine network of reserve units that Eicke used as his personal pool of battle casualty replacements to keep his division up to strength. Eicke had built up 15 regiments of reservists and two cavalry regiments during the previous two years, making him one of the most powerful officers in the SS. The other armed SS units had no such facility, and Himmler believed it was essential to take charge of them if his Waffen-SS units were not to be bled dry by heavy battle casualties. The army was still imposing restrictions on the number of recruits the SS could take, so Himmler considered it a matter of urgency to streamline the recruitment of the Waffen-SS.

While the rationalizing of the SS's personnel management system was at the heart of the dispute between Himmler and Eicke, the SS supremo also saw the *Totenkopf* commander as a potential rival for Hitler's favour and wanted to clip his wings before he became too powerful. Dietrich was also not happy with having to report to the new Waffen-SS headquarters, but he soon worked out how to ignore it and make use of his "back channels" to communicate directly with Hitler. A *Leibstandarte* guard battalion protected Hitler at all times, so Dietrich could get through to the Führer if need be.

The extra manpower authorized by the armed SS in 1939 started to come on-line in the summer of 1940. Rather than disband temporary units, such as the *Polizei* Division, that had been created in late 1939 to allow the SS to deploy three combat divisions, Himmler persuaded Hitler to keep them in place and to use the newly trained manpower to create more Waffen-SS divisions.

A fourth SS division, soon to be dubbed the *Viking* or *Wiking*, was ordered to be formed in late 1940. The SS-VT and *Totenkopf* Divisions were to be reinforced with extra firepower and specialist units. Likewise, the *Leibstandarte* was also expanded to a motorized

Right: German heavy artillery moves through a Yugoslav town during the campaign in the Balkans in 1941. The vehicles are half-track prime movers and the artillery piece is the barrel of a 150mm K 18 gun on its transporter.

Below: An SS 81mm mortar shells an enemy position in Yugoslavia in April 1941. These troops are possibly members of a heavy machine-gun company of the *Das Reich* Division, though the division's reconnaissance battalion also had a mortar platoon.

brigade. Two Totenkopfverbände regiments were transformed into the *Nord* Brigade and a third was turned into an independent Waffen-SS infantry regiment. Five Totenkopfverbände infantry and two cavalry regiments were kept under Himmler's personal control for "special duties" in the occupied territories.

The *Leibstandarte* thus grew to more than 10,000 men. It now boasted four motorized infantry battalions carried in trucks and a heavy weapons battalion. A fifth battalion was detached to guard Hitler in Berlin. The brigade's artillery now fielded 105mm and 150mm howitzers, as well as 88mm flak guns. The latter were to prove very useful in Russia when the heavily armoured

T-34 tanks appeared. Reconnaissance, combat engineer, light anti-aircraft and signal battalions, as well as a field hospital, completed the brigade's order of battle.

The *Totenkopf* Division also underwent a major expansion, receiving an anti-aircraft battalion equipped with 20mm, 37mm and 88m flak guns and a heavy artillery regiment of 12 150mm guns. A reserve infantry battalion was formed to allow a pool of battle casualty replacements to follow close behind the division.

Paul Hausser's SS-VT received a similar quantity of new equipment and capabilities as its counterparts, and was renamed the *Deutschland* Division in December 1940. This did not last long because of a fear that it would be confused with the army's *Grossdeutschland* motorized regiment. In January 1940, the division assumed the title *Das Reich*. It was ordered to transfer its *Germania* Regiment to form the core of the new *Wiking* Division. In return, it received the 11th Totenkopfverbände Regiment as a replacement.

The *Wiking* Motorized Division was a unique formation in 1940: the only Waffen-SS unit to contain foreign volunteers. In his desperate efforts to get round army recruitment restrictions, Himmler saw the possibility of recruiting pro-Nazi foreigners of what he considered to be "Aryan stock" from occupied north European countries. Nazi sympathizers from Norway and Denmark were recruited into the *Nordland* Regiment in mid-1940, and later in the year Dutchmen and Flemish-speaking Belgians were recruited into the *Westland* Regiment. During the latter half of 1940, German SS instructors had whipped

SDKFZ 221

The SdKfz 221 was a small armoured car, used primarily as a reconnaissance vehicle. It was crewed by two men; one driver sat in front, and the commander in the small turret. It was fitted with a 7.92mm machine gun in the turret, which was for defensive purposes only. Though armoured, the skin could be pierced by 7.92mm bullets, and it was thus not a battlefield vehicle. The SdKfz was in service with the SS before the first Waffen-SS panzer regiments were formed, in the armoured car companies of the reconnaissance battalions. Despite generating only 75bhp from its Horch eight-cyclinder engine, it was capable of speeds of up to 90kmh (56.25mph).

Type:	light armoured car
Length:	4.8m (15.75ft)
Width:	1.9m (6.6ft)
Height:	2.15m (7.1ft)
Crew:	2
Armament:	1 x 7.92mm machine gun
Range:	280km (174 miles)
Speed:	90kmh (56.25mph)

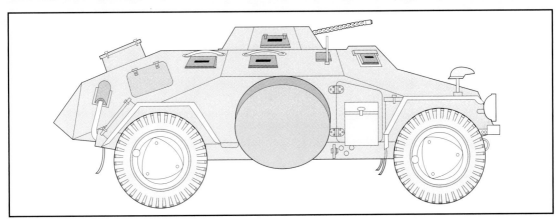

them into shape to allow the two regiments to be transferred to the *Wiking* Division under the command of Felix Steiner. He had led the *Deutschland* Regiment of the SS-VT Division with distinction during the invasion of France.

Himmler and his senior commanders went to great lengths to improve the quality of SS training. The army was persuaded to open several of its specialist training schools to the Waffen-SS, so that flak gunners, artillery men, medical orderlies, radio men and other specialists could be taught advanced skills on a par with their army counterparts. Senior Waffen-SS officers were also dispatched to army staff colleges to improve their tactical and administrative skills.

During the autumn of 1940, Hitler took the strategic decision to attack the Soviet Union. This was to be a war for racial supremacy, which Hitler said would lead to the eradication of the Jewish-Communist conspiracy that was threatening to destroy his "Thousand Year" Reich. This new empire would give him the Lebensraum or "living space" that a Greater Germany required.

The refusal of the British to surrender after Dunkirk and the subsequent Battle of Britain in mid-1940 was dismissed as little more than a side-show by Hitler, who looked to the East to fulfil his ambitions. The detailed

planning for Operation Barbarossa, as the invasion would be codenamed, took place in great secrecy. Not even the senior Waffen-SS commanders were told until a few weeks before the attack. This resulted in their training programmes being redoubled, and they also began to intensify the political and racial indoctrination of their troops. On a daily basis they were bombarded with Hitler's racial theories and hardened in preparation for the coming battle.

All through the spring of 1941, the build-up of troops and supplies continued relentlessly along the Soviet border. This build-up was interrupted by the Italian invasion of Greece, which had got bogged down during the winter of 1940 and brought British forces ashore to support the Greek Army. Neighbouring Yugoslavia was now wavering about its allegiance to the German cause, so Hitler ordered contingency plans to prevent Southeast Europe going over to the British. German panzer units in Hungary, Romania and Bulgaria were alerted to prepare for the occupation of Yugoslavia and Greece in a lightning offensive to last no longer than six weeks. Six panzer divisions (1200 tanks) and three motorized divisions were massed by the Germans around Yugoslavia, backed up by almost 1000 bombers and fighters.

To facilitate German ground operations against the Greeks and Yugoslavs, the Luftwaffe undertook intensive bombing operations on the Metaxas Line defences in the north. At the same time, the 23 divisions of the Italian Ninth and Eleventh Armies began offensive operations against Greek forces deployed in southern Albania.

THE GERMAN CONQUEST OF GREECE

— German attack
— Italian attack
---→ British retreat

0   Miles   100

0   Km   200

During February and March, the *Leibstandarte* and *Das Reich* were moved to Bulgaria and Romania respectively to spearhead the Balkans invasion, Operation Punishment. The onslaught began on 6 April with air attacks on key targets in the Yugoslav capital that lasted for two days, resulting in the deaths of 17,000 civilians.

From Bulgaria, the advance guard of Colonel-General Ewald von Kleist's panzer group raced towards the city of Skopje in Yugoslav Macedonia, which was a key railway link between Belgrade and Greece. In one day German panzers overwhelmed the stunned Yugoslav border guards and were in Skopje. The *Leibstandarte*, which had been following behind the assault wave, now took over the lead on 9 April and drove west to link up with the Italians who had begun an advance eastwards from their positions in Albania. There was almost no opposition from the Yugoslav Army units in the area; all seemed to have dissolved in panic. The SS brigade then turned south and headed to the strategic Klidi Pass which guarded the border to Greece and where Australian troops were believed to be dug in. During the

afternoon of 11 April the lead *Leibstandarte* battlegroup had their first contact with the Australian defenders.

Farther to the north, the collapse of the Yugoslav Government and military command under the weight of the relentless bombing of Belgrade forced the Germans to accelerate their invasion plans. While German, Italian and Hungarian troops struck southwards, Colonel-General Georg Hans Reinhardt's XXXXI Panzer Corps was launched from its bases around Timisoara in Romania to capture Belgrade, with the *Das Reich* Division in the vanguard.

The Yugoslav Army was wracked by ethnic divisions. Some of its Croat soldiers openly defected to the Germans, and others deserted en masse. Agents sent by SD chief Reinhard Heydrich exploited these divisions and distributed arms to local ethnic Germans, who staged several sabotage operations to help the advancing Wehrmacht. German panzers and Stukas made easy work of the Yugoslav divisions. Soon the German columns converging on Belgrade were racing each other for the honour of capturing the Yugoslav capital.

FRITZ KLINGENBERG

Fritz Klingenberg was born in Meckelenberg on 17 December 1912. In 1934 he joined the SS-VT, attending the SS-Junkerschule at Bad Tölz. As a young SS officer he was posted to the *Germania* Regiment. Within a short while, he became an inspector of the SS-VT under Paul Hausser. Klingenberg commanded a battalion of assault motorcycles after the campaign in the West, and it was with this unit that he gained fame as the man who captured Belgrade. With a small group of *Das Reich* men he took the city, simply by raising a swastika over the German Embassy and declaring the capital captured. Two hours later the mayor of Belgrade surrendered to Klingenberg, not knowing that sizeable German forces were some miles away and Klingenberg was virtually alone! For this audacious action Klingenberg was awarded the Knight's Cross. He moved back to the SS-Junkerschule at Bad Tölz in 1942, training young men to become officers in the Waffen-SS. In 1945 he assumed command of the 17th SS-Panzergrenadier Division *Götz von Berlichingen*. It was while leading this division that he was killed in action near Herxheim on 22 March 1945.

Early on the morning of 12 April, an advance guard from *Das Reich*'s reconnaissance battalion under Fritz Klingenberg approached Belgrade from the northeast. Klingenberg was anxious to enter the city, but the swollen River Danube was in his way. Using their initiative, the SS men soon commandeered a motor launch on the north bank of the river. Seven of the *Das Reich* men then crossed the Danube, and Klingenberg led them into the city. Soon after entering the city, they encountered a group of 20 Yugoslav soldiers, who without firing a shot surrendered. Klingenberg and his small team now proceeded to the German Embassy, where they unfurled a large swastika over it to declare the capture of the city. Two hours later, the mayor of Belgrade arrived at the embassy and surrendered the city to the *Das Reich* Division! Yugoslavia had held out for less than a week, and some 254,000 Yugoslav soldiers surrendered. In total the Germans suffered 558 casualties, including only 151 dead.

Farther south on the Greek border the *Leibstandarte* was finding the opposition had more fight in them. The Klidi Pass was high in the mountains and it was still covered in snow. In freezing conditions the SS assault troops infiltrated the Australian and British positions during the night of 11/12 April. Artillery barrages were used to cover the SS combat engineers as they cleared routes through the minefields to open the way for a major attack the following morning.

Tanks of the 9th Panzer Division were brought up to lead the way, with *Leibstandarte* infantry close behind. The defenders were overwhelmed in a day of intensive fighting, which saw small SS assault teams isolate and then destroy one British and Australian position after another. By late afternoon the British command ordered a full retreat, but one of the Australian battalions could not break free and was overrun with the loss of 60 prisoners.

The following day the SS men pursued the British, only to run into a British armoured brigade that was posted as a rearguard. It roughly handled the SS infantry, until a pair of *Leibstandarte* 88mm flak guns were brought up to engage the tanks. In two days of fighting that cost it 37 dead and 98 wounded, the *Leibstandarte* helped break the back of British resistance in northern Greece. As the 9th Panzer Division was swung east to pursue the British to their evacuation points around Athens, the *Leibstandarte* was sent west to help surround and destroy Greek divisions still fighting the Italians along the Albanian border.

The Greek 21st Division put up stiff resistance in the Klissurra Pass, forcing the SS men to advance on foot at night over mountain tracks to outflank their positions. With covering fire from 88mm flak guns, the SS troops then stormed the Greek lines in a dawn attack. More SS flanking attacks surrounded 12,000 Greek troops who surrendered when their escape route was closed. The *Leibstandarte* continued the movement southwards to trap more Greek troops, and on 21 April the main Greek armies in the west of the country surrendered.

Now the Germans turned their attention to the retreating British. In a daring move, a battalion of German paratroopers was dropped on the Corinth Canal bridge that dominated the roads south out of Athens, in an attempt to trap thousands of British and New Zealand troops. The *Leibstandarte* was ordered to link up with the paras and it raced 290km (180 miles) east at breakneck speed. The SS brigade's reconnaissance battalion commander, Kurt Meyer, drove his men relentlessly forward, bypassing pockets of Greek and British resistance before relieving the beleaguered paras on 26 April. After the last British troops had fled Greece, the *Leibstandarte* took pride of place in the German victory parade in Athens.

Army Group North – Totenkopf Strikes

At dawn on 22 June 1941, German aircraft and artillery began the opening bombardments of Operation Barbarossa. From the Baltic to the Black Sea, more than three million German troops attacked, taking five million Red Army soldiers largely by surprise. The Waffen-SS motorized divisions and brigades poised to attack Russia were some of the most powerful available to Hitler.

A *Totenkopf* Division driver during the opening phase of Operation Barbarossa in June 1941. The division totalled 18,754 men at the start of Barbarossa, though it suffered heavy casualties from late June onwards.

The onslaught was the beginning of almost four years of "total war" that would ultimately bring the Red Army to the gates of Berlin. Everything about the war on the Eastern Front was on a titanic scale: the distances, the number of troops involved, the intensity of the fighting and the horrific extent of the casualties.

The initial line-up of forces was of a scale that had never been seen before in the history of warfare. On the German side were 153 divisions, including 21 panzer and 14 motorized divisions containing some 3417 tanks. In the air, the Luftwaffe had almost 3800 fighters, bombers and transport aircraft available. On top of this force was added the contingents from Finland, Hungary, Italy, Slovakia and Romania that mustered several hundred thousand troops to help the Wehrmacht.

Opposing Hitler's invasion force was the Red Army, which appeared on paper to be a formidable force of some 180 divisions with some 20,000 tanks and air support from 10,000 combat aircraft. However, the Red Army was a hollow shell after many of its best officers had been executed in the purges that Stalin had unleashed in the late 1930s. Fewer than 2000 of its tanks were modern T-34s or KV-1s that could take on the latest German

Panzer IIIs or IVs on equal terms. The majority of the Red Army's soldiers were from rural peasant stock or were ill-educated factory workers. Many had received only rudimentary training to fire their rifles and had little experience operating sophisticated artillery, tanks or heavy weapons. Although Stalin loved to show off his military might in parades through Red Square or in showcase field exercises, the bulk of the Red Army rarely participated in large-scale manoeuvres or rehearsals of defensive plans. Discipline was brutal to ensure the Red Army remained under Communist Party control. Food and other provisions were in short supply. Division for division, the Red Army was hopelessly outclassed by its battle-hardened opponents in the Wehrmacht.

On the eve of the invasion *Das Reich* and *Totenkopf* each had some 16–18,000 highly trained troops. Unlike the ordinary army infantry divisions whose soldiers marched everywhere, Waffen-SS motorized units were provided with trucks to carry their troops on to the battlefield. All their artillery pieces were also towed by trucks, unlike army infantry units whose guns were pulled by horses. SS motorized infantry units were all lavishly armed with automatic machine pistols and bipod- or tripod-

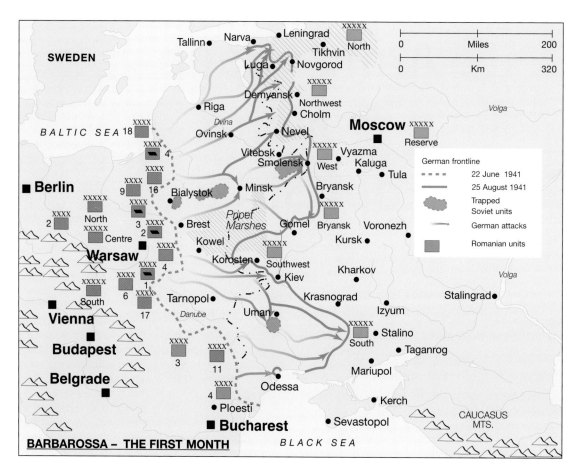

During the first period of Operation Barbarossa, Army Group North, which included the *Totenkopf* (part of Manstein's LVI Panzer Corps), advanced at a rate of 32km (20 miles) a day.

mounted MG34 machine guns, as well as 80mm and 120mm mortars. Waffen-SS troops were also some of the most highly motivated on the German side. They had all been thoroughly indoctrinated with Nazi racial superiority theories. To the members of the Waffen-SS, their Russian enemies were racial inferiors to be treated as sub-humans. The SS men were told by their officers to execute immediately any Communist Party officials they captured to break the back of any resistance. This also applied to political officers or commissars serving with Red Army units. The civilian population or captured Russian soldiers had no rights under laws of war because the Soviets had not signed up to the Geneva Convention. They were to be exploited to help the German war effort as forced labourers, and anyone who offered resistance was to be

executed immediately. Any Jews who were caught by the Waffen-SS were also to be liquidated. This brutal imperial policy soon alienated most of the civilian population in areas under German control, even in regions that had been anti-Soviet before the occupation.

Himmler summed up his attitude to the Russians during a meeting with SS generals: "It is a crime against our own blood to worry about [Russian civilians] and give them ideals, thus causing our sons and grandsons to have a more difficult time with them. When somebody comes to me and says, 'I cannot dig the anti-tank ditch with [Russian] women and children, it is inhuman, for it would kill them', then I have to say, 'You are a murderer of your own blood because if the anti-tank ditch is not dug, German soldiers will die, and they are sons of German mothers. They are our own blood.' That is what I want to instil into the SS and what I believe have instilled into them as one of the most sacred laws of the future. Our concern, our duty is our people and our blood. It is for them that we must provide and plan, work and fight, nothing else."

The fighting on the Eastern Front was also shaped by the huge distances of the theatre of operations. Once the German troops penetrated into the Russian hinterland they found their supplies lines were stretched to the limit. Ammunition, spare parts, replacement troops and equipment all became scarce commodities in frontline German divisions. Food and other basic supplies were commandeered from the local population, no matter what impact it had. As casualties took their toll and the civilian population turned against them, German troops thousands of miles from their homes began to feel isolated and psychologically besieged. They were alone, and with only their immediate comrades to help them.

So the scene was set not only for a conflict of huge size and intensity, but for a struggle that was at its heart a war of annihilation. Few rules of war applied. Both sides set about trying to eradicate each other with a degree of ferocity that had not been seen in a European conflict since the Middle Ages.

The Waffen-SS fighting divisions and brigades were posted to each of the three main German combat groups: Army Groups North, Centre and South. In the woods of East Prussia, the *Totenkopf* and *Polizei* Divisions were posted in reserve ready to exploit any successes by Colonel-General Erich Hoepner's Fourth Panzer Group as they advanced on Leningrad. The *Das Reich* Division was assigned to Colonel-General Heinz Guderian's Second Panzer Group, which was to lead the advance on Moscow.

Army Group South, which was to seize Kiev and key economic facilities in the Ukraine, contained the *Leibstandarte*, now given divisional status following the campaigns in Yugoslavia and Greece, and the newly formed *Wiking* Division. The SS units were held back from the first assault wave, and it was several days before they were fully engaged in action. The fighting in each sector was very different because of the terrain and intensity of Soviet opposition.

For the men of the *Totenkopf* Division, the advance on Leningrad, the Soviet Union's second city and cradle of the 1917 Bolshevik revolution, quickly turned into a nightmare battle of running skirmishes and ambushes in the heavily wooded and marshy terrain of the Baltic states and northern Russia. General Erich von Manstein's panzer corps initially rampaged through the Soviet border defences and advanced more than 320km (200 miles) in four days. The *Totenkopf* Division was ordered to follow behind and mop up Red Army stragglers in Lithuanian forests. The poor roads plagued the advance, and soon the SS men were running into large groups of Russian soldiers who were now starting to fight back with some determination. Many Soviet stragglers who tried to resist the SS men were dealt with ruthlessly, most being executed by their captors. It was almost a week before Theodor Eicke and his men had caught up with Manstein's panzers on the Dvina River line.

They then formed the right flank of Manstein's advance to the so-called Stalin Line, which ran south from Pskov through the heavily forested terrain that was also full of lakes. Eicke's division moved forward in two columns, and it soon ran into heavy resistance. At Dagda on 2 July, 10 SS men were killed and 100 wounded as the remains of a Soviet division decided to stand and fight. Soviet tanks joined the action, which raged throughout the night. Only the intervention of Luftwaffe Stuka dive-bombers broke the back of the resistance. Soviet artillery covered the Russian withdrawal to the Stalin Line.

Manstein's troops attacked the Stalin Line on 6 July and found themselves locked in a bitter struggle. The

THEODOR EICKE

Theodor Eicke was born in Alsace in 1892, and served as an army paymaster during World War I. He joined a Freikorps unit after the war and drifted into the SA in the early 1930s. In 1933 he moved to the SS-Hilfspolizei, whose job it was to guard enemies of the state. From this formation grew the SS-Totenkopfverbände, the concentration camp guard units. Eicke became responsible for the concentration camps in 1934, and he turned his Totenkopfverbände into disciplined, albeit pitiless, guards. The *Totenkopf* Division formed later was recruited from these guards. His men performed well enough in the French campaign, but were involved in the murder of British troops. On the Eastern Front Eicke's *Totenkopf*, steeled by his pronouncements that the war was a racial struggle to the death, excelled itself, especially at Demyansk. He was awarded the Knight's Cross in recognition of his unit's efforts, and the Oakleaves in 1942. Theodor Eicke was killed on 26 February 1943, after the aircraft he was travelling in was shot down by Soviet troops. His body was recovered from behind enemy lines by his men and buried in the military cemetery near Orelka.

A StuG III Ausf B assault gun in northern Russia during Barbarossa armed with the 75mm StuK L/24 gun. Some 320 Ausf Bs were built between June 1940 and May 1941.

Totenkopf Division was to spearhead the attack, which soon became bogged down in bloody hand-to-hand fighting of a type never before encountered by the SS men. Rather than running away, the Soviets disappeared underground into a series of bunkers and trench lines that each had to be cleared by assault teams armed with pistols, grenades and bayonets. The Soviet artillery then started bombarding their own positions as the SS men were fighting inside them, creating a horrendous slaughterhouse. Only the personal example of Eicke, who spent all day with his assault regiments, kept the advance moving forward. As he was returning from the front during the evening, his staff car drove over a mine and he had to be evacuated from the front for several weeks with severe injuries. For another three days the fighting raged over the Stalin Line as a storm drenched the battlefield in rain. A huge artillery barrage and non-stop air strikes eventually broke the back of the Soviet 182nd Rifle Division, but most of the surviving defenders eventually slipped away into the forests. The SS men were too tired by the battle to pursue them immediately. Some 82 officers and 1626 soldiers from the SS division had been killed or wounded in the 16 days since it had crossed the border.

Manstein's panzer corps now raced ahead towards Lake Ilmen and, as it tried to ford a river, it was hit by two fresh Soviet divisions, backed by a strong force of tanks. The Soviet counterattack cut Manstein's supply route. The *Totenkopf* Division was ordered to restore the front, and after heavy fighting it drove a corridor through to the trapped troops.

During the first two weeks of August, *the Totenkopf* Division was thrown into the battle of the Luga Line, the last Soviet defensive position south of Leningrad that had been built through a heavily wooded and swampy region. During daytime the SS men used artillery and airpower to take Soviet strongpoints, but at night hordes of Russian infantry would emerge from the thick forests to launch relentless human-wave attacks on the *Totenkopf*'s lines. The German advance ground to a halt as the soldiers in the frontline infantry regiments reached the limit of their endurance.

Just as Manstein was trying to smash his way through the Luga Line, the Soviets unleashed a force of eight infantry divisions and a cavalry corps around the southern fringe of Lake Ilmen. The 8th Panzer Division was temporarily surrounded and several other German divisions forced back. Manstein had to cease his northward attack and deal with the threat to his right flank. First on the scene to restore the line was the *Totenkopf*, which had to pull out of the line quickly and swing south. In a move that would become a Manstein trademark, the cunning German general did not immediately commit the SS division in the path of the Soviet advance. He held it on a flank and waited until the Soviet assault troops were fully committed to battle.

On 17 August, the *Totenkopf* struck at the exposed Soviet flank and left the Red Army troops reeling back in panic. Hundreds were captured and scores of tanks and military vehicles seized from fleeing Russians. The SS division was ordered to press deep into the Russian rear and take several key bridges that would trap all of the Soviet attack force in a pocket. Over the next two days the Germans closed the ring around the trapped Russians, sweeping the pocket with artillery and machine-gun fire. Some 1000 Russians were captured by the *Totenkopf,* and 18,000 were killed. Some 200 tanks, 300 guns and 700 trucks were left on the battlefield by the Red Army.

Manstein then ordered his panzers forward again towards Demyansk. As the *Totenkopf* followed on behind, its columns were strafed by waves of Russian aircraft and it was forced to take cover in nearby woods after Luftwaffe fighter support did not materialize. Heavy rains now fell on northern Russia, turning the battlefield into a mud bath and slowing the *Totenkopf*'s trucks. By the end of August the SS division had suffered almost 5000 men killed and thousands more wounded or struck down by illness and fatigue. The Russians now started to hit the SS men with relentless artillery barrages that lasted for hours and plunged morale to new lows.

When the rains lifted early in September, the division launched itself forward again to the southern edge of Lake

Ilmen. At first the advance went well and the SS men penetrated the Russian defences, opening a route to Demyansk. The fighting now degenerated into a series of small-scale battles to clear Soviet positions in the dense forests around the town. Eicke returned to his division during the middle of the month and found it in a desperate state.

On 24 September the Soviets took advantage of the weakened state of the German troops by launching a huge counteroffensive against the *Totenkopf*'s sector. Several brigades of fresh Soviet infantry hurled themselves at the depleted SS positions, surrounding several of Eicke's battalions. Anti-tank guns and artillery batteries were moved up to blast the Soviet infantry and tanks at close range. By evening the Russian dead were piled high in front of the SS positions. The lull was short-lived, and the Russians surged forward at first light the following day, this time led by 30 of the new T-34 tanks. Herds of pigs were also driven towards the German lines by the Soviets to clear paths through minefields. The attacks were held after the SS men allowed the Soviet tanks to close on their trenches and then destroyed them with satchel charges and hand grenades. For two more days the Soviets attacked, culminating in an assault by 100 tanks. The SS men fought fanatically, knowing that they could expect little mercy from their Soviet opponents, with one SS officer personally knocking out seven tanks on one day with demolition charges. Another SS anti-tank gunner remained at his position for two days after all his comrades had been killed, knocking out 13 Soviet tanks and driving off several attacks.

The *Totenkopf*'s defensive victory cost it another 1000 dead, but the northern sector of the Eastern Front had again been stabilized. But during October the German divisions in the northern sector, including the *Totenkopf*, were too weak to launch major offensive operations. A growing problem now was the large bands of partisans that were harassing German rear areas. The heavily forested terrain around Lake Ilmen provided great cover for the partisans, who struck at night and melted back into their sanctuaries. Eicke launched his men on "cleansing operations", in which many civilians were shot and scores of villages burnt to the ground in retaliation for partisan attacks.

The winter snows now descended on the *Totenkopf*'s sector, freezing the German advance against Leningrad. In six months of heavy fighting the division had suffered 8993 casualties, almost half of its strength.

The *Polizei* Division was also committed to action during the drive on Leningrad. It was not fully motorized, so took a number of weeks to catch up with Manstein's panzers. It participated in the battle for the Luga Line in early August, supporting the 3rd Motorized Division, and in the defensive battles around Lake Ilmen.

Soldiers of the *Totenkopf* Division during Operation Barbarossa. Against their ideological enemies the men of Eicke's command fought with fanatical determination.

The Drive on Moscow

The *Das Reich* Division formed part of the order of battle of Army Group Centre at the beginning of Operation Barbarossa. Having a strength of just over 19,000 men, it took part in the great encirclement battles waged by the Germans during the first weeks of the Russian campaign. By the time it participated in the attack on Moscow, the division had lost more than a quarter of its manpower.

A *Das Reich* motorcycle stuck fast in mud during the advance on Moscow. The autumn rains turned Russian dirt roads into quagmires, into which sank artillery pieces, wheeled vehicles and horses.

In Army Group Centre's sector of the Eastern Front, Paul Hausser's *Das Reich* was in reserve when the invasion began. It was fortunate to receive the first ever Waffen-SS assault-gun detachment, equipped with Sturmgeschütz III vehicles, a few days before it was due to move into action. These heavily armoured, self-propelled guns provided the Waffen-SS with an armoured punch that they had never had before, and reduced their dependency on the army to provide tank support.

Das Reich was assigned to the reserve corps of General Guderian's Second Panzer Group, which was positioned north of the fortress town of Brest Litovsk, ready to drive east once the city fell to German infantry. The first victim of Guderian's panzers was the Soviet Tenth Army, which was holding a salient around the city of Bialystok and was soon encircled. Guderian had his eyes firmly on an even larger group of Soviet armies positioned to defend Minsk, and he soon launched his reserve panzer corps into action. Generaloberst Hermann Hoth's Third Panzer Group completed the northern arm of the pincer movement.

Hausser's troops were soon in the vanguard of the encirclement. They raced forward at breakneck speed, shooting up bypassed groups of Russians. Speed was of the essence to Guderian's plan; by 3 July *Das Reich*'s motorcycle reconnaissance battalion had reached the River Beresina, southeast of Minsk. It was the job of other German units to clear up the Minsk Pocket that now contained some 290,000 Russians with 2500 tanks and 1500 guns. In a week of fighting the pocket was reduced by German infantry divisions, and most of the Russian troops were either killed or captured. The SS division and Guderian's panzers formed the outer crust of the German ring to stop any Soviet troops breaking through to their trapped comrades.

Das Reich's advance was characterized by brief skirmishes with confused and disorganized Soviet soldiers. It met its first serious resistance when the reconnaissance battalion tried to cross the Beresina, and a stiff fight ensued. The division was strung out in long convoys that were struggling to move at speed over the atrocious Russian road network. A Russian engineering team had time to blow the bridge over the Beresina, forcing SS engineers to repair it, delaying the advance until 5 July. Even when the bridge was built, small pockets of Russian troops continued to contest the *Das*

The initial phase of Operation Typhoon went well for the Germans, but Russian resistance and heavy rains slowed the advance. The mud prevented the Germans from exploiting their successes at Bryansk and Vyazma.

Reich attempts to secure a bridgehead to launch the advance eastwards again.

Hitler was obsessed with mopping up the Minsk Pocket, but Guderian was convinced the answer was not to stop and hold off any counterattack, but to strike fast to encircle the huge Soviet army gathering to the east at Smolensk. After several frustrating days halted southeast of Minsk, Guderian persuaded his superior, Field Marshal Hans von Kluge, of the wisdom of his plans and let him attack. Again the *Das Reich* men were in the vanguard, pushing towards Mogilev where a large Soviet force was reported to be gathering. The SS men avoided the Soviet troops, leaving them for follow-on forces, and

aimed for a crossing point over the River Dnieper at Shklov. Russian aircraft bombed the bridges over the Dnieper that the SS men were trying to capture, and again engineers had to repair them before the advance could continue towards Gorki.

Luftwaffe reconnaissance aircraft flew ahead of the SS columns looking out for any Soviet forces that might pose a threat. Guderian then joined the SS advance on 14 July as it surged even farther into the Russian interior. In little over a month Hausser's men had travelled almost 644km (400 miles). They had not suffered serious losses, but were totally exhausted by the pace of the advance.

Tanks from 10th Panzer Division took over the lead of the advance through Mstislavi and then on to Pochinok. Russians troops contested both towns and inflicted heavy casualties on the SS infantry following behind the armour. By 20 July, the 10th Panzer Division and *Das Reich* had carved a huge swathe through the Soviet positions south of Smolensk, driving to Yelnya, 48km (30 miles) to the east. Hoth's panzers were now moving around Smolensk, to close with the SS men and snap shut the jaws of another pincer movement.

Das Reich and 10th Panzer were now assaulted by a series of Soviet counterattacks aimed at keeping open a corridor to their comrades in Smolensk. Intense artillery fire kept German troops pinned down in an attempt to stop them advancing farther eastwards. The Soviets then sent in their tanks in a determined counterattack. The *Das Reich* troops clung on for two desperate days, eventually running low on ammunition. Two-thirds of 10th Panzer's tanks were knocked out in the fighting, which also resulted in 20 Soviet tanks being destroyed. *Das Reich*'s reconnaissance battalion was again in the forefront of the fighting, surviving repeated Soviet air attacks on its positions. During these desperate battles the SS division captured some 1100 prisoners.

THE SMOLENSK POCKET

Russian attacks continued against the Yelnya positions and did not cease even after 26 July, when Hoth's panzers joined up with German units to the west of *Das Reich*. The SS men were ordered to hold positions at all cost to stop the Soviets from breaking through to relieve the three Russian armies trapped in the forests to the east of Smolensk. Five Soviet infantry divisions and two tank brigades continued to batter the SS positions into early August. Guderian now turned some of his panzers southwards to crush another group of Soviet troops that were gathering around Roslavl to make a further rescue effort. The failure of this attempt only made the Soviet forces opposing *Das Reich* more desperate, and for another week, heavy fighting raged along its front.

Over 300,000 Soviet troops were now trapped and they resorted to desperate methods to escape. Thousands were killed when they tried to charge past the German units that were tightening the ring around the Smolensk Pocket. Tens of thousands escaped when a small corridor was opened on 4 August for several days. In the end, most of the Russian soldiers were doomed. The Germans declared they had captured 310,000 prisoners, 3000 tanks and 3000 artillery pieces. Those captured shared a desperate fate: denied food, medical care and shelter for months. Tens of thousands died in German prison camps.

Guderian was now ordered to swing his panzers southwards to trap an even bigger Soviet army east of Kiev. *Das Reich* did not immediately follow him, but was pulled out of the line near Smolensk in the middle of August to rest for two weeks.

At the end of August, *Das Reich* was called forward by Guderian to help his thrust southwards and relieve exhausted units. The SS men got into action on 3 September around Avdeievka, dealing with Soviet troops threatening the right flank of Guderian's panzers. Hausser was preparing his division for a major assault on the trapped Soviet troops east of Kiev when the battlefield was drenched in torrential rain. The whole of the German pincer movement ground to a halt in the mud, and the SS division was stuck fast well short of its jump-off points. When the rains lifted on 6 September, Hausser committed his troops to action even though a large part of his division was still struggling to get up to the front. Guderian channelled Luftwaffe air support to help *Das Reich* capture a key railway bridge. For the next two weeks the division continued to push southwards to squeeze the northern flank of the Soviet pocket east of Kiev, rounding up thousands of prisoners as resistance began to crumble. It was then switched east to reinforce the outer ring of the encirclement around Rommy for a pre-emptive strike against Soviet troops gathering for an offensive. By the time the Russians surrendered at the end of the month, more than 600,000 had been captured by the Germans.

THE DRIVE ON MOSCOW

Hitler was now turning his attention to Moscow, and he ordered a major concentration of panzer and motorized forces ready to strike at the Soviet capital by early October. Operation Typhoon was scheduled to begin on 30 September. *Das Reich* was assigned to follow the offensive by General Hoepner's Fourth Panzer Group, which was concentrating around Roslavl. The first objective was to surround six Soviet armies positioned between Smolensk and Vyazma. Soon, panzer spearheads were closing around their prey. In their wake came the *Das Reich* Division, which was given the job of forming a bulwark on the eastern edge of the encirclement and preventing Soviet relief columns interfering with the German operation. It was committed to action on 6 October to seize and hold the Smolensk–Moscow highway at Gzhatsk, soon reaching the outskirts of the town in the face of heavy resistance from strafing attacks by Soviet fighter-bombers.

The *Deutschland* Regiment moved to attack on 7 October, brushing past isolated pockets of Russian

Das Reich infantry follow a column of Panzer II tanks during the final phase of Operation Typhoon. By this stage the division's men were freezing, unshaven and tired.

troops. A full regimental-scale attack the following day led to the cutting of the Smolensk–Moscow road, and the division was poised to take Gzhatsk.

Tanks of the 10th Panzer Division now joined the SS men for this attack, which went in through a blizzard that had descended on the battlefield. Assault groups from the *Deutschland* Regiment rode to Gzhatsk on the back of the panzers, while to the south the *Der Führer* Regiment launched an outflanking attack to catch any Russians fleeing the town. The SS men and panzer troops rampaged through Soviet truck columns, machine-gunning hundreds of helpless Red Army men. During the freezing night that followed, Soviet troops in white camouflage launched repeated counterattacks. A build-up of Russian forces was detected the next day, and a spoiling attack was launched by the *Der Führer* Regiment that scattered the Soviet 18th Tank Brigade.

With the encirclement operation now complete and 660,000 Russians captured, General Hoepner ordered *Das Reich* to push eastwards. The division's objective was the town of Mozhaisk, which formed the centre of

the Soviet capital's outer defensive ring. Two regimental-sized battlegroups were sent to attack on 11 October, only to run into heavy Soviet resistance from infantry supported by tanks and armoured trains.

Waffen-SS 88mm flak guns were deployed forward to counter the Soviet tanks, and then tanks of the 10th Panzer Division were brought up to hit the T-34s' flanks, where their armour was weakest. The intervention of the panzers turned the battle, allowing the Waffen-SS infantrymen to penetrate into the heart of the Soviet bunker complexes. The heavy fighting brought Hausser up to the front to encourage his men but he was badly injured during one T-34 attack, losing an eye and part of his jaw to a shell fragment. The SS officer had to be evacuated from the battlefield for several weeks.

A handful of Soviet heavy tanks (probably T-35s) now appeared and attacked the *Deutschland* Regiment, until a 150mm howitzer could be brought up to knock them out. Waves of T-34s were then sent into action to push the SS regiment back. Only heavy artillery fire was able to stabilize the situation and drive off the Soviet assaults. One more day of Waffen-SS attacks, backed by Stuka dive-bombers, finally cracked the Soviet defences open to allow the division to move forward to begin its assault on the main Moscow Line defences. Backed by fire from Nebelwerfer rocket launchers, the SS troops struck at the Soviet defences around Borodino, which were held by newly arrived Mongolian troops.

Freezing rain and snow were now falling throughout the day and night, making life very miserable for the SS men, who had not yet received any winter uniforms or equipment. Fortunately, the cold weather kept the ground firm, so *Das Reich*'s supporting panzers could still roar to their assistance when heavy Russian resistance was encountered.

On 13 October the battle for Mozhaisk opened, and for five days *Das Reich* launched attack after attack to punch through the fanatical resistance. Panzers, Stukas, Nebelwerfers and every other weapon at the division's disposal had to be thrown into the battle to dislodge the Soviet troops, who were frantically trying to protect their capital. Waffen-SS assault guns now came into their own, providing vital firepower when the tanks of 10th Panzer Division were diverted to other tasks.

A SLOW, AGONIZING ADVANCE

By 19 October, Soviet defences had been smashed open and the SS division was ordered to swing south to protect the flank of Hoepner's panzers as they raced to outflank Moscow from the north. Mongolian infantry and waves of T-34s now tried to break into the SS lines. The division drove off the attacks and continued to push southeast for two days, clearing out a large section of the Moscow Line.

In the final days of October, the German troops were temporarily cheered by a sudden rise in temperature. This was actually the worst thing that could have happened for the Germans. Soon all the snow had melted and the German panzers and trucks were axle-deep in mud. For nearly two weeks Hoepner's troops sat helplessly outside Moscow, unable to move forward or even bring up fresh supplies. At night Soviet troops and partisans launched relentless hit-and-run raids on the Germans, further sapping German strength and morale. The *Das Reich* men tried to restore their fighting power for the next phase of Operation Typhoon, but they had been badly battered in the past three weeks of intense fighting, losing more than 400 dead and 5000 wounded. This was almost a third of the division's total manpower, but a disproportionate number of these casualties were in its infantry regiments, which reduced some companies to fewer than 40 men fit for action (hardly any replacements had found their way to the front yet). The division's vehicles and heavy weapons were in an equally degraded state, and only a few replacements had been received to plug the extensive battle losses. More ominously, German supply columns were now regularly being destroyed by the partisan bands that were roaming in the huge forests behind *Das Reich*'s

sector. Ammunition stockpiles were running low, making it difficult for the SS troops to attack or even to hold off Soviet assaults that were now a daily occurrence.

When the temperature started to drop in the middle of November, the ground hardened, Hoepner's panzers raced forward and Guderian's tanks struck from the southwest to try to encircle Moscow. *Das Reich* was on Hoepner's right flank and spent three weeks fighting its way through a huge belt of minefields and field fortifications. Hundreds of thousands of Muscovites had been drafted to help dig these huge ramparts that *Das Reich* shed so much blood to seize. The 7th Panzer Division managed to punch a hole and got to within 39km (24 miles) of the Russian capital before being stopped by strong defences. The panzer crews even reported back that they could see the spires of the Kremlin during the brief period they held out across the Moscow–Volga canal that formed the city's last line of defence.

THE END OF TYPHOON

In *Das Reich*'s sector, near Istra, the Soviet resistance was proving too much even for the SS men. One wrote to his mother: "These Russians seem to have an inexhaustible supply of men. Here they unload fresh troops from Siberia every day: they bring up guns and lay mines all over the place. On the 30th [November] we made our last attack – a hill known as Pear Hill and village called Lenino. With artillery and mortars we managed to take all of the hill and half of the village. But at night we had to give it up again in order to defend ourselves against the continuous Russian counterattacks. We only need to go another eight miles to get the [Soviet] capital within gun range – but we just could not make it."

The Russian winter now struck with a vengeance. At night temperatures dropped to -40°C (-40°F) and in daytime they rose to barely half that. The supply crisis meant no cold-weather lubricants or winter clothing had made their way to the frontline troops outside Moscow. Most of the Germans' tanks, artillery, heavy weapons and trucks froze solid at night, and could only be made operational by lighting fires under them. Thousands of men went down with frostbite. In the space of three weeks since the final offensive opened on Moscow, Army Group Centre had lost 55,000 dead.

By 5 December Operation Typhoon was over. The efforts of the *Das Reich* Division were in vain. Along with the other German units outside Moscow, its cold and hungry troops were struggling to survive in improvised trenches 48km (30 miles) to the west of the city. With casualties mounting, the division's ability to hold its sector of front was rapidly diminishing.

Into the Ukraine

The *Leibstandarte* and *Wiking* Divisions both made a significant contribution to Operation Barbarossa in southern Russia. The destruction of Soviet armies and the capture of hundreds of thousands of prisoners apparently signalled the collapse of the Red Army. But the Russians kept on fighting, and the Waffen-SS units began to suffer the effects of attrition as 1941 came to an end.

A *Wiking* Division machine gunner dashes forward during Barbarossa. His weapon is the 7.92mm MG34 machine gun, which is fitted with a drum magazine. It had a rate of fire of 900 rounds per minute.

The *Leibstandarte* was committed to the southern sector of Barbarossa as an element of Colonel-General Ewald von Kleist's First Panzer Group. It was assigned the mission of driving into the north of the Ukraine as part of a pincer movement to trap three Soviet armies around Uman. Its line of advance was directly south of the Pripet Marshes, which provided a natural barrier cutting off the German forces in the Ukraine from those advancing towards Minsk and Smolensk. It was the job of the *Leibstandarte* to screen the left flank of Kleist's panzer groups.

Within days of crossing the border, Kleist's troops were being vigorously counterattacked by Soviet armoured and mechanized reserves. The *Leibstandarte* had to fend off several of these onslaughts, involving huge swarms of Russian tanks and troops in the back of lorries moving towards the Waffen-SS lines. They were easily driven off, but slowed the division's advance to a snail's pace. The primitive Ukrainian road network added to the Waffen-SS men's problems, which were made worse by heavy rain.

Kleist relentlessly pressured his commanders to increase the pace of the advance to keep the Russians off-balance. By early July his spearheads were deep inside the Ukraine approaching the defences of the Stalin Line, east of Kiev. The *Leibstandarte* was sent in to breach this position on 7 July. Its reconnaissance battalion found an undefended route over the River Sluczk and it had soon bypassed many of the Soviet positions. Pressing on through thick woods, Waffen-SS armoured cars and motorcycles were closing on Zhitomir when they ran into heavy opposition from tanks and infantry. Soviet air attacks on the *Leibstandarte*'s bridges delayed the main body of the brigade coming to the reconnaissance detachment's aid until later in the day. The next day 88mm flak guns were brought up to help the reconnaissance battalion storm across the River Teterev to open the way for it to capture a key road junction outside Zhitomir.

In the third week of July, Kleist's panzer columns were again racing eastwards to close the jaws around the Uman Pocket. The spearheads of the 16th Panzer Division became overexposed and were hit by three Soviet tank divisions. *Leibstandarte* troops raced to the rescue and drove off the Russians. With this danger averted, the *Leibstandarte* turned south as the final

Two members of the *Leibstandarte* round up prisoners in July 1941. From the beginning of the campaign Waffen-SS soldiers shot many Soviet prisoners after they had surrendered.

stages of the encirclement operation unfolded. The *Leibstandarte* was moved into the line to hold the eastern edge of the pocket. Soviet tanks, infantry, cavalry and armed civilians hurled themselves at the Waffen-SS lines in waves, but most died in hails of machine-gun and mortar fire. Eventually 100,000 Russians were captured by the Germans when the pocket was finally cleared early in August.

Army Group South now surged towards the lower reaches of the River Dnieper, arriving on 21 August. The *Leibstandarte* continued the pell-mell advance, occasionally bumping into resistance from bypassed Russian units that were dispersed by artillery and mortar fire. While many of Kleist's panzer divisions were ordered north to complete the encirclement of Kiev in cooperation with Guderian's forces striking south, the remainder of his troops advanced towards the Crimea.

Leibstandarte columns followed in the wake of this advance across the barren Nogai Steppe. As they closed on the Crimea, though, Russian resistance stiffened. Prepared defensive positions manned by well-trained Soviet marines slowed the advance around Nikolayaev, although the Soviet Ninth and Eighteenth Armies were trapped around the Odessa naval base. The *Leibstandarte*

was now ordered into the Crimea, and a series of assaults had to be launched on these lines to try to blast a route south towards Perekop. Here, an 8km- (5-mile-) wide strip of land was totally devoid of cover. When *Leibstandarte* infantry tried to storm the Soviet lines on 18 September, they met a wall of lead from dug-in troops and an armoured train. After initially faltering, the SS men punched a hole through the Russian defences and captured several sectors of the trench lines. But Soviet counterattacks retook some ground.

It was now decided to screen the Crimea. The *Leibstandarte* was relieved by Romanian infantry and ordered eastwards again across the steppe towards Rostov. It had only been gone four days when a Soviet offensive broke through the Romanian lines and threatened the German supply lines. In cooperation with German mountain troops, the Soviets were thrown back in chaos into the Crimea by the *Leibstandarte*.

Kleist was now ordered to concentrate his panzer group in the Dnieper bend ready for a major encircling operation at Melitopol. The German offensive started on 30 September in response to a Soviet attack aimed at regaining the Dnieper at Nikolop. The Soviet units striking west now realized the threat to their flank and started to pull back. Dietrich's division first drove northwards to block the Soviet movement, then south to press into the flank of two retreating Soviet armies. It was caught on the open steppe and destroyed. The Soviets had built a huge anti-tank ditch around Melitopol in a desperate

A *Leibstandarte* detachment attacks a strongpoint on the Stalin Line defence system. The soldier on the right has a Flammenwerfer 35 flamethrower on his back.

attempt to hold the town, but the *Leibstandarte* columns charged into the town, machine-gunning its surprised defenders from their trucks. The SS troops were surrounded by thousands of Russians trying to surrender as resistance collapsed. Dietrich then ordered his men to press on southwards. More Soviet units were caught and scattered by the Waffen-SS men, including a whole army headquarters staff. When the encirclement was complete, more than 100,000 Russians had been trapped by Kleist's panzers.

Kleist now ordered his armoured forces to swing east again towards Rostov. The *Leibstandarte* was ordered to advance along the coast with Taganrog as its objective. By 11 October the *Leibstandarte* was outside Taganrog and had pushed a small bridgehead over the Mius River, which guarded the western approaches to the town. Three Waffen-SS battalions then stormed into the town on 17 October, and drove off a Soviet tank regiment that tried to intervene to help its defenders. The five-day battle for the town was very confused, with small groups of Waffen-SS men having to hold off huge Soviet attacks by infantry and tanks. When six men of the *Leibstandarte*'s reconnaissance battalion were overrun and executed by Soviet troops, Dietrich was enraged and ordered every Russian prisoner captured over a four-day period to be shot. More than 4000 Russians were killed in cold blood by the *Leibstandarte*.

After more than two months of relentless movement, the *Leibstandarte* was exhausted. It needed replacement troops and equipment. Despite these problems, Dietrich tried to push on to Rostov only to run into a series of Russian defensive lines, which proved too strong for his battered troops to breach. Heavy rain turned the Ukraine into a mud bath. The breakneck advance by the *Leibstandarte* had left the rest of Kleist's panzer group struggling to catch up, and it was four weeks before III Panzer Corps was moved up to continue the attack on Rostov. Dietrich's men spent almost a month kicking their heels east of Taganrog along the Mius.

On 17 November, Kleist's panzers struck out from their positions along the Mius line and lunged for Rostov. The *Leibstandarte* was in the vanguard, and its reconnaissance battalion soon punched a way through the Russian defences. It then pushed through the city to capture a key bridge over the River Ron. The rest of the division followed behind and spent several days

mopping up pockets of determined Russian resistance from the city.

This time the Soviets had prepared their defences well and had two reserve armies ready to strike back. The Fifty-Sixth Independent Army struck from the south and pinned down Dietrich's men in the city. To the north, the Thirty-Seventh Army sent waves of T-34s against three German divisions, screening the supply line into Rostov. Amid freezing weather and snow storms, the *Leibstandarte* held Rostov for 10 days before the army High Command ordered it to pull back on 28 November. Field Marshal Gerd von Rundstedt, the commander of Army Group South, had disobeyed a direct order from the Führer to hold Rostov to the last man. The field marshal was sacked, but Dietrich and his men had been saved from being trapped in Rostov by 21 Soviet divisions.

The retreat to the Mius was a depressing end to the *Leibstandarte*'s six-month, non-stop advance through Russia. Out of 9994 who had entered Russia under his command in June, Dietrich had lost 5281 killed, wounded or missing. Only 15 percent of his vehicles were in working order, and most of the division's heavy weapons also needed repair.

Hitler was furious about the retreat from Rostov and flew to Kleist's headquarters in the Ukraine to interrogate the army general and Dietrich on why his élite troops had pulled back from the city. The *Leibstandarte* commander now proved he was no "yes-man", and detailed the true state of his command to a shocked Hitler. Dietrich and his men were ordered to hold fast on the Mius. Retaking Rostov was off the agenda for the time being.

Felix Steiner's *Wiking* Division was held in Army Group South's reserve during the first five days of Barbarossa, as part of XXIV Panzer Corps. In less than six months, Steiner had built *Wiking* up to a strength of 9377 men, including 631 Dutchmen, 294 Norwegians, 216 Danes and more than 400 Finns. Although strong in manpower, the *Wiking* Division did not have as many trucks or heavy weapons as the other Waffen-SS motorized units. The unit also lacked the élan and unit spirit that its counterparts had gained from their combat experience in Poland, France and the Balkans. It moved across the border late in June in the wake of Kleist's dash for Uman. Galicia had been seized from Poland in September 1939 and the civilian population was predominantly Catholic. They initially welcomed the Germans as liberators. The region also had a large Jewish population, many of whom had fled from Poland during the German invasion two years earlier.

The *Wiking* Division had its first taste of combat on 29 June, when it was ordered to advance towards Tarnopol to mop up the remnants of three Soviet mechanized

corps that had tried to strike at the southern flank of Kleist's divisions. The *Westland* Regiment spearheaded the attack that rolled into Lvov from the west on 30 June and was soon embroiled in heavy street fighting with Soviet rearguards. In one of these battles the commander of the *Westland* Regiment, Helmar Wackerle, was killed. Tens of thousands of Soviet troops had been bypassed in the Lvov–Ternopol region and the bulk of the *Wiking* Division spent most of July sweeping the area. They also took the opportunity to stage several mass killings of Jews, including the shooting of 60 in Lvov in reprisal for the death of Wackerle. Troops of the army's 1st Mountain Division joined in this incident and other massacres by the *Wiking* Division in the Ukraine.

The *Nordland* Regiment was detached from the division during this period to help the 13th Panzer Division as it swung around north of the Uman Pocket. During early August, the reconstituted *Wiking* Division was swinging south towards Kherson on the lower Dnieper as part of the drive to trap the Soviet forces in Odessa. It was then sent northwards to the Dnieper bend to help III Panzer Corps seize Dnepropetrovsk. In heavy fighting it captured the suburb of Kamenka and then pursued the Soviet defenders out of the city into the jaws of the 13th and 14th Panzer Divisions. In cooperation with the 198th Infantry Division, it then spent most of early September mopping up around the city and helping create a bridgehead for the panzer corps to strike eastwards again.

A Stug III and Waffen-SS infantry, possibly of the *Leibstandarte*, in Cherson in August 1941. The Waffen-SS had won the town in the face of desperate Soviet resistance.

The *Wiking* Division helped in Kleist's successful encirclement operations, swinging south to close the ring around the Soviet armies at Melitopol on 30 September. It then joined XIV Panzer Corps for the next phase of the advance that took it to the northern reaches of the Mius River. Plunging temperatures in mid-November allowed Kleist's panzers to roll again towards Rostov and the *Wiking* Division was deployed as flank guard on the left wing of the German advance. It ran into heavy resistance at Astachowo to the northwest of Rostov from interlocking dug-in Soviet anti-tank guns. The Waffen-SS men had to fight for trench after trench in freezing weather. The fight for Rostov was sucking in more and more German troops, leaving the depleted *Wiking* units to hold a lengthening sector of front. On 23 November the Soviets launched their Rostov offensive, hitting Steiner's men hard and forcing them to reel back. With the *Wiking*'s position buckling, a general retreat from Rostov was ordered.

AN SS MOUNTAIN DIVISION
The final major Waffen-SS formation committed to Barbarossa was the *Nord* Mountain Division. This had been created in April 1941 by expanding the *Nord* infantry brigade with an influx of ethnic Germans who were allegedly mountaineers. Even though it was poorly trained and composed largely of middle-aged *Totenkopf* reservists, it was shipped to Norway to join the German forces assisting the Finns strike at the strategic Soviet port of Murmansk. In July 1941, the Waffen-SS men had hacked their way through dark Finnish forests to strike at the Soviet stronghold of Salla. Two major attacks were easily repulsed, badly mauling five Waffen-SS battalions. The Soviets then brought up tanks and struck back at the *Nord* Division. The inexperienced SS men panicked. Hundreds fled, and in the chaos 50 Waffen-SS men were killed and 232 wounded. Much to Himmler's fury, 147 of his Waffen-SS warriors surrendered rather than fight to the death. The division eventually recovered and fought on the Finnish front until 1944 with some distinction.

In the first six months of Operation Barbarossa, the Waffen-SS had been bloodied in the cauldron of all-out war. Its troops had surged eastwards with great professionalism and played a key part in the German victories of the summer and autumn. Of the 100,000 Waffen-SS men who had entered Russia in June 1941, almost 40,000 were now casualties, including 1238 officers. More than 13,000 had been killed in action.

Senior German Army officers were full of praise for the performance of the *Leibstandarte*, *Das Reich* and *Totenkopf* Divisions. The commanders of these divisions and their staffs were also praised for their bravery under fire. Guderian described Hausser as "cool headed". Manstein dubbed the *Totenkopf* "probably the best Waffen-SS division I ever came across". He said, "its commander [Eicke] was a brave man". "In no circumstances should we forget that the Waffen-SS, like the good comrades they were, fought shoulder to shoulder with the army at the front and always showed themselves courageous and reliable", said Manstein (though he was very critical of the poor training of some Waffen-SS officers that led to unnecessary casualties).

While the reputation of the three "premier" Waffen-SS units grew as a result of their exploits during the first six months of the invasion of Russia, the mixed performance of the *Wiking* and *Nord* Divisions indicated that the rapid expansion of Himmler's army was not without problems.

SS ATROCITIES
One area where army commanders were not so complimentary about the behaviour of the Waffen-SS was in its treatment of civilians. There was a growing number of complaints about the random and brutal killing of Jews and other civilians by Waffen-SS men. Ominously, other SS units started to appear in rear areas that operated outside the army chain of command. SS commands were set up in every sector of occupied Russia, ostensibly to coordinate "security" activity. But this was only a cover for the first elements of the Nazi campaign to cleanse Eastern Europe of *untermenschen*.

Himmler also created four special SS units, dubbed Einsatzgruppen A, B, C and D, to "clean up" occupied territory of Jews and Communist Party officials. Each group consisted of 800–1200 men and drew its personnel from the Gestapo, SD, civilian police and Waffen-SS. More than a third of the personnel for the Einsatzgruppen came from the Waffen-SS, with the personnel either drafted from depots before the invasion of Russia started or sent to them as punishment duty from units already fighting in Russia.

By the end of 1941 each of the four Einsatzgruppen had carved a trail of murder across occupied Russia, killing 500,000 people, the vast majority of whom were Jewish men, women and children (most were rounded up, taken to large pits outside towns and villages, machine-gunned and their bodies thrown into the pits). But the Einsatzgruppen were only the advance guard of Himmler's murder machine that would kill millions in occupied Russia over the following three years.

The invasion of Russia saw the Waffen-SS build a formidable reputation as a fighting force, but it also confirmed that they were warriors for a truly evil cause.

Winter in Hell

The Waffen-SS divisions that took part in Barbarossa had entered Russia with high morale and a conviction that their National Socialist zeal would easily overcome the Red Army. But six months of continuous fighting had depleted their ranks alarmingly, and the Russian winter also took its toll. Then, the "beaten" Red Army counterattacked along the whole front to drive the Germans back.

With Soviet dead lying on the snow, a *Totenkopf* machine gunner keeps watch for the next Red Army attack against the Demyansk Pocket. His tripod-mounted MG34 is fed from a 250-round belt.

The advance to the gates of Moscow in the final days of November 1941 was the high-water mark of Operation Barbarossa. Huddled together in freezing trenches with little food and ammunition, the German soldiers of the Eastern Front were soon at the end of their endurance. Thousands of men were succumbing to frostbite, and disease was rampant. Hope was in short supply.

On 5 December the Soviets struck back in dramatic fashion. In secret they had brought up 50 fresh divisions totalling 770,000 men and some 2000 tanks to form a strike force behind Moscow. While the Germans weakened themselves further in a final lunge for the city, Marshal Georgi Zhukov (who in January 1941 had been made chief of staff of the Red Army) kept his reserves out of the battle. Once it was clear that the German offensive was spent, he ordered the trap to be sprung.

Thousands of guns and "Stalin's Organ" rocket launchers pounded the demoralized German troops in the Klin salient north of Moscow, and in the Tula bulge south of the capital. Waves of new T-34 tanks raced forward with white-clad Red Army submachine-gunners riding behind their turrets. The shock was dramatic and, all along Army Group Centre's front, German units fell

back. Those that held their ground were overrun or surrounded in their improvised strongpoints. Fleeing from the Soviet tanks was an equally dangerous proposition. German units that were caught in the open at nightfall had to endure temperatures below -50°C (-58°F), further reducing their numbers and rendering their remaining equipment inoperable.

The 8000 men of the *Das Reich* Division who were still capable of fighting were caught up in this maelstrom around Istra, 49km (30 miles) to the west of Moscow. The Soviet Sixteenth Army committed two divisions of fresh troops from its Siberian reserve force against the Waffen-SS men. In a day of brutal fighting, the *Das Reich* Division was overwhelmed. Its flank was smashed open and the division had little option but to pull back. The retreat was far from orderly, and scores of SS men were captured by the Soviets and paraded in front of propaganda cameras. The images of dead and captured SS troops represented a great morale booster for the Soviet public, who were now beginning to believe that perhaps they had a chance of defeating the Nazi Blitzkrieg.

To try to create a huge water obstacle in front of their positions, the Germans now blew up the Istra

Some 95,000 men were trapped in the Demyansk Pocket. Within the pocket, Eicke's men were divided into two kampfgruppen. Here, *Totenkopf* men keep watch.

dam, turning the River Istra into a raging torrent. The *Das Reich* men and the other German units managed to hold this improvised front for just over a week, until the Soviets tanks found routes around to the north and south of their positions by moving across country. The Soviet T-34 tanks had wide tracks that made their weight-per-inch ratios lighter than that of an infantryman, so they could easily speed across the snow-covered landscape. German tanks, with their narrow tracks, would soon be stuck fast if they tried similar manoeuvres.

Faced with having the only open road to the west cut, the *Das Reich* Division again retreated towards Ruza, 64km (40 miles) to the west, where a new line was being formed against the Soviets. With its mobility and firepower severely limited by the snow, the *Das Reich* Division had to rely on its few surviving StuG III assault guns and 75mm self-propelled infantry guns to act as mobile strike forces to rush to threatened sectors of its front and repel Soviet attacks. As the retreat gathered momentum, Russian ski

troops harried the SS men with hit-and-run attacks. The *Das Reich* Division was allowed no respite.

Another Soviet offensive was unleashed on 5 January 1942 to smash Army Group Centre before it had time to recover. This time the Soviet Fifth Army assaulted the weak German divisions to the south of *Das Reich*, and threatened to overrun its supply line. Once again the desperate SS men had to retreat, this time 97km (60 miles) across the freezing steppe with Soviet ski troops and Cossack cavalry squadrons snapping at their heels.

By 12 January the division was at Gzhatsk, where its defensive line halted the Soviet offensive, which was now running out of steam through lack of supplies and heavy casualties. Zhukov, however, had another trick up his sleeve and had three shock armies poised far to the north ready to sweep down on the rear flank of Army Group Centre.

The Soviet blow struck on 2 January, and opened a huge breach in the German Ninth Army's lines north of Rzhev. Hitler raged that the Ninth Army "will not take one more step back". With few reserves available, the army group high command had to commit any soldier who could carry a gun to the battle. The only major unit uncommitted in the threatened sector was the Waffen-SS

Above: A *Totenkopf* GrW 34 80mm mortar and its crew in the Demyansk Pocket. Eicke's mortar crews were well trained, and each crew could fire up to 25 rounds a minute against attacking enemy units, up to a range of 2400m (7990ft).

Left: A *Totenkopf* night patrol returns to base following a raid on a nearby Soviet-occupied village. In the fighting in and around the Demyansk Pocket, *Totenkopf* units were subjected to incessant Red Army artillery barrages.

Cavalry Brigade under the command of Hermann Fegelein, the brother-in-law of Hitler's mistress, Eva Braun. It was dispatched across country to take on the Soviets, dragging its heavy equipment and supplies on improvised sleds. Although it cut a dash with its horses, the Cavalry Brigade was not equipped or trained to take on Soviet armoured units.

The SS Cavalry Brigade launched its counterattack on 7 January, but after a day's fighting was forced back when it ran out of ammunition. One of its battalions suffered 75 percent casualties in the horrendous fighting in the woods north of Rzhev. It was a futile effort, which did little to halt the torrent of Soviet troops heading southwards to encircle German troops sheltering around Vyazma, including the *Das Reich* Division. Hitler was furious that his orders to fight to the last man were being ignored by army commanders outside Moscow. A raft of senior generals were sacked for lack of resolution, and new men sent to put some backbone into the ranks of the troops at the front. One such man was Lieutenant-General Walther Model, who was sent to take over the Ninth Army.

He arrived in the middle of January and immediately began organizing counterattacks, but brought no reinforcements or new equipment with him. The troops at the front would have to drive back the Soviets without outside help in sub-zero temperatures and knee-deep snow.

STEMMING THE RED TIDE

The Ninth Army was ordered to launch a counterattack to trap the spearheads of the Soviet Twenty-Ninth Army approaching Vyazma. It was a daring but desperate move that needed determined soldiers. The *Das Reich* Division proved up to the job. It quickly punched a corridor to German troops to the west, including the survivors of the SS Cavalry Brigade, and closed a ring around 36,000 Soviet troops, standing ready to hold off a relief attempt by the Red Army's Thirty-Ninth Army. For more than three weeks the 650 men of the *Der Führer* Regiment and the SS Cavalry Brigade held their positions against relentless Soviet attacks. Day after day, waves of Soviet T-34s tried to blast their way past the Waffen-SS men. *Das Reich* anti-tank gunners and tank-hunting parties drove off the Soviet tanks on each occasion. Scores of Soviet tanks were knocked out in front of the German lines, but the *Das Reich* troops suffered grievously. Whole companies were wiped out in the battle, and when the Soviets gave up their attempt to free their trapped comrades the *Der Führer* Regiment was down to 35 men fit for battle. The battalions of the SS Cavalry Brigade were equally depleted to 30–40 men each.

There was still no respite for the men of the *Das Reich* Division, who were called up to fight in the Rzhev salient for just over a month. Both the Soviet and German high commands were trying to tidy up their fronts, and eliminate salients and threatening concentrations. By the end of February, the Waffen-SS division had lost another 4000 casualties and each of its frontline battalions was barely able to muster 100 men fit for action.

In the Army Group South sector, the *Leibstandarte* and *Wiking* Divisions were fully committed to the defence of the Mius River line to the west of Rostov. Although the Soviets made repeated attempts to break through the Waffen-SS lines, the German defensive positions were built on the top of a ridge high above the river. Defenders could easily pick off any attackers trying to close on them with artillery, mortars and machine guns.

THE SS DIVISIONS STAND FAST

Through the winter into the spring of 1941–42, the two Waffen-SS units held firm, and allowed other German mobile units to strike northwest to seal off a Soviet breakthrough at Izyum that threatened Army Group South's supply lines back to the Dnieper. As Soviet offensives were engulfing Army Group Centre in December 1941 and into January 1942, this storm of steel soon spread to the northern sector and almost swept away the *Totenkopf* Division. Like their comrades in front of Moscow and farther south, Theodor Eicke's men were exhausted, freezing cold and had no idea when they would be relieved. They stood shivering in their trenches on the night of 7/8 January when two Soviet armies smashed the units on either side of them. *Totenkopf* troops were able to repulse the attacks on their positions.

As the Soviet pincers closed around the German II Corps, which included the *Totenkopf*, over the next week Eicke's men were called upon to act as "fire brigades", rushed to threatened sectors to plug breaches in the line. By 20 January, 95,000 German troops were trapped in a huge pocket centred on the city of Demyansk, with air transport the only way of supplying them. Hitler refused requests from his army generals for the troops to break out. The men in the pocket were ordered to hold their positions until a relief force could be mustered. Eicke threw himself into this desperate fight with messianic zeal, organizing his division into two battlegroups that took over responsibility for defence of the pocket's western edge. Daily artillery barrages and infantry human-wave assaults were launched at the SS lines.

This was a battle of survival in every respect. Neither side was interested in taking prisoners, and when Waffen-SS positions were overrun few survivors

German frontlines
8–10 August 1941
10 September 1941
12 November 1941

KARELIAN ARMY

Suoyarvi
Kondologa
Lakhma
Lake Onega

FINLAND

Kukmoinen

7 SEP. XXXX XXXX

KARELIAN ARMY

Enso

SOUTH EASTERN ARMY

Lake Ladoga

Olonets
Komkozero
Oshta

Vyborg

XXXX 23 8

XXXXX 55

LENINGRAD FRONT

7 SEP. XXXX

XXXXX

NORTHERN FRONT

Nemzha

Helsinki

Leningrad

XXXX 42

Shlissel'burg

XXXX 54

Volkhov

ADVANCE OF ARMY GROUP NORTH

Oranienbaum

Pushkin

Tikhvin

Gulf of Finland

XXXX 8 Kunda

Narva

XXXX KS

Krasnogvardeisk

XXXX 4 SEP.

XXX X

Tapa

XXX XI

Basknarva

Kingisepp

XXXX LOG Liuban

Budogosh'

XXXX 52 SEP.

Nebolchi

ESTONIA

Gdov

Luga

XXXX LS

Chudovo

XXXX 48

Mustve

Lake Chud

XXXX 4

Novgorod

XXX ES

Lake Ilmen

XXX NAG

NORTHWESTERN FRONT

LATVIA

XXXXX

Lake Pskov

Sol'tsy
Shimsk

XXXX 11

XXXX 34

ARMY GROUP NORTH

Pskov

Dno

Staraia Russa

XXXX 11

Valdai

Bologoe

0   50   100 Miles

Slavkovichi

XXXX 34

Demyansk

XXXX 27

Lake Seligar

Ostashkov

0   80   180 Km

Novorzhev

XXXX 16

XXXX 27

Marevo

XXXX 22

XXXX 22

Kholm

Once the German frontline south of Leningrad had stabilized at the end of 1941, the *Totenkopf* at Demyansk was in an exposed position between lakes Ilmen and Seligar.

emerged from them. *Totenkopf* men were also loath to withdraw under Soviet pressure, fearing a lack of shelter from the elements if they were driven into the open and forced to endure extreme night-time temperatures.

As the siege dragged on into February, the Luftwaffe started to get its airlift organized, and daily supply flights by Junkers Ju 52 transports started to help the

Totenkopf build up stocks of ammunition and food. Winter clothing looted from the Jews of Riga was also flown in to improve the conditions of Eicke's men. The Latvian city was controlled by SS men who had served under Eicke in the concentration camps, and they were keen to help their old comrade.

In the third week of February a huge Soviet offensive surged over the *Totenkopf*'s lines, isolating many Waffen-SS positions and forcing individual units to fight desperate battles to survive. Each battalion now had to fight its own siege. There was no way to evacuate wounded SS men to hospital in Demyansk, and everyone

KARL ULLRICH

An intelligent and well-educated man, Karl Ullrich was born on 1 December 1901 in Saargemunde. An engineering graduate, he joined the SS-Pioniersturmbann of the SS-Verfügungstruppe in Dresden in 1934. Commissioned as an officer within a year, his abundant potential making itself clear during basic training, he took command of 3 Company, SS-Pionierbatallion in the SS-Verfügungsdivision. Seeing action in the West, he was awarded the Iron Cross First and Second Class for bravery under fire. He moved to the *Totenkopf* Division, and commanded a small battlegroup on the Eastern Front during 1941–42. His leadership and bravery against the Soviets during the battles in the Demyansk Pocket won him the Knight's Cross (in late February 1942, SS-Sturmbannführer Ullrich, commander of the *Totenkopf* engineer battalion, was told by radio from Hitler's headquarters of his award). By October 1944, he had led the SS-Panzergrenadier Regiment 6 *Theodor Eicke* and won the Oakleaves, and was promoted to take command of the entire *Wiking* Division. He fought a series of tough battles in Hungary and Czechoslovakia with varying success before surrendering to the Soviets in May 1945.

except the most seriously wounded had to stay in their trenches to fight off the Russians. Eicke's command was slowly dying around him, and at the end of the month he could muster only 1500 men fit for battle. For 10 days the *Totenkopf* strongholds withstood daily attempts to overrun them. They held out, but only just.

At the end of the month, Himmler had mustered 400 reinforcements to be flown in to relieve the pressure on Eicke's hard-pressed men. Their arrival, and rising temperatures, helped raise morale among the *Totenkopf* survivors. Only some 9669 men were left in the division, after it had suffered 6600 casualties during the first two months of the siege.

The Soviet forces attacking the pocket were exhausted after suffering tens of thousands of casualties, including 22,000 claimed killed and wounded by the *Totenkopf*. Only a few dozen prisoners were taken by the division, highlighting the ferocity of the fighting.

In the middle of March 1942, Hitler finally gave permission for the *Totenkopf* Division to launch a breakout attempt, codenamed Operation Gangway. This was not an escape attempt; the other German troops in the pocket had to continue to hold their positions while the Waffen-SS battled to link up with a rescue column. It took three weeks for the army rescue column to get within striking distance of the Demyansk Pocket. On 14 April, *Totenkopf* assault teams started their breakout operations, only to get stuck in mud caused by heavy rain. With all their vehicles stuck fast, Eicke's infantry now attacked on foot and swarmed over Russian defences. In several days of hand-to-hand fighting, the Waffen-SS men linked up with the rescue force on 20 April, ending 72 days of siege. Hitler was quick to lavish medals and praise on Eicke and his men, but this was a bitter pill. While other Waffen-SS divisions started to be pulled out of the line in April – to be

rebuilt as new panzergrenadier divisions equipped with armoured vehicles – the *Totenkopf* had to stay in the line holding the front around Demyansk. Army Group North was desperately short of men and equipment, making it dependent on the *Totenkopf* to turn back Soviet pressure.

The *Totenkopf* Division was now assigned to defend the Demyansk salient that stretched 72km (45 miles) behind Soviet lines. Russian attacks grew in intensity during June and July in the hope of drawing German attention and resources from the offensive towards Stalingrad. A series of battles raged around the salient for no apparent gain to either side. The result was more losses, with the *Totenkopf* suffering nearly 800 casualties in one week alone. A huge Soviet offensive on 17 July almost broke through the SS lines and wiped out two *Totenkopf* companies. The slaughter of 532 of his men in one day was too much even for Eicke, and he refused to sanction a suicidal counterattack against a breakthrough by Soviet T-34 tanks. Heavy rain now came to the Germans' assistance, and the Soviet attack got bogged down before it could make a decisive penetration to cut the *Totenkopf*'s supply corridor. By the end of July, the division could put only 2736 men in the field to fight.

Eicke was now desperately telephoning anyone in the Nazi leadership who would listen to try to get his men out of this death trap. At the end of August another wave of Soviet assaults forced the employment of the division's cooks, mechanics and other specialists to bolster the frontline. The fighting cost it another 1000 casualties.

In September, Hitler finally relented and agreed to pull the *Totenkopf* out of Russia to be rebuilt as a panzergrenadier division. There were only 6400 survivors (more than 4000 of these were non-combat specialists or walking wounded). After 18 months of combat on the Eastern Front, the *Totenkopf* Division existed in name only.

Part IV

Blood Brothers

The Aryan Brotherhood

Hundreds of thousands of non-German nationals fought in the ranks of the Waffen-SS during World War II. Some were excellent soldiers, such as those in the *Wiking* Division, while others were little more than killers in uniform. For Himmler, what began as a mission to pool Germanic blood in his Waffen-SS ended up as a desperate attempt to recruit anyone in order to stave off defeat.

A soldier of the Freiwilligen (Volunteer) Legion *Flandern* on the Eastern Front in late 1941. Recruited from Flemish volunteers, like all the national legions it suffered heavy losses on the Eastern Front.

At its peak in the autumn of 1942, Hitler's empire stretched from the Arctic circle to North Africa and from the Atlantic coast to the Caucasus mountains. The SS were instrumental in Hitler's plans to turn this empire into a racially "pure" zone, free of Jews and other *untermenschen*, or sub-humans. The Waffen-SS was now poised to undergo a major expansion to provide Germany with an élite fighting force to rival that of the Wehrmacht's panzer divisions.

The expansion of the Waffen-SS was an integral part of Hitler's plans to spread the tentacles of the SS into every aspect of the German state. Expanding the Waffen-SS to rival the Wehrmacht was mirrored in other sectors of government. The police and internal security forces had all been brought under SS control during the 1930s as part of Hitler's first moves to consolidate his dictatorship. As the war progressed, Himmler continued to spread his influence into as many other areas as possible. He took advantage of Hitler's paranoia and megalomania to convince the Führer that only the SS could be trusted to carry out his orders to the letter. The Führer was always suspicious of the army High Command after it disobeyed his orders not to retreat

from Moscow in December 1941, and was more than happy to let Himmler clip its wings. During this period the first expansion of the Waffen-SS motorized divisions into armoured units was authorized. In 1942, Himmler was also given sweeping powers to prosecute the war against the partisans, and this allowed him to raise the first Waffen-SS anti-partisan units in Eastern Europe and the Balkans.

The SS also spread its influence into every area of German life, from education and the police to the economy. Himmler was now in the process of transforming the SS from a security organization into a political and social élite. He recruited some 1200 leading German industrialists, businessmen and aristocrats into the SS as so-called honorary members. They provided Himmler with contacts and money to help expand the organization even further. In return, the SS chief was able to provide a constant flow of two million slave labourers to German industry, via the concentration camp system and through SS control of the occupied territories. The SS started to set up factories and businesses to exploit further its huge captive workforce. By 1943, the SS was one of the biggest businesses in Germany. Himmler also

AVEC TES CAMARADES EUROPÉENS
SOUS LE SIGNE ⚡⚡
TU VAINCRAS !

"You will win with your European comrades under the sign of the SS." A poster aimed at Frenchmen, and one that plays on the myth of the Waffen-SS as a Pan-European army.

moved to take control of Germany's school curriculum and marriage regulations, and he even tried to supplant the country's religious bodies by forming his own pseudo-religion based on Aryan/Germanic legends.

Himmler was perhaps the second most powerful man in Germany by 1943, and the Waffen-SS was an extension of his power base. It has to be viewed in this context to understand fully its place in German society and the Third Reich's armed forces. Many of the policy decisions taken by Himmler and Hitler concerning the expansion of the Waffen-SS had more to do with internal Nazi Party politics rather than military efficiency or effective use of scarce resources. The formation of the Waffen-SS' own special-forces troops is a typical example of this.

After Czech commandos, trained by the British Special Operations Executive (SOE), murdered SS security chief Reinhard Heydrich in 1942, rivalry between the SS and the army intelligence organization, the Abwehr, reached new levels of intensity. A department for "special troops", Amt VI-S, was set up under the RHSA

to control SS special-forces units. Otto Skorzeny was chosen to lead this organization. The tall, imposing Austrian had joined the Nazi Party even before Hitler rose to power. In the aftermath of the German invasion in 1938, Skorzeny had come to the notice of Nazi chiefs when he played a prominent part in thwarting a counter-coup by Austrians opposed to the German occupation. After seeing service with the *Das Reich* Division during the invasions of Yugoslavia and Russia in mid-1941, he gained a reputation as a dare-devil officer, but after he was injured in December 1941 he was put on light duties at the *Leibstandarte*'s depot. On 20 April 1943, Skorzeny was promoted to Waffen-SS captain and given command of Amt VI-S.

His new command was little more than an office. The Abwehr had successfully frustrated previous attempts to create SS special forces. Skorzeny moved into Friedenthal Castle near Oranienburg, and set up a training camp for the Jagdverbande (Hunting Group) 502, which was to be trained for a wide range of sabotage and subversion missions. This force became known as the Friedenthal organization. Skorzeny was obsessed by the British commandos, who since 1941 had been staging raids into Hitler's Fortress Europe. He collected captured commando weapons, silenced Sten Guns, explosives and the like. The SS was in the process of forming its own parachute force, and Skorzeny was soon given command of this unit, designated the 500th SS Parachute Battalion. He achieved lasting fame for his role in the rescue of the Italian fascist dictator, Benito Mussolini, in September 1943, although the operation itself was conducted by Luftwaffe airborne troops.

THE SS SEARCH FOR MANPOWER

Given Himmler's perpetual lust for power, it was not really surprising that he sanctioned the growth of the Waffen-SS into a force that eventually mustered over 40 combat divisions and numerous specialist units. There was, however, one fatal weakness in Himmler's plans to dominate the German state. The army High Command still formally controlled the allocation of "military age" manpower to the armed forces and the Waffen-SS. This was a constant source of tension between Himmler and the army's generals. To get around the problem, he turned to the occupied territories to attract the manpower necessary to fulfil his ambitions. Foreigners, as non-German nationals, were beyond the reach of the Wehrmacht and could be readily signed up to the Waffen-SS. The foreigners were also the key to ensuring German control of occupied Europe. Empires can often only survive with willing collaborators to do their new masters' biddings. This was particularly the case in Eastern Europe, because of the size of the territory involved and the huge populations that needed to be kept subservient to German rule. As the war dragged on and demands on the Wehrmacht grew, it became increasingly important to turn to locally recruited personnel to keep resistance in check.

While many brave men and women across Europe took up arms against their new rulers, millions of others readily decided to join the cause of the Third Reich. These men were dubbed collaborators for their treachery and so became some of Hitler's most enthusiastic supporters. There was no going back for them.

In a bizarre twist of fate, many of these men ended up in the Waffen-SS, an organization founded on Nazi racial-purity theories. Bosnian Muslims, Albanians, Hungarians, Ukranians and even Russians – all *untermenschen* according to Hitler's crazy policy of racial characteristics – ended up serving in the élite force of the Third Reich.

For Himmler, the incorporation of non-German nationals did not present any immediate ideological problems. After all, National Socialism was above all an ideology obsessed with race and the purity of Germanic blood. Himmler was determined to bring all those with Germanic blood coursing through their veins under his control. What did it matter if they were non-German nationals? Of far more importance was the fact that they were racially pure (according to Nazi ideology). For the Waffen-SS, the unifying element of race would bring foreign recruits and Germans together to fight a common enemy: Bolshevik communism. Like the crusading armies of old, the multi-national Waffen-SS would go forth as the defender of Western civilization against the barbaric hordes from the East. The names given to Waffen-SS units reflected this idea: *Germania*, *Charlemagne* and *Hohenstaufen*.

There was also a practical element to Himmler's recruitment of foreign nationals. By 1940 the Waffen-SS needed an annual addition of 18,000 recruits to maintain numbers. However, the army allowed it only two percent of German draftees – 12,000 men a year – which meant a shortfall of 6000 recruits. The SS thus had to look elsewhere.

This recruiting poster plays on the racial links between the Nordic countries of Germany, Denmark and Norway, and on the supposed threat of Bolshevik Russia.

In his efforts to recruit foreigners, Himmler was aided greatly by the work of the head of Waffen-SS recruiting, SS-Obergruppenführer Gottlob Berger. He quickly saw the solution to the SS's manpower problems: "No objections against a further expansion of the Waffen-SS can be raised by the other armed forces if we succeed in recruiting part of the German and Germanic population not at the disposal of the Wehrmacht."

But it was not until the occupation of Czechoslovakia in 1938 that Himmler had access to a source of manpower out of the grip of the generals. The so-called "ethnic Germans", or Volksdeutsche, who lived in Czechoslovakia were not officially citizens of the German Reich and therefore were not liable for conscription into the army. These were the first foreign recruits into the Waffen-SS, and they served alongside German volunteers in the early units of Himmler's élite force. At this time Himmler was considering grouping the Volksdeutsche in their own units. The conquests of Poland, Denmark, Norway, Holland, Belgium, France, Yugoslavia and Greece soon followed, bringing more potential recruits within range of Himmler's recruiting teams, and opening the door for the formation of the first foreign SS units.

As Hitler ordered the expansion of the Waffen-SS in the summer of 1940, the first foreign units were formed from Belgian, Danish, Norwegian and Dutch recruits. Himmler's racial purity requirements could be fudged because of the alleged "kindred stock" of these Germanic recruits. These men were either pre-war fascists or opportunists who wanted to show their allegiance to the New Order in Europe.

The recruits from the Low Countries were formed into the *Westland* Regiment, while the Scandinavians were assigned to the *Nordland* Regiment. They were eventu-ally linked in December 1940 with the *Germania* Regiment for the nucleus of the Waffen-SS *Wiking* 5th Motorized Division. Its commander for the next three years was Felix Steiner, who was one of the more talented Waffen-SS divisional commanders.

Himmler's lust to expand the Waffen-SS was not quenched by the formation of the *Wiking* Division, though, and he quickly moved to tap further the manpower pool of the occupied territories. He wanted to set up so-called "legions" recruited from Belgian, Dutch, Norwegian, Danish and Swedish volunteers. A French legion was initially set up under army control, before eventually being transferred to the Waffen-SS. These legions were all closely linked to fascist or right-wing nationalist groups in their home countries. Norwegian collaborator Vidkun Quisling's government, for example, was instrumental in recruiting volunteers to the Waffen-SS.

Nazi propaganda sold these foreign legions as part of a pan-European anti-Bolshevik crusade, and they were quickly dispatched to the Eastern Front to fight the Russians. Regular heroic newsreel reports recounted their exploits fighting the Red Army, although during the first two years of the Russian campaign they were more likely to be found on anti-partisan duty behind the front. Later in the war they would be given more than enough opportunities to die in battle against the Soviets.

The Flemish-speaking Belgian-Dutch legion was bound together by a common language and hatred of the old Belgian state. A French-speaking Belgian unit, drawn from the Walloon region of Belgium, was formed in 1941 under officers who were high-ranking officials in the fascist Rexist Party. It served for three years on quiet sectors of the Eastern Front until the desperate situation in the Ukraine forced the unit to be transferred to a key sector. In the process, it was expanded into Storm

LÉON DEGRELLE

Léon Degrelle was born in the small Belgian town of Bouillon in the Ardennes on 15 June 1906. Before World War II he was already heavily involved in Belgian politics as the founder of the fascist Rexist Party, and was Europe's youngest political leader. When Belgium was dragged into the war in 1940, Degrelle was arrested by Belgian loyalists as an enemy of the state and thrown into prison. Later released by German officials, Degrelle offered to raise a battalion of Walloon volunteers for the Germans. Entering the unit as a private, he worked his way up on ability alone to the highest ranks, eventually taking command of the unit. In 1943 Himmler decided that Degrelle and his men had proved themselves worthy of admission into the Waffen-SS. Personally brave, he was wounded leading from the front seven times, and was awarded the Knight's Cross for his actions in Russia. He also became one of the few non-Germans to be awarded the Oakleaves. Hitler once remarked to him: "If I had a son, I would wish him to be like you." After the war he was forced to flee to Spain. Condemned to death *in absentia* by the Belgian Government, he lived his life in exile in Spain until his death on 31 March 1994.

Brigade *Wallonien* and then fought side by side with the *Wiking* Division in the Cherkassy-Korsun Pocket. It covered the withdrawal of the *Wiking* as a rearguard. The brigade's combat exploits earned it the Führer's gratitude and its commander, Rexist leader Léon Degrelle, the Swords and Oakleaves to his Knight's Cross. The unit was destroyed in the battle for Berlin in 1945, but Degrelle managed to escape to Spain. He was one of only three of the original 850 recruits to the brigade who survived the war.

THE GERMANIC LEGIONS

Unlike the *Wiking* Division's foreign standarten which had German officers, the Scandinavian and Western European legions were led by commanders from their own countries. This meant their military usefulness was limited at first, and they had to be gently exposed to the violence on the Eastern Front to gain combat experience. The legions were organized as infantry units with light weapons and sometimes StuG III assault guns. They seldom mustered more than 2000 men at any one time. When the legions were eventually expanded into nominal divisions to satisfy Himmler's desire to create more and bigger units, they rarely contained 10,000 men each, half the strength of a German army or Waffen-SS division.

In 1943 the bulk of the legions were grouped into the Waffen-SS *Nordland* Panzergrenadier Division, which fought tenaciously on the northern sector of the Eastern Front throughout 1944. Its hour of glory came in September 1944 when its timely intervention prevented the encirclement of the Eighteenth Army. The remnants of the division went down fighting around Hitler's bunker in Berlin in April 1945.

Eventually some 50,000 Dutchmen joined the Waffen-SS, the majority of whom served in the *Landsturm-Nederland* Militia Division, which helped prop up German rule in Holland, before being sent to the Eastern Front for the remainder of the war. Belgium provided 40,000 recruits to the Waffen-SS, evenly split between Flemish- and French-speaking volunteers. Most of the Flemish speakers eventually served in the *Langemarck* Waffen-SS Division. More than 20,000 French recruits signed up to Hitler's anti-Bolshevik crusade, while Denmark and Norway each provided 6000 volunteers.

Himmler loved the propaganda value provided by these legions, as he attempted to prove that Europe was united behind the New Order. Two purely propaganda units were the so-called British Free Corps and Indian Legion, both formed from turncoat prisoners of war. They both saw very limited combat experience.

When German armies rolled east in June 1941, they swiftly conquered the Baltic states of Estonia, Latvia and Lithuania, where they were greeted as liberators following Soviet occupation. Volunteers flocked to join police and militia units being set up by the new German rulers. Soon, Himmler started to take a close interest in the Latvian and Estonian units and incorporated several into the Waffen-SS. He was particularly impressed by their zeal in helping SS Einsatzgruppen squads murder Jews in ghettos that were being set up in the region. Thanks to the ethnic affinity of the Estonian and Latvians with Scandinavia, Himmler was willing to smooth their way into the Waffen-SS. The Reichsführer-SS once remarked of the Estonians: "The Estonians really do belong to the few races that can, after the segregation of only a few elements, be merged with us without any harm to our people." The Catholic Lithuanians were beyond the pale as Slavs, as far as Himmler was concerned, so they languished in special police battalions.

Baltic units were highly prized by German commanders for their expertise in counter-partisan warfare. Eventually, they were to be formed into three Waffen-SS divisions. When German troops were trapped in the Baltic states in 1944, the Latvian and Estonian units fought on even after Germany surrendered the following year. Many took to the woods to continue fighting as partisans against the Soviets into the 1950s.

RECRUITING IN EASTERN EUROPE

According to Nazi racial classification, there were more than 2.5 million Volksdeutsche spread around Eastern Europe. Himmler quickly set about re-settling them in areas forcibly emptied of Jews and Slavs. They were also recruited in large numbers into the Waffen-SS. Early in the war they were used to provide manpower for mainstream Waffen-SS units, but in 1942 the first Volksdeutsche unit was formed. The 7th Mountain *Prinz Eugen* Division drew its Volksdeutsche recruits from Hungary, Romania and Yugoslavia. It was predominantly engaged in counter-insurgency operations against Tito's partisans in Yugoslavia, gaining a fearsome reputation as one of the most reliable and effective units in this confused and brutal war zone. In 1944, it was reinforced with drafts from the disbanded Albanian Waffen-SS unit, the *Skanderbeg* Division.

The 18th *Horst Wessel* Panzergrenadier Division was formed from Volksdeutsche recruits in Hungary during the spring of 1944, before being sent to fight on the central sector of the Russian Front. Four divisions of Hungarians were recruited from supporters of the Arrow Cross Nazi movement in late 1944 as Soviet troops

French Waffen-SS recruits swear their oath of allegiance to the Third Reich and "to unconditionally obey the Commander-in-Chief of the Armed Forces, Adolf Hitler".

invaded the country. These units were all destroyed in the fierce fighting during the first months of 1945. Czech Volksdeutsche formed the bulk of the recruits to the *Böhmen-Mahren* Brigade, which was formed in April 1945.

A luminary for Eastern European SS recruitment was Erich von dem Bach-Zelewski, the senior SS and police leader in the Army Group Centre region, who recruited the first units of ex-Soviet prisoners of war into the Waffen-SS in 1943 to fight partisans in central Russia. The so-called *Kaminski* Brigade, commanded by the Russian Bronislav Kaminski, blazed a trail of terror throughout German-occupied Russia for almost a year, killing thousands of civilians in reprisals for partisan attacks. Eventually its commander went too far – even for the SS – during the 1944 Warsaw uprising, and was executed on Bach-Zelewski's orders.

A far more impressive unit was the 14th *Galician* Division, which was recruited from Catholic Ukrainians in 1943. It was almost destroyed in the Brody-Tarnow

Pocket during the summer of 1944, when only 3000 out of 14,000 men managed to break out of the Soviet encirclement. It eventually fought in Hungary and Austria, where it surrendered to British troops. The intervention of the Vatican saved the remnants of the division from being handed over to the Soviets, unlike other units composed of turncoat Soviet citizens.

As defeat after defeat rolled back the Eastern Front in 1944, Himmler at last decided to turn the surviving two million Russian prisoners of war held by the Germans into an anti-Soviet army. After spending three years trying to work these men to death in slave labour camps, this was an amazing change of heart. Three million of these men had already died from neglect, and the survivors were becoming increasingly desperate. The approaching Soviet armies offered little prospect of liberation to captured Russian soldiers, whom Stalin had already declared to be traitors.

The former Red Army general Andrei Vlasov was persuaded by Himmler in July 1944 to tour prison camps to recruit men for a so-called Russian "army of liberation". He eventually raised two divisions out of Russian prisoners and men transferred from two Waffen-SS divisions recruited for security duties in Russia. They briefly saw action on the Eastern Front in the final months of the war. They retreated to Prague and then turned on the German garrison in the city to help Czech resistance fighters who had risen in revolt. The change of heart did not do them any good, and the US Army eventually handed them over to Russia after the war, where the majority were executed, including Vlasov.

Contrary to popular legend, the Waffen-SS did not recruit Don Cossacks. These were formed by the army and transferred to the Waffen-SS for administrative purposes only in August 1944. The XV Cossack Corps did fight alongside Waffen-SS units in the Balkans during 1944. In spite of being able to overrun Yugoslavia in a matter of weeks in April 1941, the Germans were never able to subdue the country's population. Tito's communist partisans were an aggressive force, and by 1944 some 20 German divisions, albeit not frontline units, containing 700,000 troops were tied down fighting a brutal guerrilla war. Rather than divert German soldiers from the frontline for this task, it was decided to recruit local men to fight against Tito to capitalize on the region's age-old ethnic and religious divisions. As the war progressed, the need to increase recruitment to these units became critical.

Eventually two divisions of Muslim soldiers were recruited from the region, which is today known as Bosnia, but under German rule was part of the Croatian Nazi puppet state. Himmler tried to make the units of the 13th *Handschar* and 23rd *Kama* Divisions follow the traditions of the old Muslim units of the Hapsburg Empire, which had ruled the region before World War I. Former Hapsburg officers were recruited to lead these new units. Ethnic Albanian Muslims were also recruited in 1944 into their own division, 21st *Skanderbeg*, named after the national hero of the Albanians. In addition, in a bid to use them to undermine British rule in the Middle East, Himmler drafted the Grand Mufti of Jerusalem to oversee these divisions' religious practices. This, if anything, shows the depth to which Himmler had sunk to fill out his Waffen-SS divisions.

The Muslim units proved useful in anti-partisan operations, but when faced by determined troops were less effective. They were motivated by a desire to fight their Christian Serb neighbours, who formed the core support for Tito's partisans, although the war in Yugoslavia was characterized by shifting allegiances. The Albanians, in particular, gained a gruesome reputation for committing

Infantry and panzer officers of the *Wiking* Division (note the divisional cuffband) on the Eastern Front in 1944. *Wiking* was the best foreign unit in the German armed forces.

A soldier of the 7th SS *Prinz Eugen* Division. This unit spent most of its career fighting Tito's partisans. It was virtually annihilated when it came up against the Red Army.

the end of the war, while the rest capitulated to Italian partisans, and were promptly executed.

More than 25 of Waffen-SS divisions raised during World War II contained a significant foreign element. The best units were those from Scandinavia and Western Europe, the *Wiking* Division standing out as a true élite formation on a par with the other Waffen-SS panzer divisions (it became a panzer division in 1943).

VERDICT ON WAFFEN-SS FOREIGN RECRUITMENT

As an experiment in creating a "European army" for the new Third Reich, Himmler's Waffen-SS was a failure. Nazi racial ideology meant that no attempt was made to recruit foreigners to Germany's cause until it was too late. The half-hearted attempts by Himmler to form an anti-Soviet army of Russians was typical of the attitude of the Nazi leaders. After spending three years exploiting, neglecting or systematically murdering East Europeans, the attempt by Himmler to recruit these people into the Waffen-SS seems bizarre (interestingly, the German Army made use of captured Red Army soldiers almost from the start of the Russian campaign, forming so-called *Hiwi* units for rear-area duties). Those who did join almost always did so out of desperation. It was usually a choice of signing up for the Waffen-SS or languishing in a concentration camp. Even to the last, Himmler treated these men with contempt, and considered them little more than cannon fodder (the Nazi hierarchy never considered foreign units to be nationalist formations; this was at odds with individuals such as Vlasov, who saw their units as agents for ultimate national self-determination). Hitler viewed them with even more contempt, and often complained that weapons and equipment was being allocated to foreign SS units at the expense of German units. He thought this folly, which it was, and added nothing to the German war effort.

In the closing months of the war, as it became clear that Germany was doomed, the foreigners in the Waffen-SS started to look to the future. While many were looking to save their own skins by escaping from their vengeful fellow countrymen, thousands threw themselves into the fight with renewed vigour. Knowing their fate if Germany lost the war, foreign units such as the *Wiking* Division fought fanatically to hold back the Soviets on the Eastern Front. Their sacrifice was in vain.

atrocities. Attempts to move the *Skanderbeg* Division away from Yugoslavia in 1944 to fight in the West were a disaster, ending in a mutiny, and the unit was eventually disbanded. Splits in the partisan movement led to some Serb supporters of the old Royalist regime in Belgrade to switch allegiances to the Germans. The Serbian Volunteer Corps was transferred to the Waffen-SS in 1944.

The formation of Benito Mussolini's rump fascist republic in northern Italy provided the recruiting ground for the formation of the 29th SS Waffen-Grenadier Division, which was committed to action against the Americans at Anzio in April 1944. Thereafter it fought a rearguard campaign along with other German units in Italy. Part of the division surrendered to the Americans at

Part V

High Tide
1942–1943

The Drive for Oil

In early 1942 Hitler and Stalin were each looking for a decisive victory on the Eastern Front. The German panzer divisions were rebuilt ready to launch a new Blitzkrieg, this time aimed at seizing Russia's oil fields in the Caucasus. Denied this key source of fuel, Hitler believed the Soviet war effort would grind to a halt and allow the Wehrmacht to knock the USSR out of the war.

German troops advance south during Operation Blue in July 1942. The German assault into the Caucasus involved 68 divisions with 1.4 million troops and 1495 armoured fighting vehicles, supported by 1550 aircraft.

Hitler was keen to use his élite Waffen-SS motorized divisions to spearhead this offensive, and in January 1942 authorized the formation of the first SS tank battalions for them. The four Waffen-SS motorized units – *Leibstandarte*, *Das Reich*, *Totenkopf* and *Wiking* – were still engaged on the Russian Front and could not be pulled back to Germany to be refitted and re-equipped with their new tanks. It would also take several months for the Waffen-SS to master its new equipment, so it would not have a major role in the coming offensive, dubbed Operation Blue.

Das Reich was withdrawn from the Eastern Front during April, and the *Leibstandarte* followed in June, with both ending up in France assigned to Paul Hausser's new Waffen-SS panzer corps. While the *Totenkopf* was locked into bitter fighting around the Demyansk salient until the autumn of 1942, Felix Steiner's *Wiking* Division remained in the Ukraine as part of Army Group South. It was ordered to rebuild itself in Russia, and as the spring turned to summer train-loads of replacement personnel and equipment started arriving at its bases on the Mius Front. Crucially, in April the 5th SS Panzer Battalion arrived at the division with 53 tanks. These included 12 Panzer II light

tanks, 12 Panzer IIIs armed with 50mm guns, and four Panzer IVs with short 75mm guns. It also had 12 Panzer IVs with long-barrelled 75mm cannon that could engage the feared Soviet T-34 on equal terms. The arrival of these tanks meant that the *Wiking* was the first Waffen-SS division to go into action equipped with its own tanks.

The division's two motorized infantry regiments, the *Westland* and *Nordland*, were also brought up to strength, and the assault-gun battalion received new StuG IIIs. This re-equipment programme meant that it was not sent into action against the Soviet spring offensive against Kharkov, but remained on the Mius line until June. By then it had some 18,000 men ready for action. The rebirth was not without its teething troubles, though. Many of the replacements were non-Germans from the Low Countries or Scandinavia whose military expertise was below par. Perhaps most importantly, there was not time to conduct large-scale field exercises to prepare the new recruits in the art of armoured warfare.

Operation Blue began at the end of June 1942, and at first swept all before it. The German Army Group B, with the Sixth Army in the vanguard, drove eastwards for its date with destiny on the banks of the River Volga at

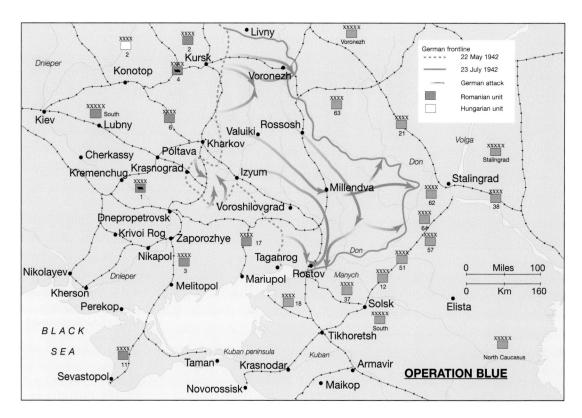

The Fourth Panzer and Second Armies advanced towards the River Don, and by 6 July 1942 the panzers had reached the city of Voronezh. To the south, Stalingrad beckoned.

Stalingrad. Army Group A turned southwards after bypassing Rostov, and headed into the Caucasus with the key oil fields as its objective. The drive to the oil fields was now codenamed Operation Edelweiss.

Colonel-General Ewald von Kleist's panzers were unleashed in the second week of July and smashed through the weak Soviet defences at Rostov. The *Wiking* Division took part in the clearing of the city before it was ordered to lead the advance southwards, with the 13th Panzer Division, as part of LVII Panzer Corps. For a month, the panzer crews and the SS men raced across the open steppe amidst huge choking clouds of dust. There was no serious Soviet resistance, and the main problem for Kleist was keeping his spearheads supplied with fuel. Luftwaffe Junkers Ju 52 transports flew thousands of fuel cans to improvised airfields to keep the panzers rolling. Camel trains were even formed to bring up fuel.

In the first week of August, the *Wiking*'s spearheads were in the foothills of the Caucasus mountains and

resistance started to stiffen in the huge sunflower fields that were all over the region. On 9 August, *Wiking* had seized the first of its objectives, the Maikop oil field, after a brief fight with Soviet defenders. German mountain troops then moved to scale Mount Elbruz, the highest point in the Causasus Mountains.

Kleist's supply lines were now starting to feel the strain of supporting troops 320km (200 miles) from their main supply bases. The *Wiking* Division and other spear-head units were bogged down in a see-saw battle to stop the Soviets retaking the Maikop oil field, so they could not break free to restart the offensive drive to seize the next set of oil fields at Grozny and then move on to the final objective of Operation Edelweiss: Baku on the Caspian Sea. Vital Luftwaffe air support was also now being diverted away to help the Germans locked in the battle of Stalingrad that was approaching its climax.

By the middle of August, Kleist's panzers had broken free and were streaming eastwards in another break-neck Blitzkrieg advance. The *Wiking* Division was close behind. By 24 August, his spearheads had come to a halt against a Soviet defensive line at Mozdok. Everything now depended on the *Wiking* Division being able to open a breach in the enemy line. After several days of gruelling

driving over desperate road conditions, Steiner's men were committed to action on the morning of 26 August. "All eyes are on your division", von Kleist signalled Steiner. "The whole operation depends on it being committed unsparingly."

Wiking was ordered to attack through the narrow Altar valley near Malgobek. The object was to reach Grozny or move south to force the entrenched Russians to retreat. Facing the SS were a collection of Soviet forces well dug in and supplied with artillery on the 300–600m (1000–2000ft) high hills surrounding the valley. The SS attack plan called for the infantry to clear the towering hills overlooking the valley, while its tanks and armoured troop-carrying halftracks raced through the narrow valley to overrun the Soviet infantry trenches and anti-tank gun pits. Steiner had strong reservations about attacking directly into the jaws of the Soviet defences.

The Waffen-SS men battled through sunflower fields and trench lines for a day, but could not reach the heights that formed the core of the Soviet defences. Heavy anti-tank gun fire stalled the *Wiking* panzers, and the Waffen-SS infantry soon faltered when they saw their tanks burning. The 13th Panzer Division was then sent into action, but to no avail. Steiner blamed the terrain and a bad plan for his troops being checked. Von Kleist was less than complimentary about the "lack of internal cohesiveness" of the Waffen-SS unit, because it contained so many half-trained non-Germans.

Wiking continued to battle against the Soviet defensive lines, and by 5 October it had taken Malgobek. Another 10 days of fierce fighting in the foothills of the Caucasus followed. Von Kleist asked Hitler for fresh panzers to

Soldiers of the *Wiking* Division during Operation Blue in August 1942. This image gives an idea of the endless steppe terrain that characterized this part of the Soviet Union.

smash through the Soviet lines, but the Führer said every spare panzer division on the Eastern Front was committed to the battle for Stalingrad. On 16 October, the *Wiking* Division went on the defensive in positions along the Terek River, less than 48km (30 miles) outside Grozny.

For almost two months the *Wiking* men fought a series of bloody skirmishes with Russian troops around Grozny. Steiner and his men received the honour of their division being retitled as a panzergrenadier formation in November (it had a strength of 15,928 men in December 1942). Supplies, particularly fuel and ammunition, were very short because of the long lines of communication down to the Caucasus and the demands of the huge battles in Stalingrad. The *Wiking*'s panzer battalion had suffered almost 50 percent losses, having only 15 Panzer IIIs and 8 Panzer IVs operational on 18 November.

When the Soviet counteroffensive struck the German Sixth Army in late November, Army Group A in the Caucasus looked vulnerable. By the middle of December, the army group was in full retreat. After first issuing his usual no-retreat order, Hitler was persuaded by the commander of Army Group Don, Field Marshal Erich von Manstein, to pull out the mobile divisions from the Caucasus to form a counterattack force to rescue the trapped troops inside the Stalingrad Pocket. The *Wiking* Division was ordered to pull out from the Grozny Front and move rapidly north towards Rostov.

Army Group South in Danger

The Red Army counteroffensive around Stalingrad trapped the German Sixth Army in the city. The whole of the German southern front in Russia was in danger of being ripped apart. Hitler, true to form, ordered Paulus in Stalingrad to hold firm as Göring's Luftwaffe tried to organize supplies to be flown into the city, while Manstein mustered his panzers to form a relief force.

A German soldier at an observation post in southern Russia keeps watch for the enemy. The frozen landscape eased movement for Soviet tanks, which meant German units could be easily surrounded.

In November 1942, seven Soviet armies had launched a counteroffensive against the Wehrmacht's Sixth Army at Stalingrad, trapping its 220,000 men inside a pocket along the frozen banks of the River Volga. Six months before, these men had been the spearhead of Operation Blue. Two German army groups, led by nine panzer divisions and seven motorized divisions equipped with some 800 tanks, at first swept all before them. Tens of thousands of Russian soldiers were trapped in pockets as German panzers manoeuvred effortlessly across the featureless steppe.

By the autumn, fanatical resistance by Red Army troops in Stalingrad had brought the German eastward advance to a halt. Street battles sucked in German division after division, until the bulk of the Sixth Army's combat troops were fighting in an area of only a few score square kilometres. No matter how hard General Friedrich Paulus drove his tired troops forward into the alleys and ruined factories of Stalingrad, the Soviet defenders refused to give up the fight. The Sixth Army's commander loyally followed his Führer's orders to fight on in the devastated city, despite warning signs that the Soviets were massing forces elsewhere for a counteroffensive.

On 19 November, the Red Army launched Operation Saturn. Hundreds of tanks surged forward across the thinly held lines of the Romanian Third Army, which had the task of holding hundreds of kilometres of front to the north of Stalingrad. The Romanians had no effective anti-tank weapons, and within hours they had either fled westwards, died in the snow or surrendered. The following day, another Soviet tank force broke through the Romanian Fourth Army, to the south of the Sixth Army. A day later the claws of the two Russian pincers met to the west of Stalingrad, trapping Paulus and his troops in the city. The 100 German Panzer III and 30 Panzer IV tanks of the three badly weakened panzer divisions in what was now known grandly as "Fortress Stalingrad" were unable to challenge the 635 Russian tanks ringing the Sixth Army, because Hitler refused to allow them to be redeployed to counter the new threat. Any sort of relief would have to come from outside the pocket.

The immediate German reserve, some 80km (50 miles) to the west of Stalingrad, was the 22nd Panzer Division, but most of its 22 Panzer III and 11 Panzer IV tanks were useless because rodents had eaten into their power cables. In any case, it was soon surrounded by

MARDER II

The Marder II self-propelled anti-tank vehicle was essentially a 76.2mm gun (taken from captured Soviet stocks) mated with a Panzer II chassis. In 1942 the decision was taken to abandon production of the Panzer II tank, and instead use the tank chassis to mount the 76.2mm gun. It entered service with anti-tank detachments in July 1942, and by March 1944 around 650 examples had been built. The Marder II carried 37 rounds of ammunition, and was manned by a crew of three. Production was cut short in 1943 to concentrate on the Wespe. The first Waffen-SS units to receive the Marder II were the *Leibstandarte*, *Das Reich* and *Totenkopf* Divisions, in the summer of 1942.

Type:	light tank destroyer
Length:	4.88m (16ft)
Width:	2.3m (7.5ft)
Height:	2.65m (8.75ft)
Crew:	3
Armament:	1 x 76.2mm
Range:	185km (115 miles)
Speed:	45kmh (28mph)

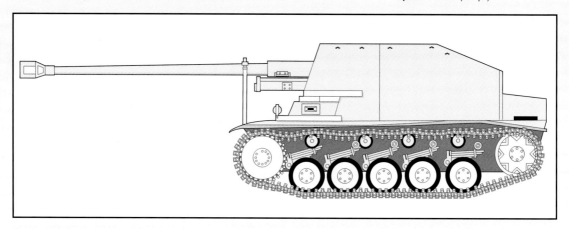

marauding Russian tanks and only just managed to escape westwards after suffering heavy casualties. The division was disbanded soon afterwards.

German forces in southern Russia had to react quickly to avoid being overrun by Red Army columns that were fanning out westwards from Stalingrad. Supply dumps and Luftwaffe air bases were hastily evacuated and small ad hoc battlegroups were formed to defend an improvised defensive line along the River Chir, to allow a rescue force for Stalingrad to be assembled. This desperate last line of resistance also protected the vital Morosowskaja and Tatsinskaja airfields, which were to be used by the Luftwaffe to fly in supplies to the Sixth Army after Hermann Göring, head of the Luftwaffe, promised that his airmen could fly in the 508 tonnes (500 tons) of supplies a day needed to keep the troops in Stalingrad fighting.

The man given the job of saving the Stalingrad garrison was Field Marshal Erich von Manstein. He was considered the best operational-level commander in the Wehrmacht. In 18 months of action on the Eastern Front, he had developed an uncannily accurate "feel" for when Soviet offensives would run out of steam. Like a cunning chess player, he was able to look several moves ahead and build plans for devastating counterattacks.

Manstein set up the headquarters for his newly formed Army Group Don on 27 November, and began calling in all available panzer divisions for the Stalingrad rescue mission, codenamed Operation Winter Tempest. A simultaneous breakout plan was developed for the Sixth Army under the codename Thunderclap. The trapped army, however, only had enough fuel for its remaining tanks to strike 32km (20 miles) westwards, so everything depended on the rescue force punching through the Russian lines, virtually up to the outskirts of Stalingrad. Two fresh panzer divisions were to be mustered for the operation from France and northern Russia, along with a pair of panzer divisions drafted from the southern Caucasus front.

Out on the freezing steppe, Manstein's grand plans had to be turned into reality by small groups of cold, tired and hungry men. Surviving the winter cold was just as much of a challenge as keeping the Russians at bay. The key battles were fought not to win the generals some "line on a map", but to control precious shelter. A unit left out in the open at night could die in its tracks. Unlike the year before outside Moscow, the Wehrmacht was now prepared for the winter and special warm clothing had been issued. Even with this equipment, however,

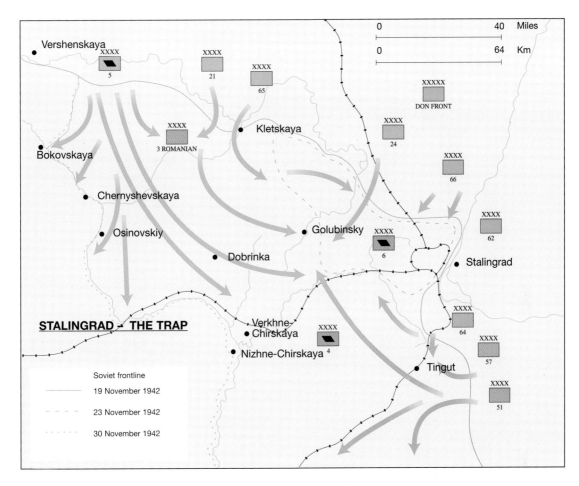

STALINGRAD – THE TRAP

Soviet frontline

—————— 19 November 1942

– – – – – 23 November 1942

· · · · · · · 30 November 1942

The Red Army offensive by the Don, Stalingrad and Southwest Fronts of November 1942 isolated the German Sixth Army fighting in Stalingrad.

soldiers could not spend more than half an hour outside shelter on guard duty at night without suffering fatal frostbite or exposure, while vehicles and heavy weapons had to be kept running and maintained 24 hours a day to stop them freezing solid. In the East during the winter, some of the most important pieces of equipment in the Wehrmacht's arsenal were its field kitchens. The delivery of hot food to frontline positions did a lot to sustain morale in truly desperate conditions, and kept men fighting beyond normal levels of endurance. Violent snowstorms could engulf units for days on end, preventing any kind of movement. One of the few benefits of the Russian winter was that it froze up the rivers and streams that criss-crossed the steppe, allowing the panzers to manoeuvre freely.

It took over a week for the first reinforcements to reach the Chir Front, when the 58 Panzer III and 6 Panzer IV tanks of the 11th Panzer Division were placed under the command of LVII Panzer Corps. The division's tanks

moved in a long column across the steppe to their assembly area just behind a weakly held front along the banks of the frozen River Chir. For a week it would be the only combat-ready tank unit in the sector, but was in no position to strike eastwards to Stalingrad by itself. The frontline was held by a mixed force of German infantry and Luftwaffe ground personnel. The Soviets were constantly probing these positions, with almost daily attacks in tank corps strength. On every occasion that the Soviets broke through, the 11th Panzer Division would mobilize its tanks to set up a blocking position. Panzers would then manoeuvre on the flanks of the Soviets, picking off enemy vehicles. The division was one of the most experienced and professional in the

PANZER III

The Panzer III was the primary tank in the Wehrmacht in the years leading up to World War II, and it saw extensive service throughout the conflict. It underwent a number of variations during its lifetime. The Panzer Ausf G (shown below) was armed with the 50mm KwK L/42 gun. The Panzer III Ausf N was armed with a short 75mm gun that fired a shaped explosive charge capable of penetrating thicker armour than the long-barrelled KwK39 L/60 which it replaced. The Panzer III saw extensive action on the Eastern Front, and 155 units were involved in the Kursk offensive of 1943. The first SS units to receive the Panzer III were the *Leibstandarte*, *Das Reich* and *Wiking* Divisions.

Type:	medium tank
Length:	5.4m (17.8ft)
Width:	2.95m (9.7ft)
Height:	2.44m (8ft)
Crew:	5
Armament:	1 x 50mm, 2 x 7.92mm
Range:	165km (103 miles)
Speed:	40kmh (25mph)

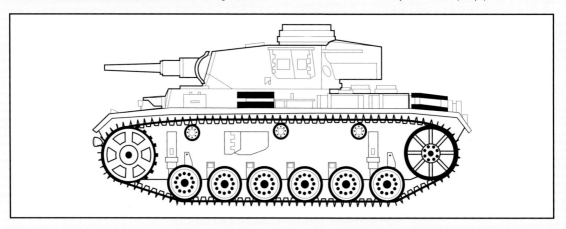

Wehrmacht, but even this could not compensate for the seemingly unlimited resources of the Red Army. For every tank the division knocked out another seemed to appear to take its place, while there were no replacements for lost German tanks. Without rest or relief, it was only a matter of time before the 11th Panzer Division would have to retreat or be destroyed.

On 10 December 1942, LVII Panzer Corps was ready to strike eastwards from its improvised forward base at Kotelnikovo towards Stalingrad. Fresh from France, the 6th Panzer Division led the offensive with its 100 Panzer III and 24 Panzer IV tanks. The already understrength 17th and 23rd Panzer Divisions were brought up from the Caucasus in support. The 17th Panzer was able to muster 30 Panzer IIIs and 18 Panzer IVs, while the 23rd could only scrape together 27 Panzer IIIs and 8 Panzer IVs. In the space of a week, the 200 tanks of LVII Panzer Corps broke through the Soviet front and pushed forward 160km (100 miles). Using classic panzer tactics, they dodged and weaved their way past scores of Red Army defensive positions. Luftwaffe tank-busting aircraft flew overhead, strafing enemy tank columns, and opening the way for the panzer divisions to push to within 48km (30 miles) of Stalingrad on 20 December. A massive Russian attack

far to the north on 16 December broke through the Italian Eighth Army's front, and Soviet armour headed for Rostov, threatening to cut off all the German forces in the Caucasus. To counter this threat, Manstein had to deploy the 6th Panzer Division north to seal the front. This was the decisive move of the campaign, because now LVII Panzer Corps lacked the strength to punch through to Stalingrad. For five days the now depleted rescue force held on to to its bridgehead over the River Aksay in the face of furious Soviet attacks.

Hundreds of T-34 tanks at a time were thrown into battle each day by the Soviets before they were knocked out. Inside the pocket, Paulus refused to order Thunderclap. He perhaps did not realize that there were no more panzer reserves available if LVII Panzer Corps failed, or maybe he feared his starving troops were not up to fighting on the open steppe. Whatever the reason, the moment was lost. After a huge Soviet attack on its bridgehead on 24 December, LVII Panzer Corps could hold out no more. Two days later it was ordered to fall back on Kotelnikovo. It left behind almost all of its tanks and thousands of dead. The 17th Panzer Division could only muster one anti-tank gun and eight operational tanks. Battalions were reduced to a few hundred men able to fight. Every battalion commander was either dead or wounded.

Meanwhile, as the 6th and 11th Panzer Divisions of XXXXVIII Panzer Corps moved westwards to plug the gap in the front created by the collapse of the Italians, they surprised a Red Army guards tank corps that had just seized a Luftwaffe airfield at Tatsinskaja. The two German divisions trapped the Russians between armoured pincers, neutralizing the threat to Rostov for the moment.

The frontline only held for a matter of days before the Soviets were attacking again. LVII Panzer Corps stood firm, but all around chaos and confusion reigned. Even the arrival of the 7th Panzer Division from France with 105 Panzer III and 20 Panzer IV tanks was not enough to stabilize the front. At the end of December, Hitler gave Manstein permission to withdraw from the Caucasus, freeing up the First Panzer Army with its 3rd Panzer Division, 16th and 26th Motorized Divisions and the *Wiking* Division for action farther north. The Führer, however, insisted that the 13th Panzer Division stay in the Caucasus to hold the Kuban Peninsula. The 11th Panzer Division had to fight a determined rearguard action to the east of Rostov in mid-January to allow the First Panzer Army to move northwards, into the Ukraine itself.

Through December and into January 1943, the Sixth Army struggled to survive in Stalingrad. Within hours of

the failure of Operation Winter Tempest, the Red Army launched a series of massive offensives aimed at destroying the Sixth Army once and for all. By this time the 100,000 or so German soldiers now alive in the pocket were so frozen and starving that they were in no position to move out of their improvised bunkers in the ruins of Stalingrad. Göring's much vaunted airlift was barely able to fly in 101 tonnes (100 tons) of supplies a day. The Luftwaffe was, however, able to bring out 30,000 wounded Germans. The airlift was put out of action for good on 22 January when the Soviets overran the last German-held airfield in the pocket.

Hitler was still optimistic that the situation could be redeemed. On 31 December 1942, he ordered I SS Panzer Corps to move from France to Kharkov in the eastern Ukraine to set up a base for a new relief effort towards Stalingrad. But on 24 January 1943, the Russians began their final offensive against Stalingrad. Within a week they had overrun what was left of the Sixth Army. Despite being ordered to fight to the last man, Paulus emerged with his staff from his bunker under a bombed-out department store and surrendered on 31 January. A day later the last pocket of German resistance in the city surrendered. Some 91,000 Germans were marched into Soviet captivity. Fewer than 5000 survived more than a few months as prisoners of Stalin.

Soldiers of the *Wiking* Division in the frozen wastes of southern Russia in late 1942. These troops are well protected from the extreme cold. In general, Waffen-SS units fared better than their army counterparts when it came to winter clothing, thanks to the SS having stolen clothing from Jews in the occupied territories.

Birth of the SS Panzer Divisions

The formation of the SS panzer corps in late 1942 signalled that the élite Waffen-SS divisions had become some of the finest units in the German order of battle. Now their fighting units would be lavishly equipped with panzers, halftracks, anti-tank guns and artillery, and the SS panzer corps would be used to turn the tide of war on the Eastern Front.

The Tiger I heavy tank first entered Waffen-SS service during the winter of 1942–43. The *Das Reich, Leibstandarte* and *Totenkopf* Divisions each received a company of 14 Tigers. This is an SS Tiger in 1944.

As the German Sixth Army was fighting for its life in the ruins of Stalingrad, in occupied France a heavily armed panzer corps was being formed from Waffen-SS units. Soon it would be loaded on to hundreds of trains and sent east to turn back the advancing Red Army.

Adolf Hitler's mistrust of the German Army had grown as the war dragged on. His arguments with senior army generals during the failed offensive against Moscow in the winter of 1941 had convinced him that a politically reliable combat force was needed if the Third Reich was to prevail in the titanic struggle with Stalin's Russia on the Eastern Front. The loyalty and obedience of the Waffen-SS to the cause of Nazism would ensure success in battle, or so the Führer thought. In May 1942, he ordered the formation of a Waffen-SS corps head-quarters that was to command the *Leibstandarte, Das Reich* and *Totenkopf* Divisions. They were to be refitted after suffering heavy casualties in Russia during the previous winter. By the summer plans had advanced apace, and the Führer now wanted his prized divisions to be equipped as panzergrenadier divisions.

All through the summer and into the autumn, new recruits and new equipment poured into the Waffen-SS

bases in occupied France, where the corps was being prepared for action. There, the three divisions and the corps staff were moulded into fighting units. This was a frantic time for the cadre of Waffen-SS veterans who had to rebuild their shattered units, while at the same time accepting new types of tanks, armoured cars, halftracks, anti-tank weapons and artillery. The tough training regime was interrupted in November 1942, when the Waffen-SS divisions were used to spearhead the occupation of Vichy France, after the Allied landings in North Africa led to the collapse of the pro-German regime. The exercise only served to show how much work was needed to prepare the divisions for action, as bottlenecks formed and units became disorganized. Once they returned to their bases, the training intensity was redoubled.

Gone were the days when the Waffen-SS only accepted volunteers who had passed rigorous fitness and ideological tests. Tens of thousands of Labour Service draftees, policemen, concentration camp guards and assorted misfits now had to be turned into élite combat soldiers. The officer ranks of the new Waffen-SS panzer force had to learn how to coordinate large numbers of tanks in battle, as well as all the skills necessary to keep tens of thousands of men supplied with all the tools of mobile warfare. As the news from Stalingrad grew worse, it became clear to the Waffen-SS veterans that they would soon be heading east again. The transformation of the armed SS from being an insignificant part of the German order of battle to becoming the potential saviour of the whole Eastern Front was rapid.

In late 1940, as Hitler was mustering his forces for Operation Barbarossa – the invasion of the Soviet Union – he ordered a massive expansion of the Waffen-SS. The *Leibstandarte* was up-rated to a full motorized division. The SS-VT was split in two to create the *Deutschland* (soon renamed *Das Reich*) and *Wiking* Motorized Divisions. The four Waffen-SS divisions were each some 16,000 men strong and now boasted 150mm howitzers, 75mm anti-tank guns and the deadly 88mm flak or anti-aircraft guns. The only tracked armoured fighting vehicles assigned to them at this point in the war were Sturmgeschütz (StuG) III assault guns armed with short-barrelled 75mm guns.

The Waffen-SS motorized divisions were in the thick of the action during the invasion of Russia in June 1941, with the *Leibstandarte* and *Wiking* Divisions fighting in the south, and the other two divisions leading the German advance in the north and central sectors. By the spring of 1942, the four divisions had suffered horrendous casualties in desperate defensive actions during the Soviet winter counteroffensive of 1941–42, and were barely functioning as fighting formations. They each mustered 2000 men fit for action. However, their tenacity in defence against massive odds, and especially their refusal to yield ground, greatly impressed Hitler.

In the summer and autumn of 1942, as stated above, the *Leibstandarte*, *Das Reich* and *Totenkopf* Divisions were withdrawn from the Eastern Front and moved to France for reorganizing as Waffen-SS panzergrenadier divisions. *Wiking* remained in the southern sector of the Eastern Front and was steadily reinforced with so-called "foreign volunteers" from occupied countries, but it was

never as powerful as the three original SS panzer-grenadier divisions.

The Waffen-SS panzergrenadier divisions were so lavishly equipped with tanks and armoured vehicles that, in reality, they were far more powerful than army line panzer divisions.

The strike power of the Waffen-SS divisions lay in their panzer regiments, which boasted two battalions of tanks. In 1942 a tank battalion had three companies – one of heavy Panzer IVs and two with lighter Panzer IIIs, each having a complement of 22 tanks. The *Leibstandarte*'s companies, however, all had Panzer IVs in frontline roles, with Panzer IIIs reduced to command tasks. For added punch, each Waffen-SS panzer regiment also had a company of the monster Tiger I tanks attached. By mid-1944 these companies had grown into battalions. This organization was constantly evolving, but it is important to realize that once a panzer regiment was committed to battle it was common for less than half of its tanks to be fit for action at any one time.

The 25.4-tonne (25-ton) Panzer IV was the main German frontline tank of the war, and it was progres-sively up-armoured and up-gunned to meet the challenge of new Allied tanks. In late 1942, the main version in service with the Waffen-SS was the Ausf G model, which boasted a long-barrelled L/48 75mm cannon. With the introduction of this version, the armour balance on the Eastern Front swung back in Germany's favour after the surprise appearance of the Soviet T-34 medium tank the previous autumn. During mid-1943, the Panzer IVs were fitted with so-called armoured "skirts" along the side of the hull and around the turret to deflect Soviet anti-tank rounds. This later feature often led to the tank being mistakenly identified by the enemy as a Tiger I. Many Panzer IIIs were also equipped with skirt armour in an attempt to keep them battle-worthy, but the tank's 50mm cannon could not knock out a T-34, which was armed with the 76.2mm F-34 gun.

The Tiger I tank was introduced into Waffen-SS service in late 1942 after making its combat debut with the army in August 1942. At some 57 tonnes (56 tons), it was truly a battlefield monster, and armed with the high-velocity 88mm cannon it could knock out a Russian T-34 at a range of almost 2000m (6560ft).

Left: A Waffen-SS panzer approaches the burning Red Army T-34 it has just knocked out. The T-34 came as a nasty surprise to the Germans on the Eastern Front in 1941.

Below: Waffen-SS infantry and Panzer III on the Eastern Front. The tank is possibly the Ausf M version, which first entered Waffen-SS service in June 1943 prior to Kursk.

Thanks to its 100mm- (3.93in-) thick front armour, the Tiger I was almost impervious to the 76.2mm cannon fitted to the Russian tanks of this period (and most Western tanks as well). In late 1944, the Tiger I was replaced with the monster Tiger II, or King Tiger tank, which was actually tactically less effective.

Contrary to popular myth, the Waffen-SS was not equipped with the famous Panzer V Panther tank until the late summer of 1943, so during the battles around Kharkov and at Kursk, the Waffen-SS had to make do with Panzer IIIs and IVs, backed up by a couple of dozen Tiger Is.

Right: The Hummel self-propelled heavy howitzer mounted the 150mm field howitzer on a Panzer IV chassis. From the spring of 1943, a single battery (six Hummels plus a gun-less munitions carrier) of these vehicles was allocated to Waffen-SS panzer divisions.

Below: A column of StuG III Ausf G assault guns/tank destroyers somewhere in Russia. Both Waffen-SS panzer and panzergrenadier divisions fielded assault gun battalions, though during 1944 the StuGs were integrated into panzer and panzerjäger battalions.

To give an idea of the tank inventories of the SS panzer divisions, in February 1943 the *Leibstandarte* had the following panzers in its order of battle: 12 Panzer IIs, 10 Panzer IIIs, 52 Panzer IVs, 9 Tiger Is and 9 command tanks. Five months later, just before the Battle of Kursk, the division could field 4 Panzer II, 13 Panzer IIIs, 67 Panzer IVs, 13 Tiger Is and 9 command tanks.

At the heart of the Waffen-SS divisions were their panzergrenadier regiments. These units were able to trace their lineage back to the original SS standarten, and they made great play of their Nazi heritage. They generally had honorific titles as well as numerical designations. For example, *Das Reich* had the *Deutschland* and *Der Führer* Regiments, *Totenkopf* had the *Thule* (later *Totenkopf*) and *Theodor Eicke* Regiments, and *Wiking* had the *Germania*, *Nordland* and *Westland* Regiments. The *Leibstandarte*, however, was unique in that all its sub-units included numerical designations and the title *Leibstandarte SS Adolf Hitler*, abbreviated to LSSAH.

HEAVY FIREPOWER

During the autumn of 1942, the panzergrenadier regiments had equipment lavished on them to turn them into self-contained armoured units in their own right. One panzergrenadier battalion in the division received armoured halftracks to allow it to go into action alongside the panzer regiment. The other battalions retained their soft-skinned transport, but also had 120mm mortars, 20mm flak guns, 75mm anti-tank guns and 150mm Bison light howitzers. These were mostly self-propelled on halftrack chassis. When fully up to strength, a Waffen-SS panzergrenadier regiment boasted some 3200 men in late 1942.

Heavy firepower was provided by the artillery regiment, which received self-propelled 105mm Wespe and 150mm Hummel howitzers, as well as wheeled versions of those guns.

Supporting the "teeth regiments" of the division were anti-tank, reconnaissance, assault gun, anti-aircraft and combat engineer (pioneer) battalions. During late 1942, the Waffen-SS started to receive the StuG III Ausf F, which featured the powerful L/48 75mm cannon, to equip its assault gun battalions (each battalion had just over 30 StuG IIIs). These vehicles packed a powerful punch and had heavy armoured protection, and so were much in demand to support panzergrenadier operations. The anti-tank companies in the panzergrenadier regiments and the divisional anti-tank battalion, as well as the reconnaissance battalion, also used the Marder III anti-tank gun, which utilized an obsolete Czech 38(t)

One of the most famous weapons of World War II – the German Flak 18 anti-aircraft gun, the deadly "88" that could also knock out any Allied tank. Each Waffen-SS panzer division had four of these guns in its flak battalion.

WESPE

The Wespe self-propelled light field howitzer was introduced into the German armed forces from February 1943. Like the Marder II, the Wespe was based on the chassis of a Panzer II tank. Its main armament came in the form of the 105mm leFH18M L/28 gun. Carrying 32 rounds of ammunition, the Wespe was used as an infantry support weapon, and was issued to panzer and panzergrenadier divisions. It saw its first major action during the Battle of Kursk in mid-1943. The Wespe was an undoubted success, and saw action on all fronts until the end of the war. The first Waffen-SS unit to receive the Wespe was the *Leibstandarte*, in the summer of 1942. It took delivery of a battalion of 12 Wespes.

Type:	self-propelled howitzer
Length:	4.79m (15.75ft)
Width:	2.24m (7.3ft)
Height:	2.32m (7.5ft)
Crew:	5
Armament:	1 x 105mm
Range:	140km (87 miles)
Speed:	40kmh (25mph)

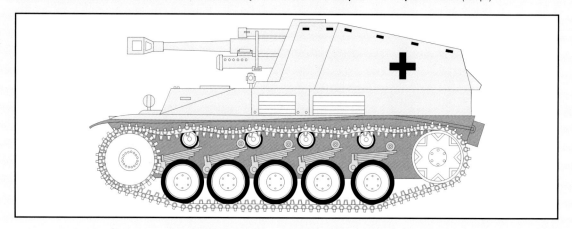

tank chassis and mounted the long-barrelled L/40 75mm or 76.2mm cannon. These bore the brunt of defensive anti-tank tasks, freeing the panzer regiment to take the lead in offensive action.

There were also strong communications, medical, supply and maintenance elements assigned to each division. Mobile repair teams were a key element, because they were able to recover damaged tanks from battlefields and return them to action within days. This ensured the divisions did not have to wait weeks for new tanks to arrive from factories thousands of kilometres from the front. At full strength, a Waffen-SS panzer-grenadier division comprised around 21,000 men. The nearest Red Army equivalent was the Tank Corps, which in 1943 boasted some 12,000 men, more than 180 T-34/76 tanks and some 60 SU-76 assault guns or SU-85 tank destroyers.

The SS Panzer Corps headquarters was activated in the summer of 1942 in Germany, before moving to France to oversee the establishment of the Waffen-SS panzergrenadier divisions. The headquarters mustered several thousand specialist staff officers and technical experts. Its core was a radio communications unit to allow the corps commander to talk to his divisions and

higher headquarters. There was also an artillery command cell to allow the firepower of all the divisional artillery regiments to be moved around the battlefield in a coordinated manner.

Depending on the battlefield situation, the corps could also take under its command army level artillery units with 210mm towed guns or mobile rocket launchers, known as Nebelwerfers. In 1942 the Waffen-SS did not have any of its own such units, but they were formed in 1943 to boost its firepower. In the middle of 1943 the first of three Waffen-SS heavy tank battalions was formed, but the battalions were not ready for action until the spring of 1944, when they went into action during the Normandy campaign.

In late 1942 the SS Panzer Corps was the only such formation in existence, but Hitler was keen to expand his private army even further, and so six months later he ordered the establishment of a second corps, to be titled I SS Panzer Corps *Leibstandarte Adolf Hitler*. The original corps headquarters was then retitled II SS Panzer Corps just prior to the Battle of Kursk in July 1943. I SS Panzer Corps was to be made up of the *Leibstandarte* Division and the soon-to-be-formed *Hitlerjugend* Panzergrenadier Division, although the two divisions did not serve together under the command of the corps headquarters until the summer of 1944, because of the need for the *Leibstandarte* in Italy and Russia. Once II SS Panzer Corps was withdrawn from Russia in the autumn of 1943, it was put in command of the *Hohenstaufen* and *Frundsberg* Panzergrenadier Divisions, which had been forming in France since December 1943. Himmler also developed plans to form a third Waffen-SS corps in the spring of 1943 comprising the Western European volunteers, and it was to be built around the *Wiking* and *Nordland* Panzergrenadier Divisions. The *Wiking* Division's commander, Felix Steiner, was eventually to take command of the corps when it was sent to the Eastern Front in December 1943. Unlike its two sister corps, III SS Panzer Corps was never afforded a high priority for equipment to allow it to become a hard-hitting armoured force.

In autumn 1943, the final stage in the evolution of the Waffen-SS armoured units occurred when the panzergrenadier divisions began to be renamed panzer divisions and were given numerical designations. For example, the *Leibstandarte* became the 1st SS Panzer Division *Leibstandarte Adolf Hitler*. The renaming was largely a symbolic act, because the Waffen-SS divisions had always been better equipped than most army line panzer divisions for well over a year. For reasons of clarity, this book will refer to them by their honorific titles only.

SS PANZER DIVISION TACTICS

To understand why the Waffen-SS panzer divisions were so successful in battle, it is essential to have some idea of the background and characters of some of the personalities who built and commanded them. While there was no such thing as a typical Waffen-SS officer, there were a number of distinctive groups.

The senior leadership in the early years were nearly all stalwart cronies of Hitler from his time in Munich during the 1920s. "Sepp" Dietrich and Theodor Eicke were old-guard Nazis, who liked to cultivate images of themselves as gruff, no-nonsense soldiers. They loved visiting the frontline trenches and swapping war stories with ordinary SS troopers. This bonhomie was largely a way to cover up for their own inadequacies as commanders and tacticians. Both, however, were sensible enough to leave complex technical problems to more talented subordinates. Others of the old Munich gang who joined the ranks of the SS remained behind in Germany and the occupied territories, supervising the mass murder of enemies of the Third Reich rather than serving at the front. Dietrich, who formed and led the *Leibstandarte* up

to mid-1943, was far from the cuddly grandfather figure that Nazi propaganda suggested. In 1941, for example, he ordered 4000 Russian prisoners to be executed in retaliation for the death of six captured *Leibstandarte* Division troopers.

The founder of the *Totenkopf*, Eicke, had a reputation as a sadist. He personally shot the SA leader Ernst Röhm during the "Night of the Long Knives". "Papa" Eicke was the first commandant of Dachau concentration camp, and by 1939 was head of the Reich's whole prison camp network. He invented the Death's Head, or *Totenkopf*, insignia that became synonymous with evil and mass murder between 1939 and 1945.

THE SS TECHNOCRATS

While the likes of Dietrich and Eicke represented the beer hall Nazi heritage of the Waffen-SS, there was also a growing breed of military technocrats that joined the organization during the late 1930s with an eye on career advancement. The most famous of these were Paul Hausser, Wilhelm Bittrich and Felix Steiner. They were all officers of the old school, having served in the Kaiser's army during World War I and then in the post-war Reichswehr. If anyone was responsible for turning the premier Waffen-SS divisions into an élite armoured fighting force, it was Hausser. He retired from the army in 1932 as a lieutenant-general, but within two years he had joined the SS and had set up the first training depot. He was soon put in charge of all Waffen-SS training, and he made a good job of it. He led the *Das Reich* Division during the invasion of Russia and was rewarded with the job of setting up the SS Panzer Corps in the summer of 1942. He led this formation during the Normandy campaign in 1944. Some of the old Munich gang did not like him because of his Prussian officer corps pedigree, but Hitler trusted him implicitly.

Bittrich was made from similar material, and replaced Hausser as commander of the *Das Reich* Division in October 1941. He was heavily involved in raising the *Hohenstaufen* and *Frundsberg* Divisions, and again replaced Hausser as commander of II SS Panzer Corps in 1944. Steiner formed the *Wiking* Division in 1940 and led it in Russia until May 1943. These men, along with Dietrich, were the most competent Waffen-SS panzer corps commanders thanks to their depth of military skill and experience.

Working behind the scenes of the Waffen-SS panzer units was a cadre of ex-army professional staff officers who kept them running at a peak of efficiency. The two most prominent were Rudolf Lehman, who was the chief of staff of the *Leibstandarte* until the summer of 1944, and Fritz Kraemer, who was chief of staff of I SS Panzer Corps for most of its existence. They effectively ran their formations to a standard that would be considered appropriate for equivalent army units.

Many of the regimental and battalion commanders in the Waffen-SS during the 1942–43 period – such as Otto Kumm, Kurt Meyer, Hermann Priess, Joachim Peiper, Theodor Wisch, Fritz Witt and Max Wünsche – would all rise to high command later in the war. They could, perhaps, be called swashbuckling characters who rose to the top through their success in battle during the Blitzkrieg years. They only knew how to soldier the Waffen-SS way: aggressively, taking risks to achieve victory. They were natural leaders who, time and again, would be at the centre of the action, ruthlessly driving their men forward and never giving up. These men kept the hard-pushed Waffen-SS panzer divisions fighting during the last two years of the war, when less motivated men would have given up.

The Waffen-SS did not create its own panzer tactics, but adapted existing army techniques to its own distinctive style of fighting. And the ability of Waffen-SS commanders to form their troops quickly into all-arms battlegroups (kampfgruppen) to deal with sudden crises or overcome difficult tactical challenges, combined with panzer tactics, paid dividends. The tight bonds of friendship between the Waffen-SS officer corps was to their advantage.

Working in kampfgruppen was the norm for the Waffen-SS panzer troops, and no major operation would be undertaken without some sort of regrouping of forces to meet specific objectives. The speed at which Waffen-SS commanders could form and launch kampfgruppen into action was often decisive on the Eastern Front, usually confounding their rigidly hierarchical Red Army opponents, who required detailed orders from higher command before any operation could be undertaken (on the positive side, deliberate planning reduced the strain on inexperienced Soviet junior officers).

Kampfgruppen were usually formed around a battalion-sized unit. For assaults and counterattacks, the main units that were used to form kampfgruppen were the division's two panzer battalions, its halftrack-mounted panzergrenadier battalion and the reconnaissance battalion. In defensive operations, the two panzergrenadier regiments bore the brunt of the fighting, with assault gun and anti-tank detachments attached to augment their firepower.

MARDER III

The Marder III was the result of Hitler's express order to switch the production capacity of the Panzer 38(t) to that of self-propelled guns. Acquiring a new design whereby the engine was moved to the centre of the vehicle and the gun was moved to the rear, the Marder III went into action with both panzer and infantry divisions from May 1943. Armed with the 75mm Pak 40/3 gun, it was an effective anti-tank weapons platform. It was superseded in May 1944 by the Jagdpanzer Hetzer, by which time 975 units had been produced. By the war's end, some 300 units were still in service. The last two Marders left in Waffen-SS service, in mid-March 1945, were fighting with the *Totenkopf* Division.

Type:	self-propelled anti-tank gun
Length:	4.65m (15.25ft)
Width:	2.16m (7ft)
Height:	2.48m (8.1m)
Crew:	4
Armament:	1 x 75mm
Range:	185km (115 miles)
Speed:	42kmh (26mph)

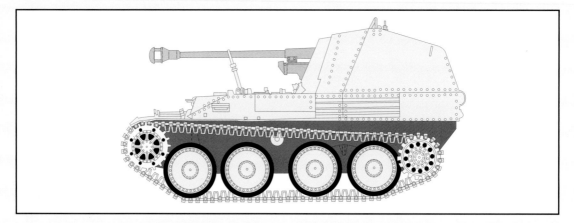

Forming a kampfgruppe was a routine event, and there were well-established procedures for it. The divisional commander would first draw up his tactical plan, setting objectives for his regiments. He would then assign divisional assets from his specialist battalions, or elements of other regiments, to specific regimental commanders. The regimental commander, in turn, would divide up his newly assigned assets between his battalion commanders.

The kampfgruppe commander had full tactical command of all the units and equipment assigned to him for the duration of an operation, and only once the mission was completed would they be returned to their parent units for re-assignment. A kampfgruppe was usually named after its commander, which emphasized his instrumental role in its actions. The commander was responsible for all tactical planning and the issuing of operational orders. This meant Waffen-SS battalion and regimental commanders had to be knowledgeable about the all-arms tactics and the capabilities of tanks, infantry, artillery, engineers and anti-tank weapons.

While most kampfgruppen were set up as a result of deliberate planning, a number were formed on an ad hoc basis when communications with higher headquarters were lost. Often during sudden enemy breakthroughs, an assortment of units would find themselves cut off. It

Above: The first Waffen-SS Nebelwerfer battalions were formed in 1943. In the spring of 1945 Himmler took the decision to amalgamate the battalions into a single brigade.

Below: SS troops prepare to load a six-barrelled Nebelwerfer 41 rocket launcher. When fired it loosed a salvo of six rockets and produced a nerve-wracking sound. Unfortunately, it also kicked up large clouds of smoke.

WERNER OSTENDORFF

Born on 15 August 1903, Werner Ostendorff began his military career in 1925 when he joined Jäger Regiment 1 before transferring to the Luftwaffe in 1934. Commissioned into the SS in 1935, he served at the officer school at Bad Tölz, and with the *Der Führer* Regiment. He held various other posts in the early war years, including taking command of the Fliegerabwehr-Machinengewehr-Abteilung when it was formed in early June 1939. During the Polish campaign he acted as a staff observer with Panzer Division Kempf. When the *Das Reich* Division was formed, Ostendorff became its senior staff officer, and won the Knight's Cross for his actions in leading a small mixed battlegroup into action. In mid-1942, he became the Chief of Staff to Hausser's SS-Generalkommando and served with this unit at Kharkov and Kursk. In November 1943, he was given command of the newly formed 17th SS Panzergrenadier Division *Götz von Berlichingen*, leading this unit in action in Normandy. In February 1945 he took command of the *Das Reich* Division, but was soon wounded in action. This very capable staff officer died of his wounds in a field hospital in Austria on 5 May 1945.

would then be the job of the senior commander on the ground to take charge and organize the defence.

An important part of any kampfgruppe was a half-track-borne artillery observation party from the division's artillery regiment. The divisional artillery commander would then assign artillery batteries and ammunition supplies to support specific operations. The allocation of fire support was carried out in much the same way as kampfgruppen were formed, with those units in greatest need getting the lion's share of firepower. Luftwaffe forward air controllers would also regularly be assigned to work with kampfgruppe commanders, directing cannon-armed Junkers Ju 87 Stuka dive-bombers and Henschel Hs 129 ground-attack aircraft to their targets, by radio from their armoured halftracks.

Waffen-SS battle tactics were designed to capitalize on the capabilities of SS divisional equipment and flexible unit organization. Its attack tactics were an evolution of the successful German stormtrooper tactics developed during the final years of World War I, and then refined in the interwar period.

It was the job of the reconnaissance battalion to find weak spots in the enemy's position and then quickly report back to the division intelligence staff on the best way to approach and attack the opposition. The weakest point in the enemy's frontline would then become the target of the division's main effort, or schwerpunkt (literally, centre of gravity; thus point of maximum effort). Surprise was essential, since it required the penetration of the enemy line on a narrow front by superior and fast-moving forces.

A powerful kampfgruppe would then be assembled to lead the attack, with a range of capabilities to allow it to bridge rivers, breach minefields and then smash the enemy's resistance. A kampfgruppe had to be self-contained to allow it to overcome sudden obstacles or surprise enemy counterattacks. Once committed to action, this assault force would receive the bulk of the division's artillery support. If a decisive breakthrough was achieved, then more kampfgruppen would be dispatched to capitalize on the initial success.

TACTICAL FORMATIONS

If possible, Waffen-SS commanders would choose to mount their breakthrough attacks against thinly held sectors of the enemy front, so their combat power would not be dissipated before the start of the decisive phase of the operation. To ensure the breakthrough was successful with the minimum of losses, the Waffen-SS and army developed the panzerkeil (armoured wedge) tactics. The most heavily armoured tanks in the division, usually Tigers, would lead the attack because of their relative invulnerability to enemy anti-tank rounds. Following behind would be lighter tanks and infantry in halftracks. Riding alongside the infantry would be combat engineers, ready to move forward to clear any minefields, clear obstacles or bridge gaps. The kampfgruppe commander would be located just behind the lead tanks, to coordinate the various combat elements under his command.

"No plan survives contact with the enemy", stated Helmuth von Moltke (1800–91), Prussian field marshal, and so divisional commanders would be constantly monitoring the progress of an attack on the radio net to see how the operation was developing. They were always looking for opportunities to unhinge the enemy's defences, even if this meant sudden changes of plan to capitalize on surprise events. Here, the kampfgruppe system came into its element again, because units

Above: The 105mm le FH 18/40 gun was the standard German light divisional howitzer throughout the war. Each SS panzer battalion had three battalions of 12 each.

Below: All Waffen-SS panzer divisions had an anti-tank battalion made up of a self-propelled company and two companies of anti-tank guns (as here).

could be quickly switched to those kampfgruppen with the best chance of success. The Waffen-SS always reinforced success, pumping reinforcements into breaches in the enemy lines and then pressing on deep into vulnerable rear areas. This type of fast-moving operation often meant that kampfgruppen might be temporarily out of contact with regimental or divisional headquarters, so Waffen-SS commanders were given great latitude to exploit the situation as best they could.

Contrary to popular belief, Waffen-SS panzer commanders preferred not to attack Soviet positions head-on, but rather tried to find undefended gaps in their positions so they could rapidly move deep behind their lines. It was the job of the reconnaissance battalion to push ahead of the lead kampfgruppe to find routes for it to move forward, avoiding minefields, anti-tank ditches and heavily defended positions.

On the Eastern Front, strictly regimented Soviet forces were often completely confused and defeated by these tactics. Even very small kampfgruppen could cause damage out of all proportion to their size, because of their ability to dodge and weave their way past enemy defences and strike at key points such as command posts, supply dumps and bridges. With their

So-called schürzen armoured aprons fitted to the side of panzers gave them additional protection from enemy anti-tank rounds. The lead tank in the picture is a Panzer IV, which also has additional armour around the turret (later Panzer IVs also had thicker frontal armour).

communications to headquarters severed and their lines of retreat cut, Soviet regiments or even divisions could be rendered ineffective. They would then be trapped in pockets to be liquidated at a later date by follow-up infantry units.

In defensive operations, the Waffen-SS aimed to fight in an equally flexible and mobile way as it did during offensive operations. It was the job of the panzergrenadier regiments to hold ground, but counter-attacks played a key role in defeating Soviet breakthroughs. Aggressive use of artillery was the first line of defence, breaking up enemy concentrations in assembly areas before they moved forward. Once attacks were under way, the rapid calling down of artillery and mortar fire on enemy infantry could cause havoc and heavy casualties. It was the job of the Marder self-propelled anti-tank guns, StuG IIIs and 88mm flak guns assigned to the panzergrenadier regiments to defeat enemy tank attacks.

STOPPING ENEMY TANKS

If the enemy attack was pressed forward, then the panzergrenadiers would be ordered to hold their ground to try to separate the enemy tanks from their supporting infantry. Usually Soviet tank crews would press on forward deep behind the German frontline, even if their tank-riding infantry had been mortared and machine-gunned as they crossed the panzer-grenadiers' trench line. For Waffen-SS soldiers, letting Red Army tanks roll over their foxholes and trenches before dealing with follow-on infantry required not only skill but also nerves of steel.

More Marder self-propelled antitank guns, StuGs and 88mm flak guns would now be in a position to block the Red Army tanks as they moved around the division's rear area. Carefully prepared tank-killing zones would be created in which the heavy anti-tank weapons could deal with any threats at long range.

Only as a last resort would the Waffen-SS division commit its panzer regiment in "penny packets" to deal with small numbers of enemy tanks. The panzers, usually teamed with the halftrack battalion, would be held back to counterattack against any enemy penetrations that looked like creating dangerous breakthroughs, or to strike deep into the heart of the enemy's own defences to turn the tables on them.

On 31 December 1942, attempts by the German Army to break through to the trapped Stalingrad garrison had failed, and Hitler turned to the SS Panzer Corps to restore the situation. The *Leibstandarte* and *Das Reich* Divisions were loaded on to almost 500 trains and shipped eastwards from 9 January 1943 onwards. *Totenkopf* (which on its own required 120 trains to ship it to the East) was given an extra month's grace after Eicke persuaded the Führer that he needed more time to lick his division into shape for combat. He also raided the French countryside for cars and trucks to ensure his division had adequate transport.

It took almost a month for I SS Panzer Corps to travel across Nazi-occupied Europe to the Eastern Rampart of the Third Reich. In the snow-covered wastes of the eastern Ukraine, the veteran Waffen-SS officers steadied their raw troopers as the day approached when they would meet the advancing Red Army. They would not have long to wait.

Above: Waffen-SS SdKfz 251 halftrack armoured personnel carriers in central Russia in 1943. It was not until late 1942 that the Waffen-SS received its first SdKfz 251s.

Below: Waffen-SS SdKfz 251s in action, probably at Kursk in 1943. On the battlefield the SS panzergrenadiers in each SdKfz 251 would accompany the panzers into combat.

First Blood of the SS Panzer Corps: Kharkov

In early 1943 the Germans were on the verge of losing the war on the Eastern Front. The defeat at Stalingrad and the subsequent Soviet offensive in the Ukraine threatened the whole southern sector of the front. The situation was saved by the leadership of Erich von Manstein and his masterful use of the newly raised I SS Panzer Corps, which retook Kharkov in spectacular fashion.

Waffen-SS infantry and a StuG III assault gun during the offensive to retake Kharkov in early 1943. The newly arrived SS corps was quickly thrown into battle against over-extended and exhausted Soviet units.

In January 1943, Soviet armies had been running rampant in the Ukraine, with the Wehrmacht falling back in disarray after the massive defeat suffered by the German Army at Stalingrad. While finishing off the remnants of Paulus' battered army, the Russians extended their offensive to the Ukraine, smashing weak German, Hungarian and Italian armies in their path.

Soviet forces began the final phase of their offensive on 14 January with a massive attack on the over-stretched German, Hungarian and Italian armies dug in along the River Don. Lieutenant-General F.I. Golikov's Voronezh Front and Lieutenant-General N.F. Vatutin's Southwest Front rolled over the defenders with ease, and within two weeks had pushed 160km (100 miles) westwards. They were now poised to cross the River Donets, which barred the way to Kharkov and the strategically crucial River Dnieper crossings.

To counter this advance, the Germans rushed reinforcements from all over Europe in a desperate bid to rebuild the Eastern Front. North of Kharkov, the army's élite *Grossdeutschland* Motorized Division, supported by the 88th and 168th Infantry Divisions, held the Belgorod area. Two divisions of the SS Panzer Corps, which had just arrived from France, were deployed along the Donets blocking the direct route to Kharkov.

Under SS-Obergruppenführer Paul Hausser, I SS Panzer Corps was superbly equipped with new tanks, armoured halftrack personnel carriers, self-propelled artillery and Nebelwerfer multi-barrel rocket launchers. Holding the Donets line were the *Leibstandarte* and *Das Reich* Divisions. The 1st SS Panzer Regiment of the *Leibstandarte* was the strongest tank unit in the corps, with 52 Panzer IVs, 10 Panzer IIIs and 9 Tiger Is. *Das Reich*'s 2nd SS Panzer Regiment had 81 Panzer IIIs and only 21 Panzer IVs, backed up by 10 Tiger Is.

The journey from France took almost two weeks, and many of the 200 trains carrying the division were re-routed to avoid Royal Air Force (RAF) bombing and Soviet partisan attacks. These disruptions meant that the divisions arrived at the railhead in Kharkov in dribs and drabs. The first elements to arrive were from the *Leibstandarte*'s 1st Panzergrenadier Regiment, which threw an improvised defensive ring around Kharkov along the frozen banks of the River Donets. Next off the trains on 29 January were the armoured cars and motorcycles of the *Leibstandarte*'s reconnaissance battalion,

SDKFZ 251

The Schützenpanzerwagen (SdKfz) 251 was an armoured halftrack vehicle, with standard wheels on the front axle and tracks at the rear. Essentially designed as an armoured personnel carrier, the SdKfz 251 entered service with the Waffen-SS in 1942. The versatility of the basic vehicle allowed it to serve as the platform for a wide range of different weapons, including a 75mm infantry support gun, a flamethrower, a flak gun and even a multiple rocket launcher. An interesting variant was the "UHU", which carried a huge infra-red searchlight designed to operated alongside tanks equipped with infra-red sights. In total some 15,000 were produced during the war.

Type:	armoured personnel carrier
Length:	5.8m (19ft)
Width:	2.1m (6.9ft)
Height:	1.75m (5.75ft)
Crew:	12
Armament:	2 x 7.92mm
Range:	300km (186 miles)
Speed:	52kmh (32.5mph)

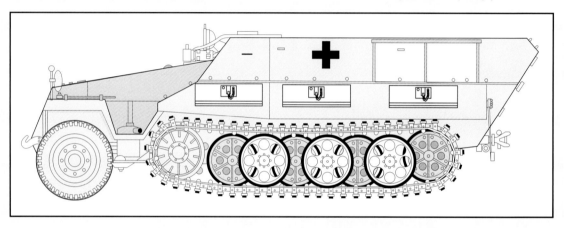

and they were dispatched to set up a covering screen 80km (50 miles) to the east, to give early warning of any approaching Russians. At the same time the *Deutschland* Panzergrenadier Regiment, of the *Das Reich* Division, was also sent to extend the screen northwards.

As the Waffen-SS troops fanned out across the winter wasteland, they had a series of vicious encounters with the advance guard of the Soviet XVIII Guards Corps. Intermingled with the Russian troops were retreating columns of the hard-pressed German 298th and 320th Infantry Divisions, who had marched across the steppe to seek safety in the west. The German infantry columns were shepherded back towards Kharkov. In a couple of cases, the Waffen-SS reconnaissance troops mounted raids to rescue recently captured infantrymen, racing into Soviet positions on their motorcycles and raking them with machine-gun fire.

The reconnaissance screen fell back deliberately towards Kharkov, and by 4 February 1943 I SS Panzer Corps was almost fully deployed in its main defensive position along the Donets. South of Kharkov there was a void of 160km (100 miles) between the Waffen-SS corps and the left flank of the First Panzer Army. Manstein was moving up units of the Fourth Panzer Army to fill the gap,

but they would take time to arrive, leaving Kharkov very exposed to encirclement by Golikov's tanks in the interim.

Hausser's Waffen-SS troops held their front along the Donets with grim determination against furious attacks by the Soviet XII and XV Tank Corps from Lieutenant-General P.S. Rybalko's Third Tank Army until 10 February (each tank army had two tank corps, a separate tank brigade and support units). This brave stand only played into the Soviets' hands. Russian troops were pushing around the flanks of Hausser's corps and there was a real prospect of Stalingrad being repeated, albeit on a much smaller scale. Major-General K.S. Moskalenko's Fortieth Army, with IV Tank Corps in the lead, ejected the *Grossdeutschland* Division from Belgorod and sent it heading south to Kharkov.

In their positions east of the city, the Waffen-SS divisions inflicted heavy casualties against Soviet human-wave attacks. Hausser, now dubbed "Papa" by his men, took great delight in visiting the frontline to watch the action. He was reportedly particularly impressed by the performance of the new MG 42 belt-fed machine gun, which was used in action by the Waffen-SS for the first time by the *Leibstandarte*'s 1st Panzergrenadier Regiment on 4 February. Hundreds of

SOVIET UKRAINE OFFENSIVE

Soviet frontline
- – – – – 29 January
- ·············· 9 February
- —— 20 February
- ——→ Soviet attack

In early 1943, two Red Army fronts tore a hole in the German frontline and threatened the whole of the Ukraine. Unfortunately for the Red Army, its armoured spearheads pushed too far west and outran their supply lines.

dead Russians were later found piled in front of the Waffen-SS position.

To the south of the Waffen-SS, Vatutin took advantage of the lack of opposition in front of him to push his troops tirelessly forward. The Sixth Army, with two tank corps, two infantry corps and a cavalry corps, raced for the Dnieper crossing at Dnepropetrovsk, while Lieutenant-General M.M. Popov's Front Mobile Group of four tank corps pushed south, aiming for Krasnoarmeiskoye and the Sea of Azov.

Overestimating the capabilities of his SS troops, Hitler ordered them to attack southeast to close the gap with the First Panzer Army. Two groups were formed for the operation. A strong covering force was to remain around Kharkov under the command of *Das Reich*, which also included the *Leibstandarte*'s 2nd Panzergrenadier Regiment and elements of the division's Tiger tank company, artillery and flak regiments. Hausser's corps headquarters and the *Grossdeutschland* Division also remained in the city, along with the 298th Infantry Division.

The covering force fought an increasingly desperate defensive battle, and the frontline had to be pulled back to free troops for the coming operation to the south of the city. By 12 February, the Soviet VI Guards Cavalry

Corps had punched a hole in the line separating the *Leibstandarte* from the 320th Infantry Division. Surrounded and burdened with thousands of wounded men, the army division needed help fast. A kampfgruppe was formed under SS-Sturmbannführer Joachim Peiper, then commander of the 2nd Panzergrenadier Regiment's armoured personnel carrier battalion, to rescue the division. He was given a column of ambulances and a detachment of StuG III assault guns for the mission. The kampfgruppe punched through the Russian front after destroying several tanks, and pushed 48km (30 miles) behind enemy lines to find the beleaguered infantry division. After loading up the ambulances, Peiper's men headed back to German lines, but a Soviet ski battalion had moved into place to block their path and destroy the main bridge over the River Udy, which the Waffen-SS column had to cross to return to Kharkov. The Waffen-SS kampfgruppe attacked and cleared out the Russians in house-to-house fighting, before repairing the bridge for the ambulances.

However, the improvised structure could not take the heavy Waffen-SS assault guns and armoured halftracks, so Peiper ordered his men back behind Russian lines to find a more suitable crossing. They returned to the

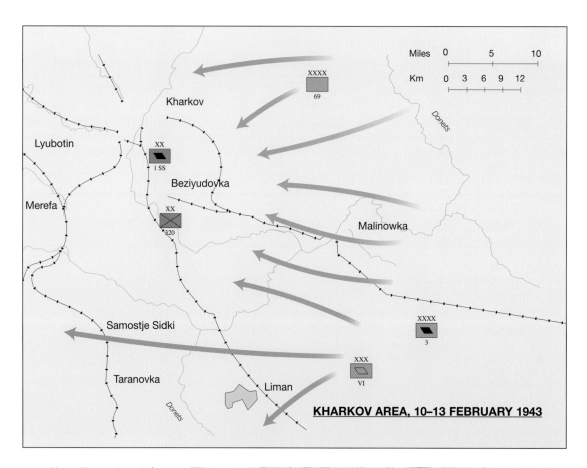

KHARKOV AREA, 10–13 FEBRUARY 1943

Above: The weakened German forces trying to hold Kharkov were threatened with encirclement and annihilation as Red Army formations approached their positions.

Right: A makeshift Waffen-SS defensive position on the outskirts of Kharkov in February 1943. Rather than being trapped, in the middle of the month Hausser gave the order to abandon the city. He thus saved I SS Panzer Corps from certain destruction.

Leibstandarte's lines after suffering only a handful of casualties and rescuing the 320th Infantry Division, which was soon able to return to frontline duty after being fed and housed by the Waffen-SS supply units. This was only a temporary respite for Hausser, though. To the north of Kharkov, the *Grossdeutschland* Division was being pushed back into the northern outskirts of the city. No forces could be spared to counter this dangerous pincer movement because of Hitler's insistence that I SS Panzer Corps' attack group continue with its southward push from Merefa. This would involve the commitment of the *Leibstandarte*'s powerful panzer regiment for the first time.

The large attack group, under the *Leibstandarte*'s commander, SS-Obergruppenführer Josef "Sepp" Dietrich, was ordered to lead the attack forward on 11 February. Pushing directly southwards into the flank of the Soviet VI Guards Cavalry Corps was the *Leibstandarte*'s 1st Panzergrenadier Regiment with its lorry-borne infantry, and the 2nd Battalion of the division's panzer regiment. *Das Reich*'s *Der Führer* Panzergrenadier Regiment reinforced this effort, while SS-Obersturmbannführer Kurt "Panzer" Meyer led the *Leibstandarte*'s reconnaissance battalion deployed on the right to seal the Russian incursion with a large flanking move. He was given a panzer battalion to support this daring move.

Heavy snowdrifts slowed the advance and made it impossible for the Waffen-SS panzers to take the lead in the attack for the first few hours. Stuka dive-bombers strafed Russian columns, and the Waffen-SS units made good progress, clearing the enemy from village after village. By early evening Meyer and his men had all but completed their encircling move, while the main attack columns surprised and destroyed a number of Russian formations. On 12 February, Meyer's advance continued under the cover of a massive snowstorm. Russian and German tank columns became intermingled in the poor visibility, but the Waffen-SS column pressed on regardless. The following day, Meyer's kampfgruppe found itself cut off in Bereka, which blocked the Soviet line of retreat from the pocket created by the Waffen-SS operation. During the night, six tanks of the *Leibstandarte*'s Panzer Regiment, under Max Wünsche, broke through the Soviet ring to reinforce Meyer, and he then used the tanks to sweep the neighbourhood of Soviet infantry. For the next two days the attack group tightened the grip on the trapped Russian cavalry corps, and swept village after village for stragglers. *Leibstandarte* panzers led these attacks, neutralizing isolated Russian tanks so the panzergrenadiers could move forward in their armoured halftracks. By the time the Waffen-SS had finished its work, the 7000 Soviet soldiers of VI Guards Cavalry Corps had been scattered, 10 of its 16 tanks destroyed, 3000 troops wounded and a further 400 captured. Other Russian troops were moving forward to help their comrades, however, and soon the Waffen-SS group found itself under attack on three fronts. It was now time for the German forces to fall back.

Two soldiers of I SS Panzer Corps west of Kharkov in February 1943. They each carry an MP40 submachine gun, a 9mm weapon that had a cyclic rate of fire of 500rpm. The magazine held 32 rounds.

PAUL HAUSSER

Paul "Papa" Hausser was born on 7 October 1880, and served with the Imperial German Army during World War I. He won both First and Second Class Iron Crosses for his actions, and finished the war as a major. He remained in the Reichswehr after the war and retired as a major-general in 1932. His vast experience was highly sought after by the fledgling SS-Verfügungstruppe (SS-VT), and he joined the SS in 1934, becoming commandant of the SS-Junkerschule at Bad Tölz. In 1936, he was appointed Inspector-General of the SS-VT. Hausser was given command of the *Das Reich* Division in 1941, and won the Knight's Cross for his leadership. In February 1943, he disobeyed a direct order from Hitler and withdrew from the city of Kharkov, only to launch a counteroffensive and retake the city the next month. He was awarded the Oakleaves for this brilliant action (though out of pique Hitler delayed his award by four months). After the Allied invasion in the West in June 1944, he commanded the Seventh Army, and was seriously wounded leading the Falaise breakout. He was awarded the Swords for his bravery. For the remainder of the war, he commanded Army Group G. He died on 21 December 1972.

The main Soviet force dodged Hausser's punch, slipping in behind the advancing Waffen-SS men to try to cut them off from Kharkov and split up the already fragmented German front even more. In these see-saw battles the superior equipment, training and determination of the Waffen-SS tank crews usually meant they came out on top, but their panzer kampfgruppen could not be everywhere, and by 14 February Kharkov was virtually surrounded. To compound the problem, an uprising had broken out in the city and Hausser feared that his corps headquarters units, *Das Reich* and *Grossdeutschland*, would share the same fate as Paulus at Stalingrad. He wanted to order an evacuation through a narrow corridor to the southwest. Repeated orders from Hitler to hold the city to the last man and bullet were ignored: Hausser issued the orders to pull out on 15 February. By the time Hitler found out and had issued countermanding orders, the *Das Reich* Division was on its way to safety and there was no going back. The *Das Reich* and *Leibstandarte* panzergrenadiers set up an improvised defence line to the south of Kharkov, but Soviet tanks were close on their heels, inflicting a steady stream of casualties before the Waffen-SS units could break clear.

With I SS Panzer Corps safely out of Kharkov, Manstein was able to complete the reorganization of his panzer divisions for their counterstroke. An unannounced visit by Hitler, furious at the loss of Kharkov, to Manstein's headquarters at Zaporozhye on 17 February interrupted the field marshal's preparations. Hitler had intended to dismiss Manstein for the loss of the city and order an immediate northwards attack by I SS Panzer Corps to retake Kharkov. Fortunately for the field marshal, the sound of Russian artillery near his command post brought the Führer to his senses and he left in a hurry, to allow Manstein to get on with sorting out the Soviets. Manstein

was also helped by the fact that the *Totenkopf* Division got stuck in mud after a sudden thaw during the day, making it unavailable for Hitler's proposed attack.

Manstein's plan called for two Waffen-SS divisions to strike southwest from Krasnograd into the western flank of the Soviet Sixth Army, while the Fourth Panzer Army drove northwards to push the remaining elements of the western Soviet attack force onto the guns of the Waffen-SS panzers. Farther east, the First Panzer Army would take the offensive against Popov's Front Mobile Group and complete the destruction of the Soviet forces west of the River Donets.

The Russians proved easy meat for the panzers. After two months of continuous fighting, Popov's group was down to 50 worn-out tanks and 13,000 men fit for battle. Lieutenant-General F.M. Khatritonov's Sixth Army was in an equally parlous state, with many of its 150 tanks stranded through lack of fuel. Of most help to Manstein, however, were orders from Vatutin (who was still convinced the Germans were retreating) for the Soviet troops to keep advancing.

As this battle was developing, Hausser set about reorganizing his corps for offensive action. The *Leibstandarte* was to be the anvil of the offensive based around Krasnograd, while *Das Reich* and the newly arrived *Totenkopf* Division swung south and then northwards, forcing the Russians back on to the guns of the *Leibstandarte*. The arrival of the *Totenkopf* at Krasnograd on the morning of 19 February, with its 81 Panzer IIIs, 22 Panzer IVs and 9 Tiger Is, completed I SS Panzer Corps' order of battle for perhaps its most famous victory. In the afternoon Manstein ordered the attack to proceed.

A 96km (60-mile) road march brought *Das Reich* and *Totenkopf* to their jump-off positions at Novomoskovsk on 20 February. Pushing westwards, they sliced through the immobilized XXV Tank Corps and IV Guards and XV Guards Rifle Corps near Pavlograd. These units were in bad shape after Luftwaffe anti-tank aircraft caught the Russian armour by surprise earlier in the morning. XXXXVIII Panzer Corps was already attacking from the south, so the Waffen-SS attack sliced into the side of the already stalled Russian columns. *Totenkopf* was assigned the northern axis of the attack, and *Das Reich* pushed farther south and then turned eastwards to Pavlograd, before swinging northwards. The Waffen-SS men raced forward at such a breakneck speed that Soviet and German troops often became intermingled. A panzer kampfgruppe of *Das Reich* spearheading the division's advance seized a key bridge outside Pavlograd on 22 February. Two *Das Reich* Panzer IIIs and a Tiger held the bridge for several hours, destroying three T-34s that tried to take the bridge back.

The two Waffen-SS divisions trapped the Soviet I Guards Tank Corps and two rifle divisions. The Waffen-SS Tigers and Panzer IVs knocked out the Russian tanks and anti-tank guns with ease at long range with their powerful 88mm and 75mm cannons, before panzer-grenadiers closed in to mop up pockets of isolated Soviet infantry who offered resistance in the snow-bound villages. Elements of Soviet divisions were smashed in the attack, with most of the men just abandoning their

tanks and vehicles and fleeing into the surrounding forests. For five days the two Waffen-SS divisions meandered through huge columns of abandoned and destroyed vehicles, machine-gunning small groups of Russian soldiers hiding amid the carnage. The Soviet Sixth Army had ceased to exist.

The Soviets exacted a heavy price from the *Totenkopf* Division for its victory, however. The division's commander, SS-Obergruppenführer Theodor Eicke, flew forward in his Fieseler Storch light aircraft to visit his spearhead units on 26 February. The infamous SS general ordered his pilot to land near a village that he believed was occupied by *Totenkopf* troops. In fact, the men on the ground were a group of cut-off Russian soldiers, and Eicke's aircraft was ripped apart in mid-air by anti-aircraft artillery fire as it approached the ground. The following day Waffen-SS troops cleared the village and recovered the mutilated body of the former concentration camp commander.

From the north, the *Leibstandarte* Division was conducting an aggressive defence of its line in the snow,

This map graphically illustrates the plight of the *Leibstandarte* and *Das Reich* Divisions trapped in Kharkov, and shows that Hausser was right to abandon the city.

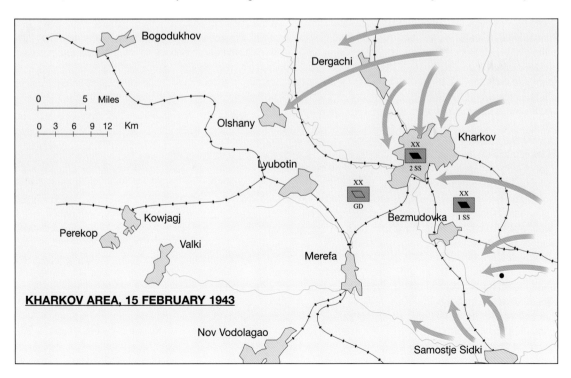

KHARKOV AREA, 15 FEBRUARY 1943

aimed at neutralizing the advance elements of the Soviet Third Tank Army. *Leibstandarte* kampfgruppen were launched forward on a daily basis to destroy large Soviet formations spotted by Luftwaffe aerial reconnaissance. The Waffen-SS men infiltrated at night through the thinly held Soviet front to ambush the enemy. Bursting from forests, the kampfgruppen usually took the Russians by surprise, and within minutes their panzers and armoured halftracks would be among the enemy positions, spreading destruction. Their job complete, the Germans would then pull back to regroup and rearm for the next foray.

On 17 February the *Leibstandarte*'s reconnaissance battalion, reinforced with panzers, wiped out a Soviet infantry regiment in the first big raid. Three days later Peiper's armoured infantry battalion cleared out 750 Russians, three tanks and dozens of anti-tank guns from a heavily defended village during a night attack.

SS-Obersturmbannführer Kurt "Panzer" Meyer was given command of a kampfgruppe of panzers and reconnaissance troops on 19 February, tasked with destroying a large enemy force advancing west. His panzer company destroyed a Russian battalion in the afternoon.

At dawn on 21 February, his column had taken up ambush positions near the town of Jerememkevka. Meyer spotted a long column of Soviet troops moving across the snow-covered steppe, totally unaware of the imminent danger. The attack began with a daredevil charge into the middle of the column by a reconnaissance team in VW Schwimmwagen amphibious jeeps, led by Meyer himself. One vehicle was blown up by a mine, but within minutes the others were among the stunned Russians, raking them with machine-gun fire. Panzer IV tanks then burst out of the woods at the head and tail of the column, cutting off any hope of retreat. Several hundred Russians were slaughtered and a dozen artillery pieces captured. The following night Meyer's force launched another raid on an unsuspecting Russian column, with similar results. The fighting on the northern sector of the division's front was also intense, with the panzer regiment having to be sent to relieve its pioneer battalion, which had been surrounded by a surprise Soviet attack.

On 23 February Meyer's battlegroup was ordered forward, again ambushing a Soviet divisional headquarters and a whole divisional artillery group. A surprise panzer attack charged into a Russian-held town, and within five hours the *Leibstandarte* men had killed 1000 enemy soldiers and captured 30 heavy artillery pieces.

Above: Soldiers of I SS Panzer Corps in the snow during Manstein's counter-offensive to retake Kharkov in late February.

Right: A brief rest for an SS Panzer III as Manstein's corps approaches Kharkov. During this period the *Das Reich* and *Totenkopf* Divisions trapped two Soviet armies and destroyed around 600 enemy tanks, 600 anti-tank guns and 400 artillery pieces.

While the *Leibstandarte*, *Das Reich* and *Totenkopf* Divisions were striking back at the Soviet spearheads south of Kharkov, on the right flank of the German front the *Wiking* Panzergrenadier Division was involved in a series of brutal skirmishes to hold back the enemy advance. A powerful Soviet tank force, led by III and IV Tank Corps and supported by hundreds of ski troops, was pushing south into the breach in the German line, just to the west of the First Panzer Army. Manstein hoped to seal the gap in the front from the west with I SS Panzer Corps, and from the east with the armoured units of the Fourth Panzer Army being brought up from the Caucasus.

HOLDING THE LINE

By 8 February, the Soviets had taken the key rail junctions at Krasnoarmeiskoye and Gishino, in a surprise push 80km (50 miles) behind the left flank of the First Panzer Army. First on the scene to counter this dangerous incursion was the *Wiking* Division, closely followed by the 7th and 11th Panzer Divisions. These were not fresh and superbly equipped divisions. They had been in action continuously for almost three months, and were down to only 2000 fighting troops each. *Wiking* alone could not muster more than five battered old Panzer III tanks fit for action. The Waffen-SS men could barely stabilize the front, let alone press forward to clear out the incursion. Only his strong artillery regiment enabled the *Wiking*'s commander, SS-Obergruppenführer Felix Steiner, to contain the Russian tanks.

On 12 February, the *Wiking* Division launched an outflanking attack into the eastern edge of Krasnoarmeiskoye itself and northwards to Gishino, but it broke down in the face of fanatical Soviet resistance. For the next week, the Waffen-SS men and an army infantry division fought vicious street battles to contain the Soviet forces from breaking out of the town. X Soviet Tank Corps arrived to support the advance from Krasnoarmeiskoye, but the Soviet troops in the region were also very weak by this time, with no more than two dozen tanks available to fight the Waffen-SS troops.

The 7th Panzer Division was now thrown into the battle, attacking into the east of the city, while the *Wiking* Division tried to storm in from the west. Luftwaffe Stukas supported the assault, but the Russians held firm. XXXX Panzer Corps now ordered the *Wiking* and the 7th Panzer Divisions to bypass Krasnoarmeiskoye. In a Blitzkrieg-style advance they were to defeat the Soviets in a battle of manoeuvre. The attack opened on 19 February with a sweep north from Krasnoarmeiskoye across the open steppe, trapping several thousand Russians and 12

tanks. A large Soviet force broke out two days later. Now the remaining elements of the Popov Mobile Group turned tail and headed north as fast as possible.

The rearguard of X Tank Corps, with 16 T-34s, tried to halt the *Wiking* Division on 21 February. Again *Wiking* swept around the Soviet defences and rolled northwards. This was a no-holes-barred pursuit. The handful of Waffen-SS tanks of the division's only panzer battalion led the way, supported by armoured cars and motorcycle troops. Every couple of kilometres, the advance guard would run into the remains of a Soviet vehicle column, either abandoned because of lack of fuel or devastated by Luftwaffe air strikes. The Waffen-SS men did not stop to investigate but pressed on. They did not outnumber the enemy, so victory would only come by moving faster than the Soviets, and keeping enemy commanders confused as to where they would strike next.

The *Wiking*, 7th and 11th Panzer Divisions caught up with the remains of four Soviet infantry divisions and four tank corps at Barvenkovo on 25 February. More than 50 T-34s were dug in to the south of the town, but they had run out of fuel so could not manoeuvre against the rampaging panzers. In a three-day battle, the 11th Panzer Division attacked directly from the south, while the *Wiking* and 7th Panzer Divisions swept around the Russians' flanks. The Soviets, however, kept open a corridor to the Donets at Izyum, and most of their troops managed to escape the pincers – but all their tanks had to be left behind.

MANSTEIN HALTS THE SOVIET OFFENSIVE

By the end of the February the first phase of Manstein's offensive was complete. The Russian thrust to the south had been defeated and the gap in the German front closed by the dramatic intervention of I SS Panzer Corps. The German High Command claimed 615 enemy tanks, 354 artillery pieces, 69 anti-aircraft guns destroyed, 23,000 Russians dead and 9000 prisoners, during the first phase of the counterattack. Manstein now turned his attention to the large Soviet armoured force guarding the southern approach to Kharkov. In an ill-considered move to blunt the German drive, Rybalko's Third Tank Army swung south to take on I SS Panzer Corps. In a matter of days his army would be cut to pieces.

The attack got under way on 24 February, with heavy tank attacks against the northern flank of the *Leibstandarte* Division. The frontline panzergrenadier units had to call up panzer support to drive off the Soviet 11th Cavalry Division, for the loss of five tanks and 500 dead. A panzer attack the following day surprised a Soviet artillery regiment and destroyed more than 50 howitzers. An

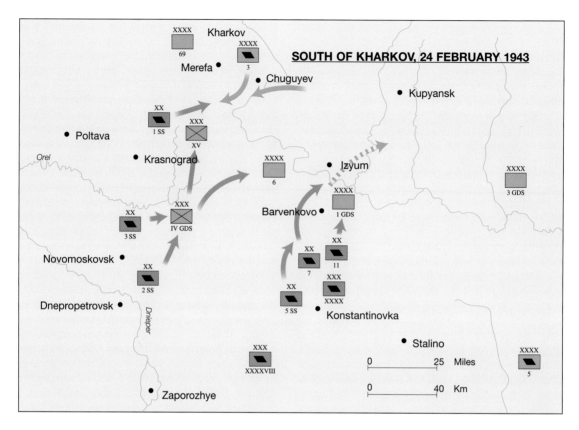

SOUTH OF KHARKOV, 24 FEBRUARY 1943

As the end of February 1943 approached, Red Army units to the south of Kharkov were being isolated and destroyed piecemeal by I SS Panzer Corps and XXXXVIII Panzer Corps.

attack force of 30 German tanks used a valley to advance behind the Russian artillery, and when they broke cover the Soviets fled. Soviet pressure on the *Leibstandarte* Division continued on 26 February, with an attack by T-34 medium and KV-1 heavy tanks. A total of 12 vehicles were destroyed by SS anti-tank teams.

The Soviets now pushed their last tank reserves southwards in a bid to drive a wedge between the *Leibstandarte* and its sister divisions, which were moving northwards after they had finished clearing up what was left of the Soviet Sixth Army. Hausser ordered the *Leibstandarte* to pull back on 28 February to entice the Russians to move farther south into a trap. Three days later, I SS Panzer Corps was advancing again. The Luftwaffe caught the Russian tanks in the open and broke up their attack formations.

The *Leibstandarte*'s panzers then moved eastwards, destroying nine tanks and fifteen anti-tank guns. A link-

up with the *Der Führer* Panzergrenadier Regiment, of the *Das Reich* Division, was made on 3 March. Meyer's reconnaissance battalion achieved another link-up with *Totenkopf* later in the day, to complete the ring around a huge pocket of Soviet troops. For two days infantry elements of I SS Panzer Corps cleared up the pocket, but there were not enough troops and so thousands of Russians escaped. In the *Leibstandarte*'s section of the pocket, prisoners from four Russian infantry divisions and a tank brigade were picked up. VI Guards Cavalry Corps managed to escape the trap, but large parts of IV, XXII and XV Tank Corps were destroyed. A further 61 Soviet tanks, 225 guns, 60 motor vehicles and 9000 dead were left on the icy battlefield.

Rybalko's defeat left Kharkov wide open, and Manstein soon set his panzers rolling north again to capture the prize. He planned to push I SS Panzer Corps forward to bypass Kharkov from the west, and then swing east around the top of the city to the Donets and block the escape route of its defenders, as XXXXVIII Panzer Corps assaulted the city from the south. To complete the victory, the reinforced *Grossdeutschland* Division, which had recently received a new tank detachment of 42 Panzer IVs and 9 Tigers, would strike north to Belgorod to block any interference with the attack on Kharkov. It was to be supported by the *Totenkopf*'s reconnaissance battalion during this phase of the operation. Only the imminent arrival of the spring thaw could save Kharkov from the Germans.

Hausser now pulled together his panzer corps into an attack formation, with the *Totenkopf* on the left, *Leibstandarte* in the centre and *Das Reich* on the right. Rocket launchers were positioned to support the attack, and Tiger I tanks moved forward to spearhead the assault operation.

According to plan the first attack went in on 6 March, and four days later the Waffen-SS panzers had reached a line level with Kharkov. To the east, the army panzer divisions were held up for five days by a determined stand by the 25th and 62nd Guards Rifle Divisions.

Heavy air strikes preceded the Waffen-SS advance, with *Das Reich* receiving priority support. The Soviet defences were weak and disorganized, so the German advance pushed all before it. Again, the *Leibstandarte*'s reconnaissance battalion was teamed with a strong panzer detachment to spearhead the division's advance. Meyer had the use of Tiger I tanks for the first time. South of the town of Valki, Meyer's kampfgruppe was confronted by a "pak-front", or network, of 56 76.2mm anti-tank guns. With panzergrenadiers sheltering behind the turrets of the tanks, Meyer ordered his panzers to charge forward. Their speed meant Waffen-SS men overran the anti-tank guns easily, but two dozen T-34 tanks lay in wait ahead, hidden in a village. The Panzer

IVs started to take casualties before a Tiger was called up. The lead Tiger got to within 100m (328ft) of the village when a T-34 opened fire. It hit the Tiger on the turret, but the Soviet 76mm shell barely scratched the German tank's paint. The Tiger blasted the T-34 with its 88mm gun, blowing off the turret and taking half of a nearby house with it. During the next hour the Tigers cleared out a dozen T-34s and the rest fled at high speed. The remainder of the kampfgruppe was, meanwhile, clearing out the last Soviet infantry and gun crews who had hidden in the village as the tank duel raged in its streets.

The following day Meyer's men were again confronted by a pak-front on the outskirts of Valki. A tank attack was ordered, but several panzers were lost to enemy fire before they overran the gun pits. German tanks literally crushed the anti-tank guns under their tracks when the Soviet gunners refused to flee.

Das Reich's *Der Führer* Panzergrenadier Regiment led the division's attack, and it was soon within striking distance of the western outskirts of Kharkov. The *Totenkopf* Division was not making as good progress out on the left wing because of heavy resistance from VI Guards Cavalry Corps. The *Totenkopf*'s reconnaissance battalion was also fighting alongside the *Grossdeutschland* Division's left-flank units and was unable to help out, after getting bogged down for several days in a battle with three Soviet infantry divisions.

At this point Nazi politics and pride entered the tactical equation, and threw a massive spanner in the works of Manstein's counteroffensive. Stung by his ungraceful

A Waffen-SS casualty is evacuated by horse transport during the battles around Kharkov. Though the retaking of the city was a triumph of mechanized warfare, I SS Panzer Corps suffered 11,500 casualties in its efforts, testament to the doggedness of the Soviet Red Army.

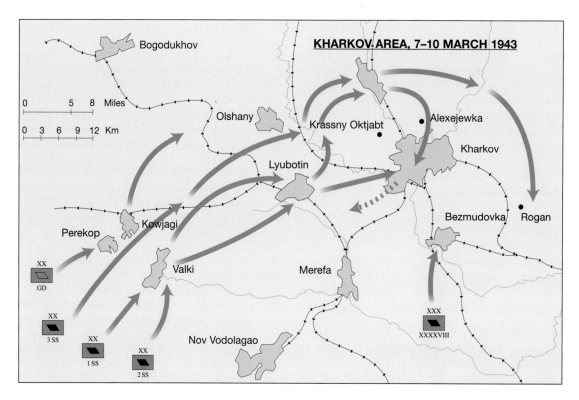

As Red Army resistance outside the city disintegrated, I SS Panzer Corps and XXXXVIII Panzer Corps were free to close in on Kharkov, along with the *Grossdeutschland* Division.

---

departure from Kharkov three weeks earlier, Hausser was determined not to allow the army to share in the glory of recapturing his prize. In direct disobedience of orders to keep his tanks out of the city, Hausser planned to send the *Das Reich* Division into Kharkov from the west, while the *Leibstandarte* pushed in from the north. The *Totenkopf* was to continue its original mission to encircle the city.

For five days the Waffen-SS men battled through fanatical resistance in the concrete high-rise housing blocks that dominated the approaches to the city centre. The remnants of the Soviet Third Tank Army, reinforced by armed citizens, fought for every street and building.

By 10 March the *Totenkopf* and *Leibstandarte* had cleared the town of Dergachi, 16km (10 miles) to the north of Kharkov, of Soviet defenders, opening the way for the *Leibstandarte* to swing southwards down two main roads into the heart of the city. Two large kampfgruppen were formed, based around each of the division's panzer-grenadier regiments, for the assault operation and they were reinforced with strong assault gun, 88mm flak gun

and Nebelwerfer rocket launcher support. A third kampf-gruppe made up of the reconnaissance battalion and a panzer battalion, led by Meyer, was to push farther eastwards and then enter Kharkov to close the escape route of the defenders. This took him through a heavily wooded and swampy region, which required plenty of guile and cunning to navigate safely. The column got hopelessly disorganized in the woods, as the tanks were pressed into service to drag bogged-down reconnaissance jeeps out of the mud caused by an early thaw. Meyer, of course, was at the head of the column and, as he emerged from the forest, a large Soviet infantry regiment blocked his path. Fortunately, a roving Stuka patrol intervened and devastated the Russian column.

The Soviets rushed reinforcements, including a tank brigade and an élite brigade of NKVD security troops, into the city to try to set up an improvised defence line. Hausser was determined not to let the Russians build up their strength, so the *Leibstandarte* and *Das Reich* Divisions were ordered to press on with a night assault during the early hours of 11 March. The two main *Leibstandarte* assaults immediately ran into heavy resistance, backed by tank counterattacks all along the northern edge of the city. Assault guns were brought up to deal with the enemy tanks, but a vicious duel developed during the day with many Waffen-SS vehicles being put out of action. Progress could only be made with the support of the Nebelwerfer rocket launchers, but even then no breakthrough was achieved.

The key attack, as always, was led by Meyer. With his small column of motorcycles, jeeps, halftracks, two Marder self-propelled anti-tank guns and nine tanks, he set off in darkness to raid the city. His kampfgruppe weaved its way past a number of Soviet positions, until a pair of T-34s spotted it and opened fire, destroying a panzer. In the confusion, a Soviet anti-tank crew opened fire and destroyed their own tanks, inadvertently clearing the way for Meyer. He then pressed his column on into the city and it had reached the cemetery by midday, but had to halt when its tanks ran out of fuel. It then formed an all-round defensive position and waited for relief. Meyer's force was besieged in the cemetery overnight by thousands of Russian troops and armed civilians. The Germans furiously dug in to escape the effects of mortar and artillery fire that was raking their positions.

Hausser now received orders instructing him to call off the attack by *Das Reich*'s *Der Führer* Regiment, but the Waffen-SS commander ignored them. The battle continued to rage in the city throughout the night. To the west, the *Leibstandarte*'s two panzergrenadier regiments began their advance again, this time supported by panzers and 88mm flak guns in the front-assault echelons. Snipers in high-rise flats were blasted with quad 20mm flak cannon mounted on halftracks, while the panzers and flak guns defeated Soviet counterattacks by roving groups of T-34s. The *Leibstandarte*'s Tigers spearheaded the attacks, acting as mobile "pillboxes". The armoured monsters could park on street corners and dominate whole city blocks, while being impervious to enemy fire of all types. Later in the day, Joachim Peiper's armoured personnel carrier battalion was at last able to break through the Red defence to established a tenuous link with the impetuous Meyer trapped in the cemetery. It brought in much needed ammunition and fuel, before evacuating the wounded. Meyer's depleted kampfgruppe had to remain in position to block any moves by the Russians to reinforce their defences in the centre of the city.

During the night and into the next day, several Waffen-SS kampfgruppen swept through central Kharkov. Every block had to be cleared of snipers, dug-in anti-tank guns and lone T-34 tanks. The *Leibstandarte* commanders drove their men forward into attack after attack to prevent the Soviets reorganizing their defence. The *Der Führer* Regiment continued to press in from the west to add to the pressure on the Russians in the tractor factory area in eastern Kharkov. The bulk of the *Das Reich* Division was pushing south of the city to cut through large Soviet defensive positions and complete the German ring around the city. *Das Reich*'s tanks cleared a key hill to the southeast of Kharkov on 14 March, destroying 29 anti-tank guns and scores of bunkers, to break the back of Soviet resistance.

Within the city, the Soviet defenders were still putting up a tenacious resistance. They quickly withdrew from threatened areas, and then used the sewers and ruins to move in behind the Waffen-SS troops. Peiper's armoured halftrack battalion proved invaluable because of its relative invulnerability to rifle fire from the scores of Soviet snipers who were still at large in areas "cleared" by the *Leibstandarte*. Resistance from the population was intense, and thousands of Kharkov's citizens joined in the battle to prevent their city becoming part of the Third Reich again.

The brutal nature of the fighting in Kharkov was emphasized by the fact that more than 1000 Waffen-SS men were killed or wounded. On 14 March the operation to seize the city was complete, and German radio began issuing gloating bulletins about the Soviet defeat. At the Führer's headquarters in East Prussia, plans were being made for a bumper issue of medals to the "heroes" of I SS Panzer Corps.

The main group of Soviet forces in the city was now pulling back southwards into the face of the advancing

A knocked-out Soviet KV-1 heavy tank outside Kharkov in March 1943. During the Kharkov battles many Red Army troops abandoned their vehicles and escaped on foot.

XXXXVIII Panzer Corps. There was now the possibility of the Germans catching elements of more than 10 enemy divisions and tank corps in a pocket.

On 13 March the *Totenkopf* Division completed its wide sweep north of Kharkov, with SS-Obersturmbannführer Otto Baum's panzergrenadier regiment, backed by a panzer battalion, capturing the Donets crossing at Chuguyev to tie the noose around Rybalko and his men. The *Totenkopf* attack punched south and eastwards to link up with the 6th Panzer Division advancing northeastwards. The *Das Reich*, *Totenkopf*, 6th Panzer and 11th Panzer Divisions then proceeded to chop up the huge Soviet force hiding in the pocket south of Kharkov. Stalin gave Rybalko permission to give up the defence of the city and break out to the east. The trapped Russians made desperate efforts to escape, staging massive human-wave assaults to break past the *Totenkopf*'s blocking positions along the Donets.

The German noose was not pulled tight enough, and five days later the remnants of the Third Tank Army completed their breakout past Chuguyev, which was then held by weak army panzer divisions. Unlike Hitler, Stalin realized the importance of getting skilled troops out of pockets rather than leaving them to their fate (Rybalko survived the ordeal and went on to command his army with distinction at Kursk during the summer). The exposed *Totenkopf* Division would have been in real trouble if the Soviets had tried to break through to the forces trapped near Kharkov with their reserve Guards tank corps, but it was held back to secure the north Donets line.

To complete the German victory, Hausser dashed panzer kampfgruppen north to link up with the *Grossdeutschland* Division, which had been taking on Soviet armoured units defending Belgorod. An unofficial "race" developed between the *Leibstandarte* and the élite army division for the honour of seizing the last major centre of Soviet resistance in the Ukraine.

The first line of Soviet resistance, some 16km (10 miles) north of Kharkov, was rolled over on 16 March by the *Leibstandarte*'s 2nd Panzergrenadier Regiment, supported by a huge barrage of Nebelwerfer and artillery fire, as well as by wave after wave of Stuka dive-bombers. A line of Soviet anti-tank guns and infantry bunkers ceased to exist. Next day, Peiper's kampfgruppe was unleashed northwards with strong armoured support, including the *Leibstandarte*'s Tiger detachment. This powerful force made easy meat of another enemy anti-tank gun position during the afternoon.

After a pause during the night to rearm and organize air support, Peiper was off again. On cue, more Stukas attacked a large road-block just after dawn on the morning of 18 March. With the road now clear, Peiper ordered his armoured force forward again. He did not stop until his tanks and armoured carriers were in the centre of Belgorod at 11:35 hours. Eight T-34s encountered on the drive north were destroyed by the Tigers – all other Soviet positions had been ignored. "Sepp" Dietrich flew north in his Storch aircraft to congratulate Peiper on his success. The German coup de main operation may have taken the Russians by surprise, but during the afternoon they pulled themselves together and launched a string of armoured counterattacks. The *Leibstandarte*'s panzers repulsed all the attacks, destroying 14 tanks, 38 trucks and 16 anti-tank guns.

It was not until later in the afternoon, however, when the *Das Reich*'s *Deutschland* Panzergrenadier Regiment linked up with Peiper's kampfgruppe, that the German position in the town was fully secure. The Russians continued to harry Peiper's men in the town, and he was forced to conduct a number of panzer sweeps of the countryside to expand the German grip on the region. During one such operation a pair of Tiger I tanks was attacked by Russian tanks, who destroyed an accompanying armoured halftrack before they were driven off for the loss of 10 tanks, 2 armoured cars and 10 trucks.

Peiper's dash to Belgorod had been possible thanks to a return of winter weather, but in the final days of March the temperature was rising and the snow disappeared. It

A StuG III Ausf F of I SS Panzer Corps in winter camouflage, March 1943. Its gun is the 75mm StuK40, which could easily knock out Soviet T-34 and KV-1 tanks.

A Panzer III and panzergrenadiers of the *Leibstandarte* Division advance into Kharkov in March 1943. The recapture of the city prompted Hitler to state that the I SS Panzer Corps was worth 20 Italian divisions, a not entirely inaccurate assessment.

was replaced by deep mud, which made all movement off roads, even by tracked vehicles, almost impossible. The *Totenkopf* and *Das Reich* Divisions fought a series of bitter infantry battles to establish a firm frontline along the Donets, east of Kharkov, for several days, but the spring campaign season was all but over.

Back in Kharkov, Waffen-SS panzergrenadiers combed the ruins of the city for the few remaining pockets of Soviet troops, and were also settling some old scores with its citizens. The desecration of the graves of Waffen-SS men killed during the January battles, and the mutilation of the bodies, made the *Leibstandarte* loath to show any quarter to captured Russian soldiers. Several hundred wounded Soviet soldiers were murdered when Dietrich's men occupied the city's military hospital. Any captured commissars or senior Russian officers were executed as a matter of routine, in line with Hitler's infamous "commissar order".

Special German Gestapo squads, SS Sonderkommando security units and Einsatzgruppen with mobile gas chambers followed close behind the victorious German troops, to ensure there was no repeat of February's uprising. An estimated 10,000 men, women and children perished during Hausser's short reign of terror in the city of Kharkov.

On 18 March, the German High Command claimed that 50,000 Russian soldiers had died during Manstein's counteroffensive, along with 19,594 taken prisoner and 1140 tanks and 3000 guns destroyed. An impressive total but, when compared with the 250,000 Germans lost at Stalingrad, it is clear that the Soviets benefited more

from the Kharkov battles. The Russians, their military production in full swing, could also replace their losses more easily.

I SS Panzer Corps had demonstrated that it was one of the world's foremost armoured formations, holding out against superior odds and then counterattacking with great skill and élan. Its success was not achieved cheaply, though. Some 11,500 Waffen-SS men were killed or wounded during the two-month campaign in the Ukraine. Some 4500 of these were borne by the *Leibstandarte*, emphasizing its key role at the centre of all the major battles of the campaign. Indeed, the majority of the casualties were in the combat units of the three Waffen-SS divisions. Not to be forgotten is the role of the *Wiking* Division serving with the First Panzer Army. It lost thousands of men in a series of small skirmishes, but was still able to take the offensive and defeat superior odds.

Manstein was justifiably dubbed "the saviour of the Eastern Front" for his efforts in turning back the Russian tide. Hitler declared I SS Panzer Corps to be "worth 20 Italian divisions". Of more importance to those divisions, though, was the Führer's express order to General Zeitzler, his Army Chief of Staff, that "we must see that the SS gets the necessary personnel". And, in preparation for the summer campaign season, it was also to be given priority when it came to delivery of the latest Panzer V Panther tanks, much to the annoyance of the army. A combination of mud and exhaustion brought military operations to a halt on the Eastern Front in mid-March 1943. Both sides needed to reorganize and re-equip for the forthcoming campaign season.

The Battle of Kursk

For the assault against the Kursk salient, codenamed Operation Citadel by the Germans, II SS Panzer Corps was reinforced by hundreds of tanks and vehicles and thousands of new recruits. During the actual battle the SS panzer divisions battered their way through the dense Soviet defences, only to be stopped in a huge tank battle at the village of Prokhorovka.

An SS grenadier surveys the Soviet tank he has just knocked out at Kursk. He appears to have used a Panzerfaust, which, if correct, would have been one of the first production models of this weapon.

During July 1943, the eyes of the world were on a nondescript stretch of undulating steppe around the previously unknown Russian city of Kursk. The run-down and unremarkable city, however, would soon enter military history as the centre point of the most decisive battle of World War II. Here, the might of the German Wehrmacht would stage its last major strategic offensive of the war on the Eastern Front. The Red Army held its ground, and within weeks would stage its own massive counteroffensive that eventually drove all the way to the heart of the Third Reich, to Berlin itself. After Kursk, Stalin's armies would hold the strategic initiative on the Eastern Front.

In the build-up to the battle both sides massed their best troops, tanks, artillery and aircraft. By early July, the Germans had concentrated 43 divisions, with 2700 tanks and assault guns, supported by 1800 combat aircraft. Barring their way were 100 Russian divisions and 5 tank armies, with 3306 tanks and 2650 aircraft. Within days these gigantic war machines would clash to decide the fate of the world.

The origins of this titanic clash stretched back to the winter battles around Kharkov in February and March 1943. German counterattacks pushed back the Soviet spearheads that had surged westwards during the winter. By the time the spring thaw made all movement off roads impossible, the Wehrmacht had regained lost ground and stabilized the front. But the Soviets retained control of a huge salient that bulged more than 80km (50 miles) westwards into German-held territory.

To the German High Command, the 160km- (100-mile-) wide salient was a prize that could not be resisted. A rapid panzer advance, punching inwards from either shoulder of the salient, would trap hundreds of thousands of Russian troops and, in turn, shorten the German front. This would free more than 15 divisions and allow a new offensive to be mounted on the Eastern Front, one that would finish off Stalin's resistance once and for all. For Adolf Hitler, the proposed Kursk Offensive offered a chance to turn the tide of war in Germany's favour to counter growing Anglo-American power in the West (the campaign in North Africa had ended in Axis defeat in May 1943). If Russia could be defeated, then the might of the Wehrmacht could be turned westwards in time for the expected cross-Channel invasion in 1944. German success on the Eastern Front was also seen by the Führer as an essential gambit to keep key Axis allies –

Romania, Hungary, Italy and Finland – fighting on Berlin's side. Hitler was also convinced that the raw materials and industrial resources of the Ukraine would be decisive in the "war of production" between the Axis and the Allies.

Hitler's generals were divided about how to proceed. His field commanders in the East wanted an immediate offensive in April, to exploit their victories around Kharkov and catch the Soviets before they had time to rebuild their strength. Others wanted to husband the precious panzer divisions and use them to launch a decisive counterstroke against the expected Soviet summer offensive, to capitalize on the Wehrmacht's experience and expertise in armoured warfare.

The Führer was at first undecided. As ever, he was keen to attack, but wanted any offensive to be a dramatic success which would signal that Germany was still the dominant military power in the world. For this reason he was determined to use Germany's newest "wonder weapons" to inflict a punishing defeat on the Red Army. The new 45.72-tonne (45-ton) Panzer V Panther tank and Ferdinand super-heavy assault guns/tank destroyers were to spearhead the attack. Hitler placed great store on the Panther, and repeatedly delayed the offensive to ensure that large numbers of the new tank would be ready to spearhead the assault operation. While preparations for the offensive began in April, it was not until the first days of July that Hitler gave the go-ahead.

The plan's strategic concept was essentially very simple. Colonel-General Walther Model's Ninth Army was to push southwards into the northern shoulder of the salient. At the same time, Field Marshal Erich von Manstein's Army Group South would strike northwards to link up with Model's men, trapping the Soviet defenders holding the line west of Kursk. Both attack forces were to contain strong armoured reserves, which would be on hand to defeat any Russian counterattacks. Operation Citadel was to be a repeat of the classic Blitzkrieg victories of 1941–42, when huge Soviet armies had been encircled with ease by marauding panzer forces.

Model's assault force eventually grew to include some six army panzer divisions, two panzergrenadier divisions and thirteen infantry divisions. Two battalions of the monster Ferdinands would spearhead an assault force that contained more than 700 tanks and 250 assault guns.

The most powerful elements of the German attack force, however, were concentrated on the southern axis, where Manstein had three army panzer corps and three infantry corps. He also had command of the SS Panzer Corps, which had grown into the most powerful tank formation in Europe, with 430 tanks and assault guns ready for action on the eve of battle. III and XXXXVIII Panzer Corps, of the Fourth Panzer Army, boasted more than 870 tanks and assault guns at the start of Operation Citadel, the codename of the German offensive. In reserve was XXIV Panzer Corps with another 150 tanks. In total, Manstein had amassed some 1500 armoured vehicles for

Newly produced Tiger I tanks loaded onto rail transport for shipment to the panzer divisions earmarked to take part in the Kursk offensive. The SS panzer corps at Kursk fielded 41 Tigers.

KURSK: SOVIET DEFENSIVE BELTS

XXXXX WESTERN FRONT
• Zhizdra

XXXXX BRYANSK FRONT

• Bryansk
XXXXX ARMY GROUP CENTER

• Orel

• Ponyri

Sevsk
XXXXX CENTRAL FRONT

XXXXX STEPPE FRONT

• Kursk

• Rylsk
XXXXX VORONEZH FRONT

• Oboyan

• Sumy

• Prokhorovka

• Belgorod

NORTHERN DONETS

XXXXX ARMY GROUP SOUTH

Main defence belt
Second defence belt
Third defence belt
First front position
Second front position
Third front position
Steppe Front position

• Kharkov
XXXXX SOUTHWESTERN FRONT

The Soviet plan at Kursk was quite simple: to wear down the German panzer divisions as they tried to batter their way through carefully prepared defence lines.

---

his weary divisions out of the line to be rested and rebuilt. The *Leibstandarte*, *Das Reich* and *Totenkopf* Divisions were pulled back to billets in Kharkov and neighbouring towns, which only a few months before had been battlegrounds. A major reorganization of the corps was ordered by the Führer, who wanted to build up his beloved Waffen-SS so he would not have to rely on the army and its generals, who in his mind only seemed to want to retreat.

At the end of March, the Führer informed the *Leibstandarte* Division's commander, SS-Obergruppenführer Josef "Sepp" Dietrich, that his unit would be the core of a new corps, to be known as I SS Panzer Corps *Leibstandarte Adolf Hitler*. Scores of staff officer from Dietrich's division would form the new corps staff, while hundreds of officers and noncommissioned officers were to be drafted to form a training cadre to establish the new Hitler Youth SS panzergrenadier division. A number of artillery, assault gun and anti-tank battalions were also transferred from the *Leibstandarte* to the new division, to provide the core of its specialist regiments.

As a result of these developments, Hausser's formation was renamed II SS Panzer Corps, even though it was the first such headquarters to be set up by the Waffen-SS.

As trainloads of *Leibstandarte* veterans headed westwards, those who remained behind were ordered to prepare their units for action in a few weeks' time. Thousands of replacement soldiers were now arriving on a daily basis. These were mostly a mix of raw conscripts and drafted Luftwaffe ground personnel. Gone were the days when the Waffen-SS could pick and choose who served in its ranks. When Dietrich greeted the first batch of ex-Luftwaffe men in Kharkov, he asked for volunteers for the panzergrenadiers. There were few takers – most of the new Waffen-SS men wanted to serve in maintenance and repair teams. In future the replacements were not to be given a choice regarding which units they would serve in. Most of these recruits were directed to the *Leibstandarte* Division because of the heavy casualties it had suffered during the previous two months.

A constant stream of trains arrived at Kharkov with new tanks, artillery, vehicles and other equipment. Waffen-SS repair teams worked overtime to get the scores of tanks damaged in action back to fighting

---

the attack, including the first 200 Panthers which were formed into a special brigade to support the Army's *Grossdeutschland* Panzergrenadier Division.

The Luftwaffe built up a major force of tank-hunting aircraft to provide close air support to the assault troops. These assets included 37mm cannon-armed Junkers Ju 87G Stukas and 30mm cannon-armed Henschel Hs 129s. Manstein had more than 1000 Luftwaffe combat aircraft to support his offensive, and a string of radar stations were positioned around the southern flank of the salient to give prior warning of Russian air activity.

The surrender of 230,000 German troops in Tunisia in May to British and American forces stiffened Hitler's resolve to launch Operation Citadel. In his mind there was no time to spare before Anglo-American forces made landings on mainland Europe.

During the final days of March 1943, SS-Obergruppenführer Paul Hausser was able finally to pull

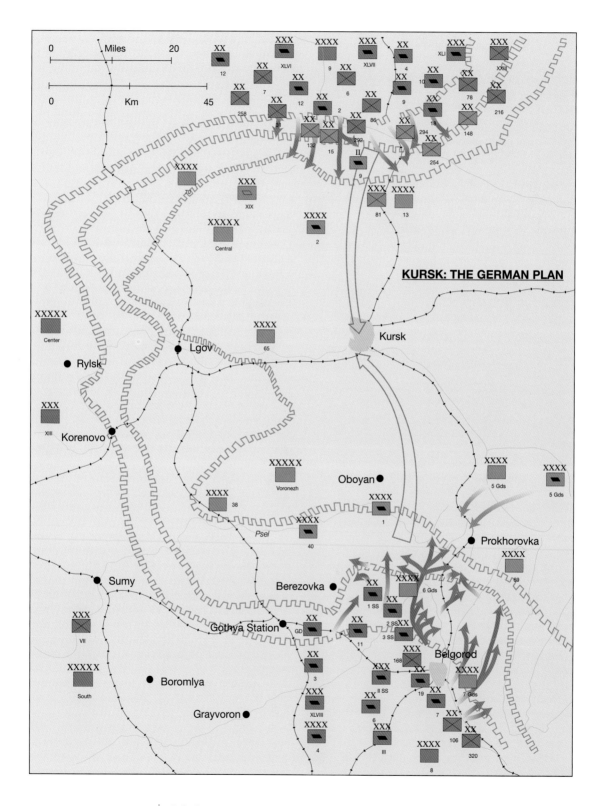

KURSK: THE GERMAN PLAN

SYLVESTER STADLER

Sylvester Stadler was born on 30 December 1910 in Steiermark, Austria. He joined the Austrian SS in 1933 and was posted to Germany for military training. Showing leadership potential, he was enrolled into the SS-Junkerschule at Bad Tölz in 1935. In 1940 he was assigned to the *Der Führer* Regiment and then transferred back to the *Deutschland* Regiment later that year. Wounded in action, he became an instructor at the SS-Junkerschule at Bad Tölz. He returned to his post in March 1942, and saw action during the battles for Kharkov and was awarded the Knight's Cross for his exemplary leadership. Stadler became *Der Führer*'s regimental commander in June 1943, and led the regiment during the Battle of Kursk. He was awarded the Oakleaves in 1943. Stadler took command of the newly formed 9th SS Panzer Division *Hohenstaufen* in May 1944, but was severely wounded in the fighting in Normandy. He recovered, though, and returned to command the *Hohenstaufen* until the war's end. Stadler was one of the most outstanding divisional leaders of the Waffen-SS, and fully deserved his reputation as a brave officer. He died on 23 August 1995, aged 85.

The theory and reality at the Battle of Kursk. The hollow purple arrows represent the German plan to destroy the Soviet salient; the solid arrows are actual German advances.

condition. No one trusted them to be returned in time for the coming offensive if they were shipped back to workshops in Germany.

The panzer regiments of the Waffen-SS divisions were extensively reorganized to absorb their new equipment. The *Leibstandarte* and *Das Reich* Divisions were both ordered to send the first battalion of their panzer regiments back to Germany, for training in the use of the new Panther tank. This process would not be complete by the time Operation Citadel began, contrary to the many accounts of the Battle of Kursk which state that the Waffen-SS divisions fielded hundreds of the new tanks during the offensive. In fact, the Panther would not make its appearance on the Eastern Front in Waffen-SS service until the middle of August 1943.

The Waffen-SS was also not equipped with hundreds of Tiger I tanks at Kursk: only three companies of the heavy tanks saw service with II SS Panzer Corps during July 1943. Each division did have a battalion of Sturmgeschütz (StuG) III assault guns and a strong contingent of Marder III self-propelled anti-tank guns.

By the time Operation Citadel got under way, the *Leibstandarte*'s panzer regiment boasted a single battalion, with 67 Panzer IV and 13 Panzer III tanks, along with 13 Tiger Is. The *Das Reich* Division was less well equipped, with only 33 Panzer IVs, 62 Panzer IIIs and 14 Tiger Is. To boost its fighting power, the division pressed 25 captured T-34s into service. The *Totenkopf* Division still had two battalions in its panzer regiment, but 63 of

its tanks were Panzer IIIs. It also had 44 heavier Panzer IVs and 15 Tiger Is.

The *Wiking* Division's panzer unit had been upgraded to regimental status; however, it had yet to grow beyond battalion strength. In July 1943 it could only muster 23 Panzer III and 17 Panzer IV tanks. It had no Tigers, and was kept in reserve throughout the Kursk offensive.

To increase the firepower of Hausser's corps further, the army provided two heavy artillery and two rocket launcher regiments, as well as a special command headquarters to coordinate fire missions of all artillery units in the corps. This meant that huge amounts of firepower could be brought down on individual targets in a very short space of time.

To prepare his command for battle, Hausser ordered a series of training exercises to be held. Noncommissioned officers drilled the new recruits to turn them into combat soldiers. Tank driving and gunnery courses were run on the new vehicles and weapons being delivered to the Waffen-SS. Senior commanders were given top-secret briefings on the Operation Citadel plan, and were shown scores of Luftwaffe aerial photographs of the Soviet defences in their respective sectors.

Company and battalion field exercises were held on the steppe around Kharkov to familiarize the troops with equipment and practice the tactics to be used during the coming battle. Finally, divisional and corps "command post" exercises were put on to acquaint the Waffen-SS commanders and staff officers with the plan. They based their planning on intelligence that said four Russian infantry divisions were holding the enemy's first defensive line in II SS Panzer Corps' sector. Two more held the second line, and behind them were two tank corps with at least 360 tanks. After defeating these

Both sides tried to snatch prisoners for intelligence purposes prior to the Battle of Kursk. These Russians, taken by the Waffen-SS, are waiting to be sent to the rear for interrogation.

forces, counterattacks were to be expected from several more enemy tank corps. Although many Waffen-SS men were confident regarding their own equipment and abilities – arrogance was a common trait among Hitler's "master race" – some of the older veterans knew the coming battle would be like no other they had previously faced.

By the end of June, II SS Panzer Corps was warned to be ready to move forward to its assembly area in a few days. The Führer decided on 21 June – almost two years to the day since the start of his invasion of Russia – to launch the operation on 5 July. The Waffen-SS divisions started to move from their billets around Kharkov to their assembly areas near Belgorod in a series of night-time road moves. During daylight hours they remained out of sight in forests, waiting for X-Day, as the start day of the operation was codenamed, to dawn.

On the other side of the frontline, Marshal of the Soviet Union Georgi Zhukov was ready and waiting for the German offensive. The victor of the battles of Moscow and Stalingrad also recognized the importance of the Kursk salient, and was not prepared to give it up

lightly. He knew the Germans would attack, and saw the chance to engage their precious panzer divisions in a war of attrition. Once they had been worn down, he would launch his reserves in a massive offensive along the whole length of the Eastern Front, to inflict a strategic defeat of such magnitude that the Third Reich would not be able to recover.

Zhukov was appointed personally to coordinate the defence of Kursk, and he was given unlimited resources to do the job. Unknown to the Soviet commander, his biggest help came from his British allies, who for three years had been reading all of the Third Reich's secret radio communications traffic. The British had broken the Germans' Enigma code using an early form of computer, but they were unwilling to reveal to Stalin the full extent of their code-breaking success, and so created a convoluted means to pass so-called "Ultra" material to Moscow. This involved establishing contact with a ring of Soviet agents in Switzerland, codenamed Lucy, and drip-feeding them Ultra decodes relevant to the war in Russia. The Lucy agents were convinced they were receiving documents from disgruntled German officers within Hitler's inner circle. The result was that within days Moscow had verbatim transcripts of high-level orders being sent from Hitler's headquarters to his senior commanders on the Eastern Front. These included all

Behind the German frontline at Kursk prior to the launch of Citadel. A group of SS soldiers confer on the left, while in the background is a halftrack prime mover.

the plans for Operation Citadel, including details of units, objectives, logistic information and, crucially, the date for the start of the offensive. Hitler's desire to micro-manage the war down to the lowest level played into the Soviets' hands. They knew every move of almost all German units, often before the commanders of those units themselves. Indeed, Manstein's success during the Kharkov offensive has been attributed to the fact that he did not consult the Führer on many of his moves, so they were not compromised by the Lucy Ring and thus caught Red Army commanders by surprise.

With this vital information to hand, Zhukov was able to plan his defence in a methodical way. The key to his plan was the need to prevent the German panzers from breaking free and manoeuvring against the Soviet rear areas. He recognized that Soviet units were inferior to the Germans when it came to mobile warfare, and he wanted to close down the battle into a series of local set-piece actions. A network of strongpoints, each reinforced with scores of anti-tank guns, was built around the Kursk salient. Each strongpoint was mutually supporting, so once the Germans attacked one they would be raked by well-aimed fire from another. The Germans were to be given no chance to put their mobile Blitzkrieg tactics into action, especially rampaging into the rear of Soviet positions. Zhukov wanted to capitalize on his soldiers' dogged determination in defensive operations. He wanted to trade their lives and their anti-tank guns for panzers. Russia had a massive supply of men and hardware at this stage of the war. This was to be the Verdun of the Eastern Front – a battle of attrition rather than a fast-moving tank battle.

For three months the Russians poured men and machines into the Kursk salient to build a string of defence lines almost 48km (30 miles) deep. Millions of mines were laid along the length of the salient, and behind them thousands of anti-tank guns and artillery pieces were sited in hundreds of strongpoints. Positioned between the defence lines were tank brigades, ready to launch immediate counterattacks, and behind the four main defence lines were tank corps held in reserve to seal any German breakthroughs. Hundreds of kilometres to the rear was the Fifth Guards Tank Army, Zhukov's strategic reserve, which was being held ready to deliver the coup de grâce. Once committed, the Soviet strategic reserve would decide the fate of the war on the Eastern Front.

Waffen-SS Panzer IIIs on the eve of Citadel. Despite the addition of Tigers, the majority of tanks in the inventories of the Waffen-SS panzer divisions at Kursk were Panzer IIIs.

In II SS Panzer Corps' sector, the Soviet Sixth Guards Army created what was intended to be a death trap for the Waffen-SS men. Facing the brunt of the German attack were the soldiers of the 67th and 52nd Guards Rifle Divisions. They manned a series of strongpoints along a ridge line, which allowed them to observe the approach routes to the southern shoulder of the Kursk salient and call down massive barrages of artillery and multi-barrel Katyusha rocket launcher (the so-called Stalin's Organ) fire on German assembly areas. Two anti-tank regiments and two tank regiments were spread out among the first-echelon divisions to stiffen their resistance. The tanks and anti-tank guns were emplaced in bunkers to protect them from shell fire. Along the front were some 290km (181 miles) of trench lines. Hundreds of kilometres of anti-tank ditches were dug to channel

Above: SS grenadiers hitch a lift on a Panzer III during the Battle of Kursk. As can be seen by the expression on the men's faces, morale was very high at the start of the battle.

Right: Panzers and panzer-grenadiers in an SdKfz 251 halftrack of the *Das Reich* Division at Kursk. Overhead, the advance of the division was covered by Ju 87 Stuka dive-bombers.

the German attack towards tank-killing zones. More than 1000 machine-gun nests and mortar batteries were positioned to cover the mine belts, to stop German combat engineers clearing paths through the 140,000 mines. Some 300 pillboxes and over 3000 individual bunkers protected several thousand riflemen and tank-hunting squads armed with anti-tank rifles. Some 9.6km (6 miles) behind the main defence line were three infantry divisions, a tank brigade and two more regiments of anti-tank guns. They had prepared similarly strong defence lines to their comrades in the frontline, although the mine belts were thinner with only 30,000 mines. Throughout the Sixth Guards Army's sector, there were more than 400 anti-tank guns between 45mm and 76mm calibre, some 778 mortars and almost 500 artillery pieces between 76mm and 203mm calibre. They were all in prepared positions, and their target-spotting teams had had three months to pre-register ranges and targets.

DEFENCE IN DEPTH

Nearly 48km (30 miles) behind the front were the so-called rear-defence lines, which were sited on a number of key rivers, blocking the advance to Kursk itself. These contained a far higher density of mines, machine guns, mortars and anti-tank guns than in the second line. Not content with this density of fortification, Zhukov ordered another defensive sector – of three lines – to be built at the the base of salient, in case the Germans punched through the initial defence lines. To add to the Germans' problems, all the construction work on the Soviet defensive positions was to be conducted at night or under camouflage nets so Luftwaffe photographic reconnaissance would not be able to pinpoint them. Hundreds of dummy trench lines, bunkers and minefields were also prepared to confuse German intelligence. When the Germans attacked they would have little idea of the real tactical layout of the Russian positions, beyond what they could see from their own trenches.

From the Lucy Ring reports and tactical intelligence from prisoners and deserters, Zhukov knew almost to the hour when the German assault would begin. The Soviet commander, however, was far from complacent. Once the battle started he knew that anything could happen.

By the evening of 3 July, II SS Panzer Corps was deployed in its assembly areas and final orders were issued for the initial assault. On the left was the *Leibstandarte*, in the centre was *Das Reich* and the *Totenkopf* was deployed on the right. All were to attack simultaneously to batter through the Russian defences.

The attack was to start just before midnight on the evening of 4 July, with battalion-sized infantry assaults going in to seize a number of key Soviet positions to allow artillery observers to be sited so they could call in fire to cover the attack against the main Russian defence line. Soviet artillery barrages started to fall on the Waffen-SS divisions' assembly areas just after dusk, causing minor casualties and confusion, but they were not intense enough to stop the main attack. The first attacks went in on schedule, with small groups of panzergrenadiers infiltrating through minefields and rushing the enemy trenches. In two hours of hand-to-hand combat, the outposts were captured and the main attack of the *Leibstandarte* Division was ready to roll at just after dawn – 04:05 hours – on 5 July.

THE GERMAN OFFENSIVE BEGINS

Each of the division's panzergrenadier regiments was given a major Russian strongpoint as an objective. The Waffen-SS panzer regiments and armoured troop-carrier battalions were kept in reserve to exploit any breakthrough created by the panzergrenadiers. For 50 minutes before the attack the massed artillery of the corps blasted the objectives, and in the final five minutes of the barrage Junkers Ju 87 Stuka dive-bombers joined the attack. The bombardment demolished whole sections of trench line and scores of anti-tank guns, stunning the Russian defenders. Once the *Leibstandarte*'s attack was under way, the artillery and Stuka support was switched to "soften up" the defences in front of the *Das Reich* Division, which was due to attack at 08:15 hours.

Tiger Is, StuG IIIs and Marders then rolled forward with the first wave of panzergrenadiers to give them close support as they moved into action. This was the so-called panzerkeil, or wedge, tactic. The presence of the armoured firepower was the key to the success of the assault, with the Tigers and other vehicles acting as mobile pillboxes. They destroyed scores of machine-gun nests in quick succession to allow the panzergrenadier assault teams to move in to clear out the trench lines with hand grenades and flamethrowers. Dozens of anti-tank guns were destroyed by the giant tanks, which were impervious to Soviet fire. These assault operations took until well into the afternoon, and cost the *Leibstandarte* Division some 500 casualties alone. The close-quarter fighting was vicious and few Soviet soldiers showed any inclination to surrender, with just over 100 being captured by the Waffen-SS during the day. By mid-afternoon, the *Leibstandarte* and *Das Reich* Divisions were ready to start the next phase of the operation: launching their panzer reserves forward. *Das Reich*'s panzers got stuck in a previously undiscovered minefield, and the *Leibstandarte*'s surged ahead until they ran into the pak-front of the

Waffen-SS grenadiers at Kursk. The SS units encountered stiff resistance on the first day of the battle, being hit by concentrated artillery fire and strafing by Soviet aircraft.

Soviet 28th Anti-Tank Brigade. Two Tigers were damaged by the expertly dug-in anti-tank guns, before the *Leibstandarte*'s commanders ordered the advance halted until infantry could be brought up during the night to clear out the enemy's second-line defences.

The *Leibstandarte* and *Das Reich* Divisions were the most successful units on the German southern wing on the first day of the offensive. Their army comrades on each wing got bogged down in the thick mud and the numerous Soviet minefields.

Throughout the night, the Waffen-SS commanders reorganized their forces to punch through the second line of enemy defences as soon as it got light. Again a massive artillery and rocket launcher bombardment was planned, to be followed by an infantry assault with Tiger tank support. It took almost two hours for the *Leibstandarte*'s panzergrenadiers to clear paths through the Soviet mine belts and blow holes in the barbed-wire entanglements. Daylight came, and in four more hours of fighting the Waffen-SS men cleared out the enemy bunkers and gun positions.

Meanwhile, the *Das Reich*'s *Der Führer* Panzergrenadier Regiment was repulsed with heavy losses when it tried to take a strongpoint in its sector. A divisional-sized artillery fire mission was needed to clear the way forward.

SS-Standartenführer Theodor Wisch, the *Leibstandarte*'s new commander, was forward in his armoured halftrack watching the battle, and once the panzergrenadiers had cleared a passage through the enemy position he gave orders for his panzer kampfgruppe to motor northwards. It had barely moved a few hundred metres forward when more than 45 T-34s charged out of a wood directly at the Waffen-SS tanks. Eight were knocked out by the panzers, while Stuka dive-bombers picked off another three before the Soviet tanks retreated. The panzers were rearmed and refuelled in the forward battle zone from halftrack supply vehicles, before moving forward again later in the afternoon, with panzergrenadiers providing support in armoured carriers. They only got a few kilometres north before the force ran into a massive pak-front and huge minefield. Four tanks and many halftracks were lost to mines. At the same time as the *Leibstandarte* Division's panzers were rolling forward, *Das Reich*'s panzer kampfgruppe and reconnaissance battalion were ordered to exploit the breach created by their own panzergrenadiers. They destroyed 10 Soviet tanks, but were stopped in their tracks by anti-tank fire which hit a number of Tigers. Again the Soviets had managed to halt the German attack and prevent the panzers breaking into the open countryside.

Out on the Waffen-SS right flank, the *Totenkopf* Division was still battling to cut through the 52nd Guards Rifle Division, which was tenaciously holding its main defence position. Attacks in the late morning broke the back of the defence, though, and the *Totenkopf* was able to make big gains. However, in the afternoon large Soviet counterattacks by II Guards Tank Corps battered the division's right flank. Waves of armour surged forward, with some attacks involving more than 300 Soviet tanks.

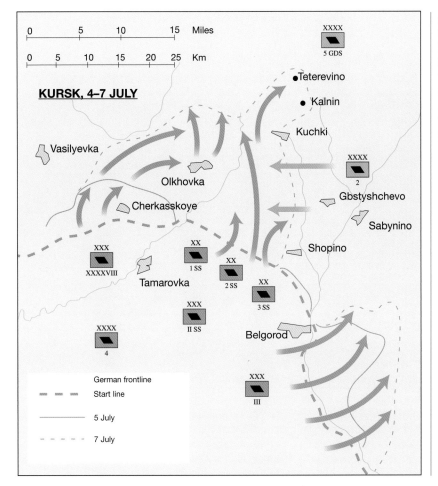

KURSK, 4–7 JULY

0 5 10 15 Miles

0 5 10 15 20 25 Km

Vasilyevka

Olkhovka

Cherkasskoye

Teterevino

Kalnin

Kuchki

Gbstyshchevo

Sabynino

Shopino

Tamarovka

Belgorod

German frontline
Start line
5 July
7 July

As II SS Panzer Corps drove deeper into Soviet lines, it began to encounter increasing numbers of Red Army tanks and suffered substantial losses. The *Leibstandarte*, for example, was experiencing a 10 percent loss rate.

During the night of 6 July, the Russians reinforced V Guards Tank Corps with three brigades in preparation for a major counterattack against the Waffen-SS. Small, probing attacks were launched in the dawn light by individual tanks, supported by squads of tank-riding infantry. At 06:00 hours the *Leibstandarte* and *Das Reich* panzer kampfgruppen were ordered forward. In the morning gloom Soviet tank brigades attacked the Waffen-SS panzers from three sides. They surged forward in waves, to be hit by a wall of fire from the German panzers. The main assault wave was made up of dozens of T-34s. They were picked off one-by-one by the panzers, but still kept attacking. The *Leibstandarte*'s Tiger company was in the thick of the action, alone accounting for more than 30 T-34s.

In spite of their terrible losses, the Soviet tanks were soon among the German formations. Panzergrenadiers picked off those tanks that came close and shot any tank-riding infantry on their hulls. The battle raged all day. More than 90 tanks and 60 artillery pieces were lost and 600 Russians were captured in the battle, which decimated XXXI Tank Corps and III Mechanized Corps. Their actions, however, successfully blocked the German advance into the heart of the Soviet third defence line.

The tank dogfight between the Waffen-SS and Russian T-34 crews continued overnight and into the morning of 8 July. Whole battalions and brigades of T-34s would suddenly appear from forests and villages to charge the panzer kampfgruppen, which were at the tip of a 19.2km- (12-mile-) deep breach in Soviet lines gouged out by II SS Panzer Corps.

The *Leibstandarte* and *Das Reich* panzer kampfgruppen moved around the exposed steppe, destroying dozens of Soviet tanks with their long-range weapons. To increase the firepower available, the *Leibstandarte*'s

A StuG III and Waffen-SS infantry in a captured Soviet trench at the Battle of Kursk. As the grenadiers take the opportunity to rest, the StuG's commander keeps watch for the enemy.

assault gun battalion was moved up to the spearhead of the division.

The panzers and assault guns could not be everywhere, though, and individual Russians tanks easily penetrated the thinly stretched defences of the *Das Reich*'s and *Leibstandarte*'s panzergrenadier regiments. Anti-tank guns and hand grenades drove off most of the Russian attacks. Four T-34s managed to sneak through the German defences, and get within a few hundred metres of the *Leibstandarte*'s divisional headquarters, before they were knocked out by tank-hunting teams armed with hollow-charge mines.

Hausser was determined to press forward the attack, and so just before midday the *Leibstandarte* and *Das Reich* armoured kampfgruppen were ordered to wheel northwestwards. Their objective was to seize the crossings over the River Psel and breach the Russian third line, thus opening a clear route northwards. The panzers, led by the *Leibstandarte*'s Tigers, destroyed 22 T-34s as they moved across the open steppe towards the river. As the assault groups approached the Psel valley, they ran into an anti-tank brigade hidden among the villages and woods along the valley. A network of mines and bunkers forced the panzer commanders to rein in their tanks. A small squad of *Das Reich*'s panzergrenadiers did score a major success when they moved through a minefield and captured a Soviet divisional command post and a general. The Soviet defence did not crack, though, and the German drive north had been blocked.

Over on the eastern flank, the *Leibstandarte*'s assault gun battalion led a panzergrenadier attack northeastwards, which allowed several villages to be cleared of isolated pockets of Soviet infantry.

By the evening of 8 July, the two lead Waffen-SS divisions had destroyed more than 120 tanks, but 76 of their panzers were badly in need of repairs. Many of the panzer companies were down to half strength, and time was needed to patch up the scores of battle-damaged tanks that were filling up the repair workshops.

As the battle raged on at the schwerpunkt, Hausser put in train plans to relieve the *Totenkopf* Division and move it up to punch a hole through the defences along the Psel. The *Totenkopf* Division had been holding the

PANTHER

The Panzer V, commonly known as the Panther, was one of the finest tanks of the war. Developed as a result of German forces encountering the Red Army T-34 in battle, the Panther was Germany's answer to the Russian tank. Despite early teething troubles and a poor showing at Kursk, the Panther was an awesome machine. Equipped with a long 75mm KwK42 L/70 gun and 80mm (3.14in) thick armour, the Panther was capable of knocking out any Allied tank while being impervious to all but the largest-calibre anti-tank weapons. More than 5000 units were produced from January 1943, and it saw extensive service with the élite Waffen-SS divisions from late July 1943.

Type:	heavy medium tank
Length:	8.86m (29ft)
Width:	3.27m (10.75ft)
Height:	3m (9.84ft)
Crew:	5
Armament:	1 x 75mm, 2 x 7.92mm
Range:	200km (124 miles)
Speed:	46kmh (29mph)

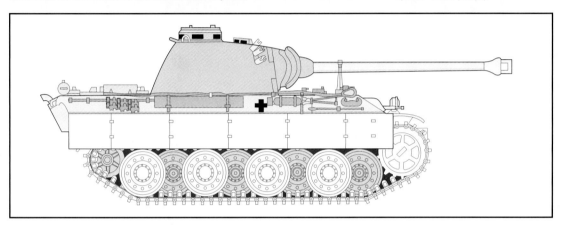

right flank of II SS Panzer Corps since the start of the offensive, and it spent most of the day handing over its sector to an army infantry division. The safe completion of this manoeuvre was only possible thanks to the intervention of the Luftwaffe. During the morning, three cannon-armed Hs 129 tank-hunting aircraft were patrolling to the east of the *Totenkopf*, when they spotted a Soviet tank brigade of 60 T-34s forming up ready to smash into the flank of the Waffen-SS corps. More aircraft were summoned and, in less than an hour, the whole brigade was destroyed by 30mm cannon fire, or forced to scatter into woods and gullies to hide from the aircraft. The attack totally disrupted the preparations of II Guards Tank Corps to pressurize the *Totenkopf*, allowing the Waffen-SS unit to disengage successfully from the front.

The first regiment of the *Totenkopf* Division was in position ready to attack the Psel line early after dawn on 9 July, along with the *Leibstandarte*'s 1st Panzer-grenadier Regiment. It didn't have enough strength to punch through the heavily reinforced Soviet defence line, though. A bridge across the Psel had been blown to prevent a crossing. By mid-afternoon, the Waffen-SS attack had been called off to allow preparations to be made for a more substantial attack the following day. The

Totenkopf made a night-time raid to seize a key hill above the Psel, but it was driven back. The Soviets kept up their pressure on the right flank of Hausser's corps, sending repeated human-wave attacks against the 167th Infantry Division that had just relieved the *Totenkopf*. Thousands of Russian infantrymen, many of them press-ganged civilians, were killed by well-aimed artillery fire that was called down within a few hundred metres of the German frontline.

The Soviets were also feeling the strain of battle by this time. Their third line of defence was holding up – but only just. Zhukov had committed all his local reserves. A final decision was now made to send in the strategic reserve. The three tanks corps of the Fifth Guards Tank Army received orders to move westwards to engage the Waffen-SS, and stop them taking a town called Prokhorovka. It would be three days before they were in a position to strike. In the meantime, the troops at the front would have to hold on.

Manstein also realized that the battle was approaching a critical point, and he had prepared orders for XXXXIV Panzer Corps, with the *Wiking* Division in the lead, to start moving towards Belgorod, ready to exploit any breakthrough by Hausser's spearheads. Reports from the northern shoulder of the Kursk salient were not encouraging. The German offensive was stalled, and Soviet troops were even starting to drive forward.

Amid heavy summer rain showers, II SS Panzer Corps moved forward again in a coordinated attack to crack open the final line of Russian resistance. The *Totenkopf* Division was now fully deployed to the left of the *Leibstandarte*, and it was launched forward to seize a bridgehead across the Psel. The *Theodor Eicke* Panzergrenadier Regiment led the attack, which was preceded by heavy artillery fire. Assault guns provided close support as the panzergrenadiers stormed the heavily defended villages along the Psel. The Soviet XXXIII Rifle Corps held out for the morning, trading artillery and mortar fire with the Germans, as well as launching a number of counterattacks. Totenkopf commanders led their men forward again in the afternoon, and two bridgeheads were established. It took several hours before bridging equipment could be brought up to allow armour to cross the swollen Psel, to press home the advance. Heavy rain delayed the work, which meant the bridge would not be ready to carry tanks for another day.

Troops of II SS Panzer Corps pass through a burning Russian village at Kursk. Massed, heavy Red Army artillery, combined with minefields, slowed the SS advance to a snail's pace.

More artillery was brought forward to soften up the Russians to allow the *Totenkopf* to expand its bridgeheads. Stukas joined the assault during the afternoon, and by early evening a third breach had been made in the Soviet defence line. At nightfall three Waffen-SS panzergrenadier battalions were over the Psel, and they held off repeated counterattacks as darkness approached.

On the main road to Prokhorovka, the *Leibstandarte*'s 2nd Panzergrenadier Regiment, reinforced with Tigers, assault guns and Marders, prepared for a dawn attack. Panzers, reconnaissance troops and infantry in armoured halftracks stood ready to exploit the breach. All the division's artillery regiment, backed by rocket launchers and Stukas, pounded the Soviet defence lines on a wooded hill. A battle raged on the slopes and in the woods between Waffen-SS panzergrenadiers and Soviet infantrymen. Soviet artillery joined in the battle, directed from the hills along the northern bank of the Psel. The accurate shell fire brought the *Leibstandarte*'s casualties to more than 200 for the day. Dug-in T-34s had to be destroyed individually by the Tigers, to allow the hill to be taken by the late afternoon. More than 50 Soviet tanks were knocked out and 23 assault guns destroyed. By the time darkness returned to the battlefield, there was still no breakthrough and the panzer kampfgruppe had still to be deployed.

To the south, the *Das Reich* Division was ordered to strike directly eastwards to seize high ground overlook-

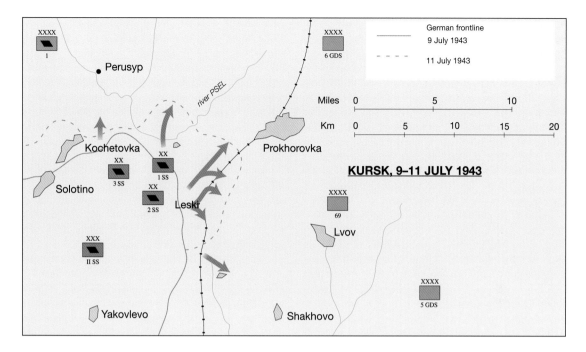

ing the main positions of the Waffen-SS corps. The *Deutschland* Panzergrenadier Regiment made some progress at first, but very strong anti-tank resistance prevented much progress being made thereafter.

Soviet counterattacks on the Psel bridgehead opened at 08:00 hours on 11 July with a heavy tank attack that was driven off by the *Totenkopf*'s anti-tank gunners, who knocked out 27 Russian tanks. This allowed work to continue on the bridge, which was capable of carrying the heavy Tiger tanks. Heavy rain and Soviet shelling continued to hamper the work of the Waffen-SS engineers, who did not finish their work until just before midday. The division's 94 tanks then began to cross the river, and plans were put in motion for a major offensive the following day. Victory seemed to be within sight.

The *Leibstandarte* pushed forward again to take the last hill-top pak-front before Prokhorovka. Two panzergrenadier battalions led the attack on the hill, which was bristling with anti-tank guns. They laid down a withering wall of fire that stalled the Waffen-SS attack. Then a wave of T-34s was sent into action against the Germans.

Rocket fire and Stuka support was requested to neutralize the resistance in a barrage that began at 09:00 hours. The air support was directed with great precision by a Luftwaffe forward air controller in an armoured half-track with the attack troops. The arrival of a detachment of Tiger attacks added to the weight of the assault. Within the hour, the panzergrenadiers had penetrated the

By the time II SS Panzer Corps approached the village of Prokhorovka, many of its men were exhausted from almost continuous combat since the beginning of the battle.

Russian trench system and were clearing bunker after bunker. The fighting flowed back and forth as the Russians threw more men into that battle. Stuka raids continued throughout the morning.

Now the *Leibstandarte* panzer kampfgruppe was thrown into the battle, and this turned the tide in the Germans' favour for good. Soviet tank counterattacks against the flanks of the *Leibstandarte* were repulsed. The Russians lost 21 tanks and more than 30 anti-tank guns. More than 200 Waffen-SS men were killed or wounded during the bitter fighting for the hill. This degenerated into a tank duel along the length of the division's front, involving attacks by small groups of tanks.

Satisfied with their success over the Psel and in front of Prokhorovka, Hausser's staff now set about planning the following day's drive to complete the piercing of the Soviet third defence line. More artillery was to be brought up to blast the Russians out of their bunkers on the hill above the *Totenkopf*'s bridgehead. Once this was complete, the *Leibstandarte* and *Das Reich* Divisions would surge forward to seize Prokhorovka. With the resistance destroyed, the panzers were to be unleashed into the open country beyond.

The Waffen-SS panzer regiments were rested during the night to prepare them for the coming major attack. Repair teams worked to ensure the maximum number of panzers were available. During the evening the *Leibstandarte* mustered 5 Panzer IIIs, 47 Panzer IVs and 4 Tiger Is ready for action; *Das Reich* fielded 34 Panzer IIIs, 18 Panzer IVs, 1 Tiger I and 8 captured T-34s; and the *Totenkopf* had operational 54 Panzer IIIs, 30 Panzer IVs and 10 Tiger Is. II SS Panzer Corps was also able to field 60 StuG IIIs and a similar number of Marder self-propelled anti-tank guns. In total, Hausser would have more than 300 armoured vehicles available for action.

He and his staff were convinced they were only a few hours away from achieving the decisive break-through and ultimate victory on the Eastern Front. They had no idea that only a few kilometres from the *Leibstandarte*'s advance posts, a force of more than 800 tanks and assault guns was massing to strike at them the following morning.

THE FIFTH GUARDS TANK ARMY
Marshal Pavel Rotmistrov had just led his Fifth Guards Tank Army on a 320km (200-mile) road march to Prokhorovka, and had spent the day preparing to launch it into action. He brought with him the fresh XVIII and XXIX Tank Corps and the Fifth Guards Mechanized Corps. To bolster his attack wave, he was assigned II Tank Corps or II Guards Tank Corps, which had already been blooded in the past week's clashes with the Waffen-SS. This force included 500 T-34s, with the remainder being light T-70s or lend-lease British Churchill and American General Lee tanks. Rotmistrov was Stalin's most experienced tank commander, and he set about preparing his mammoth tank force for action with great professionalism. The road march was accomplished in conditions of great secrecy under heavy fighter cover, and when his tanks halted to rest and refuel they were hidden in forest assembly areas. They gathered in the gullies and forests to the east and north of Prokhorovka under the cover of darkness, and awaited their orders.

Their commander recognized that, tank crew for tank crew, his men were no match for their German opponents. Only a few months before many had been factory workers who had built their tanks and then driven them to the front. Rotmistrov realized that once under way, his force would soon run out of control. Most Soviet tanks did not have radios, and commanders controlled their subordinates by means of coloured flags. Rotmistrov gave his corps and brigade commanders simple orders,

little more than specific objectives and axes of advance. The main way he could influence the battle was by tightly controlling the timing of when he committed his tank brigades, so the Soviet marshal set up his forward command post on a hill southwest of Prokhorovka, from where he could see all the key terrain and get a "finger tip" feel for the course of the battle. The Soviet marshal spent most of the night making final preparations for the mass attack, which was to start just after 06:00 hours the following morning, 12 July.

PROKHOROVKA – EVE OF BATTLE
The Battle of Prokhorovka effectively took place in an area little more than 8km by 8km (5 miles by 5 miles) – it was smaller than the battlefield at Waterloo. The terrain where the main engagement of the battle was to unfold was flat and rolling. The main Waffen-SS tank forces were concentrated on a hill 1.6km (1 mile) southwest of Prokhorovka. The ground slopped gently down towards the village, but then a small ridge line created an area of dead ground, behind which Rotmistrov had concentrated his main tank strike forces – XVIII and XXIX Tank Corps. A railway line and embankment, running southwest from Prokhorovka, created a natural division of the battlefield, meaning the Russians had to employ two distinct axes of attack. The railway line also formed the divisional boundary between the *Leibstandarte*, north of it, and *Das Reich*, to its south.

To the northwest of this gladiatorial arena was the River Psel, and the high ground on the northern bank of the river dominated the assembly area of the main Waffen-SS assault force – the *Leibstandarte* Division. The high ground was far too distant for direct tank fire from it to be a threat, but it provided a superb artillery observation vantage point. Whoever controlled this high ground dominated the battlefield. The valley along the Psel, with its small woods and villages, also provided a covered approach route to infiltrate behind the high ground above Prokhorovka.

South of Prokhorovka was a series of forested hills, running in a north–south direction. They were intersected by deep gullies and streams, making them poor ground for tanks.

Above the Psel, infantry battalions of the Soviet XXXI Tank Corps, without tank support, kicked off the Russian offensive by attacking during the night. The *Totenkopf* Division saw off the attack after hand-to-hand fighting in the villages around its bridgehead. In the face of heavy Soviet artillery, air raids and Stalin's Organ fire, the *Totenkopf* Division's panzergrenadiers began their attack as scheduled just after dawn. The division's panzer regiment

A member of the *Leibstandarte* described the fighting at Prokhorovka thus: "They were around us, on top of us, and between us. We fought man-to-man."

was now over the River Psel, and was poised to strike out once a route through the Soviet defences became apparent. Elements of the *Totenkopf*'s panzer kampf-gruppe were committed at 07:15 hours, and they helped punch a first hole in the Soviet line.

All during the night, the forward outposts of the *Leibstandarte* were sending back reports to their head-quarters, saying they were hearing noise from large numbers of tanks. In places Soviets tanks tried to probe the German line and, as dawn broke, scores of Russian fighter-bombers attacked the division's frontline posi-tions, artillery fire bases and supply columns. It was becoming clear that something was wrong, but the Germans had no idea what it was. The division's panzer kampfgruppe was ordered to proceed with its early morning attack directly towards Prokhorovka, with the Tiger tank company in the lead. The *Das Reich*'s *Deutschland* Panzergrenadier Regiment was lined up as well, ready to advance northwards on the south side of the *Leibstandarte*.

Almost like clockwork, at 06:30 hours both the *Leibstandarte*'s panzers and the Soviet XXIX Tank Corps were waved forward by their commanders. In the morn-ing haze, the Waffen-SS panzer crews spotted a mass of tanks 4.8–6.4km (3–4 miles) directly in front of them, on the far side of the valley. Some 60 tanks – a whole brigade of XXIX Tank Corps – were heading straight for them. Artillery fire and Katyusha rockets started to land among the German tanks. At the extreme limit of their range – 2000m (6562ft) – the 50 or so Waffen-SS tanks started to pick-off the Soviet armour. Rotmistrov had briefed his tank commanders not to stop to trade fire with the Germans, but to charge at full speed to make it more difficult to be hit, and to allow them to get into a position to hit the enemy tanks at close quarters on their more vulnerable side armour. The charge of the T-34s was a death ride. The Russian crews followed their orders to the letter, but by 09:00 hours the steppe was littered with burning hulks. The *Leibstandarte* tank crews had destroyed their enemy for almost no loss thanks to their long-range gunnery skills.

Rotmistrov's first wave also hit the *Das Reich* Division, with a brigade of XXIX Tank Corps taking a pounding from the *Leibstandarte*'s artillery as it moved forward. Then the *Das Reich* panzers put down withering fire to halt their attack. Rotmistrov now started to launch his

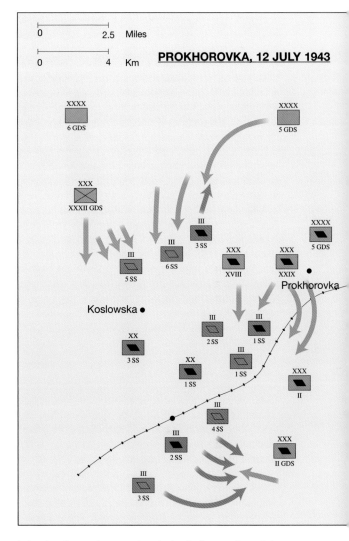

PROKHOROVKA, 12 JULY 1943

brigades forward on an hourly basis in an attempt to batter through the German lines.

Next on the receiving end of an attack from XVIII Tank Corps was the *Totenkopf*'s *Theodor Eicke* Panzer-grenadier Regiment in the Psel valley. Two Soviet infantry regiments, backed by 50 tanks, pushed forward into the *Totenkopf*'s right flank at 07:45 hours, to be seen off by the division's assault gun battalion.

At almost the same time, artillery and rocket fire rained down on the *Leibstandarte*'s 1st Panzergrenadier Regiment, which was holding the ground to the right of the division's panzer kampfgruppe. After an hour of soft-ening-up artillery fire, the Russian armour was sent into action. The defenders were given a warning from a Luftwaffe reconnaissance patrol that a tank brigade was approaching along the railway line. Some 40 T-34s of XXIX Tank Corps were then among the German trenches. More were following behind in a second wave, along with hordes of Red infantry. Waffen-SS tank-hunting teams went to work taking on the Russian vehicles, but five Marder self-propelled guns were needed to see off the tanks.

Farther to the east, the *Leibstandarte*'s panzers were now attacked from two directions by more than 70 tanks of XVIII Tank Corps. An advance guard of seven panzers was overrun in the charge, losing four tanks to point-blank fire as the T-34s surged past. The remaining three panzers were ignored by the Russian tanks, which were now heading directly for the main panzer kampfgruppe. The "lost" panzers turned to follow the T-34s, picking off 20 of them before the main panzer line opened fire with a mass volley. Stunned by the sudden burst of fire, the Russians halted to trade fire with the Germans. The 33 tanks of the panzer kampfgruppe now counterattacked, moving into flanking positions and raking the mass of confused Russian tanks with gunfire. After three hours of swirling action, the Germans claimed to have knocked out 62 T-70s and T-34s.

CLIMAX AT PROKHOROVKA

The *Totenkopf* Division continued to be pressed by XVIII Tank Corps, which committed its 32nd Motorized Infantry Brigade at 10:00 hours to another battle in the Psel valley. Some 50 tanks, including T-34s, T-70s and Churchills, were again driven off by the *Totenkopf*, which claimed 20 kills. At almost hourly intervals, Soviet infantry attacks were launched against all sides of the *Totenkopf*'s bridgehead to keep the pressure on the German left flank. Harassing artillery fire was also regularly directed at the two tank bridges to try to prevent reinforcements moving into the bridgehead.

The *Leibstandarte*'s commander, Theodor Wisch, was forward monitoring the battle from a hill just behind the panzer kampfgruppe. He watched as a group of T-34s managed to break free from the battle with the *Totenkopf* and swing right into the *Leibstandarte*'s flank held by its reconnaissance unit. A handful of Russian tanks managed to get past the reconnaissance battalion's anti-tank guns, and charged forward into the division's rear area, shooting up trucks and small groups of Waffen-SS men until they were put out of action by the *Leibstandarte*'s artillery regiment firing its guns in the anti-tank mode.

By early afternoon the battle in front of Prokhorovka reached its climax, first with Russian infantry supported by tanks advancing directly out of the town towards the *Leibstandarte*'s panzergrenadiers. A panzer counter-attack broke up the infantry formation, and 40 tanks were claimed destroyed at long range. An hour later, the panzer kampfgruppe was moved northeastwards to clear out the 100 or so Soviet tanks believed to be hiding in the Psel valley. The *Leibstandarte*'s three remaining Tigers were then placed at the front of the panzerkeil. The force had only moved a few hundred metres when directly ahead more than 100 T-34s could be seen charging towards the German formation. This was the last hurrah of Rotmistrov's XVIII Tank Corps, and would see the destruction of the whole of the 181st Tank Brigade.

TIGERS VERSUS T-34S

At a range of 1800m (5905ft), the Tigers started to take their toll on the Russian tanks. One after another the T-34s exploded in huge fireballs. Still the Russians kept coming. At 1000m (3280ft), every shot from the Tigers' 88mm cannons was scoring a hit. Up to 10 tanks a minute were being hit as the Soviet brigade continued to surge forward. The Russians tried to return fire, but they were firing on the move, and few of them were able to hit any of the German tanks. Now the famous incident occurred when a T-34 tried to ram the Tiger of the famous *Leibstandarte* tank commander, SS-Untersturmführer Michael Wittmann, at high speed. The Tiger survived the impact and was able to back off from the wrecked Russian tank before its ammunition exploded. The 181st Tank Brigade failed to penetrate the German line, and for much of the afternoon the *Leibstandarte*'s panzers hunted down its remnants along the northern edge of the battlefield.

A tank brigade tried to launch an attack from the Psel valley later in the afternoon, but its T-34s barely got forward from their assembly area before accurate German 88mm fire from the Tigers broke up the attack. In the Psel valley the remnants of several Soviet tank brigades and battalions were trying to sort themselves out after being rebuffed with heavy losses during the day's battles. Commanders were trying to muster scratch battalions from the survivors, in order to rejoin the fight. Two more attacks were attempted towards the end of the afternoon, only to get the same reception from the German tanks. The Soviet tank crews were now starting to show a healthy respect for the Waffen-SS panzers, and made few attempts to emerge from cover. In addition, the *Leibstandarte* Division's artillery regiment started to direct regular barrages into the area to make sure that the Russian troops kept their heads down.

On the *Das Reich*'s front the battle was equally fierce, with two tank corps and several infantry divisions trying to batter through its position from late in the morning. The brunt of these attacks were borne by the division's two panzergrenadier regiments, *Der Führer* in the south and *Deutschland* to the immediate right of the *Leibstandarte*, which set up a series of defensive fronts in the woods and gullies south of Prokhorovka. II Tank and II Guards Tank Corps had already been blooded against the Waffen-SS over the previous week, and were now more cautious in exposing their tanks to German firepower.

A series of coordinated brigade-sized infantry and armour attacks was launched throughout the day, beginning at 11:40 hours with a push against *Der Führer*'s second battalion led by 30 T-34s. At the same time, an infantry attack hit *Deutschland*'s front.

Barely had the *Das Reich* Division seen off these human-wave infantry assaults when *Der Führer* was bounced by a two-pronged attack. The regiment's front was engulfed by thousands of Russian infantry charging forward at the Waffen-SS lines. One German battalion also counted 40 Russian tanks advancing towards its lines among the infantry. In the north of the regiment's sector, another 70 tanks tried to push through to the Belgorod–Prokhorovka railway line at 14:00 hours.

Waffen-SS assault guns and anti-tank guns were pushed forward to repulse the Russian attacks, which went on well into the afternoon. At 15:00 hours, *Das Reich*'s panzer kampfgruppe was mustered from its reserve positions to counterattack and neutralize the Soviet threat once and for all. Two Soviet tank brigades were decimated in the sweep and 21 T-34s destroyed. This calmed the situation for a few hours. The Soviets were not finished yet, though, and they pushed forward again at 17:00 hours to try to force a breach between

Das Reich and the 167th Infantry Division. As nightfall approached, the Soviet attack on *Das Reich* had well and truly run out of steam.

Over on the western flank of the battlefield, the *Totenkopf* Division was still battling to break out of its bridgehead. As the pressure mounted on German defences in front of Prokhorovka during the morning, the division was ordered to swing a kampfgruppe back across the Psel to strike into the Soviet armour using the valley as a base to attack the *Leibstandarte* Division. This attack made some progress and kept the Soviets bottled up in their "valley of death" for the rest of the day. The schwerpunkt of the division's efforts was to the north, and at 12:30 hours its panzer kampfgruppe was launched northwards through a huge barrage of Katyusha rocket fire. The *Totenkopf*'s panzers, with their 10 Tiger tanks in the lead, swept all before them. The advance rolled 3.2km (2 miles) north to cut the main road north out of Prokhorovka, and only the onset of darkness brought it to a halt. The division's panzers claimed the destruction of 27 Russian tanks in the advance. Follow-up panzergrenadiers made slower progress in the face of determined Soviet infantry, who fought to the last in the villages and woods around the bridgehead. This meant only a narrow corridor could be kept open from the bridgehead to the panzer spearhead to the north. Soviet

---

Two SS soldiers examine a knocked-out T-34 at Kursk. The T-34 crews negated the long range of the guns of the German Tigers and Panthers by closing with them quickly.

The aftermath at Prokhorovka. German SS grenadiers approach knocked-out T-34s. Losses on both sides were high, but the Soviets had halted II SS Panzer Corps.

counterattacks and artillery barrages rained down on the *Totenkopf* Division well into the night, inflicting heavy casualties. The division's panzers suffered badly, with more than 45 out of 94 tanks being put out of action, including all of its Tigers. Heavy rain showers washed the battlefield during the early evening, extinguishing many of the 400 burning tank hulks that were arrayed in front of the German lines. In the rain, repair crews from both sides tried to recover the remains of the damaged tanks to patch them up for the next day's combat.

A string of top Soviet generals visited the battlefield to congratulate Rotmistrov on his great "victory". He had stopped the élite of Hitler's hated SS in their tracks and still held Prokhorovka. When Rotmistrov toured his shattered command to see for himself if it could be made ready for action the following day, he could be forgiven for thinking he had suffered a massive defeat. XXIX Tank Corps had lost 60 percent of its tanks, and XVIII Tank Corps had suffered 30 percent losses. On 13 July, Rotmistrov admitted that his tank army could only field 100 to 150 combat-ready tanks out of the 850 committed for action at Prokhorovka on the previous day. The remainder had been destroyed or were too badly damaged to be considered fit for action.

Controversy has surrounded German tank losses in this crucial battle, with Rotmistrov and other Soviet histories claiming the Waffen-SS lost more than 300 tanks, including 70 Tigers, during the action in front of Prokhorovka on 12 July. German records, however, paint a different picture. The Germans admitted to losing 70 to 80 tanks on that day, the majority of which were from the *Totenkopf* Division. The *Das Reich*'s mechanics had already repaired scores of tanks damaged earlier in the offensive, so that on the morning of 13 July they actually had more tanks available than on the day before; while the *Leibstandarte* Division was only some 17 tanks down on the previous day's total.

When Hausser saw the tank kill claims coming from the battlefield, he could scarcely believe his eyes. The *Leibstandarte* Division alone claimed 192 Soviet tanks destroyed. The Waffen-SS general thought this was scarcely credible until he visited the battlefield and walked around the hulks, numbering them with chalk to confirm the kills. Rotmistrov's own admissions of his tank losses tally in many ways with German figures, indicating that his tank charge, when considered on its own, might be classed as one of the most disastrous actions in military history.

On 13 July, Hitler summoned his Eastern Front commanders to his East Prussian headquarters to issue new orders. Three days before, British and American troops had landed in Sicily, and the Ninth Army on the northern shoulder of the Kursk salient had been hit by a massive Soviet offensive that sent it reeling backwards in confusion. Hitler wanted to strip the Eastern Front of troops to shore up the Mediterranean. The Battle of Kursk was over.

Part VI

Retreat
in the East
1943–1944

The Mius Front

In the aftermath of the Battle of Kursk, the *Totenkopf* and *Das Reich* Divisions were sent south to strengthen the Mius Front, which was being assaulted by large Red Army forces. The two Waffen-SS divisions managed to achieve their objective, but in doing so suffered heavy losses in both men and vehicles, losses that could not easily be replaced.

A *Totenkopf* Tiger I on the Mius Front in July 1943. The SS panzer divisions retained their Tiger companies until early 1944, when they were withdrawn and organized into independent heavy tank battalions.

Barely two weeks after the end of Operation Citadel, II SS Panzer Corps was thrown into a new battle. In three days of fighting along the River Mius Front, in the southern Ukraine, Adolf Hitler's élite Waffen-SS panzer divisions would suffer more casualties than during the two-week swirling tank battles south of Kursk. Thrown into a bloody frontal assault, the *Totenkopf* and *Das Reich* Divisions suffered thousands of casualties from dug-in Soviet anti-tank guns and machine-gun nests. The Waffen-SS divisions eventually drove the Soviets from their bridgehead across the Mius, but the Führer's "Fire Brigade" lost irreplaceable men and equipment at a crucial time when the fate of the Eastern Front hung in the balance.

It took the Waffen-SS only a few days to disengage from the Prokhorovka region after Adolf Hitler cancelled Operation Citadel on 17 July 1943. Plans were now prepared for counteroffensives to destroy the Soviet bridgeheads across the Mius and the Donets at Izyum. The *Leibstandarte* and *Das Reich* Divisions, with the 17th Panzer Division and 333rd Infantry Division in support, were to crush the Izyum incursion with an assault beginning on 24 July. This was to be a quick containment operation, lasting only a few days, to allow II SS Panzer Corps to be free to deal with the Mius Front.

No sooner had the Waffen-SS troops been deployed in their attack positions than the order arrived from the Führer's headquarters cancelling the operation. He had other work for them. The *Leibstandarte* was loaded onto trains, minus its tanks which were to be handed over to the *Das Reich* and *Totenkopf* Divisions, and sent west to help shore up Mussolini's fascist regime in Italy after the Allied invasion of Sicily in early July 1943. The Izyum counterattack would be left to the élite Waffen-SS *Wiking* Division and the 17th Panzer Division. In two weeks of bitter fighting the two formations contained the Soviet bridgehead, but did not have the strength to wipe it out.

The remaining units of II SS Panzer Corps were now loaded onto trains again and sent off to the Mius Front, where a more serious crisis was developing that threatened to break open the southern front of Field Marshal von Manstein's Army Group South. For the Waffen-SS men this was a confusing time – they received little information apart from the time their trains were leaving for "destinations unknown". Once they arrived they were expected to be ready for action in a few hours.

The last 160km (100 miles) of the River Mius flow almost exactly along a north–south course into the Gulf of Taganrog. The German "new" Sixth Army had been defending this line since the spring, with 10 under-strength infantry divisions and a single weak panzergrenadier division. The Mius was the last natural obstacle before the great River Dnieper, and Hitler believed it was the key to protecting the Ukraine's natural resources and industrial potential from the Red Army.

THE MIUS POSITION
In mid-July 1943 the river was reduced to barely a trickle. It was only some 50m (164ft) wide and a few centimetres deep. The Sixth Army had spent almost six months building up its defences on the high ground on the western bank, but the 12.8km- (8-mile-) long slope up from the river meant the German positions were dangerously exposed to Russian observation and artillery fire. The high ground was featureless, with only a handful of small villages and ravines providing any protection from artillery fire. However, huge wheat fields with nearly ripe crops covered the slopes, making it very easy for infantrymen to disappear from view. Along the river bank there was little cover, and the only way for the Germans to protect themselves was to dig deep trench lines and bunkers. They also planted numerous minefields to channel any attacks into killing zones. In the run-up to Operation Citadel, the Mius Front was a backwater, with few reinforcement troops and tanks being sent to help bolster the Sixth Army. It had much in common with the fictional section of the Eastern Front portrayed in the 1977 Sam Peckinpah movie, *Cross of Iron*.

The Soviet High Command had great plans for the Mius Front. They saw it as a key pressure point to draw away the German panzer reserves if their front around Kursk was ever seriously threatened. In a classic campaign of maskirovka, or deception, they carried out all the preparations for their Mius offensive in full view of the Germans. Tank and truck convoys moved into position at night with headlights on. Radio conversations detailing attack plans were made with no attempt to encode secret information. Artillery positions were set up in the open and stockpiles of ammunition were not hidden. As the giant tank battle at Prokhorovka reached its climax, the Soviets ordered their troops on the Mius to attack. There were tank reserves on hand to exploit any breakthrough, but the incursion would, hopefully, panic the Germans into moving panzers away from the decisive front. Tens of thousands of Red Army soldiers would die in the coming weeks to satisfy the Soviet master deception plan.

The opening attack on 17 July went like clockwork for the Soviets. Several small-scale attacks on the northern and southern wings of the Mius line were easily repulsed. In the centre of the front, between the towns of Kuibyshevo and Dmitrievka, the Russians threw their II Guards Mechanized Corps into action, with 120 T-34 and 80 T-70 tanks in the first assault wave. They smashed through the German first line with ease. Although briefly delayed by German minefields and infantry counter-attacks, the Soviet advance seemed unstoppable. On 18 July, the commander of the Sixth Army, Infantry General Karl Hollidt, threw in his only reserve, the 16th Panzergrenadier Division, with its 40 or so tanks. The division was given little time to prepare or plan the operation, and it was a total disaster. Overnight, the Soviets had brought up scores of anti-tank guns, and the German division's panzer battalion had barely crossed its start line when it ran into a hailstorm of fire. In the space of a few minutes it lost more than 20 tanks, and had to pull back in disorder. The Soviets pressed forward to exploit their advantage, seizing the summits of the ridges high above the River Mius.

THE DEFEAT OF THE 23RD PANZER DIVISION
Manstein now sent Hollidt the 23rd Panzer Division to give him more armour to turn back the Soviet tide. However, its attack on 19 July was just as disastrous as the efforts of the 16th Panzergrenadier Division, losing 28 of its 50 tanks in a direct frontal attack on the Russian line. Again the Soviets pressed home their advantage, with a major attack by IV Mechanized Corps being mounted on 22 July. Its 140 tanks rolled forward to take on the Sixth Army's remaining 36 panzers. Only the arrival of XXIV Panzer Corps' headquarters units saved the day. It organized a rapid, improvised defensive line of 88mm flak guns and Sturmgeschütz (StuG) III assault gun batteries to repel the Soviet tank armada. Now it was the Germans' turn to inflict havoc on the Soviets. The 88mm flak gunners used their powerful weapons to great effect, picking off 93 Soviet tanks and breaking the back of the enemy attack. With its last reserves of tanks shattered, the Red Army offensive ran out of steam.

After its diversion to the Izyum Front, II SS Panzer Corps was not available to lead the Mius counterstroke until 29 July. The *Totenkopf* Division, led by SS-Brigadeführer Hermann Priess, arrived on the Mius Front first, followed by elements of *Das Reich*. Hollidt was a firm believer in the principle of launching immediate counterattacks to dislodge any Soviet incursions to prevent the enemy fortifying their positions. In the past, rapid counterattacks had always driven the Soviets back

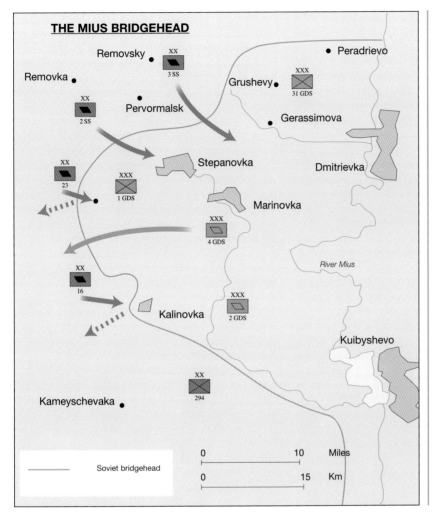

THE MIUS BRIDGEHEAD

Remversky

Removka

2 SS

Pervormalsk

23

1 GDS

Stepanovka

Marinovka

4 GDS

16

Kalinovka

2 GDS

294

Kameyschevaka

Peradrievo

Grushevy

31 GDS

Gerassimova

Dmitrievka

River Mius

Kuibyshevo

3 SS

Soviet bridgehead

| 0 | 10 | Miles |
| 0 | 15 | Km |

Eliminating the Red Army bridgehead cost the *Totenkopf* and *Das Reich* Divisions heavy losses in both manpower and vehicles, losses neither unit could afford after their efforts at the Battle of Kursk.

in confusion. Hollidt's experience with the 16th Panzergrenadier and 23rd Panzer Divisions did nothing to change his mind. II SS Panzer Corps would therefore be sent straight into action, with no time to familiarize itself with the ground or scout out the enemy's weak points. Hollidt was not interested in a deep, flanking attack. He wanted a frontal assault, and he wanted it on 30 July. Never inclined to miss a chance to prove that they could do what the army had failed to accomplish, the Waffen-SS commanders went about their new mission with gusto.

The *Totenkopf*'s objective was a ridge line in the centre of the Russian position. A complete Soviet anti-tank brigade with scores of 76.2mm high-velocity anti-tank guns, supported by dug-in T-34s and elements of five infantry divisions, had had five days to turn the Waffen-SS

division's objective into a fortress. Immediately to the south, *Das Reich*'s *Deutschland* Panzergrenadier Regiment was to assault the heavily fortified town of Stepanovka, to seize a nearby hill which was the highest point in the Mius region. The Soviet defenders knew their trade, though, and they had created a mutually supporting network of pak-fronts, so any German tanks that tried to attack one anti-tank battery could be hit in the flank by accurate fire from another battery.

The *Totenkopf*'s attack was to be spearheaded by SS Panzer Regiment 3, with its 49 Panzer IIIs, 9 Panzer IVs and 10 Tiger Is. The division's two panzergrenadier regiments, *Theodor Eicke* and *Totenkopf*, followed behind in echelon to clear out Soviet infantry positions. As usual, the Tigers were positioned at the front of the *Totenkopf* panzerkeil.

As the attack rolled forward just after dawn on 30 July, everything seemed to be going well until the panzers moved into range of the pak-fronts. A furious barrage of accurate heavy anti-tank rounds started to rain down on the German tanks. Russian infantry then joined in, with their anti-tank rifles aimed at the panzers' thinner side armour. To compound the problem, heavy artillery started to land among the attack formation, forcing the panzergrenadiers to run for shelter.

The Russian fire forced the panzers to try to take cover in ravines or folds in the ground. Each tank was now taking multiple hits, and it was difficult to find any cover from the fire, which was coming in from both the front and side. Whole Soviet anti-tank batteries were concentrating their fire on individual German tanks, until they either pulled back or were knocked out. Even the heavily armoured Tigers found they could not survive this ordeal. Then, the *Totenkopf*'s tank crews found they had blundered into a minefield. Tank after tank had its tracks blown off, and the immobilized panzers were easily picked off. In less than two hours the attack had all but ground to a halt, with some 48 tanks, including 8 Tiger Is and scores of other light armoured vehicles, being put out of action.

It was now up to the panzergrenadiers to take the lead. Combat engineers came forward under heavy Soviet machine-gun and mortar fire to clear assault lanes through the minefields. Artillery and rocket fire was brought down on the Soviet line to cover the advance, but the fire support broke down when one of the Nebelwerfer launchers exploded, throwing the German fire base into confusion. Now Soviet Stormovik fighter-bombers appeared over the battlefield in large numbers to strafe the Waffen-SS attack troops.

By the middle of the day, the Soviet defence was holding firm and the battlefield was being obscured by the smoke from dozens of burning German tanks. A rare Stuka dive-bomber attack in the early afternoon allowed the *Totenkopf* Regiment's combat engineers to clear two lanes through the minefield. Some of the few remaining panzers were brought up to support the panzergrenadier attack. The Russians now staged a counterattack with half a dozen T-34s, but it was quickly beaten back by the panzers. By the time it started to get dark, the *Totenkopf* Division had made no serious impression on the main Soviet defence line. Its panzer regiment had lost almost all of its tanks, although many would be repaired over the coming days, and just under 500 men had been either killed or wounded. The division's panzergrenadier companies were devastated, some losing more than 60 combat soldiers out of an original strength of 90 men.

The *Das Reich* Division's attack on Stepanovka was equally unsuccessful. It had two kampfgruppen available

A destroyed Soviet T-34 on the Mius Front. In total the Germans knocked out 585 tanks in the Mius battles. An impressive total, but bought at a high price considering that the two SS panzer divisions could muster only just over 20 tanks at the beginning of August 1943.

PAK 43

The Panzerabwehrkanone 43 entered service in late 1943, and proved itself to be the best anti-tank gun of World War II. With its 88mm high-velocity barrel, the Pak 43 was the only German weapon able to penetrate the thick and well-sloped armour of the Soviet heavy tanks. It also had excellent long-range firepower, with one gun knocking out six T-34s at a range of 3500m (11,483ft). Its low profile allowed it to be hidden easily in foliage, and much harder to spot on the battlefield. Though transported on wheels, it was usually dug into position before deployment. It saw action on every front during the war, and proved to be a challenging adversary for US and Soviet formations alike.

Type:	anti-tank gun
Length:	6.61m (21.7ft)
Traverse:	56 degrees
Weight:	3650kg (8048lb)
Elevation:	38 degrees
Rate of fire:	10rpm
Calibre:	88mm
Max. range:	4000m (13,123ft)

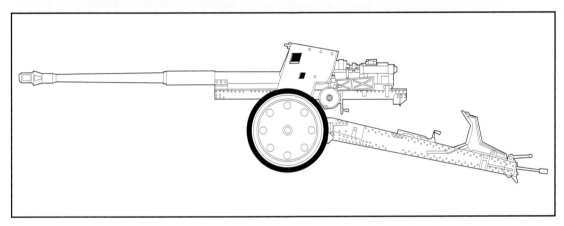

for action, because most of the *Der Führer* Panzergrenadier Regiment was stuck on muddy roads far to the north. The *Deutschland* Panzergrenadier Regiment was to storm into Stepanovka, backed by the division's assault gun battalion. Panzer Regiment 2, the reconnaissance battalion and the armoured personnel carrier battalion of the *Der Führer* Regiment would make a sweep to the south of the village, to take the key hill that dominated the whole region.

Preceded by a snap artillery barrage from *Das Reich*'s self-propelled artillery battery, the *Deutschland* Regiment successfully charged into the town, but then its problems began. The Soviets had fortified every building and the Waffen-SS men soon found themselves fighting for their lives. Mines, booby traps and snipers were waiting for them in large numbers. The attackers barely managed to push into the town deeper than a few streets. *Das Reich*'s panzer kampfgruppe fared slightly better than the *Totenkopf*'s tanks, though. In spite of losing 25 tanks in minefields, it was able to capture two hill-top strongpoints before its attack got bogged down.

German casualties in Stepanovka were mounting at an alarming rate, with many companies now commanded by junior lieutenants or senior noncommissioned officers due to losses among senior officers. Not even the deployment of the reconnaissance battalion's 20mm flak guns in the direct fire role was able to dislodge the Soviet defenders from their bunkers and tunnels.

By the end of the day, *Totenkopf* had suffered 320 casualties for little gain. The *Totenkopf*'s commander, Priess, was determined to press ahead with the assault and decided that more guile was needed to winkle out the Soviets from their defensive positions. He ordered his panzergrenadiers to launch a surprise "silent" night assault to clear out the Soviet defences. While the initial assault got into the Russian trenches undetected, the Soviets reacted quickly and drove the Germans back with a very prompt counterattack. The incident, however, distracted the Russians long enough for *Totenkopf*'s combat engineers to clear more than 2000 mines and create new lanes through the minefields.

The Waffen-SS attack on 31 July was far better planned, with a 45-minute artillery fire preparation by all of II SS Panzer Corps' artillery and rocket launchers. Stuka dive-bombers were on call in strength for the first time in the operation. This time, also, a huge rolling barrage was employed to shield the remaining *Totenkopf* panzers and supporting infantry as they moved forward.

Servicing a Tiger I in the field. Despite its ability to knock out anything the Allies could throw at it and its armour thickness, the Tiger suffered from being mechanically unreliable.

The attack breached the first Soviet defence line but it soon stalled. Again casualties were horrendous, with one Waffen-SS assault battalion reduced to fewer than 100 men. The division was now down to one Tiger, nine Panzer IVs and five Panzer III tanks.

In the *Das Reich* Division's sector, the Russians launched no less than 14 counterattacks, backed by more than 70 tanks, as they tried to turf the Waffen-SS out of Stepanovka. Fighting during the afternoon was halted by a torrential downpour that turned the battlefield into a quagmire. The storm at one point put the *Totenkopf*'s divisional headquarters out of action, when a violent flash-flood surged down the ravine in which it was positioned, washing away radio antennae and command trucks.

The day's action was hardly encouraging for the Waffen-SS, with another 400 men killed or wounded and 24 more tanks destroyed. Another 80 tanks were in workshops under repair. If this rate of loss continued, II

SS Panzer Corps would cease to exist as an effective fighting force. Manstein was so concerned that his élite armoured reserve was being bled white for no gain that he visited Hollidt's headquarters to order the offensive to be called off. He needed the Waffen-SS panzer divisions to deal with an anticipated Soviet offensive at Kharkov.

In a tense conference on 31 July, Hausser insisted that his men could finish the job. The commander of the *Der Führer* Regiment, SS-Obersturmbannführer Sylvester Stadler, was produced to convince the field marshal that his fresh troops could turn the tide. His enthusiasm swayed Manstein into allowing the offensive to continue for a "few more days". Radical new tactics were now to be used to prevent a repeat of the past two days' slaughter.

Stadler was allowed to spend the rest of the day making a thorough reconnaissance of the sector south of Stepanovka. At 04:00 hours on 1 August, the two unblooded battalions were launched forward to seize the high ground below the town, with *Das Reich*'s panzer kampfgruppe in support.

Simultaneously, 600 German guns and Nebelwerfers launched a massive barrage along the entire length of the Russian frontline. Hundreds of anti-tank gun pits and infantry bunkers that had been pinpointed during the previous two days' battles were targeted during the barrage. In the sector to be assaulted by Stadler's troops, the Nebelwerfers laid a huge smokescreen to cover their dash across open ground. The tactics worked, and within a few minutes the Waffen-SS men were over the enemy's barbed wire, throwing grenades into their trenches and bunkers. A couple of hours of fierce hand-to-hand fighting followed as Stadler and his men swept into the Russian strongpoint. Defeated, the Soviet infantry retreated down the hill, leaving Stadler with control of the summit. He barely had time to admire the superb view of the battlefield, though, when a massive Soviet artillery fire mission landed on the position, forcing his panzergrenadiers to take cover in the old Russian trenches. Stadler's small command team dived under an abandoned T-34 tank. Disaster then struck, when a Soviet shell destroyed all his radios. German artillery observers on nearby hills had no idea that the Waffen-SS had taken the hill, and decided to join in the battle, blasting the strongpoint with their own fire. Only the firing of a signal flare brought this madness to an end. Now a human-wave attack by Soviet infantry, backed by T-34s, started to move up the hill. A few assault guns appeared, and they knocked out the Russian tanks that had survived the carnage and pressed home their attack.

CLOSING IN ON STEPANOVKA

In parallel with Stadler's attack, *Das Reich*'s panzer kampfgruppe attacked eastwards to bypass Stepanovka and push through to take the Soviet anti-tank guns holding up the *Totenkopf* Division in the flank. Heavy anti-tank gun fire halted the panzers south of Stepanovka as they moved forward. The panzergrenadiers dismounted from their armoured personnel carriers and assaulted the small pak-front blocking the way forward. Stukas were called in to blast a hole in the Soviet defence line, opening the way for the panzers. The job of leading the advance now fell to a Waffen-SS assault gun battery. Its StuG IIIs swept all before them, and were soon raking the Soviet anti-tank brigade's positions blocking the *Totenkopf* from the rear. The latter was at last able to move forward. Its panzergrenadiers sealed the ring around Stepanovka during the afternoon, allowing the *Deutschland* Regiment to clear the town of its last defenders.

Farther to the north, the *Totenkopf*'s remaining 19 panzers were at last moving forward. The morning's massive artillery preparation and the success of the *Das Reich*'s attacks significantly reduced the weight of fire that the Soviet defenders could lay down. Stuka attacks

neutralized many pockets of resistance, and the Nebelwerfers were used to screen the German tanks from anti-tank gun fire.

By 16:00 hours, the main Russian strongpoint blocking the SS advance was cleared. A massive Soviet counter-attack now materialized. Several regiments of Russian infantry surged up the hill. The few remaining German tanks turned their machine guns on the mass of infantry covering the hillside. The intervention of the Luftwaffe was decisive, when a wave of Stukas dived on the Russian attack group. For the men of the *Totenkopf* Division, the air strike could not have come a moment too soon. Only a few hundred German troops were inside the captured strongpoint, and they would have had no chance of survival if the Russians had reached them.

From their hard-won vantage points, the Waffen-SS assault troops could now see huge Russian convoys moving across the Mius bridges. The Red Army was in full retreat from its bridgehead.

THE MIUS FRONT IS STABILIZED

II SS Panzer Corps spent another day on the Mius Front, helping the Sixth Army mop up the last pockets of Russian resistance on the west bank of the river. It had already received new orders to pull out of the Mius Front and move northwards to counter a fresh Soviet offensive around Kharkov that was growing into a major threat. Only the *Totenkopf* and *Das Reich* Divisions would be committed to this new battle. Hitler wanted Hausser's headquarters to move immediately to northern Italy, to shore up his forces being mustered to repel the imminent Allied invasion of the Italian mainland.

The *Totenkopf* Division lost 1500 dead and wounded. This was three times the number of its casualties during Operation Citadel. Crucially, most of the losses were among the division's combat regiments, particularly the panzer regiment and panzergrenadiers. The losses in junior officers and company level commanders were grievous indeed. The Waffen-SS ethos of leadership from the front was proving to be very costly. *Das Reich*'s losses were nearly as bad, bringing its total dead and wounded during the previous month up to 2811.

The two divisions' tank losses were horrendous, with the *Totenkopf* only being able to muster 23 tanks fit for action on 2 August 1943. *Das Reich*, likewise, could only field 22 tanks. Prior to the Mius operation, the combined II SS Panzer Corps armoured strength had been some 190 tanks and assault guns. While many of the damaged Waffen-SS tanks and assault guns were repaired, the scale of the slaughter inflicted by the Russian defences along the Mius was unprecedented.

Retreat to the Dnieper

While the bloody battles raged along the River Mius Front, the Soviet High Command used the breathing space caused by the departure of the Waffen-SS panzer divisions in the northeastern Ukraine to prepare for the decisive offensive to break the German hold on the Eastern Front once and for all. Again, Hitler would turn to his Waffen-SS formations to save the day.

Digging a trench in anticipation of Red Army attacks in August 1943. When the Soviet attack came at the beginning of that month, it tore a huge gap in the German line between Orel and Belgorod.

The Soviet First Tank Army, Sixth Guards Army and Fifth Guards Tank Army, which had escaped the German coup de grâce at Prokhorovka by Adolf Hitler's decision to call off Operation Citadel prematurely, were quickly rebuilt for offensive operations. Men and resources were allocated to the units decimated at Kursk to bring them up to strength for Operation Rumyanstev, as the Soviets codenamed their new offensive.

The offensive was to break along an axis from Belgorod to Kharkov, and then fan out westwards to drive the German Army Group South back to the River Dnieper. To ensure the success of the operation, Stalin massed 650,000 men and 2300 tanks north of Belgorod. They faced a shell-shocked Fourth Panzer Army and Army Detachment *Kempf*, which had been granted no respite since the end of Operation Citadel. They mustered only around 200,000 men and fewer than 300 tanks between them. The army panzer divisions committed to Operation Citadel had suffered far heavier casualties than the Waffen-SS, and still had not received any replacement tanks or men. In most sectors, the Soviets were able to achieve a local supremacy in tank strength of 12 to 1.

When Operation Rumyanstev was unleashed on 3 August 1943 it achieved dramatic successes. The brunt of the Soviet assault fell to the west of Belgorod against the sectors of XXXXVIII Panzer Corps and LII Corps respectively. The 19th Panzer Division could only put 28 tanks into action against the main Soviet axis of attack. It took the Russians only a matter of hours to crack open the German defences, and once a breach developed there was no way to seal it. A torrent of T-34s was unleashed.

The German XI Corps fought a dogged rearguard action along the Donets above Belgorod, and then pulled back to Kharkov, repulsing repeated attempts to outflank its front. The 6th Panzer Division, 503rd Heavy Panzer Battalion with Tiger I tanks, and numerous independent assault gun battalions saved the day on numerous occasions as XI Corps fell back southwards.

In XXXXVIII Panzer Corps' sector, chaos reigned. The commanders of both the corps and the 19th Panzer Division were killed in the confusion when their staff cars were ambushed by Soviet tanks. The isolated divisions of the corps fought desperate rearguard actions as they tried to retreat to safety in the south. A gap more than 32km (20 miles) wide had been torn in the German front,

Right: As no fewer than
eight Soviet armies closed
in on Kharkov, the battered
panzer divisions of the
Waffen-SS tried desperately
to shore up the front.

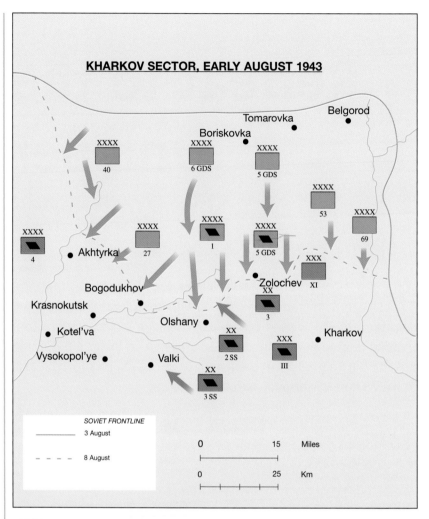

KHARKOV SECTOR, EARLY AUGUST 1943

Belgorod

Tomarovka

Boriskovka

XXXX
40

XXXX
6 GDS

XXXX
5 GDS

XXXX
53

XXXX
69

XXXX
4

XXXX
27

Akhtyrka

XXXX
1

XXXX
5 GDS

XXX
XI

Bogodukhov

Zolochev

XX
3

Krasnokutsk

Olshany

Kotel'va

XX
2 SS

XXX
III

Kharkov

Vysokopol'ye

Valki

XX
3 SS

SOVIET FRONTLINE

———— 3 August

- - - - 8 August

0   15   Miles

0   25   Km

Right: Waffen-SS panzergrenadiers rush past a
burning T-34 during the
Kharkov battles at the
beginning of August.

and the Soviet First Tank Army was advancing southwards at breakneck speed to exploit this very favourable situation. The Fifth Guards Tank Army was following close behind, ready to swing eastwards and encircle Kharkov itself.

Field Marshal Erich von Manstein now started to muster his panzer strike force to seal the gap in the line and defeat the Soviet tank armies. III Panzer Corps under Lieutenant-General Hermann Breith was ordered to take charge of the operation to defeat the Soviet thrust. He was to have the *Totenkopf*, *Das Reich* and *Wiking* Divisions for the mission, as well as the 3rd Panzer Division. However, at this time all the Waffen-SS divisions were still en route by train from the Izyum and Mius Fronts. In the meantime, the 3rd Panzer Division would have to hold the ring as best it could.

Although it could only put 35 tanks in the field, the 3rd Panzer Division was a seasoned unit and it put up a good fight, staging a rearguard action on 5 August against a push by the Soviet XVIII Tank Corps of the Fifth Guards Tank Army. The division repulsed this attack, and became a firm anchor on the right flank of III Panzer Corps.

Farther to the west, there were no German forces to stop the First Tank Army seizing the key rail junction at Bogodukhov on 6 August. Over the next two days the lead elements of the *Das Reich* Division started to arrive south of Kharkov, and they were fed piecemeal into the battle to try to shore up the front to the west of the city. Luftwaffe aerial reconnaissance was providing Breith with valuable photographs that showed thousands of Russian tanks moving southwards to the west of Kharkov.

SAVING KHARKOV

By 8 August *Das Reich* was deployed in strength, with four Tigers and 20 assault guns in action. Even though its panzer regiment was still to arrive, the division was able to inflict heavy losses on the Soviet III Mechanized Corps and XXXI Tank Corps, which were spearheading the First Tank Army's advance. VI Tank Corps, however, was still advancing southwards unopposed.

It was now the turn of the *Totenkopf* Division to enter the battle, and try to close down the Soviet breakthrough. During the night of 8/9 August the division deployed across VI Tank Corps' axis of advance, ready to stop it in its tracks. The *Totenkopf* Panzergrenadier Regiment was to form the centre of the defence, with the reconnaissance battalion screening its left flank and the *Theodor Eicke* Panzergrenadier Regiment digging in on the right. In reserve was a company from SS Panzer Regiment 3 with 12 tanks. The remainder of the regiment's 14 Panzer IIIs and 27 Panzer IVs were still en route.

The Soviet 112th Tank Brigade charged at the front of a German-held village during the afternoon, with hundreds of "tommy gun"-armed infantry riding on the hulls of dozens of T-34 tanks. A furious battle raged in the streets of the village, at the centre of the *Totenkopf* Regiment's position, as small groups of Waffen-SS men destroyed the Soviet tanks with hollow-charge mines and machine-gun teams dealt with the tank-riding infantry. As this battle raged, two more Soviet tank brigades pushed west of the village, forcing back the *Totenkopf*'s reconnaissance battalion.

More German forces were arriving all the time, with the *Wiking* Division turning up to bolster the 3rd Panzer Division's front on the right flank of III Panzer Corps. It arrived just in time to meet an all-out offensive along the whole of the corps' front on 10 August. In furious fighting, the 3rd Panzer and *Das Reich* Divisions held their lines, claiming 46 and 66 Soviet tanks destroyed respectively.

A DESPERATE STRUGGLE

Although the *Totenkopf* held its front, three Soviet tank brigades swept past its left flank, pushing 16km (10 miles) forward. SS Panzer Regiment 3 now intervened in the battle to cut off the Soviet spearhead. In a desperate battle in vast cornfields, the Waffen-SS tanks sliced into the flank of the Soviet 1st Tank Brigade. Two panzer kampfgruppen fought throughout the day, knocking out scores of tanks and machine-gunning hundreds of Soviet troops. These interventions brought the Russian drive south to a halt – just. More disjointed and desperate fighting continued during 11 August, as the small *Totenkopf* units tried to establish a continuous front.

The *Wiking* and *Das Reich* Divisions remained on the defensive, dealing with direct enemy frontal attacks across open cornfields by groups of 25–30 tanks and hundreds of infantry. Their panzers broke these attacks up with long-range fire. The *Totenkopf* Panzer Regiment and combat engineers continued their desperate counterattack, accounting for 134 tanks of the 268 with which the First Tank Army had started the day.

With the First Tank Army taking heavy losses, the Soviet High Command ordered Marshal Pavel Rotmistrov's Fifth Guards Tank Army to swing in behind it and then take over the advance. XVIII and XXIX Tanks Corps took the lead on 12 August and pushed southwards, just as III Panzer Corps launched itself forward into what was left of the First Tank Army.

Army Tiger tanks from the 503rd Heavy Tank Battalion joined the *Theodor Eicke* Regiment to slice into the flank of the First Tank Army, destroying scores of T-34s and forcing the 112th Tank Brigade to retreat northwards.

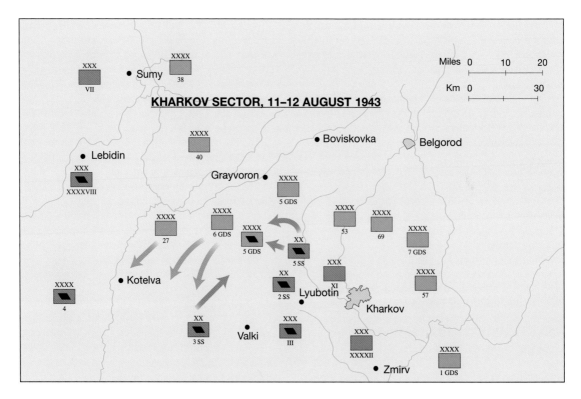

KHARKOV SECTOR, 11–12 AUGUST 1943

By the middle of August the Waffen-SS panzer divisions were fighting desperately to prevent Kharkov from being encircled by Red Army formations.

Totenkopf panzers continued to clear out a group of VI Tank Corps troops cut off farther south, and also destroyed a relief column. The *Theodor Eicke* Regiment's westward advance was now reinforced by the *Totenkopf* assault gun battalion, which knocked out 25 Soviet tanks that tried to press home a counterattack.

This advance was joined by the *Das Reich* Division, which was now attacking in a southwesterly direction. Its 22 panzers and 23 assault guns led a kampfgruppe formed around the *Der Führer* Panzergrenadier Regiment, which smashed into the lead tank brigade of the Fifth Guards Tank Army moving south to help its beleaguered comrades. The Germans claimed the destruction of 70 Russian tanks and the death of the corps commander in the turret of his burning T-34. Many of these tanks belonged to XVIII Tank Corps, which had joined the battle late in the afternoon.

The *Wiking* Division also advanced during the day against a prepared Soviet defence line held by infantry units of the Soviet XXIX Tank Corps. SS Panzer Regiment

5 led the attack, but its 24 Panzer IIIs and 17 Panzer IVs could not punch through the strong Soviet anti-tank defence network.

During the early hours of 13 August, the Russians again pressed forward regardless of losses. The fresh V Guards Tank Corps and 6th Motorized Brigade were used to batter their way past the *Totenkopf*'s reconnaissance battalion, and then push even farther south. III Panzer Corps' attack was now gathering momentum, though, as the *Totenkopf* and *Das Reich* Divisions pushed from east to west, with the aim of cutting off the Russian spearheads.

With Tiger tanks and assault guns in the lead, the Waffen-SS assault columns sliced through the shell-shocked elements of the First Tank Army that barred their way. Scores of T-34s were knocked out to bring the combined "kill" total for the two Waffen-SS divisions in a 48-hour period to 200 tanks. *Wiking*'s panzergrenadiers also advanced, pushing back a Soviet infantry division guarding the western approach to the town.

As the *Totenkopf* advance gathered pace, its small panzer kampfgruppe stalked the shattered remnants of the Soviet tank brigades through sunflower fields. The Russians usually fled before the rampaging panzers. During the afternoon, a group of 30 T-34s tried to take on

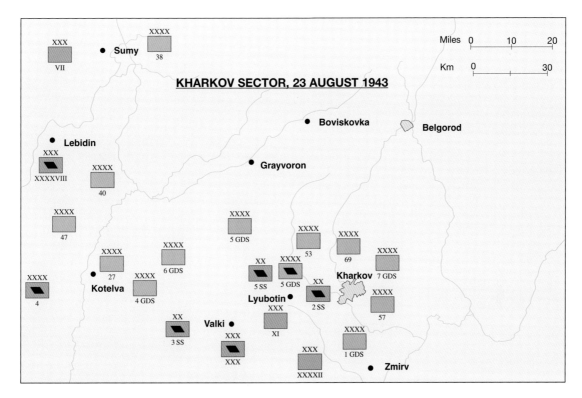

KHARKOV SECTOR, 23 AUGUST 1943

the panzers head-on. In a brief engagement the German Tigers and Panzer IVs formed a firing line, while the *Totenkopf*'s Panzer IIIs manoeuvred against the enemy's vulnerable flanks. The Soviets didn't realize the danger they were in and charged straight into the killing zone. None of the T-34s escaped the battle.

Over the next two days the *Totenkopf* and *Das Reich* Divisions completed the encirclement of the 52nd and 90th Rifle Divisions, along with the remnants of V Guards Tank Corps. Some 4500 corpses, along with the remains of 21 T-34s and scores of artillery pieces and trucks, were found in the "pocket" as it was being combed for survivors by the Waffen-SS.

Now the Waffen-SS divisions were ordered to turn north to chase away the remnants of the First Tank Army's shattered brigades. Both the *Totenkopf* and *Das Reich* Divisions used their last remaining Tigers to spearhead the drive. *Wiking* Division's panzergrenadiers could not hold off the strong Russian infantry attacks, so *Das Reich* had to send a panzergrenadier kampfgruppe to close a 1.6km (1-mile) breach in its sister division's front.

On 20 August, the *Totenkopf*'s panzer kampfgruppe forced a crossing of the river line and then turned westwards to start rolling up the Russian defences blocking the advance of the rest of III Panzer Corps. Now the *Totenkopf*

Surrounded by strong Soviet forces and with no hope of reinforcements, the Germans were forced to abandon Kharkov. They would never return.

Division moved north to link up with the army's *Grossdeutschland* Panzergrenadier Division that was pushing west. This move trapped two Soviet rifle divisions and a tank corps in a mini pocket. Most of the trapped Soviet tanks were eventually destroyed, but almost all the infantry were able to escape into the forests.

In the swirling tank battles west of Kharkov, two Soviet tank armies had been all but destroyed, losing a combined total of more than 800 tanks in a two-week period. Soviet infantry divisions between Belgorod and Kharkov could now put only 4000 men into the frontline. III Panzer Corps' counterstroke had succeeded beyond the wildest dreams of its commanders.

With its attack to the west of Kharkov thwarted, the Soviet High Command now decided to switch the main effort of its offensive to the city itself. The Seventh Guards and Fifty-Seventh Armies were launched forward with support from the First Tank and Fifth Guards Tank Armies. They boasted a combined armoured force of more than 500 tanks, and had soon pushed the five weak infantry divisions of the German XI Corps back into a narrow horseshoe-shaped defensive line around the outskirts of the city. To protect the vulnerable flanks of the city, every available 88mm flak gun and assault gun was deployed to hold off the Soviet assault.

Das Reich's panzer regiment and assault gun battalion were posted to the northwest sector of the city to guard the suspected approach route of the Fifth Guards Tank Army through a series of ripe corn and sunflower fields. Heavy air raids by Stuka dive-bombers, and minefields, broke up the tank formations of the Fifth Guards Tank Army's assault on 18 August. Marshal Pavel Rotmistrov called off his attacks, and was forced to reorganize his plan for the next day.

As dawn broke, small groups of Soviet tanks started to use ravines and stream beds to move through the cornfields to attack the German frontline. Waiting for them were the dug-in 88mm flak guns, along with 71 Panthers, 25 assault guns, 32 Panzer IVs and Tigers of the *Das Reich* Division. Wave after wave of T-34s tried to charge out of the cornfields to try to cross the few hundred metres to close with the main German defence line. During the course of the day the Germans claimed 184 T-34s destroyed by their guns.

Undeterred by these losses, Rotmistrov drove his men and tanks forward again on 19 August. This time they tried to push down the railway line into the north of Kharkov. The result was the same, with the Panthers and 88mm flak guns destroying scores of tanks at a range of

2000m (6561ft). Few of the Soviet tank crews even got within range to return fire before their T-34s were turned into raging infernos. On this day the Germans claimed 154 Russian tanks destroyed.

During the following day, the Red armour laid low and prepared for another attack. Once darkness fell, hundreds of Russian tanks surged forward through the cornfields. The panzer gunners could only see their targets in the light of muzzle flashes from other tanks or anti-tank guns. Soon they were among the German tanks, and the two armoured forces started firing at each other at point-blank range. After dawn the German line was secure, with 80 more Russian tanks burning in front of *Das Reich*'s position. XI Corps, however, had to order tank and infantry sweeps to clear pockets of Soviet troops that had infiltrated its lines. Flamethrower teams and 88mm guns were used to hunt down the dozen or so Soviet tanks that were still loose behind German lines south of Kharkov.

The Soviet Fifty-Seventh Army was also pressing Kharkov from the southeast, and after it had cut the railway line into the city it was only a matter of time before it fell. By 21 August, the Kharkov garrison had all but exhausted its reserves of artillery ammunition. Manstein now gave the order to pull out of the city. During the early hours of 23 August, Soviet troops drove out the last German rearguards and raised the Red Banner over Dzerzhinsky Square.

The vicious fighting around Kharkov had exhausted both the Soviet and German armies. For three weeks the

A German Pak anti-tank gun knocks out a Soviet tank during the retreat from Kharkov. Judging by the empty shell cases on the right, this crew has engaged several other targets.

northern wing of Army Group South had been able to stabilize its front. In the south, the weak Sixth Army now became the focus of Soviet attention. It lasted only a few weeks under relentless pressure before its units were streaming westwards in disorder. This defeat exposed the northern wing of Manstein's army group. With no reserves available to plug the gap, Hitler reluctantly agreed on 15 September to allow Manstein to pull his troops back behind the Dnieper.

The *Wiking*, *Das Reich* and *Totenkopf* Divisions were now operating under the command of the Eighth Army (formerly Army Detachment *Kempf*) during the withdrawal back to the Dnieper at Kremenchug. The three SS panzer divisions were now badly weakened by three months of constant combat. They barely mustered 25 tanks and 12 assault guns each, while their panzergrenadier battalions often had no more than 100 men apiece.

In mid-October 1943, the Soviets renewed their offensive in the southern Ukraine. After crossing the River Dnieper, the Red Army rolled over the weak LVII Corps with another huge tank armada and headed westwards towards Krivoi Rog. Field Marshal Manstein again gathered his panzer fire brigade to stabilize the front. XXXX Panzer Corps, with the *Totenkopf* Division as its spearhead, scythed into the flank of the Soviet assault force. Six weak German panzer divisions smashed two Soviet tank corps and nine rifle divisions, taking 5300 prisoners and destroying 300 tanks in the process. The *Totenkopf* Division remained on station in the Dnieper bend for the remainder of 1943.

These battles cost the *Totenkopf* dearly, though, and by this time it was approaching breaking point. The *Das Reich* and *Wiking* Divisions were in a similar position. *Das Reich* was to be pulled out of Russia and rebuilt in France. SS-Obersturmbannführer Heinz Lammerding, however, remained behind with a kampfgruppe to help hold the Dnieper line to the south of Kiev. In only a few weeks it would find itself fighting for its life.

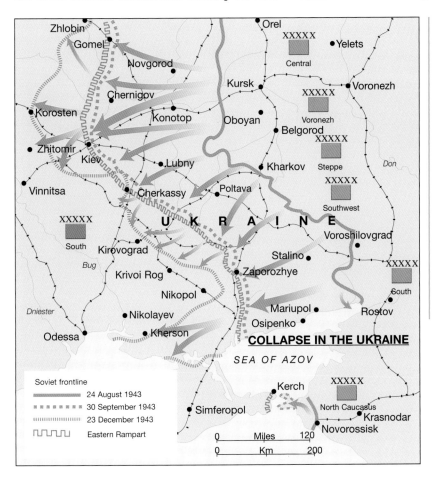

By the end of 1943 Soviet forces had sent their enemies reeling west. The German defensive line grandly titled the Eastern Rampart existed only in Nazi propaganda.

COLLAPSE IN THE UKRAINE

Soviet frontline
- 24 August 1943
- 30 September 1943
- 23 December 1943
- Eastern Rampart

0   Miles   120
0   Km   200

The Battle for the Ukraine

By the third year of the war on the Eastern Front, Soviet military production was running in high gear, turning out more than 20,000 tanks and heavy assault guns in 1943 alone. This mass of materiel, combined with German losses at Kursk, made the Wehrmacht extremely vulnerable in the East. This was highlighted in November 1943, when the Red Army launched an offensive in the Ukraine.

An officer of the *Leibstandarte* Division in November 1943, a photograph that amply conveys the temperatures soldiers had to endure during the winter season on the Eastern Front.

In early November 1943 the Soviet High Command launched a massive offensive to seize Kiev, the Ukrainian capital. The Red Army pushed across the Dnieper and threatened to open a breach between the Wehrmacht's Army Group South and its neighbour to the north, Army Group Centre. The brunt of the attack fell on the 11 infantry divisions of the German Fourth Panzer Army. When 20 Russian infantry divisions, backed by four tank and one cavalry corps, rolled forward, the German VII Corps was lucky to get out of Kiev without being surrounded and wiped out. Two weak army panzer divisions failed even to dent the Soviet armoured juggernaut as it rolled westwards for 112km (70 miles), capturing the key railway junctions of Fastov and Zhitomir. More than 1000 Soviet tanks were loose behind German lines, and they threatened to turn south and roll up all of Field Marshal Erich von Manstein's army group.

Hitler had already released the 1st SS Panzer Division *Leibstandarte Adolf Hitler*, as the premier Waffen-SS armoured formation was now titled, from its occupation duties in Italy for service on the Eastern Front, when the Soviet offensive burst around Kiev. The *Leibstandarte*, with its powerful panzer regiment equipped with 95

Panther, 96 Panzer IV and 27 Tiger I tanks, would provide the heavy armoured punch for the counteroffensive being planned by Manstein. Two army panzer divisions, the veteran 1st Panzer and the newly formed 25th Panzer, would support the attack. The 1st Panzer boasted 95 Panzer IVs and 76 Panthers, while the 25th Panzer had 93 Panzer IVs and an attached heavy tank battalion armed with 25 Tiger Is. Going into action alongside this force were elements of three other weak panzer divisions: the Waffen-SS *Das Reich* Division with 22 Panzer IVs, 6 Panzer IIIs and 10 Tigers, and two army divisions – the 7th and 19th Panzer – with 40 tanks between them.

To lead the attack, Manstein appointed the veteran army panzer commander General Hermann Balck. His XXXXVIII Panzer Corps in theory would have almost 500 tanks available for the operation, but they would take several weeks to assemble and ready for action.

The terrain west of Kiev was very different from the open steppes to the east, with huge forests stretching for kilometres across the countryside. Small Ukrainian towns sat on most of the road junctions and around a number of strategic bridges. Throughout November 1943, temperatures were hovering just above freezing,

The attack of XXXXVIII Panzer Corps at the end of 1943 was aimed at retaking Kiev, but Soviet forces were too strong and the German panzer divisions, including the *Leibstandarte*, were far too weak.

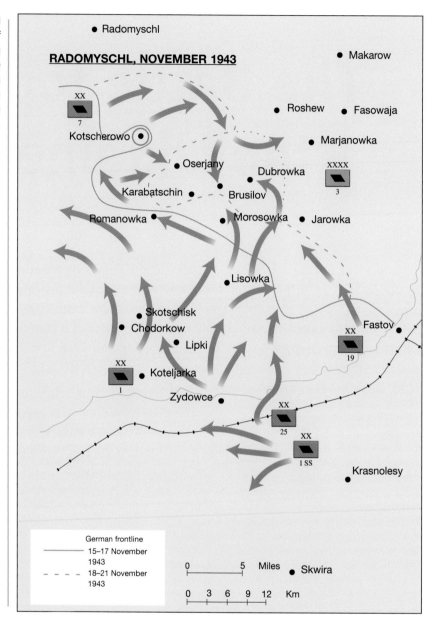

which meant sudden thaws and rain turned most roads and fields into thick mud quagmires that sucked in even tracked vehicles. The arrival of freezing winter weather was keenly anticipated by all Eastern Front tank commanders, because it would enable rapid movement off roads across the frozen ground.

At the end of the first week of November, Manstein ordered his counterattack force to assemble around the town of Fastov, which at that time was located on the left flank of the Soviet incursion into the German lines. The only forces available, the advance elements of the 25th Panzer Division and the *Das Reich* Division, were hastily thrown into action. They suffered heavy losses when their armour was delayed and the lorry-borne panzer-grenadiers found themselves locked in battle with hundreds of T-34s. Their holding action bought Balck time to gather his divisions, though, and they were sent rolling forward on 15 November. The Russians had not been in position long enough to dig in their pak-fronts, so to the *Leibstandarte*'s panzer crews the advance resembled the "good old days" around Kharkov the previous spring. SS-Sturmbannführer Joachim Peiper was now leading the division's panzer regiment. He was soon to be in the centre of the action.

Two powerful kampfgruppen were formed for the Waffen-SS advance, built around each of the *Leibstandarte*'s panzergrenadier regiments. Each one had a panzer battalion and assault guns attached to spearhead their advance. With Tigers and Sturmgeschütz (StuG) IIIs leading the way, the kampfgruppen easily punched holes in the thinly held Soviet front and headed north.

Heavy Soviet counterattacks were thrown at the *Leibstandarte*'s pincers, but the Waffen-SS men pressed on. Speed was their best ally. As the German panzer units closed in on Brusilov, the Soviet defence became more desperate. Several Soviet brigades were thrown into action to stop the *Leibstandarte*'s wide pincer move. Tigers, Panthers and StuG IIIs saw off these attacks, knocking out scores of T-34s in the process.

A final push was made on 22 November to close the ring, with Tiger tanks leading the advance of the southern pincer. They blasted their way through a pak-front holding open the Russians' escape route, knocking out 24 tanks and 2 assault guns. Peiper, with a kampfgruppe of Panzer IVs and panzergrenadiers riding in armoured halftracks, led the advance northwards during the following afternoon, to link up with the advance guard of the army's 1st Panzer Division which was probing the northern suburbs of Brusilov. The impetuous Peiper raced forward, but he was held up by huge swamps north of the town. His kampfgruppe then destroyed nine T-34s and 24 anti-tank guns during this sweep, and saw off another Russian attempt to break through to the forces now trapped in Brusilov, destroying six more tanks in the process. Trapped in the pocket were elements of seven major Soviet units. German Army divisions were used to comb the pocket – they cleared out several thousand prisoners and 3000 Russian dead littered the battlefield. The Germans claimed 153 tanks and more than 320 artillery pieces destroyed. Thousands more Russian troops escaped through the swamps to freedom.

The *Leibstandarte* Division was now regrouped for a further push northwards, to the heavily defended town of Radomyschl. On 29 November Peiper's panzer regiment and the reconnaissance battalion led the way. His Tigers punched a hole through a thick pak-front south of Radomyschl, but as resistance stiffened the attack was called off.

An SdKfz 251 halftrack mounting a 20mm gun of the *Leibstandarte* Division during the drive to Radomyschl. This vehicle would be part of the division's flak battalion.

A new plan called for XXXXVIII Panzer Corps to move 64km (40 miles) westwards in front of the Russians, and then hit their exposed western flank, rolling up their new frontline of anti-tank guns and dug-in tanks. With the Ukraine now firmly in the grip of a heavy winter frost, the *Leibstandarte* Division moved at night to its jump-off point north of Zhitomir on 6 December. Peiper was again to lead the attack with his panzer regiment, armoured troop carrier battalion and the reconnaissance battalion.

The Waffen-SS tanks pressed home their advantage during the following day, but then ran out of fuel during the afternoon and had to be resupplied before the advance could continue. Stung by criticism, Peiper pushed his men forward with a vengeance on 7 December, covering more than 32km (20 miles) and cutting the road north out of Radomyschl. He then pushed southwards to reach the outskirts of the town, before turning east to close the ring around what was left of the Soviet Sixtieth Army.

For almost a week, the *Leibstandarte* Division held the ring around the Russian forces trapped in Radomyschl. The division's panzers were also used to force back Russian troops to the north of the town, and smash the remaining enemy armoured reserves. The advance was successful at first, but Peiper's tank crews got bogged down in a series of costly but inconclusive engagements.

Almost a month of intense combat had taken its toll on the mighty *Leibstandarte* Division. Its tank strength now stood at some 20 tanks fit for action, with almost

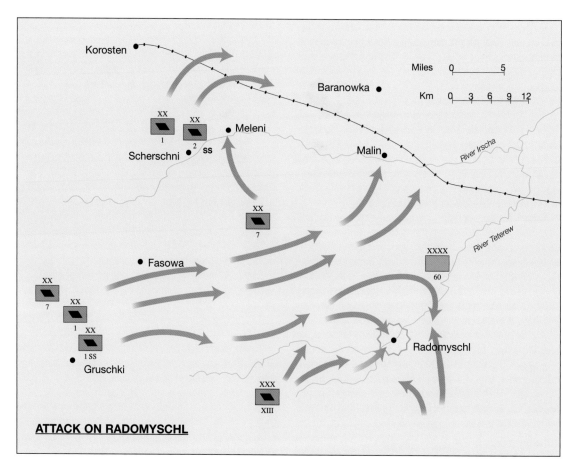

ATTACK ON RADOMYSCHL

Between 26 November and 23 December 1943, the panzers of the *Leibstandarte* Division, part of XXXXVIII Corps, defeated superior Red Army armoured forces.

200 tanks under repair. The panzergrenadier regiments were equally stretched, and each could only muster 500 men fit to fight.

Another Soviet tank force was now located gathering to the northwest around Meleni, and so Balck called off his attacks on Radomyschl. The *Leibstandarte* and 1st Panzer Divisions were ordered to launch another of the general's favourite pincer moves, to be ready for action on 19 December. The attack rolled forward under a barrage from 30 artillery batteries and scores of Nebelwerfer launchers. At first the *Leibstandarte* panzergrenadiers surprised the Russians and cleared out a score of trenches with little opposition. Then the panzer kampfgruppe moved forward until it ran into a huge pakfront of anti-tank guns. Three Soviet armoured corps and

elements of four infantry corps were in the salient being pushed in by the three German divisions.

During the following morning, the *Leibstandarte*'s losses mounted, until by the end of the day the division had only 20 tanks left fit for action, including 3 Tigers. It accounted for 17 T-34s, 4 assault guns and 44 artillery pieces destroyed. The following morning one panzer company of six tanks fended off a huge Soviet tank attack, destroying twenty-one T-34s in the desperate battle.

XXXXVIII Panzer Corps could only maintain its attack for two days, but it had inflicted big losses on the Soviets, with the 1st Panzer Division smashing a two corps-sized attack and knocking out 68 tanks on 22 December. The following day Balck halted the attack so he could use his three panzer divisions to form a mobile reserve, ready to parry another Soviet attack force that was gathering to the south in XXIV Panzer Corps' sector. During the previous two months Balck and his élite panzer divisions claimed to have destroyed or captured 700 Soviet tanks and 668 anti-tank guns.

But the storm broke on 24 December 1943 – 1000 Soviet tanks smashed southwest towards Manstein's headquarters at Vinnitsa, 80km (50 miles) away. On 27 December the Russian force rolled on into Kazatin. The 1st Panzer Division pushed south to retake the town and the *Leibstandarte* manoeuvred in front of Berdichev to stop a massive column of tanks heading towards it.

On 29 December the Russians attacked in strength, launching more than 150 tanks along the length of the *Leibstandarte*'s front. That morning it could only get four Tigers, eight Panzer IVs, seventeen Panthers, fifteen StuG IIIs and four Marder self-propelled anti-tank guns into the line to meet the Soviet onslaught. Two assault guns and a couple of 88mm guns had to meet an attack by forty T-34s. They knocked out nine of them, and then the intervention of a Tiger destroyed eight more, driving off the attack. A pair of Panthers saw off a breakthrough during the afternoon, and the 88mm flak guns also accounted for many T-34s. In total, some 59 Russians tanks were knocked out in front of the division's line. During the early evening, however, a force of 65 enemy tanks had skirted round the northern end of the *Leibstandarte*'s line.

The Waffen-SS held the line with grim determination during 30 December, but the pressure became unbearable on the final day of 1943. Hundreds of T-34s surged forward, to be met by a hail of fire which knocked out 25 of them. As darkness descended, the division was ordered to fall back as part of a deliberate withdrawal by XXXXVIII Panzer Corps from Berdichev. During the five days of the battle the Russians had lost more than 200 tanks in front of Balck's corps front. But the Germans had also lost equipment, which could not easily be replaced.

The *Leibstandarte* Division was pulled out of the line near Berdichev in the first days of January 1944, and then moved north to try to close a gap in the front between XXXXVIII Panzer Corps and LIX Corps. By the time the *Leibstandarte* Division was pulled out of the line for rest and refitting itself, it had claimed 288 Soviet tanks destroyed since the start of its Christmas offensive. Away from the frontline, the *Leibstandarte* Division was soon able to repair its damaged vehicles, and on 21 January 1944 it had 22 Panthers, 25 Panzer IVs, 1 Tiger and 27 StuG IIIs ready for action. All these vehicles would soon be needed on the Eastern Front.

Right: A Tiger I and grenadiers of the *Leibstandarte* on the steppe near Radomyschl in late 1943. Factory records show that the division took delivery of eight Tigers at this time.

Below: A mixture of Tigers and Panthers of XXXXVIII Panzer Corps at the end of 1943 near Radomyschl. At this time the *Leibstandarte* had a battalion of Panthers in its order of battle, organized in four companies.

Kessel Battles

Weakened by a steady stream of losses since the Battle of Kursk in July 1943, the Wehrmacht's Eastern Front was in tatters by January 1944. It was held by a rag-tag collection of divisions that were lucky to each number 5000 fit soldiers. Even the élite panzer divisions of the Waffen-SS were barely able to scrape together 30 worn-out tanks that could be defined as "combat ready".

A Waffen-SS 20mm Flakvierling 38 in the Cherkassy Pocket in early 1944. This gun was usually issued in platoon strength to the HQ companies of SS armoured artillery and panzer regiments.

Kessel is the German word for kettle. It is also the German military term for a "battle of encirclement". The analogy is appropriate. Once caught in a pocket by enemy pincers, any trapped troops are put under increasing pressure until a boiling point is reached. In the face of dwindling supplies, the trapped troops would either have to break out or face destruction. It was an experience that would be familiar to the soldiers of Army Group South in the first few months of 1944.

The Soviet breakthrough southwest of Kiev during December 1943 pushed the German Fourth Panzer Army back 160km (100 miles), leaving the Eighth Army's right flank dangerously exposed. In January 1944, it was the only German formation with a foothold on the southern banks of the River Dnieper. Hitler refused to let it withdraw to safety, and it was therefore only a matter of time before the Soviet High Command closed the net around it. The core of the Eighth Army's defence was the Waffen-SS *Wiking* Division. Usually, it had only a dozen Panzer IIIs, eight Panzer IVs and four Sturmgeschütz (StuG) IIIs ready for action on any day during January 1944. The division also boasted the Walloon Assault Brigade made up of Nazi volunteers from southern Belgium.

The Soviets made their first attempt to surround the Eighth Army in early January, with another steamroller offensive aimed at smashing XLVII Panzer Corps deployed to defend Kirovograd, which protected the route to the German rear. More than 600 Russian tanks opened a huge breach in the German line and trapped 4 German divisions in the sprawling industrial city. "Kirovograd sounds too much like Stalingrad for my liking", was the comment of the garrison commander, who took advantage of a breakdown in radio communications with higher command to order his troops to march to freedom. They successfully broke out with all their tanks and heavy artillery. The line was rebuilt after Field Marshal Manstein moved in two fresh divisions to mount a counterattack. Leading this effort was the *Totenkopf* Division, which had been brought up from the lower Dnieper. Just as the Soviets were preparing for a final push, the *Totenkopf* burst upon them and scattered several Russian divisions. It was only a temporary respite, though.

Manstein now tried to turn the tables on the Soviet First Tank Army that was pushing southwards into the Eighth Army's exposed left flank. He pulled together a scratch force of three "divisions", under army panzer

Right: The contribution of the *Totenkopf* Division was vital in stabilizing the German front near Kirovograd in early January 1944.

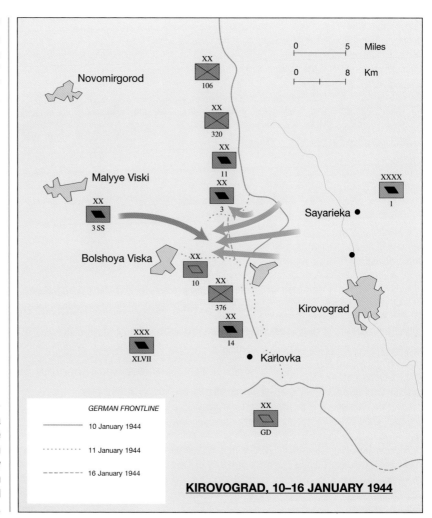

Novomirgorod

Malyye Viski

Bolshoya Viska

Sayarieka •

Kirovograd

• Karlovka

XX
106

XX
320

XX
11

XX
3

XX
3 SS

XXXX
1

XX
10

XX
376

XX
14

XXX
XLVII

XX
GD

```
0        5   Miles
0        8   Km
```

GERMAN FRONTLINE

——————— 10 January 1944

·············· 11 January 1944

– – – – – – 16 January 1944

KIROVOGRAD, 10–16 JANUARY 1944

Below: Unidentified Waffen-SS grenadiers watch a panzer attack in the Ukraine in early 1944. The barren landscape was lashed by freezing winds, which increased the windchill factor considerably.

General Hermann Breith, and launched them east into the flank of the Russian force. Heavy mud delayed the deployment of the *Leibstandarte* Division into position to lead Breith's III Panzer Corps. Backed by the Wehrmacht's only artillery division, the Waffen-SS troops sliced into the flank of the Soviet spearhead. Thick mud made the going heavy, but with its Tigers in the lead the division swept all before it. By 28 January it had closed the ring around several Russian divisions. The Germans claimed 8000 Russians dead, 701 tanks destroyed and 5436 prisoners.

This success was occurring at the same time as another Soviet advance was moving to trap the German Eighth Army on 24 January. Two armoured pincers sliced into the thinly held flanks of the army and met up on 28 January to close the noose around 56,000 men of the German XI and XLII Corps, forming what has since become known as either the Korsun or Cherkassy Pocket. The only German armoured unit in the pocket was the *Wiking* Division.

Just as at Stalingrad, Hitler ordered the troops in the pocket to stand firm and wait for a rescue force to restore the front behind them. In the meantime, an air bridge would keep them supplied with food, fuel and ammunition. It was a fantasy. Soviet fighters started to take a huge toll on the Luftwaffe supply aircraft. On the ground, more than 500 Soviet tanks were ringing the pocket, and Manstein could only muster four worn-out panzer divisions to mount a rescue mission. Hitler would give him no fresh troops from Western Europe because of the Anglo-American threat to France. Breith, meanwhile, was ordered to complete his operation against the encircled Russian force to the west and then batter his way through to the Eighth Army.

The army's 16th and 17th Panzer Divisions spearheaded the break-in operation, with the composite "Bake" Heavy Panzer Regiment in the lead. This unit was at this time the most powerful German tank unit on the Eastern Front, boasting 47 Panther and 34 Tiger I tanks, supported by armoured infantry and self-propelled units. Attacking northwards on 4 February in an attempt to turn the tables on the Soviet tank force and trap it in a pocket, the rescue force at first made good progress. A sudden thaw then turned the battlefield into a quagmire. III Panzer Corps' advance literally got bogged down. Wheeled fuel tankers and ammunition trucks just could not move. Even tracked vehicles had difficulties. At times fuel for the tanks had to be carried forward to the front in buckets or cans. The *Leibstandarte* Division battled on for 32km (20 miles). Its Tiger company destroyed 26 Soviet tanks as it established a bridgehead over the River Gniloy Tikich on 8 February 1944.

With its northward advance stalled, III Panzer Corps now moved the *Leibstandarte* Division and the army's 1st Panzer Division southwards so they could attack directly eastwards towards the pocket. This switch confused the Soviets, and the advance moved forward again, with the Waffen-SS on the left and the 1st Panzer on the right. Again frost helped the tank advance, and the 1st Panzer Division was able to throw a bridgehead over the Gniloy Tikich at Lyssinka, only 8km (5 miles) from the trapped troops. A huge pak-front of 52 anti-tank guns and 80 T-34s barred its way, though. The 16th Panzer Division and the Bake Regiment tried to outflank the enemy defences by pushing north, but they were soon stopped by heavy enemy fire.

As the *Leibstandarte* Division tried to keep up with the advance, it was hit by huge Soviet tank attacks. First V

A Waffen-SS Tiger in the Ukraine, February 1944. The Tiger's lack of manoeuvrability and slow speed meant it always operated with supporting lighter tanks, such as Panzer IVs.

Rifle Corps, followed by XVI Tank Corps, surged forward. It was all the understrength Waffen-SS division could do to hold off the non-stop attacks that swept forward out of the thick forests.

The battle went on for days. Soviet tanks washed around the small German units holding open the 1.6km- (1-mile-) wide corridor eastwards. Several times the Russians cut the corridor, and counterattacks had to be mounted to clear out their infantry and tanks. By 16 February, the 1st Panzer Division, helped by *Leibstandarte* panzergrenadiers, was holding on to its bridgehead by its fingernails. Only 60 men and a dozen Panther tanks were across the river, holding off daily attacks by V Guards Tanks Corps. III Panzer Corps just did not have enough strength to mount the final push to open a corridor to the trapped troops. During the afternoon, Manstein ordered XI and XLII Corps to break out west that evening. He avoided consulting the Führer's headquarters to prevent his orders being countermanded.

Inside the pocket, General Wilhelm Stemmermann was not going to repeat the mistakes of Field Marshal Freidrich Paulus at Stalingrad, and he immediately prepared to follow Manstein's orders. There was no time to lose.

The trapped troops were organized into three assault columns and a rearguard for the breakout. *Wiking* formed the southern column. Its last remaining Panzer IIIs and StuG IIIs led the advance, which began at 23:00 hours on 16 February. The first assault went in silently, with German infantry bayoneting Soviet sentries. This established

Panzers and halftracks in the Cherkassy Pocket. During the breakout from the pocket in February 1944, the *Wiking* Division's panzers sacrificed themselves to aid the escape.

paths through the Soviet inner ring, and then the *Wiking*'s tanks fanned out to provide flank protection for the ragged column.

The other two columns, made up of two infantry divisions, used guile to slip through the Russian lines to link up with 1st Panzer Division. *Wiking*'s column soon ran into trouble when a storm of Russian machine-gun and tank fire started to rake it. SS-Obergruppenführer Herbert Gille, *Wiking*'s commander, ordered one of his battalions to deal with this threat, while the rest of his division skirted around to the south of the Russian blocking position. When the Waffen-SS grenadiers reached the Gniloy Tikich, they abandoned all their heavy equipment and swam the freezing river before finding safety.

It was then the rearguard's turn to move out, and soon the two infantry divisions were being bombarded from the blocking position that had hampered *Wiking*'s escape attempt. They, too, broke and ran for the Gniloy Tikich. The few kilometres to the river were soon littered with abandoned trucks, cars, wagons, artillery pieces and tanks, as well as the bodies of 15,000 dead Germans. Among them was their commander, Stemmermann, who died when a tank shell ripped into the wagon he was travelling in.

Throughout the night and into the morning, the pathetic survivors of the pocket staggered past the men of the 1st Panzer and *Leibstandarte* Divisions. The hardened panzer troops were shocked at the poor morale of the survivors. They started to talk about "Kessel shock" – a penetrating fear of capture by the Soviets that overrode normal discipline and led to the breakdown of unit cohesion in time of crisis.

The 1st Panzer Division held its bridgehead open for two more days, though only some 30,000 men found their way to German lines. The *Wiking* Division was shattered, and was now reduced to less than half of its established strength. Only 600 troops out of the Walloon Brigade's 2000 men escaped. The survivors were soon shipped away from the front, and III Panzer Corps pulled back to establish a defence line ready to repel the inevitable next Soviet offensive.

As usual, the Russians massed huge breakthrough forces close to their chosen pressure points. Whole divisions of artillery blasted the German lines for days, and then several hundred T-34s were launched forward to drive over the ruins. The targets were two weak infantry corps, which soon folded when the Soviet attacks went in on 4 and 5 March 1944. In a matter of days Zhukov's tank corps covered more than 160km (100 miles), and most of Manstein's army group – 22 divisions – found itself cut off in a huge Kessel or pocket centred around the town of Kamenets Podolsk. The cut-off troops included the cream of the Wehrmacht's panzer divisions, as well as both the *Leibstandarte* and *Das Reich* Divisions. Command of the trapped troops fell to the First Panzer Army's commander, Colonel-General Hans Hube. The one-armed tank commander had actually served under Paulus at Stalingrad, and he would soon put into practice some of the lessons he had learnt in that Kessel battle. Just before Stalingrad fell, Hitler ordered Hube to be evacuated because he had earmarked him for rapid promotion.

Still serving with III Panzer Corps, the *Leibstandarte* Division was in the path of Zhukov's massive southward pincer. With only a dozen operational Panthers and a handful of other tanks and assault guns to hand, the division had no hope of stopping the several hundred Russian tanks that streamed through the breach in the Eastern Front. The Waffen-SS played an instrumental part in rescuing several army infantry divisions that looked as if they might be overrun. At this point it became the cornerstone of the west-facing front of the pocket. Over on the eastern edge of the pocket, the *Das Reich* kampfgruppe was in an equally precarious position, with six Panthers, five Panzer IVs and four StuG IIIs ready for action. The small *Das Reich* contingent desperately fought alongside a number of improvised kampfgruppen to hold a firm front facing eastwards, as more than 400 Russian tanks battered at Hube's beleaguered command.

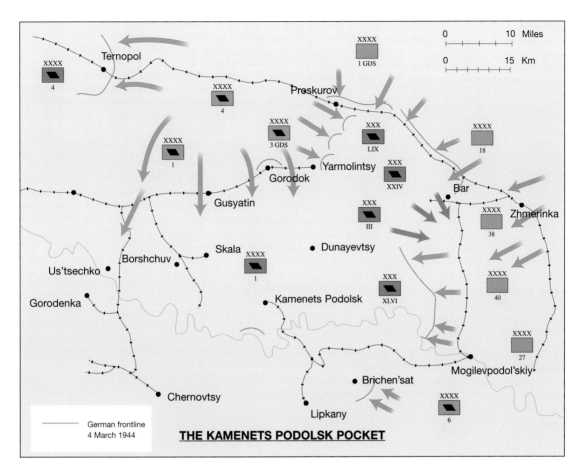

THE KAMENETS PODOLSK POCKET

German frontline
4 March 1944

Hube and Manstein, however, were determined not to repeat the mistakes made at Stalingrad. They first of all refused to follow Hitler's orders and declare the pocket a "fortress", one that had to be defended to the last man. Hube's pocket was going to be a "mobile pocket" – it would keep moving so the Russians would not be able to trap it, and then concentrate their forces against it.

For more than two weeks Hube kept his army moving southwards, and then westwards to keep the Russians guessing about the exact location of his divisions. Air supply was organized properly, with each division having its own Luftwaffe team which set up improvised airstrips each day. Fuel and ammunition were flown in and the wounded evacuated. By this stage of the war the Luftwaffe had finally mastered this type of operation, and the air bridge provided Hube's men with just enough supplies for them to keep fighting and moving. The continual movement was also good for morale, and Hube's army did not suffer any of the panics that were seen in the Cherkassy Pocket.

In March 1944 the entire First Panzer Army was trapped in a pocket, including the *Leibstandarte*. However, the Fourth Panzer Army acted as a relief force which extracted the trapped forces at the end of March 1944.

The obvious escape route for Hube's men was to head south, where a number of bridges over the River Dniester into Romania remained open. Zhukov therefore concentrated the bulk of his tanks against these crossings, rather than reinforcing the eastward-facing defences of his pincers. Manstein devised a plan for Hube to attack directly westwards, cutting through the Russian lines to escape and meet up with rescue forces moving east.

Hitler hated the plan because it gave up huge amounts of territory. For days he sat on his hands and refused to make a decision. On 24 March Manstein threatened to issue the breakout orders anyway, unless Hitler agreed to his plan. On this rare occasion the Führer backed down. Field Marshal Manstein got his

HERBERT GILLE

Herbert Otto Gille was born in Gandersheim on 8 March 1897. He joined the Imperial German Army in 1910 and was commissioned into the artillery, seeing action during World War I. In 1934 he joined the SS, becoming a battalion commander at the Doeberitz infantry training school. Transferring to the *Der Führer* Regiment, he was involved in the Polish and French campaigns. In 1941 he moved to the *Wiking* Division, where he won the Knight's Cross for his actions on the Eastern Front. In December 1942 he took command of the *Wiking* Division, and was awarded the Oakleaves for his leadership at Kharkov. For leading the breakout from the Cherkassy Pocket after the death of Stemmermann, Gille was further awarded the Swords. In the spring of 1944, he led an operation to rescue German troops besieged in the city of Kowel, successfully relieving them. For this act he was awarded the Diamonds. With Dietrich, he was the only other Waffen-SS man to win this award. In August 1944, Generalleutnant Gille took command of IV Panzer Corps until he was arrested by US troops. He was released in 1948 and lived out the rest of his life in Germany. He died on 26 December 1966.

freedom of movement and his reinforcements – II SS Panzer Corps. It would begin to move to the Eastern Front from France immediately, with the two well-equipped but unblooded Waffen-SS Divisions: the 9th *Hohenstaufen* and the 10th *Frundsberg* Panzer Divisions.

Inside the pocket, two assault groups were formed to batter past the Soviet defences. The *Leibstandarte*, then part of Kampfgruppe *Mauss*, fell back from its positions on the western flank of the pocket and deployed as part of the flank guard. The Corps Group von Chevallerei's élite Waffen-SS division helped hold open the escape corridor for almost 12 days against repeated attacks by the Soviet Third Guards Tank Army. The *Das Reich* Division stayed as the rearguard on the eastern edge of the pocket.

Central to Manstein's breakout plan was the deployment of II SS Panzer Corps to punch a corridor through from the west and take the pressure off Hube's hard-pressed troops in the pocket. On paper, II SS Panzer Corps was a formidable force, but its leaders and soldiers were largely untried in combat. Their commander, SS-Obergruppenführer Willi Bittrich, was one of the most professional officers in the Waffen-SS, but many of his divisional and regimental commanders were very raw. Bittrich's corps boasted an impressive array of weaponry, with *Hohenstaufen* fielding 21 Panthers, 38 Panzer IVs, 44 StuG IIIs and 12 Marder self-propelled anti-tank guns, while *Frundsberg* could put 44 Panzer IVs and 49 StuG IIIs into action.

By 3 April, Bittrich's men had finished unloading their tanks from trains in Lvov, and the following day they moved forward into action. The weather was terrible, with thaws one day followed by heavy snow the next. For the first day of the operation, the Army 506th Heavy Panzer Battalion took the lead with its Tiger Is battering away

through a large pak-front of anti-tank guns. Now the *Frundsberg* Division took over the advance for the final 32km (20 miles) to Hube's men. It then immediately ran into a concealed pak-front, and so the division's reconnaissance unit was sent forward to pinpoint the enemy gun pit and bunker positions. Panzers were then brought up to blast the enemy anti-tank guns one by one. Soon the tanks were rolling eastwards again, with the divisional commander, SS-Gruppenführer Karl von Treuenfeld, leading the advance with the first panzer company. He decided that the link-up could be achieved sooner if a direct route across country was taken. The Waffen-SS general managed to get through to Hube's 6th Panzer Division with five tanks, but he was soon cut off from his division by a massive Soviet infantry attack. The Waffen-SS tank crews had to fight dismounted from their immobile panzers to deal with Soviet tank-hunting squads that lurked in the woods and forests along the column's route. Bittrich came forward to sort out the mess.

By 6 April Bittrich had cleared the Soviet infantry brigades in the woods around the town of Buchach, which was the objective of Hube's columns. A supply column with 610 tonnes (600 tons) of fuel then moved down the corridor to refuel Hube's tanks and trucks, which were almost running on vapour. Over the next three days all the trapped German divisions were able to pass safely into the area held by II SS Panzer Corps. The rescue operation was a major success for Manstein, but the Führer saw it entirely differently. The "saviour of the Eastern Front" was relieved and replaced by Field Marshal Walther Model, who had a reputation for issuing "fight to the last man and bullet" orders. He was more to Hitler's liking.

Attention now turned to tidying up the new frontline, where dozens of small German detachments had been cut off. On 11 April, the *Hohenstaufen* Division was

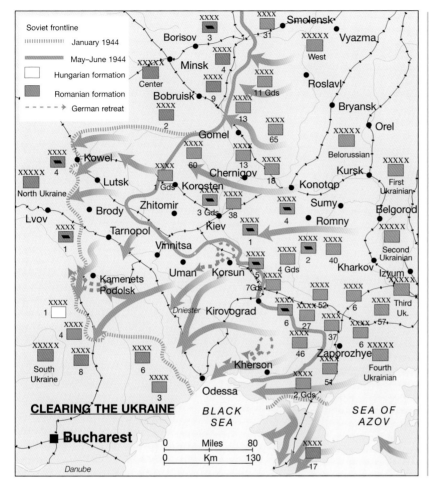

Soviet frontline

|||||||||||| January 1944

▓▓▓▓ May–June 1944

☐ Hungarian formation

▓ Romanian formation

– – – → German retreat

CLEARING THE UKRAINE

Despite Hitler's frequent interference and "no retreat" orders, and superior Red Army forces, German commanders managed to conduct a fighting withdrawal from the Ukraine in early 1944.

ordered to spearhead the rescue of 4000 Germans trapped in Ternopol. The operation was far from a success. On the first day the division got stuck in another quagmire, and then ran into heavy Soviet resistance. The attack got moving again, though, and pushed to within 8km (5 miles) of the trapped troops. This time the Soviet ring held. The garrison attempted to break out but was massacred in the process. Only 53 men made it through to the Waffen-SS lines.

The desperate state of the Eastern Front meant that even the remnants of the *Wiking* Division were mustered to fight in support of the rescue effort. Many soldiers still did not even have personal small arms after losing them in the Korsun/Cherkassy Pocket. Fortunately, the division had just been augmented by a fresh armoured regiment with 79 Panthers, which had been forming in Germany since December 1943. The division was committed to an operation to relieve the cut-off town of

Kowel on the Ukrainian-Polish border, which had been surrounded by a Soviet spearhead since mid-March. Gille's men finally relieved the garrison on 6 April. It was a victory of sorts, but the division had suffered many casualties, not just killed but also wounded, which meant the loss of veterans to hospitals and dressing stations.

On the southern wing of Army Group South, the *Totenkopf* Division was fighting a desperate rearguard battle around Kirovograd as the Eighth Army fell back to the River Dniester. For most of April, it retreated into Romania and on several occasions had to fight desperate actions to avoid being trapped in pockets.

By May 1944, the Ukraine, which the Führer had been desperate to hold no matter what the cost, had been cleared of German forces, and within a few days the Crimea had also fallen. A succession of massive Soviet offensives had literally smashed their way through Manstein's Army Group South.

Retreat from Leningrad

Army Group North fought a long, attritional war in its efforts to take Leningrad between 1941 and 1944. The Waffen-SS contribution to the siege was at first small, but grew steadily to become III SS Panzer Corps. By mid-1944, the corps, along with the whole of the army group, was fighting for its life in the face of massive Soviet offensives. It ended the war trapped in the Courland Pocket.

Two members of the Latvian Waffen-SS on home soil in 1944. Behind them lies a knocked-out Soviet T-34 tank, which has received a hit on its turret. The submachine gun is a 9mm MP40.

Hitler's ambitions to capture Leningrad, the birthplace of the Bolshevik revolution, had been thwarted in the autumn of 1941 by the city's heroic resistance and the need to divert vital panzer divisions for the assault on Moscow. By the summer of 1942 the siege of the city had been a bloody sideshow, as the fate of the war on the Eastern Front was decided in the south during the battle for Stalingrad.

If he could not take Leningrad, then Hitler was determined to make sure its residents paid for their defiance of the Third Reich. He ordered German troops to press the siege of Leningrad mercilessly. Waffen-SS involvement in the battles around Leningrad was initially small, but it grew during 1942 and by the winter of 1943 III SS Panzer Corps was committed to holding a key sector of the siege lines around the city.

Historic Leningrad was built on a 80km- (50-mile-) wide isthmus between the Gulf of Finland and Lake Ladoga. To besiege the city, German troops had surged north to Lake Ladoga in November 1941 to cut its road and rail routes to the south and east. Finnish troops had taken their revenge for the 1939 invasion of their country by the Soviets, and had joined forces with the Germans

in June 1941 to close off Leningrad from the north. The only way into the city was by air or by boat across Lake Ladoga, until it froze. Truck convoys could then be sent across the famous "Road of Ice" to ease the plight of its desperate citizens and to arm its defenders. The first winter of the siege was the worst, with hundreds of thousands of civilians dying from German shelling and bombing or simply starving to death.

For the German troops manning the siege lines around the city, conditions were equally primitive as they tried to survive the horrendous Russian winter and fight off almost constant Soviet attacks. Unlike the German forces in the central and southern sectors, the troops of Army Group North were at the back of the line when replacement weapons, equipment and clothing were distributed. Army Group North's status as a secondary theatre of operations meant few panzer divisions were deployed to support it.

The contribution of the *Totenkopf* Division to the battles south of Leningrad has been mentioned earlier, but it was not the only Waffen-SS division assigned to the sector. The *Polizei* Division had been committed to fighting around Lake Ilmen during the autumn of 1941. It saw heavy fighting in this sector as the Soviet winter offensive was unleashed in November and December. In late January 1942, the Soviet Second Shock Army launched a major offensive to punch through to Leningrad by opening a breach in the German line north of Novgorod. As well as relieving Leningrad, it was hoped that thousands of German troops would also be trapped by this manoeuvre.

DESTROYING THE SECOND SHOCK ARMY

After a good start, 30,000 Soviet cavalrymen broke through the German lines and 70,000 infantrymen soon followed to form a 64km (40-mile) salient. The advance guard of the relief force was only 97km (60 miles) from Leningrad when the Germans struck back. Eight German divisions, including the *Polizei*, were soon pulled out of the line and sent to seal off the Russian incursion. By 15 March, the Germans were ready to go back on the offensive and the *Polizei* Division led an assault group to cut the supply line of the Second Shock Army. In freezing weather the Waffen-SS men were able to close the gap on 20 March, trapping 100,000 Russians in a desolate winter wasteland. The Russians still had plenty of fight left in them, and had soon opened a new supply route to their troops over a frozen lake. When the thaw began in April, the Second Shock Army was trapped. The Waffen-SS troops joined forces with army troops to close a tight ring around the Russians, who were now running short of food, ammunition and medical supplies. The agony of the Second Shock Army lasted until July 1942, when the Germans finally snuffed out all resistance. There was one last mass escape attempt by the trapped troops, which allowed thousands of Russians to get to freedom. Out of the 100,000 who joined the battle in January, more than 55,000 were killed or captured. The latter included the Second Shock Army's commander, Lieutenant-General Andrei Vlasov. He would later help Himmler recruit an army of Russians to fight the Soviets.

During the summer, the Russians turned their attention to the shortest land route to Leningrad by punching a corridor through the German-occupied Siniavino salient, which brought Nazi forces to the southern shore of Lake Ladoga. The *Polizei* Division, fresh from its successes against the Second Shock Army, had been brought up to man a key siege line along the Neva River, south of Leningrad. Foreign Waffen-SS volunteers from the Dutch legion, Flemish legion, Norwegian legion and two Latvian battalions were also now in action on the Leningrad Front, fighting on a number of sectors with varying degrees of success.

The Soviets staged a two-pronged attempt to break the siege, striking from both west and east on 27 August. The eastern strike force made good progress before being stopped by German counterattacks. In the west, the *Polizei* Division stood firm along the Neva when three Soviet divisions tried to form a bridgehead over the river. Two more Soviet divisions did manage to force a bridgehead on 3 September, which held out for nine days until heavy counterattacks by the Waffen-SS forced them back across the river in some disorder. For several more weeks the Soviets kept up their attacks, until they ran out of steam. The German forces slowly gained strength and forced the Soviets back to their starting points. The siege of Leningrad would continue through another winter.

THE SOVIET JANUARY 1943 OFFENSIVE

The Soviets waited until January 1943 before attempting again to punch through the Siniavino salient. This time they mustered a far stronger attack force, including more than 500 tanks. On 13 January some 2885 Soviet guns opened up with a huge artillery barrage aimed at the German siege lines, including the *Polizei* Division that was still holding the line along the Neva. The Germans had now built a series of strongpoints along the siege lines either side of the Siniavino salient. These proved very difficult for the Soviets to overcome, and they suffered huge casualties trying to do so. The German strongpoints ultimately could not contain the Soviet troops and, five days later, two attack groups linked up to open a land corridor to Leningrad. To deal with the crisis, the *Polizei* Division was pulled out of the Neva line and sent into action to try to drive back the Soviet attack. The Waffen-SS failed to push back the Soviets, but it did stop them widening their 8km- (5-mile-) wide land corridor to Leningrad. The fighting around the Siniavino salient lasted for two weeks, and it totally exhausted both the Germans and Soviets. German artillery was still able to sweep the corridor and Soviet casualties were horrendous as they tried to push supply convoys into Leningrad. The Red Army lost more than 115,000 casualties during the battle.

With the Battle of Stalingrad drawing away German reinforcements, Army Group North was unable to replenish its losses from these battles, so when the Soviets struck again in February they had more success. The *Polizei* Division was hit by a Soviet infantry division and a ski brigade in February and forced back from the Neva. The Russians penetrated 5km (3 miles) into the Waffen-SS lines before reinforcements could be mustered to stabilize the situation. These battles cost the Germans heavily, and the Spanish 250th Infantry Division that went

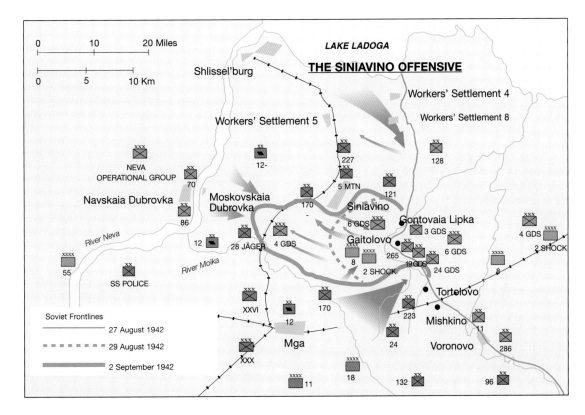

THE SINIAVINO OFFENSIVE

to the *Polizei* Division's assistance suffered 3200 casualties. On 19 March the Soviets struck once more, and the *Polizei* Division's lines were again penetrated. To push them back the 502nd Heavy Panzer Battalion sent its Tiger I tanks into action, backed by Flemish-speaking Belgian Waffen-SS volunteers of the Flandern legion. The appearance of the monster Tiger tanks sent the Russians reeling back in chaos to their start lines.

These bitter battles took a heavy toll on the *Polizei* Division and it was now able to muster only a few thousand frontline fighting troops. In the spring, plans were announced to pull the division out of the line and reform it as a panzergrenadier division. Cadres of the division began moving from Russia to Croatia in the summer, but a battlegroup remained behind to man the Neva line until the spring of 1944.

To bolster the siege lines around Leningrad, the SS chief Himmler ordered the newly formed III SS Panzer Corps to move from Croatia in December 1943. The former *Wiking* Division commander, Felix Steiner, was now in command of the corps and he soon reinvigorated the German defences around the southern rim of the Leningrad siege lines, and opposite the Oranienbaum bridgehead to the west of the city.

Between 19 August and 9 September 1942, the Red Army launched its Siniavino offensive in an attempt to relieve Leningrad. However, it was halted by a German counterattack.

Steiner's corps was only a shadow of the powerful SS panzer formations that were mustered to fight at Kursk and in Normandy. Apart from his corps headquarters staff, Steiner only brought with him one major unit, the 11th *Nordland* Panzergrenadier Division, to relieve the pressure on the remnants of the *Polizei* Division.

Nordland was the second Waffen-SS division composed mainly of Western Europeans, primarily from Scandinavia and the Low Countries, and it included Danes, Dutch, Estonians, Finns, French, Swedish and Swiss volunteers. It was formed in the summer of 1943 by combining several Waffen-SS volunteer legions. Its core unit was the *Nordland* Regiment, which was composed of Western European volunteers that had formerly been attached to the *Wiking* Division. Volunteer legions from Norway and Denmark were also absorbed into the division, along with volunteers from Hungary and Romania. It was far from lavishly equipped and manned, mustering only 11,500 men when it left Croatia for the

FELIX STEINER

Felix Steiner was born on 23 May 1886 in East Prussia. He saw fighting during World War I in the German Army, and was in officer training when war broke out. He saw action on both the Eastern and Western Fronts and stayed in the Reichswehr after 1918. Steiner became a member of the Nazi Party in the early 1930s and joined the SS. When war broke out in 1939 he was commanding the SS Regiment *Deutschland*. In the autumn of 1940, he was promoted to SS-Gruppenführer and ordered to form a new SS division made up of foreign volunteers. This became known as the *Wiking* Division, and Steiner was its first commanding officer. He led it into battle on the southern sectors of the Russian front between 1941 and 1943, where it performed well. In 1943, his experience in forming a new formation was again put to use as he was ordered to create III SS Panzer Corps. By the end of the war he was in command of an entire army near Berlin. He was absolved of any war crimes during the subsequent Nuremburg trials, and retired to write two books about the *Wiking* Division's exploits in the USSR. He died at his home on 12 May 1956.

Russian Front. The division did not yet have its own panzer battalion, and its only armoured fighting vehicles were a couple of dozen StuG III assault guns.

By the end of December 1943, Steiner's corps headquarters had taken over control of the Oranienbaum Front, with the *Nordland* Division, a regimental-sized battlegroup of the *Polizei* Division, and the 9th and 10th Luftwaffe Field divisions under its command. Army Tiger I tanks of the 502nd Heavy Tank Battalion and 88mm flak guns of the 11th SS Flak Battalion were also attached to Steiner's command. A brigade of 5000 new Dutch SS volunteers was also in the process of arriving to augment the existing Dutch legion that was already fighting outside Leningrad.

Army Group North was also able to draw upon a variety of other Waffen-SS units that were formed largely from recruits from the Baltic states. The 2nd SS Motorized Brigade was a Latvian unit that had originally been raised for internal security tasks in the summer of 1943. More Latvians were grouped into the 15th SS Grenadier Division. In the rear of the army group was an SS police squad led by Freidrich Jeckeln, one of the first Einsatzgruppe commanders, who was charged with keeping German lines of communication clear of partisans. This unit was sent to the front in December 1943 to counter a Soviet breakthrough at Nevel, in the south of the army group's sector. Forming in Estonia was the 20th SS Grenadier Division, built from more local volunteers who were far from keen to see Soviet rule return to their country. The *Polizei* Division's former commander, Karl von Pfeffer-Wildenbruch, was in the Baltic states setting up VI SS Corps that would eventually take command of locally recruited Waffen-SS units.

No amount of ornately titled units could compensate for the fact that the army group was a wasting force,

denied replacement troops, supplies and new equipment. So when the Soviets launched their new offensive in January, the Red Army soon gained tactical and operational advantage. A build-up of troops was first detected on the eastern sector and the *Polizei* Division battlegroup was rapidly deployed as a reserve to the threatened sector. Then, on 14 January, the Soviets launched a massive coordinated offensive along the length of Army Group North's front. The Second Shock Army burst out of the Oranienbaum bridgehead and rolled over the 9th and 10th Luftwaffe divisions on the extreme right of III SS Panzer Corps. They were literally crushed by artillery barrages, waves of T-34s and infantry assaults. The two units ceased to exist as fighting formations. Huge columns of Russian tanks were now streaming southwards, and driving a wedge between Steiner's Waffen-SS men and the rest of the army group. Steiner ignored orders by Hitler for his troops to fight to the last man, and he ordered a retreat. Bowing to the inevitable, Hitler agreed to allow the army group to withdraw to the Panther Line, which was being built either side of Lake Peipus, 100km (62 miles) to the rear. Hitler's orders were largely academic. The Soviet offensive was so overpowering, though, that there was little chance of it being halted east of the Panther Line.

Steiner and his men kept one step ahead of the Soviets and conducted a skilful retreat. As heavy weapons and vehicles were pulled back west, Waffen-SS detachments, such as the 23rd Panzergrenadier Regiment *Norge*, blew up bridges, mined roads and sabotaged any military equipment that could not be evacuated, such as dug-in Panther tanks. By the end of January the corps was safely behind the Narva sector of the Panther Line, between the Baltic Sea and Lake Peipus. Soviet troops of the Forty-Seventh, Second

Two soldiers of III SS Panzer Corps in northern Russia in January 1944. In the background are two disabled KV-1 tanks (note the rear-mounted machine guns).

Shock and Eighth Armies attempted to outflank the Narva defences by landing at Mereküla in February, but the Waffen-SS men were ready for them and the Soviet landing force was devastated with 350 Russians killed and 200 captured. The 2nd SS Brigade, 15th Division and the *Polizei* Division battlegroup were less lucky and spent six weeks retreating to Pskov with the remnants of the German Eighteenth Army. The "roving pocket" was almost surrounded near Luga, but dodged past the Soviet spearheads to make it back to the Panther Line by the beginning of March. As well as keeping one step ahead of the pursuing Soviet tanks, the German troops had to battle past moving bands of Soviet partisans who ambushed them in the huge forests that dominated the region.

DEFENDING THE PANTHER LINE

Once behind the Panther Line defences, the Waffen-SS units were in the forefront of efforts to drive off Soviet probing attacks that were launched with great regularity during March and April. The narrow Narva position was a natural defensive line, which the Soviets could not outflank, so the Waffen-SS defence held firm against repeated attacks.

Farther south, VI SS Corps was thrown into the line to take over command of the 1st SS Brigade and the Latvian 15th Division. It held out against two major Soviet attacks in March and sealed a dangerous penetration of the German front, supported by the *Polizei* Division battlegroup.

During the late spring and into the summer, Soviet forces were gathering their strength for a major offensive that would decisively defeat the German Army on the Eastern Front. In June the first phase unfolded with the launching of Operation Bagration, which swept all of Army Group Centre. In mid-July, Army Group North was hit. The forces south of Lake Peipus were forced to fall back when their southern flank was exposed.

In the Narva bridgehead, Steiner's Waffen-SS men had tried to build up their defences and had been reinforced with new Western European volunteers, including the Belgian Storm Brigade *Wallonien*. A dozen Panther tanks from the 11th SS Panzer Battalion bolstered the defence, as well as heavy guns from the 54th SS Heavy Artillery Regiment. When the Soviets threw a series of massive tank attacks against the Narva bridgehead in July, this engagement became known as the "Battle of the European SS" because so many foreign volunteer contingents were involved. What was left of the *Nordland* Division, plus the Dutch and Belgian brigades and the Estonians, all put up furious resistance. In one battle, for example, they knocked out more than 100 T-34s that charged the German lines.

While Steiner's men were holding their own, farther south Soviet spearheads were approaching Riga and threatening to cut off all of Army Group North from the main German forces in Lithuania and East Prussia. The situation looked desperate when Steiner was ordered to mobilize his motorized units and race from Narva to Riga

The Soviet offensive was vast in scale and intensity, and finally freed the city of Leningrad. It also marked the beginning of the Red Army's campaign to liberate the Baltic states.

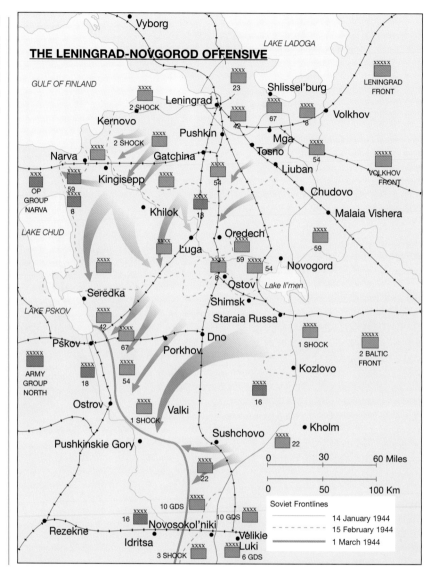

THE LENINGRAD-NOVGOROD OFFENSIVE

to set up an improvised defensive line to hold open an escape corridor. On 16 September, Steiner's corps, with the *Nordland* Division in the lead, began its 250km (155-mile) forced march and arrived in Riga from the north as Soviet troops were entering the city from the east. Steiner and his men had arrived just in time to hold open the vital escape route. As the Waffen-SS corps withdrew, it again destroyed anything of military importance: railway lines, bridges and oil refineries.

Along with the 14th Panzer Division, and the 11th and 225th Infantry Divisions, the 10,000 men of Steiner's corps defended Riga for two weeks against human-wave infantry attacks backed by heavy bomber raids. Steiner now led what was left of his corps into the Courland Peninsula to the west of Riga. It was trapped there with the rest of the army group when Soviet tanks reached the Baltic north of Memel at the end of October. A strong defensive corridor had been thrown up across the entrance to the peninsula and a large Soviet attack was driven back. In the Courland Pocket were III SS Panzer Corps and VI SS Corps. The latter comprised the 15th and 19th SS Divisions, while III SS Panzer Corps was made up of the *Nordland* Division and the 23rd SS Panzergrenadier Division *Nederland*.

In January 1945, Steiner was recalled to Germany to head up the newly formed Eleventh SS Panzer Army, and many of his units followed soon after. With Soviet troops now on the border of Germany, the fate of the army group trapped on the Courland Peninsula was precarious. The foreign volunteers who remained in Courland were looking for a means to escape the inevitable defeat. Some Scandinavian and Western European Waffen-SS started to take to boats to sail across the Baltic to safety in neutral Sweden. For the Estonian and Latvian Waffen-SS volunteers, there was no escape. Many, having been released from their oath of enlistment by their German superiors, now drifted

Two Tigers and accompanying infantry in the Courland Pocket in early 1945, a photograph that illustrates the misery of much of the fighting on the Eastern Front.

away and took refuge in the forests of their home countries to form partisan bands to fight a guerrilla war against the Soviets. Some were still fighting in the 1950s with the help of the American Central Intelligence Agency (CIA). The Americans and British saw these men as valuable allies in the Cold War against the Soviets. They turned a blind eye to their new allies' previous involvement in Hitler's élite force.

Poland, 1944

After their mauling on the Eastern Front in early 1944, the Waffen-SS panzer divisions were rested and rebuilt to bring them up to strength. Their services were soon required when the Soviet 1944 summer offensive, codenamed Bagration, broke like a thunderclap on the Eastern Front. The SS divisions fought desperately to preserve the shattered front and hold back the Red Army.

A soldier of IV SS Panzer Corps in northern Poland in late 1944. Soviet offensives had brought the Red Army to the borders of Germany itself, and not even the efforts of the Waffen-SS could reverse the tide.

On 22 June 1944, the Soviet High Command unleashed Operation Bagration. In two weeks, the Wehrmacht's Army Group Centre was dissected with almost surgical precision by Soviet pincer moves that lanced into its flanks and then chopped the weakened German forces into a series of pockets. The battle destroyed 28 German divisions and 350,000 German soldiers were either killed or captured, including 47 generals. Almost overnight, a third of the German Eastern Front had ceased to exist. Desperate measures were needed to restore the situation. Hitler turned to Field Marshal Walther Model – his master of last-ditch defence – to save the day. Soon, he would turn to the only two Waffen-SS panzer divisions then available on the Eastern Front. They would be at the centre of his efforts to form a new defence line.

The remnants of the *Leibstandarte* and *Das Reich* Divisions were immediately shipped westwards after they escaped from the Kamenets Podolsk Pocket in April, to be rebuilt to meet the Anglo-American cross-Channel invasion. *Wiking* spent most of May and early June hunting partisans in the forests of eastern Poland. New tanks, trucks, artillery and weapons arrived steadily

to bring it back up to something like a respectable strength by the end of June. The *Totenkopf* Division also received more than 6000 replacements from other Waffen-SS units and the concentration camp organization. Its most prized new asset was the return of its panzer regiment's 1st Battalion, with 79 new Panther tanks. The battalion had been training on the new tanks in Germany for several months, and it would significantly enhance the division's strike power.

As well as rebuilding the *Totenkopf* and *Wiking* Divisions, plans were made to send another SS panzer corps to the Eastern Front to lead the two divisions. IV SS Panzer Corps was formed in 1943 to train Waffen-SS forces in Western Europe, and would eventually be committed to action in Poland in August 1944, under the command of SS-Obergruppenführer Herbert Gille.

As Operation Bagration gathered momentum and the German front began to crumble, the *Totenkopf* Division was ordered to form a defence line near the Polish city of Grodno and to provide a safe haven for the remnants of the German Fourth Army, which were fleeing west ahead of the Russian advance. More than 400 tanks were soon thrown against the *Totenkopf*'s rearguard. It held them off for 11 days, until the division was ordered to fall back towards Warsaw. At this point the Luftwaffe's *Hermann Göring* Panzer Division moved up to support the *Totenkopf*, and for almost a week the two divisions held Siedlce, 80km (50 miles) east of Warsaw, in the face of attacks by the Soviet Second Tank Army (the German panzer units had arrived at the key road and rail junction on 24 July, only hours ahead of the Soviet XI Tank Corps). Luftwaffe Stuka dive-bombers also provided support in these battles.

As this battle was raging, on 27 July the Soviet High Command launched III and XVI Tank Corps, supported by VIII Guards Tank Corps, with a combined strength of some 500 tanks, in a wide flanking movement to the south. This move caught the Germans by surprise, and two days later Soviet tanks had advanced 48km (30 miles) and were in the suburbs of the Polish capital, Warsaw.

THE WARSAW UPRISING

Again, Model ordered his panzer divisions to race back to head off the Soviet spearheads. The *Totenkopf* and *Hermann Göring* Divisions, now joined by *Wiking*, were launched into a desperate counterattack to drive back the Soviet spearheads from the River Vistula. The *Wiking* Division had arrived by train in western Warsaw on 27 July, and moved through the city to take up defensive positions to hold off the Russians. The city was tense, and on 1 August the freedom fighters of the Polish Home Army rose in rebellion. All over the city guerrilla fighters attacked German-held buildings and started to fortify "liberated" zones in the city and along the western bank of the Vistula, which cut Warsaw in two. The Polish leaders depended on the swift arrival of Soviet tanks on the western side of the Vistula. However, the Home Army had failed to read the flow of the battle on the eastern bank of the Vistula between the Germans and the Soviet Second Tank Army.

As Soviet tanks cautiously entered Praga, the eastern suburb of Warsaw, during the morning of 31 July the prospects for an early liberation of Poland's capital seemed high. Unknown to the Russians, they were about to encounter a whirlwind. The *Totenkopf*, *Wiking* and *Hermann Göring* Divisions were attacking, as well as two army panzer divisions. The Soviet III Tank Corps only just managed to escape the German pincers, and by the end of the day the Soviets had been evicted from Praga. The attack was decisive and sealed the fate of the Warsaw Rising, even before it had begun. With the Germans now entrenched in Praga in strength, there was no hope that the Russians would be able easily to link up with the Polish Home Army.

The Soviets now tried a wide encircling move to the north of Warsaw. By 4 August, IV SS Panzer Corps, now with the *Totenkopf* and *Wiking* Divisions under its command, had already been ordered by Model to set up a blocking position north of the city, and was ready and waiting when the Soviet storm burst on 14 August. For a week the Waffen-SS formation held off 15 Russian infantry divisions and 2 tank corps. A Waffen-SS counterattack on 11 September drove the Soviets back, and again defeated a link-up with the Polish Home Army.

The *Totenkopf* and *Wiking* Divisions were the linchpins of the German operation to crush the Warsaw rising, even though they did not actually take part in the fighting against the Polish Home Army. By preventing a link-up with the Red Army, they consigned the population of the city to two months of siege.

RETRIBUTION

On 2 August, SS-Obergruppenführer Erich von dem Bach-Zelewski was appointed to put down the uprising – no matter what it took. Civilians and prisoners were indiscriminately butchered by Bach-Zelewski's SS special police squads and Sonderkommando. On 2 October the Poles – starving, with their ammunition supplies exhausted and all hopes of rescue by the Red Army extinguished – came out waving white flags. Hitler ordered that all of the city's population be deported. Many of them ended up in SS death camps.

IV SS Panzer Corps, flushed with victory, remained on duty in northeastern Poland for the rest of 1944, where it tried to hold the line against repeated Soviet offensives that started on 10 October. It had to fall back at the end of that month, but the front soon stabilized as the Russian drive ran out of momentum once more.

The Soviet High Command was now preoccupied with clearing out the Balkans. Russian troops swept through Romania, Yugoslavia, Bulgaria and up to the borders of Hungary. In October 1944 the Hungarians were wavering, so Hitler ordered the launch of Operation Panzerfaust to seize key points throughout the country's capital, Budapest. Adolf Hitler's daring Waffen-SS commando leader, Otto Skorzeny, led a raid to seize Hungarian government leaders. Other SS and army units then occupied the city and prepared it for defence. At this point Soviet troops were only a few kilometres from Budapest, and by Christmas the city would be encircled. When that happened some 70,000 German troops would be trapped.

The combat performance of the Waffen-SS divisions was the only bright spot in a gloomy strategic situation on the Eastern Front. At the end of 1944, the Eastern Front had been pushed back to the borders of Germany

Operation Bagration destroyed the German Army Group Centre. Red Army forces committed to the offensive numbered 1,254,000 men, 2715 tanks and 1355 assault guns.

itself. Soviet troops were poised to strike at the very heart of the Third Reich.

As the collapse of Army Group Centre was being played out, the head of the Waffen-SS special forces, Otto Skorzeny, deployed several of his commando teams, or jagdverbande, to try to establish contact with isolated pockets of German troops. Skorzeny's jagdverbande were formed to operate in specific regions. Units included an "eastern" battalion trained to operate on the Russian Front, a "southeastern" battalion trained to work

in the Balkans, a Central European unit and a West European unit. The Luftwaffe wing, Kampfgeschwader (KG) 200, was assigned to work with Skorzeny to fly and parachute his men far behind enemy lines.

KG 200 flew deep behind Soviet lines and dropped the Waffen-SS teams on their dangerous missions. All except Jagdverbande Southeast were quickly cornered by the Red Army and wiped out. When the Soviets smashed the German forces in Romania in August, Jagdverbande Southeast was destroyed.

The Waffen-SS and the Partisan War

The Waffen-SS war against anti-Nazi partisans in Russia and Yugoslavia was a complete disaster. Faced with an enemy that was both elusive and tenacious, SS units responded with ever greater use of terror. This only served to alienate further the indigenous population, creating an ever-larger potential pool of recruits for those waging war against their German occupiers.

The SD searches for suspected partisans in Poland in 1940. Any piece of evidence, however flimsy, was enough to incarcerate suspects and their families, often in concentration camps.

At the height of the Nazi Blitzkrieg campaigns in October 1941, German rule stretched from the Bay of Biscay to the outskirts of Moscow. Hitler's soldiers did not bring freedom or liberation to the peoples of Europe, but oppression. Arbitrary arrests, torture and forced labour soon became commonplace across the continent. Yet although the Germans had defeated almost every army in Europe, they could not so easily break the spirit of resistance that was growing by the day.

Armed resistance to German rule took on many forms, ranging from localized acts of sabotage to large-scale guerrilla warfare. German strategy for defeating partisans was fatally flawed from the beginning, because of Hitler's racial views and his open contempt for the peoples of Eastern Europe, whom he regarded as *untermenschen* or subhumans. Conventional strategies of counter-insurgency warfare, involving winning over rebellious populations with rewards or political concessions, were rejected by Hitler, who only wanted to subjugate and then exterminate peoples who did not belong to his Aryan master race.

As German troops rampaged through Europe, anyone who showed any sign of resisting Nazi rule, or was even judged to be capable of acting as a catalyst for resistance, was dealt with ruthlessly. Thousands were executed in random shootings and others arrested, tortured and shipped out to concentration camps. The only attempt to enlist local allies involved the setting up of pro-Nazi puppet regimes in Western Europe. In the East, such a luxury was not attempted; even anti-Soviet Slavs were still *untermenschen* in Hitler's view and did not warrant any political role. Police auxiliaries were recruited in Eastern Europe, but they were only used at first to help SS Einsatzgruppen to massacre Jews and other "racial inferiors". This role tapped into the latent anti-semitism in the Ukraine and the Baltic states, and indeed many of these auxiliary forces outdid their German masters in brutality. In the long term, this did nothing to win over the population to the German cause, and only served to create more discontent and further stoked the fires of resistance in the occupied territories.

Once the partisan war was under way in earnest, German forces followed a policy of showing no mercy to anyone who engaged in partisan activity or was suspected of supporting them. Captured partisans were routinely executed, and whole villages were razed to the

Right: Jews taken prisoner during the Warsaw ghetto uprising in 1943. Moments after this photograph was taken, these Jews were machine-gunned.

Below: A member of the Jewish resistance in Warsaw, the Jewish Fighting Organization, gives himself up to German troops. Himmler said of the ghetto: "The former living quarters of the 500,000 *untermenschen* must disappear; the city of Warsaw, always a dangerous seat of decay and subversion, must be reduced in size."

ground for providing comfort to enemies of the Third Reich (or even for being suspected of doing so).

Occupied Russia and Yugoslavia were the main theatres of partisan conflict for most of the war, although French and Greek partisans escalated their struggle into open warfare as German forces retreated during the summer of 1944. There was some partisan action in Italy from late 1944 onwards, but this was not on the scale of the conflict in Yugoslavia or Russia. By 1943, huge areas of Russia and Yugoslavia were in the hands of partisan forces and more than a million German soldiers, along with locally recruited auxiliary forces, had been diverted to combat the partisan threat. As the problem intensified, the Waffen-SS was increasingly drawn into this brutal and seemingly endless struggle.

Russia was by far the biggest theatre of partisan warfare for the Germans, and from late 1941 the Waffen-SS was actively involved in the struggle to crush this threat to Nazi rule. German plans to rule occupied Russia called for a sector, or operations zone, 160km (100 miles) behind the frontline to be controlled by the army. Each of the three army groups – North, Centre and South – had an army rear-area commandant who was responsible for ensuring the lines of communications to the fighting troops remained open. Three divisions of security troops were assigned to each army group to allow the commandants to protect key bridges, roads, railway junctions and supply dumps. These were largely second-rate units, often made up of medically downgraded recruits who suffered from flat feet and stomach ulcers, and who lacked heavy weapons and armoured vehicles.

Behind the operational zone, the Germans divided Russia into two Reich commissariats, with one covering the Baltic states and Belorussia, known as the Ostland Commissariat, and the other responsible for running the Ukraine. These were civilian branches of the German Government, and were responsible for the economic exploitation of Eastern Europe's population and natural resources. German civilian police units and locally recruited auxiliary police units were nominally responsible for security in the two commissariats, but they were soon overwhelmed by the task as partisan bands spread throughout Russia and the Baltic states. The German system of government and exploitation in the USSR was modelled on that set up in Poland after September 1939, where the Reich General Government had been established to control the rump of the country after the occupation. In Poland, the SS had deployed 12 police regiments and 14 battalions of locally recruited police, dubbed "Schumas".

Overlaying the military and civilian administration of Eastern Europe, Reichsführer-SS Himmler had set up a system of parallel control via representatives dubbed the "Higher SS and Police Leaders". They were posted to a series of headquarters that mirrored every level of army and civilian administration in the East, so Himmler's men were able to act quickly to stamp out any sign of resistance. In theory, they had the job of coordinating the activities of the Gestapo, the SD, German civil police, army and locally recruited auxiliaries. They thus soon became a law unto themselves.

In the first months after Operation Barbarossa, the Higher SS and Police Leaders and their staffs were pre-occupied with coordinating the activities of the four Einsatzgruppen that were combing occupied Russia to eliminate its Jewish population. This took a year or so, and then the SS hierarchy in the East turned its attention to setting up ghettos in several major cities and towns to accommodate Jews forcibly evicted from their homes in Western Europe, before they could be shipped to the extermination camps.

The core of the SS occupation force was provided by 14 SS police regiments in Belorussia and seven locally recruited "rifle regiments". A major effort was made to recruit Schuma battalions from the Baltic states. Some 26 Schuma battalions were eventually deployed in the Baltic states; 64 others, comprising some 26,000 men, eventually operated elsewhere in occupied Russia alongside the SS police.

Waffen-SS and army units transiting through occupied Russia or garrisoned behind the front for training and recuperation were often mobilized by the local Higher SS and Police Leaders to participate in various missions. It was a brave Waffen-SS or Wehrmacht officer who refused to carry out the requests of the personal representatives of Himmler. These tasks could range from anti-partisan sweeps to the premeditated massacres of Jews.

The most infamous incident of this type occurred in Poland with the crushing of the uprising in the Jewish ghetto in Warsaw in April 1943. When the surviving 60,000 Jews in the ghetto decided to fight back rather than meekly be transported to Nazi death camps, the SS leadership in Poland mobilized a task force of 800 Waffen-SS troops, 800 SS policemen, 100 Wehrmacht soldiers and 340 Ukrainian and Baltic auxiliaries to crush the rebellion. This force first surrounded the ghetto and then systematically burnt and demolished every building inside to flush out the resistance. Over a month later, the SS police general Jürgen Stroop boasted that his men had rounded up 56,000 prisoners, and killed 7000 in the course of the operation. The one-sided nature of this struggle is reflected by the fact that Stroop's men only managed to recover nine rifles and 59 pistols, along with several hundred hand grenades and improvised weapons from the ruins of the ghetto. The erasing of the Warsaw ghetto was a massacre, not a battle.

In Russia, the Higher SS and Police Leaders soon became key figures in the partisan war. As far as Himmler and the SS were concerned, the campaign to eliminate

OSKAR DIRLEWANGER

Dr Oskar Dirlewanger was one of the most unsavoury men to have been associated with the Waffen-SS. Born on 26 September 1895, he was a very brave and intelligent individual. However, for all his natural gifts, he was also singularly unsuited to civilian life. His violent and perverted tendencies (he served a prison sentence for molestation) found a niche in Nazi military life. Using old contacts who had risen in the Nazi Party, Dirlewanger was given a reserve Waffen-SS rank and headed a unit known as the *Dirlewanger* Brigade. This unit was made up of the dregs of society: murderers, concentration camp prisoners and many other assorted "undesirables". Dirlewanger's men acquired a reputation for brutality and violence. As partisan hunters they took part in operations in the Balkans and on the Eastern Front. Dirlewanger won the Knight's Cross in September 1944 for his actions, and this is probably the most positive thing that can be said about him. He died on the night of 4/5 June 1945 after Polish forces captured him and tortured him to death. A gruesome end for a man who excelled at and lived by violence.

the Jews was identical to the struggle against the parti-sans. In July 1941 Himmler appointed a top SS officer, Erich von dem Bach-Zelewski, to be Higher SS and Police Leader in the Army Group Centre rear operations zone. His first job was to comb the Pripet Marshes look-ing for Jews. In September 1941 he declared his philosophy, stating that "where there is a Jew, there is a partisan, and wherever there is a partisan there is a Jew".

Bach-Zelewski basically took over all anti-partisan operations in central Russia during 1941 and into 1942, organizing joint sweeps of partisan-controlled territory with Waffen-SS troops and army units. He was provided with a number of Waffen-SS units, including a motorized infantry brigade and the cavalry brigade led by Hermann Fegelein. Along with assorted police units, the SS general had some 36,000 men under his direct command and could also call on several thousand army soldiers. Fegelein was particularly zealous in his work, launching a series of killing actions in the Pripet Marshes that left 1000 suspected partisans, 699 Red Army soldiers and 14,178 Jews dead.

THE PARTISAN THREAT GROWS

Bach-Zelewski's men soon found themselves caught in a maelstrom of partisan fighting during the winter of 1941, as tens of thousands of Soviet troops who had been bypassed by the panzer spearheads started to band together, along with peasants alienated by German oppression, and strike back. German garrisons were raided, railway lines blown up, truck convoys ambushed and collaborators assassinated. Belorussia was the centre of partisan activity against the Germans, and the region's huge forests offered them the perfect sanctuary. By the end of 1941, the partisan bands were receiving help from the Soviet High Command and their attacks were coordinated with Red Army offensives. These bands at first only mustered a few hundred men, but by the time German troops were driven off Russian soil in the summer of 1944 several hundred thousand partisans were in operation.

By early 1942 Bach-Zelewski's Waffen-SS men were no longer facing unarmed Jewish villagers who meekly lined up to be machine-gunned, but well-armed and motivated partisans. When the Waffen-SS men suffered casualties at the hands of the partisans it enraged Bach-Zelewski, who ordered even more barbaric reprisals. If partisans fired on German troops from villages, then the village was torched and the villagers' crops and cattle confiscated, before the population was either conscripted as forced labour or executed. Huge swathes of central Russia were laid bare and tens of

thousands of people were forced to flee to towns controlled by the Germans, or to the forests to take shel-ter with the partisans.

In September 1942, the partisan problem was so out of control that Himmler was able to persuade Hitler that it was all the army's fault and that he should be put in charge of the partisan war. Himmler appointed Bach-Zelewski as his chief of anti-partisan units on the entire Eastern Front.

Over the next three years the Germans mounted 43 large scale anti-partisan operations in Russia, the vast majority in the Belorussia region. Bach-Zelewski was no SS bureaucrat but a man who led from the front. He was often found at the head of anti-partisan sweeps, and he particularly liked to fly over partisan-controlled territory in his Luftwaffe Fieseler Storch light aircraft looking for possible targets. One of his favourite tricks was to machine-gun villages from his aircraft in the hope of prompting any partisans taking shelter into returning fire. This would give him the justification to move in his troops to liquidate the offending village's population.

THE FAILURE OF ANTI-PARTISAN MEASURES

As the partisan war escalated through the summer of 1942, it was soaking up an increasing number of German Army troops. With the Red Army resurgent, the Wehrmacht needed every man at the front, and a new source of manpower was sought to take over the burden of fighting the partisans. Himmler now turned to the auxiliary Schuma police units. Ukrainian Catholics from the Galicia region and the Baltic states were initially a fertile recruiting ground for these auxiliary units, and Himmler was soon admitting them into the ranks of his Waffen-SS.

Ultimately, the German anti-partisan effort in Russia was a major disaster. The brutal tactics of Bach-Zelewski and his Waffen-SS soldiers totally turned the population against the German cause. At the height of the decisive 1943 summer campaign season, for example, the parti-sans were able to disrupt German supplies in key sectors and severely hamper the ability of the Wehrmacht to resist the advance of the Red Army. Stalin, although initially suspicious of the partisans (they were behind the German lines and thus outside his area of control), was soon lavishing praise on their ability to cause the Germans trouble. The Waffen-SS was a major factor in losing Germany the partisan war in Russia.

In Yugoslavia, the partisan war again sucked in large numbers of Waffen-SS troops as the conflict escalated out of control, because of heavy handed German responses to attacks on their troops. The basic German

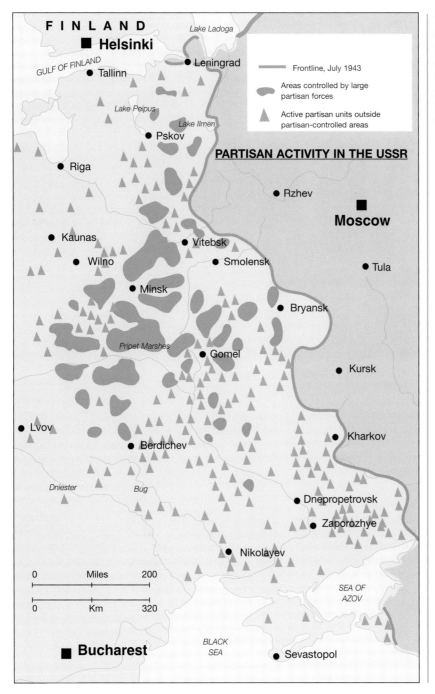

The scale of partisan activity behind German lines in July 1943. The partisans diverted large numbers of Wehrmacht troops away from the frontline, and also had a damaging effect on German morale.

PARTISAN ACTIVITY IN THE USSR

strategy in Yugoslavia was one of "divide and rule", using locally recruited forces to avoid having to divert large numbers of Wehrmacht troops from the Eastern Front for occupation duties in what was considered a strategic backwater. Yugoslavia's complex ethnic mix played into the Germans' hands, and allowed them to break up the country. The Germans gave the Dalmatian coast, Kosovo and what is now Slovenia to the Italians. Romania,

The Germans' answer to partisan attacks – public executions. In their anti-partisan sweeps the army and SS were largely indifferent to the guilt or innocence of victims.

Bulgaria and Hungary were rewarded with chunks of territory along their borders. The rump of Serbia and Bosnia was placed under direct German rule. Croatia became an "independent" fascist state.

Responsibility for internal security was initially in the hands of the Wehrmacht, which was primarily interested in keeping open lines of communications to Greek ports to supply German troops fighting the British in North Africa. The SS presence was restricted at first to intelligence and secret police operatives, whose main interest was in playing one ethnic group off against the other. Higher SS and Police Leaders headquarters were set up in each of the main regions of Yugoslavia and they operated independently of the Wehrmacht High Command in the country. The SS drafted in several of its police regiments and strong contingents of Gestapo agents to give their leaders in Yugoslavia some backup. They soon got to work arresting and executing anti-German elements throughout the country. Not surprisingly, this generated both fear and resentment among large segments of the population.

By late 1941, the first partisan bands were attacking German and Italian troops throughout the country. The Yugoslav partisan movement was at first split between royalist groups of mainly Serbian origin and the communists led by Josip Broz, better known as Marshal Tito. Skilful manoeuvrings by the Germans brought many of the royalists, or Chetniks, over to their cause, which led Hitler to think he had little to worry about in Yugoslavia. The Croats had been pro-German since before the 1941 invasion, and they proved some of the most loyal allies during the anti-partisan campaign in Yugoslavia. Tito's communist partisans soon proved highly effective, and their nationalist ideals inspired an increasing number of Yugoslavs to resist their occupiers. His partisans became a thorn in the side of German occupation forces in the Balkans. In three years of war, Tito managed to raise a large partisan force in the mountainous interior of Yugoslavia, tying down 700,000 German and allied troops by early 1944.

In early 1942, the growing partisan threat and the apparent inability of the Wehrmacht garrison to deal with it led Himmler to take a greater interest in events in Yugoslavia. The Waffen-SS was ordered to raise a division specifically to help in the anti-partisan effort. The 7th SS Mountain Division *Prinz Eugen* was mobilized in Serbia in March 1942, recruited mainly from so-called ethnic Germans (Volksdeutsche) from Southeastern Europe, with a core of Austrians to provide the mountaineering expertise. Its first commander, Artur Phleps, would become a key figure in the German Yugoslav campaign. A few dozen captured French Renault and Soviet tanks were provided to give the division some armoured firepower. Higher SS and Police Leaders also set about recruiting Croats into the local police, including some moulded into a pseudo SS-style unit dubbed the Einsatzstaffel, and 15,000 auxiliary policemen who formed 15 Schuma-style battalions. Some 10 Serbian auxiliary battalions and 2 Albanian police regiments were created. These men formed the nucleus of future Waffen-SS divisions recruited from Yugoslavia.

The *Prinz Eugen* Division took part in a series of German search-and-destroy operations in the mountains along the Serbian-Montenegrin border during the autumn of 1942. These were aimed at surrounding suspected partisan bases, and then sweeping through them to capture or kill any partisans and civilians suspected of aiding them. At first the operations were small-scale affairs involving a few battalions, but as the size of the partisan bands began to expand the Germans had to resort to multi-divisional operations.

By the winter of 1942–43, the Germans were having to draw in an increasing number of Wehrmacht, Waffen-SS, Italian and locally recruited troops to generate the manpower for setting up effective cordons around partisan bases. In response, the partisans infiltrated networks of spies into the Italian and locally recruited forces to give them advance warning of German-led operations against them. German commanders then set up special forces squads to penetrate partisan-held areas, and to provide detailed intelligence of partisan deployments to allow effective offensives to be launched.

Even with these innovative tactics, as well as having command of the air and the sea, the Germans were unable to contain Tito's partisans. The nimble partisans always seemed to be able to escape from the traps set for them by the Germans. The division of authority between the SS and the Wehrmacht High Command in Yugoslavia was a major factor in the German strategic failure. The military response to Tito's partisans was

Soviet partisans. By the middle of 1943, there were an estimated 700,000 partisan fighters operating behind German lines in the Soviet Union.

bedevilled by the conflicting policies of the SS and the Wehrmacht. Both organizations pursued different agendas, with the SS policy of terror stoking the resistance to the Wehrmacht, who were trying to pacify the country. Theoretically, Waffen-SS combat units operated in Yugoslavia under tactical control of the Wehrmacht when they were participating in anti-partisan operations, but in reality they split their time between following army and SS orders.

Himmler expanded his involvement in the Yugoslav theatre during the summer of 1943, when he formed V SS Mountain Corps headquarters to take command of Waffen-SS units fighting Tito's partisans. He had also begun to form a new division of Bosnian Muslims to capitalize on their hatred of the Croats and Serbs. Titled the *Handschar* Division, the new unit was formed in France and had specially designed uniforms, including fez headwear. The veteran *Prinz Eugen* divisional commander, Phleps, was put in charge of the corps headquarters that started to move to Yugoslavia in the autumn of 1943.

Italy's surrender in September 1943 forced the Germans to expand dramatically the size of their zone of control in Yugoslavia. This resulted in V SS Corps being given responsibility for the Dalmatian Coast, with the *Prinz Eugen* Division as its core unit because the *Handschar* Division was still in France after a mutiny severely disrupted its training.

During the following winter the corps took over responsibility for all of Bosnia, and set up its headquarters in Sarajevo. Its main job was to try to keep open strategic road and rail communications through the country's mountainous interior, which proved a thankless and never-ending task.

Major anti-partisan operations conducted by V SS Corps in late 1943 included Operation Autumn Storm, which was supposed to lead to the destruction of the partisan units in eastern Bosnia. The German units had to comb an enormous area, so the bulk of Tito's men slipped through their narrowing ring. The partisans suffered 9000 casualties in the course of the operation, and were immediately pursued in Operation Snowstorm: twin drives to the west and northwest. Concluded by the end of December, these operations cost the partisans an additional 2000 men. The *Prinz Eugen* Division was in the thick of the action, alongside Wehrmacht units fighting under SS command. Terrible winter weather conditions took a heavy toll on German and partisan forces alike.

Despite five large-scale offensives mounted by Axis forces in Yugoslavia, Tito's partisan movement survived and thrived.

ANTI-PARTISAN OPERATIONS IN YUGOSLAVIA

GERMANY

SLOVENIA
Ljubljana

HUNGARY

ROMANIA

Trieste

Zagreb

CROATIA

Fiume

BOSNIA-
HERZEGOVINA

Belgrade

Bela Crkva

Valjevo

Zadar

Jajce

Sarajevo

Ljubovija

Prozor

Ancona

Jablanica

Foc̆a

Pljevlja

Ras̆ka

Nis

ITALY

Split

Kolas̆in

Novi Pazar

Dubrovnik

Niks̆i̇c

MONTENEGRO

Skopje

Axis-occupied

Independent state of Croatia

Offensives against Tito's partisans

1   Sept–Dec 1941

2   January 1942

3   June 1942

4   Jan–March 1943

5   May–June 1943

ALBANIA

MACEDONIA

Tirana

| 0 | Miles | 150 |
| 0 | Km | 240 |

Ferocious fighting took place in remote mountain regions, where troops had to carry all their supplies and ammunition on their backs or loaded onto mules. The German command of the air gave them some advantage, although the partisans' local knowledge meant they were usually one step ahead of their pursuers. Few prisoners were taken by either side and the Germans also dealt ruthlessly with any local civilians they suspected of giving succour to the partisans. This led to strong suspicions that the enemy casualty figures claimed by the Germans for their anti-partisan forces also included thousands of innocent civilians.

Though badly battered in these operations, the major partisan units retained their cohesion and Tito's troops were still an effective fighting force. The partisans were now operating in division-sized units, with around 20,000 troops concentrated in mountain bases, and were increasingly being supplied by air by British and American aircraft flying from bases in Italy. Time was running out for the Germans in the Balkans.

In April 1944, V SS Corps organized a major sweep against partisan units in northern Bosnia, under the codename Operation Maypole, which again failed to trap its prey. German intelligence discovered the location of Tito's mountain headquarters in the town of Drvar, in what is now western Bosnia, and German Army

Partisans in Yugoslavia. In their attempts to play on ethnic divisions in the country, plus their usual heavy handedness, the Germans aided recruitment to the partisan movement.

---

commanders in the Balkans organized a corps-sized operation to surround and then destroy the partisan base. As the ground operation got under way, the 500th SS Parachute Battalion was to land by glider around Tito's headquarters and capture the partisan leader, as well as British, Russian and American advisors working with him.

Operation Knight's Move was compromised from the start by partisan agents who spotted the movement of the ground troops towards Drvar, so when the first gliders started landing on 24 May 1944 they were met by fully alert defenders. The first wave of SS men was massacred by Yugoslav fire, allowing Tito to escape down a rope ladder. He was soon on his personal train and heading for safety. More paratroopers landed and soon they were fighting hand-to-hand with the partisans. By the time the ground column relieved the SS detachment, it was all but wiped out. More than 250 Germans were killed and 880 wounded in the operation.

During the summer of 1944, the partisan war escalated dramatically and V SS Corps' troops were involved

in almost weekly anti-partisan sweeps around Sarajevo and eastern Bosnia. It was now joined by the *Handschar* Division, as well as by the newly formed Albanian (*Skanderbeg*) and Croat (*Kama*) Waffen-SS divisions. The intensity of the partisan fighting in Yugoslavia and Russia was recognized in 1944 when veterans of the conflict were given their own decoration, the Anti-Partisan Badge. Within the Waffen-SS and SS police, the badge was highly prized because it acknowledged the ferocity of the fighting against the partisans. The SS, however, still showed contempt towards their partisan foes, who were dubbed "bandits" or "illegal combatants" who did not warrant any rights under the rules of war. Captured partisans were either executed on the spot or dispatched to slave-labour camps.

As in Russia, the German anti-partisan campaign in Yugoslavia was doomed to failure because no real effort was made to win the population over to Berlin's cause. The barbaric behaviour of German units, particularly SS police and Waffen-SS divisions, and their local allies, was in fact instrumental in helping the partisans portray themselves as fighting a "war of national liberation".

V SS Corps, and in particular the *Prinz Eugen* Division, ultimately played an important role in allowing thousands of German troops to escape from Greece, but in the end this made little difference to the outcome to

Despite having 700,000 troops in Yugoslavia by 1944, Axis forces were not able to defeat Tito. By 1945 partisan forces (shown here) had become a professional army.

the war in the Balkans. The drive by Soviet troops into Romania and Bulgaria in the autumn of 1944 threatened to trap 350,000 German troops in Greece. This included the remnants of the Waffen-SS *Polizei* Division that had been part of the German garrison in Greece since late 1943. Bulgaria changed sides and its troops invaded the region, now known as Macedonia, to try to cut the escape route of the German forces that were in full retreat from Greece. The *Prinz Eugen* Division moved into Macedonia and set up a bridge-head in the Vardar corridor to allow the German withdrawal to proceed successfully.

Soviet tank columns were now approaching Belgrade across the Danube plain, and V SS Corps was re-deployed to try to establish a solid front south of the city in the Nis region. It spent two months fighting a determined rearguard action against pursuing Soviet, Bulgarian and Yugoslav troops as the Germans retreated into Hungary. During these battles, V SS Corps' commander, Phleps, was captured and summarily executed by Soviet troops.

Part VII

Defeat in the West

1944

Rebuilding the Panzer Divisions

From the hedgerows of Normandy to the icy valleys of the Ardennes, the Waffen-SS panzer divisions proved to be the toughest opponents the Western Allies faced during the final year of the war. By 1944 the premier Waffen-SS divisions were among the strongest and best-led formations in the German order of battle, and proved to be tenacious foes.

A StuG III assault gun of the 16th SS Panzergrenadier Division *Reichsführer-SS* being loaded onto rail transport for shipment to Italy in early 1944. The division had a StuG battalion comprising three batteries.

Buoyed by the success of the Waffen-SS at Kharkov in 1943, Hitler wanted more Waffen-SS panzer divisions. Hausser's corps headquarters, now dubbed II SS Panzer Corps, was itself pulled out of Russia after the failed Kursk offensive and moved to France to begin raising another two Waffen-SS divisions, the *Hohenstaufen* and *Frundsberg*. In the autumn of 1943 a new designation system was introduced, with the panzergrenadier divisions officially being renamed panzer divisions. For example, the premier Waffen-SS unit became the 1st SS Panzer Division *Leibstandarte-SS Adolf Hitler* (LSSAH).

Although it was not affiliated to the two Waffen-SS panzer corps, the 17th SS Panzergrenadier Division *Götz von Berlichingen* was also formed at this point, and it would later go on to play a prominent part in the battles on the Western Front during the following year.

The new Waffen-SS panzer units were initially slow to take shape, with new recruits and equipment arriving in dribs and drabs. As winter approached, and it became clear that the British and Americans would soon launch their invasion of France, the pace of training and equipping increased. Soon new tanks, armoured halftracks and other weapons were flowing to the Waffen-SS in France.

The *Hitlerjugend* Division received the highest priority for men and equipment. Its cadre of *Leibstandarte* instructors was soon whipping the young 17- and 18-year-olds of the division into shape. Lack of time meant the division concentrated on battlefield skills, not parade drills. Tactical exercises with live ammunition were the norm. Panzer crews were sent to tank factories in Germany to help build the vehicles they would soon drive into battle.

The *Hitlerjugend* Division was soon conducting complicated battalion, then regimental, and finally divisional, exercises. By the spring of 1944, the division boasted nearly 20,000 soldiers and an almost complete inventory of vehicles and equipment, as well as a high standard of training.

The *Frundsberg* and *Hohenstaufen* Divisions were not quite as lavishly equipped and trained, but nonetheless they were to benefit from a trip to the Eastern Front in April 1944 to help the First Panzer Army break out of a Soviet encirclement. They saw limited action and allowed Hausser's successor, Willi Bittrich, to see his units in battle and to sideline a number of incompetent unit commanders. The troops themselves fought well

Right: A Tiger I of one of the SS heavy tank battalions that was formed in Germany in early 1944. These units were numbered 101st, 102nd and 103rd.

Below: An 88mm Nashorn tank destroyer in action on the Eastern Front. These vehicles were organized into independent units attached to corps and armies. They also fought in the West in 1944.

and showed much potential. They stayed in the Ukraine on temporary "loan" to the Eastern Front until early June, when they were recalled to France to fight in Normandy. On their return they would put up an impressive performance, on a par with the other Waffen-SS units. Bittrich's headquarters team was also first rate, and would later inflict the only strategic defeat on the Allies during the northwest European campaign. This famous defeat was one that would take place at Nijmegen and Arnhem in September 1944.

Languishing in the south of France, the 17th SS Panzergrenadier Division was at the bottom of the list for receiving new equipment. Its inventory was to number only a single assault gun battalion of StuG IIIs by the time the Allied landings occurred in Normandy in June.

Shattered by their experiences on the Eastern Front, the *Leibstandarte* and *Das Reich* Divisions were pulled back to France in the spring of 1944. There, they would be rebuilt so that they could act as the spearhead for Hitler's counter-invasion strategy. The half-starved and lice-infested remnants of the two divisions were in no shape to do much beyond clean and repair their paltry stocks of weapons and vehicles.

Then the Waffen-SS replacement and supply system started to kick in. The new soldiers and equipment were suddenly beginning to arrive in large quantities. Time was short, however, and the quality of the new recruits left a lot to be desired. Most of them were drafted youngsters, or former Luftwaffe (air force) and navy personnel. They were not of the same ilk as the volunteers who had made their way into the ranks of the élite Waffen-SS divisions earlier in the war. The cadre of *Leibstandarte* and *Das Reich* veterans had to begin almost from scratch. They found themselves teaching these new Waffen-SS men basic soldiering skills while also having to indoctrinate them into the special philosophy of their "divisional family".

Crucially, by the late spring of 1944, France and Belgium were hotbeds of resistance sabotage activity, and the Allied air forces had started to concentrate their air attacks on communications links in the run-up to D-Day. This made it almost impossible for the two divisions

HETZER

The Jagdpanzer 38 (t) "Hetzer" (baiter) was developed as a dedicated tank hunter, capable of defeating the Allied powers' latest armour. Based on the redesigned hull of the Czech PzKpfw 38 (t), the Jagdpanzer 38 (t) entered German service in July 1944. It was armed with the 75mm Pak 39 L/48 anti-tank cannon and protected by sloped armour, reaching 600mm (23.6in) in thickness at the front. Crewed by four men, it carried 41 rounds of ammunition and had a 7.62mm machine gun for close protection and anti-air defence. Some 1577 vehicles of this type had been produced by the war's end, seeing service with the Waffen-SS on the Eastern and Western Fronts.

Type:	tank destroyer
Length:	6.27m (20.6ft)
Width:	2.63m (8.6ft)
Height:	2.1m (6.9ft)
Crew:	4
Armament:	1 x 75mm, 1 x 7.92mm
Range:	161km (100 miles)
Speed:	26kmh (16mph)

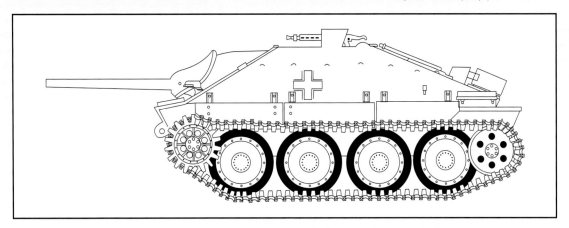

to take their young recruits out on large-scale manoeuvres. When the invasion came, they would go into battle with half-trained units that were unused to operating together. This would put even greater strain on the remaining Eastern Front veterans.

By the late spring of 1944, the five Waffen-SS panzer and one panzergrenadier divisions earmarked to repulse the impending Allied invasion of France boasted some of the most powerful weapons in the German arsenal. The most common tank was the Panzer V Panther. With its sloped armour, wide tracks and powerful, long 75mm cannon, it could outshoot, outmanoeuvre and out-armour almost every Allied tank.

The Panther could take out the most common Allied tank, the Sherman, at a range of 2000m (6562ft). In marked contrast, a Sherman tank had to close to within 500m (1640ft) to stand a chance of penetrating the sloped side armour of the German monster. The lighter Panzer IV was more evenly matched with the Sherman but, as it was equipped with a 75mm gun, would still enjoy a considerable advantage in range. Also, the protection afforded by its add-on armoured skirts was highly efficient in neutralizing both the hollow-charge bazookas and the PIAT guns that would be aimed at them in France.

The most feared tank in the German arsenal was the Tiger I, with its famous 88mm cannon. Its 100mm (3.9in) frontal armour rendered most Allied tank guns useless. The only thing that stood a chance of piercing the frontal armour of the Tiger was the British 17-pounder gun, a weapon that boasted a revolutionary discarding tungsten sabot round. Contrary to popular belief, the monster Tiger II tank never served with the two Waffen-SS heavy panzer battalions in the fighting in Normandy. One army battalion was directed to the Western Front, but it never got to Normandy, as it was caught up in the German rout during August 1944. The Waffen-SS would not see the benefits of these giant tanks until they used them in the Ardennes offensive of December 1944.

Waffen-SS units also had large numbers of Jagdpanzer IV, StuG III and Marder self-propelled guns at their disposal. These machines were constructed on converted tank chassis, but lacked rotating turrets. Their heavy cannons were mounted low in their hulls, and this had the advantage of making them easy to camouflage. They were found to be ideal as defensive weapons. The Jagdpanzer IV was based on a Panzer IV chassis and it had the same long-barrelled 75mm cannon as the Panther and thick, sloped armour.

Tiger Is, Panthers and other vehicles en route from Germany to the West for the Waffen-SS divisions and heavy tank battalions being organized to meet the Allied invasion.

The StuG III was smaller, being based on the obsolete Panzer III, but it had a useful 75mm cannon. The Marder was a lightly armoured tank hunter, built on a Czech tank chassis, and mounting the incredibly powerful 76.2mm anti-tank gun, the design of which had been captured from the Russians.

The most powerful anti-tank units in the Waffen-SS divisions were the 88mm flak guns of the divisional anti-aircraft artillery battalion. These guns could punch through the armour of any Allied tank at an unrivalled range of more than 2500m (8202ft).

At the heart of each Waffen-SS panzer division were two panzergrenadier or mechanized infantry regiments, each of which had an anti-tank company, supplied either with Marders or towed Pak 40 anti-tank guns. Panzergrenadier companies were lavishly equipped with the shoulder-fired Panzerschreck anti-tank rocket launcher, which was copied from the American bazooka, or the "throw-away" one-shot Panzerfaust anti-tank

rocket. These weapons turned every infantry squad into a tank-hunting unit.

One panzergrenadier battalion in each division was mounted in armoured SdKfz 251 halftracks, known as SPWs, to allow it to accompany the panzer battalion close to the enemy. The other five panzergrenadier battalions were carried in soft-skinned trucks. The divisional reconnaissance battalion also had armoured halftracks, as well as Marders.

Supporting the frontline Waffen-SS troops was an array of powerful artillery systems. A number of self-propelled howitzers called Wespes, with 105mm guns, and Hummels, with 150mm weapons, were mixed with towed 105mm and 150mm guns in divisional artillery regiments.

Each panzergrenadier battalion also had its own infantry gun company which boasted self-propelled 150mm and 75mm guns, as well as 120mm heavy mortars. Corps-level firepower was provided by Nebelwerfer multiple rocket launchers.

Their experience of three brutal campaign seasons in Russia had transformed the Waffen-SS panzer divisions into some of the most professional armoured formations the world has ever seen. Under experienced commanders – such as Hausser, Dietrich, Bittrich, Kurt "Panzer"

Meyer and Joachim Peiper – the Waffen-SS panzer divisions were trained up and inspired to become masters of their art.

Central to German armoured doctrine was the idea of the all-arms battlegroup (or kampfgruppe). Unlike in Allied armies, it was considered routine for the Waffen-SS quickly to form kampfgruppen. These battlegroups would combine tank, panzergrenadier, anti-tank, reconnaissance and artillery units and would operate under a single commander. There was no set size or shape of a kampfgruppe, as these variable factors would depend on the mission and the enemy being faced.

The close-knit Waffen-SS "family" made the formation and functioning of kampfgruppen even more effective than it was in the Wehrmacht panzer units. These Waffen-SS officers had all served with each other for several years. As a result, they knew exactly how their comrades operated, and could easily become a member of each other's command team. Thus, they were able to conduct complex tactical manoeuvres through brief verbal orders that had been issued over the radio net.

Time and time again during the campaigns in the West after D-Day, Waffen-SS kampfgruppen, despite being rapidly formed, would save the day for the German Army. On the Allied side – in contrast to the Germans' units – the formal and laborious "orders groups" were the norm, making it difficult for their operations to be rapidly improvised.

BATTLEFIELD TACTICS

Mission command (or auftragstaktik) was at the heart of German Army tactics. Commanders were given an objective to reach and were left to formulate a plan of operation that would achieve the High Command's intent. During both defensive and offensive operations, German commanders would decide where exactly the schwerpunkt (point of main effort) was to be. Once this had been identified, they would concentrate as much of their resources as possible in order to secure it.

In the defensive battles in Normandy, this usually resulted in the Germans trying to hold a key piece of high ground that dominated a large area. Holding the high ground would give an important advantage: devastating artillery as well as tank fire could be brought to bear against the enemy, effecting its retreat.

When the Waffen-SS moved to attack, the same principle was used. However, in their manoeuvres the bulk of the German offensive power would be concentrated against the weakest point in the Allied line. Once success had been achieved, an overwhelming force would be concentrated to reinforce these gains.

The Waffen-SS had learnt on the Eastern Front that its tanks were true battle-winning weapons, in both the attack and defence role, as long as they were concentrated and used en masse. A division's panzer battalion would only be committed to action if it could achieve decisive results. It was not to be wasted away in penny packets, holding ground or on limited attacks. The job of holding ground was to be left to the panzergrenadiers, which were to be supported by the anti-tank units. These two units in turn would often find themselves supported by the flak battalion's 88mm guns, operating in the direct-fire role.

RETHINKING THE BATTLEFIELD

Once it had been committed to action, a panzer kampfgruppe would usually boast elements of the SPW battalion, anti-tank guns and self-propelled artillery. This self-contained force would be able to deal with any likely enemy threat and hold ground once the operation had achieved its objective.

On the whole, the experience the Waffen-SS had gained in Russia was invaluable when it came to fighting the relatively inexperienced British and American divisions that had landed in Normandy. However, no matter how much they had learnt, there was one major shortfall: these SS men had never been forced to face massed Allied airpower. The paralyzing effect of the overhead presence of British Typhoons or American Mustangs was to force a rethink by the Waffen-SS commanders. They realized that they would have to change the way they moved their troops around the battlefield. It soon became apparent that the massed tank attacks that had worked so well for them on the Eastern Front were, once executed in the West, very vulnerable to Allied air attacks.

One thing the Waffen-SS – particularly its officer corps – never lacked in abundance throughout the war was fighting spirit. A major factor in nurturing and maintaining the fighting spirit of the Waffen-SS panzer divisions was their strong sense of unit identity. Both officers and noncommissioned officers alike served almost exclusively in the same regiment or division throughout their time in uniform. They had come to know and trust their comrades in arms, and had shared successes and hardships. Each division also had its own distinct set of characteristics.

The *Leibstandarte* was the élite of the élite. It was the first unit to be formed and the Führer took a personal interest in the division that bore his name, giving it priority for recruits and equipment.

Das Reich had been hardened by years on the Eastern Front, but by 1944 was an unhappy unit under a martinet commander, Heinz Lammerding. The *Hitlerjugend* adopted many of the traditions of the Nazi Youth movement and was not strong on military formalities. Many of its officers were former *Leibstandarte* men who were determined to prove themselves as good as their old comrades.

The *Hohenstaufen* and *Frundsberg* Divisions were new units but, despite this, were very professional in the way they conducted themselves. In 1944, soldiers of the Waffen-SS panzer divisions all believed that they were serving in the best units in the world. Every soldier considered himself to be utterly invincible.

The leadership of the Waffen-SS panzer force had developed and matured during the course of the war. There were a number of distinct groups within the Waffen-SS, and they all – to varying degrees – meshed together to produce very effective fighting units. There was a rump of senior officers who were all hardcore Nazis, such as "Sepp" Dietrich, who had loyally served Hitler for two decades.

Senior officers such as "Sepp" Dietrich had power, position and lavish property under Hitler's regime. Moreover, they were passionate believers in Hitler's cause, particularly his racial war against the Jewish and Slav *untermenschen* in the East. Men such as Dietrich never had any pretensions to be military geniuses, and relied on professional soldiers including Hausser, Bittrich and Fritz Kraemer to run things for them. Dietrich was later to enjoy promotion to the rank of SS-Oberstgruppenführer, or the equivalent of an army lieutenant-general, which many considered to be a serious case of over-promotion. However, what mattered most to Hitler was Dietrich's loyalty, not his tactical skill.

Hausser and Bittrich were the military intellectuals of the Waffen-SS. Hitler, however, never quite trusted them. He once called Hausser "crafty fox" in a very uncomplimentary way. However, they were practical, down-to-earth soldiers, and by 1944 they were no longer convinced that Germany would be able to win the war. There was a small core of Himmler cronies in the Waffen-SS panzer divisions. They found their way into senior command posts through Himmler's patronage, and because of this nepotism were considered "untouchable", even if they proved to be totally incompetent. Lammerding of *Das Reich* and the *Hitlerjugend* Division's Mohnke were examples of the individuals who would fit into this category.

Almost all Waffen-SS combat regiments and battalions in France in 1944 were commanded by hardcore

HUMMEL

The Hummel self-propelled gun mounted a standard 150mm heavy field howitzer in a lightly armoured rear fighting compartment on a Panzer IV chassis. The gun was mounted in the middle of the vehicle over the engine, which gave the Hummel a very high silhouette. The Hummel was first delivered to units in the spring of 1943, and each of the Waffen-SS panzer divisions had a single battery of six Hummels plus one gun-less Hummel munitions carrier (each Hummel carried only 18 rounds for the main gun). The Hummel first saw action at the Battle of Kursk in July 1943. Between December 1942 and late 1944, 666 Hummels were built.

Type:	self-propelled heavy howitzer
Length:	7.17m (23.5ft)
Width:	2.97m (9.74ft)
Height:	2.81m (9.2ft)
Crew:	6
Armament:	1 x 150mm, 1 x 7.92mm
Range:	215km (134 miles)
Speed:	42kmh (26.25mph)

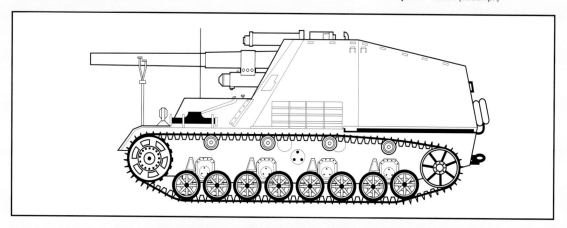

Waffen-SS panzergrenadiers riding in SdKfz 251 halftracks on the Eastern Front. By early 1944, the SS panzer divisions were the finest formations in the German order of battle.

veterans. These were men who had worked their way up through the ranks of their divisions. Most of them had started their military life as junior officers in the opening days of the war and, by a process of natural selection, ended up shouldering much of the responsibility for the fight against the Allies. The likes of Meyer, Peiper, Fritz Witt, Max Wünsche, Teddy Wisch and tank ace Michael Wittmann were all in their late twenties or early thirties, and could only be described as "natural leaders of men".

These highly skilled soldiers were men who led from the front. As a result of their actions, they took great pride in accumulating injuries and medals at an alarming rate. They were expert practitioners of armoured warfare. Often their presence on the battlefield was enough to turn around a calamitous situation and restore the troops' morale.

Unlike British and American officers – who did not wear their medals on the battlefield – Waffen-SS officers made a great show of their decorations. This was particularly the case if they had won the famous Knight's Cross for bravery in battle (worn at the neck). Some of them even wore them with their camouflage combat smocks. They were totems of their own bravery in past battles, and their appearance also served to make their followers aspire to win these medals.

Unlike some of the older Waffen-SS hands, they had far from given up the fight, and now that the opportunity to achieve fame and notoriety had arisen, they were hungry for glory. Their wishes would soon come true.

For the rank-and-file men serving in the Waffen-SS, their enthusiastic willingness to fight was due to a combination of various factors. Since Hitler's accession to power, the population of Germany had been subject to daily bombardments of Nazi propaganda. The school and university systems were fertile recruiting ground for the Nazi Party, and the indoctrination of those young-sters was a major objective for Hitler's henchmen. The outbreak of war accelerated this process of indoctrina-tion. Once the Allied bombers started raiding major German cities in massive numbers from late 1942 onwards, the German people could see for themselves what little pity they would evoke from such a ruthless enemy. The men who had served on the Eastern Front also realized that Germany would be shown no mercy if the Soviets ever broke through and were allowed to push into the Reich. It was a fight to the finish.

Invasion Front

On the eve of the June 1944 Allied invasion of Northwest Europe – codenamed Overlord – the rebuilt Waffen-SS panzergrenadier and panzer divisions formed the armoured spearhead of Field Marshal Gerd von Rundstedt's plan to smash the invasion bridgehead. But the German High Command was divided on when and where the invasion would take place, fatally weakening German chances.

A German sentry, stick grenade tucked into his belt, on the Normandy coast in 1944. The Waffen-SS made up six of the eleven panzer and panzergrenadier divisions on the Western Front in June 1944.

In the spring of 1944, at depots and training camps all over Belgium and France, veteran Waffen-SS instructors were hard at work trying to knock thousands of new recruits into shape to meet the coming Allied invasion of Northwest Europe.

Due to the lamentable state of German intelligence, Field Marshal Erwin Rommel, the commander of Army Group B, had no firm intelligence about where the Allied troops would come ashore. Aerial photographs showed huge camps in southern England packed with tanks, artillery and supplies, while ports around the British coast were chock-a-block with ships and landing craft. All that was certain was that this immense force would attempt to open the long-awaited second front in a matter of months.

For the "Desert Fox", time was of the essence. When he toured France on an inspection of the Atlantic Wall coastal defences during December 1943, Rommel was far from impressed. France had long been a backwater of the war. It was where German units would be sent to recuperate after suffering a mauling in Russia. Since being appointed commander of the invasion coast, which stretched from the French border to northern Holland,

Rommel had been trying to knock the last vestiges of complacency out of his rag-tag collection of just under 60 divisions. He ordered a major effort to reinforce the beach defences with minefields and fortifications. Millions of tons of concrete were poured into the ground to build bunkers and gun positions overlooking every possible landing site on the French coast. Inland, Rommel wanted strong armoured forces close at hand to defeat any Allied troops that did manage to get ashore.

The Waffen-SS provided the bulk of Rommel's armoured reserve, comprising six of the eleven panzer and panzergrenadier divisions available to the Western Front. Except for a brief period in Italy when he worked with the *Leibstandarte* Division, Rommel had never commanded Waffen-SS divisions, but he quickly formed a favourable impression of them and their commanders. Touring their training grounds, Rommel could see their superb equipment and rigorous training schedules quickly bearing fruit. That was more than could be said for a number of army divisions. Rommel was shocked at the state of the infantry divisions manning the invasion defences along the coast, which were staffed mainly by former Russian and Polish prisoners. Their fighting potential was minimal. Some of

Though the Germans had enough panzer divisions to destroy the Allied bridgehead in Normandy, there were arguments in the High Command as to how they should be deployed against the Allies. This indecision would prove fatal to the Germans in Normandy in June 1944.

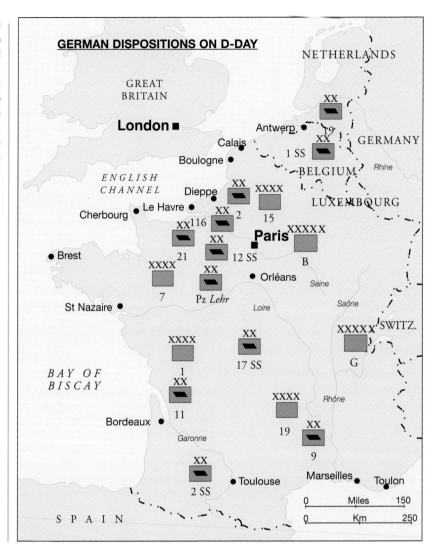

GERMAN DISPOSITIONS ON D-DAY

the army panzer divisions were not much better, with the famous 21st Panzer Division having to make do with captured French tanks and trucks in many of its battalions. Such problems only increased Rommel's reliance on the Waffen-SS, which had first call on replacement manpower, new weapons and equipment.

Rommel threw himself into his mission with a vengeance, setting a punishing schedule of inspection visits around France and trips to the Führer's headquarters in East Prussia to secure more men and resources for his command. He spent hours locked in fruitless meetings with Hitler to secure backing for his counter-invasion strategy. From his experience in North Africa and Italy, Rommel believed that the Allies had to be defeated on the

landing beaches, otherwise they would be able to consolidate a bridgehead and bring their overwhelming superiority in materiel to bear against the thinly stretched German defenders. Rommel believed he would have little chance in a war of attrition in France. Any invasion would have to be smashed within 24 hours, so the panzer divisions should be based close to the coast, ready to strike.

Rommel's immediate superior in France, the 71-year-old Gerd von Rundstedt, disagreed, and argued that it would be better to mass all the panzer reserves inland as a huge strike force, and then launch one knock-out blow against the Allied bridgehead. Luftwaffe bombers and Admiral Karl Dönitz's U-boat fleet would also be able to cut Allied supply lines, leaving them isolated in France.

FRITZ WITT

Fritz Witt was born in Hohenlimburg on 27 May 1908. He joined both the SS and the Nazi Party in December 1931, and in 1933 he became a member of the SS Stabswache Berlin, one of only 117 individuals chosen. He was given a commission in 1934, and joined the *Deutschland* Regiment. Leading this unit during the invasion of Poland, he was awarded both the Second and First Class Iron Crosses. In September 1940 he won the Knight's Cross for his actions in France. In October 1940, Witt returned to the *Leibstandarte* and took part in the fighting in the Balkans. Transferred to the Eastern Front, his battalion grew to become the SS-Infanterie Regiment 1, and he was promoted to SS-Obersturmbannführer as its first commanding officer. He won the Oakleaves in 1943 for his various actions in Greece and on the Russian Front. In July 1943, Witt was promoted to SS-Oberführer and given command of the 12th SS Panzer Division *Hitlerjugend*. In April 1944 he was further promoted to SS-Brigadeführer, but was killed two months later on 14 June 1944 after sustaining shrapnel wounds to the face in an Allied naval bombardment during the fighting in Normandy.

Arguments raged between Rommel and his commander-in-chief. Allied airpower would slaughter the panzer columns as they marched to the coast, said Rommel. The "Desert Fox" had little confidence in German air and seapower being able to influence the coming battle. SS-Oberstgruppenführer Paul Hausser and SS-Obergruppenführer Josef "Sepp" Dietrich, the commanders of the two SS panzer corps, also weighed in to the argument on the side of Rundstedt. Their experience in Russia told them that a mass attack would have more chance of success. Rommel countered that they had never had to fight under Allied air supremacy.

The lack of intelligence on Allied intentions also complicated Rommel's planning. While most German commanders in France were convinced that the Allies would strike across the Straits of Dover to seize the Pas de Calais, the possibility of an invasion farther west in Normandy could not be excluded.

With his generals unable to agree on a common strategy, Hitler not surprisingly was able to force his own plans on the invasion-front commanders. Even though his astrologer told him to expect an invasion in Normandy, Hitler decreed that the bulk of the German forces in the West would be based within striking distance of the Pas de Calais. This included the two SS panzer corps, until II SS Panzer Corps was temporarily dispatched to the Eastern Front in April 1944. He backed Rundstedt's idea of a concentrated counterattack.

In April 1944, Hitler took on board some of Rommel's ideas and decided to move some panzer units westwards to cover the Normandy beaches. The *Hitlerjugend* Division was shipped to new bases northwest of Paris, within a day's drive of Normandy, and Dietrich soon followed with his corps headquarters. Dietrich's other division, the *Leibstandarte*, was still refitting and remained behind in Belgium. Dietrich's force of one SS division, the corps heavy tank battalions and three army panzer divisions was poised to strike at any landing in Normandy. Hitler gave Rundstedt and Rommel the authority to move the three army divisions, but the Führer had to give his approval for any other panzer units, including the Waffen-SS, to move towards any invasion beach. This was a classic Hitler muddle. It meant Rommel would have insufficient forces to kill off any Allied bridgehead at birth, while Rundstedt was unable to muster his 11 panzer division force to strike at the Allies en masse. This convoluted command arrangement would bedevil the German response when the invasion did occur in June 1944.

These arguments were far from the minds of the Waffen-SS tank crews and panzergrenadiers training in France and Belgium in the spring of 1944. They were focused on the coming battle with the British and Americans. Day after day, their commanders stressed that the outcome of the war would turn on the coming battle. If the Allies could be quickly thrown back into the sea, then Germany would have won a key breathing space to turn its attention eastwards once again and drive back the Soviets, who were already on Poland's eastern border.

For the Waffen-SS, their Führer's struggle against the Soviets was a crusade for racial survival. The threat from the Western Allies was a diversion from this battle that had to be resolved quickly, to release them once again to take on the Russians. On his inspections, Rommel told the Waffen-SS men that the Allies would not be able to recover from the defeat of their invasion. If the Allies failed to secure a bridgehead in Europe, it could take years for them to regain their strength to make another attempt (which was correct), perhaps forcing them to sue for peace, or so said Hitler.

The Battle for Caen

In four days of bitter fighting following D-Day, the Hitlerjugend Division effectively brought the Allied advance to a halt on the outskirts of Caen. For a unit in action for the first time, it was a remarkable performance. Caen was Montgomery's objective for the attacks on 7 and 8 June, but the young soldiers of the 12th SS Panzer Division had other ideas.

A *Hitlerjugend* trooper lays out a swastika flag as a recognition symbol for Luftwaffe aircraft. This must be before 6 June, as after D-Day the Allies had total air superiority and the Luftwaffe had disappeared.

In its billets northwest of Paris, the men of the *Hitlerjugend* Division could clearly hear the waves of Allied bombers passing overhead on the morning of 6 June 1944. This raid was heavier than usual. Throughout the early hours of the morning, a steady stream of phone calls alerted the division to the fact that parachute landings were taking place all over Normandy. The divisional commander, 36-year-old SS-Brigadeführer Fritz Witt, put his command on alert. Commanders frantically roused their troops from bed, and reconnaissance parties were formed, ready for any move to counter the invasion.

In the German High Command, confusion reigned. No one was sure where the Allies had landed or in what strength. Rommel, Rundstedt and Hitler all prevaricated, fearing the landing in Normandy was just a feint to distract attention from an assault in the Pas de Calais, or in the mouth of the Somme. A reconnaissance force was sent to the coast south of the Somme at 02:30 hours but the rest of the *Hitlerjugend* Division had to wait for orders. Reports were coming in every couple of minutes, but there was still no concrete information on the Allied attack.

At 05:00 hours orders were issued for the division to begin concentrating at Lisieux in eastern Normandy. It took several hours for the troops to get on the road, and they spent the rest of the day moving westwards under relentless Allied air attack. Swarms of fighter-bombers – "Jagdbombers" or "Jabos" as they were known to the German panzer crews – were scouting ahead of the Allied bridgehead on the lookout for German columns. Some 20 vehicles were destroyed and more than 80 *Hitlerjugend* soldiers killed or wounded in the attacks. More important than the materiel and human losses was the delay caused as the Waffen-SS columns had to stop, take cover and weave their way past twisted and smoking wreckage. Refugee columns clogged the roads, and this was responsible for further hindering the movement of German troops towards Normandy. As a result of these obstacles, it would be nightfall before the division found itself anywhere near striking distance of the Allied bridgehead.

The German High Command was still locked in confusion about what to do with the panzer reserves. By mid-afternoon on 6 June, it was clear that the Normandy landing was in fact no feint. Although the Germans did not have precise information, Allied records showed that 55,000 men were firmly established ashore in five main bridgeheads. Only in the late afternoon were the first

KURT MEYER

Kurt Meyer was born on 23 December 1910 in Jerxheim. Originally a police officer, he joined the *Leibstandarte SS Adolf Hitler* in 1934 and became one of the most charismatic men in the Waffen-SS. He established a reputation for daring and élan that made him popular with the men under his command. He made his name during the Balkan and Greece campaigns where, as an SS-Sturmbannführer, he took the unorthodox step of pushing his faltering men forward against Greek fighters by lobbing grenades behind his troops to force them to attack. For his part in the *Leibstandarte*'s success in Greece, he was awarded the Knight's Cross. His actions during the invasion of the USSR earned him the Oakleaves. In 1943, Meyer was moved to provide experience in the newly formed *Hitlerjugend* Division. The death of divisional commander Fritz Witt saw him promoted to SS-Brigadeführer and take command of the *Hitlerjugend* Division. He was tried after the war for his troops' actions in the murder of Canadian POWs, and spent 10 years in prison. He was released in 1955, and died on his 50th birthday in December 1960.

orders for counterattacks issued to the panzer reserves. The 21st Panzer Division was already in action north of Caen against the British bridgeheads. Accordingly, the *Hitlerjugend* and Panzer Lehr Divisions were ordered to move against the British beaches. They were under the command of "Sepp" Dietrich's I SS Panzer Corps.

The *Leibstandarte* Division remained in Belgium to counter the threat of an Allied landing in the Pas de Calais, the region that so dogged Hitler. In the meantime, the *Das Reich* and the 17th SS Panzergrenadier Divisions began moving northwards from southwest France. Despite their determination, it would be at least a week before they managed to reach the invasion front. It would also be six days until Hitler finally agreed to release II SS Panzer Corps from the Eastern Front. Far from being able to hammer the Allies with a knock-out blow, the Germans ended up committing their reserves piecemeal in a desperate bid to shore up a crumbling front.

While Dietrich was easily able to establish contact with his old comrade, Witt, he nevertheless had great problems in trying to link up with the 21st Panzer Division or the remnants of the infantry divisions resisting the British north of the large Norman city of Caen.

Dietrich and other staff officers from the Waffen-SS crisscrossed the German front in order to try to pull together some sort of cohesion. All during the night they worked out various formulae for counterattack plan after counterattack plan. But all of their plans were rapidly overtaken by events. The commander of the 21st Panzer Division could not be found at his command post, and this would frustrate further plans to mount a joint attack with the *Hitlerjugend* Division.

Of even more concern was the fact that the arrival of the *Hitlerjugend* Division was still stalled because of the chaotic conditions on the roads. The Panzer Lehr Division was even farther behind, and would not arrive at the front for days. In the meantime, thousands more Allied troops and tanks were rapidly pouring ashore.

The planned mass panzer attack for the following day had to be scrapped. The most that could be expected was for the *Hitlerjugend* Division to go in, with support from 21st Panzer. The first kampfgruppe of the *Hitlerjugend* Division to reach the front was based on the 25th SS Panzergrenadier Regiment, commanded by the famous SS-Standartenführer Kurt "Panzer" Meyer.

Only 34 years old, Meyer was an aggressive and determined officer who would claim fame for being the youngest German divisional commander of World War II.

Hitlerjugend troops in action to the west of Caen in early June. This is a 75mm leIG 18 infantry gun, possibly of the division's 12th SS Reconnaissance Battalion.

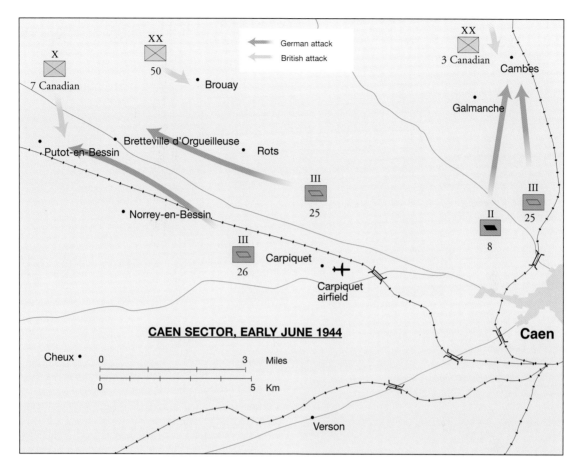

CAEN SECTOR, EARLY JUNE 1944

Supreme self-confidence – which, some said, bordered on arrogance – was Meyer's trademark, and when he arrived at the 21st Panzer's headquarters during the early hours of 7 June in order to coordinate the coming attack, he did not win any friends. He took one look at the situation map and left the army officers in no doubt as to how totally unimpressed he was by their assessment of the threat posed by Allied forces.

Meyer was to push forward on the left flank of the 21st Panzer, after forming up on the western edge of Caen itself. His objective was simple: to reach the coast. By first light, only a few companies of the 25th Regiment were in place on the start-line, with the remainder still moving around the southern suburbs of Caen. In the meantime, the petrol shortages and traffic chaos meant that the 26th SS Panzergrenadier Regiment and the *Hitlerjugend*'s Panther tank battalion would not be in position to attack until the following day at the earliest.

This was to be a worrying time for Meyer as he surveyed the battle front from his command post in the

In early June, the *Hitlerjugend* Division successfully defeated a number of large-scale Allied attacks to the northwest and north of Caen.

Ardennes abbey, 4.8km (3 miles) outside Caen. At 10:00 hours, his Panzer IV battalion with 50 tanks finally arrived, followed by more of his Waffen-SS panzergrenadiers.

The attack was fixed for 16:00 hours, with two panzergrenadier units advancing line abreast. They were to be supported in their efforts by large numbers of heavy tanks and artillery. During the early afternoon, Meyer watched from the abbey's high tower as the Canadian 3rd Division – which was known to contain three full infantry brigades and was backed by hundreds of tanks – started to form up for a major attack. Blissfully unaware that the *Hitlerjugend* Division was in its path, the Canadian 9th Brigade and a regiment of tanks began their advance. To observers, they looked as unthreatening as a unit that was on a training exercise during peacetime.

Making a split-second decision, Meyer junked his deliberate attack plan and instead decided to lay a devastating ambush for the Allied force. By now this force had bypassed one of his advance panzergrenadier units and was heading deep into the German rear with Carpiquet airfield as its objective. All of Meyer's 88mm-armed tanks and anti-tank guns that were in hull-down positions on a ridge near the abbey were ordered to hold their fire until the Canadian 9th Brigade and the tanks drove into the centre of Meyer's killing zone. The Panzer IV companies were ordered to move quickly along the hedge-lined roads before taking up vantage fire positions on the flanks of the Canadian line of advance.

Meyer waited until the Canadians were within 200m (656ft) of his lines before giving the order "Achtung panzer – marsche!". Panzer crews powered up their engines and moved into position.

Fire started raining down on the Canadian brigade. Stuart and Sherman tanks began to explode after taking devastating hits from the *Hitlerjugend* panzers. Then Meyer's I Battalion of panzergrenadiers was launched into the shell-shocked remains of the Canadian 9th Brigade.

The battle lasted for six hours as the two forces became intermingled. Company sized groups of Canadians were surrounded by Meyer's troops in the small Normandy villages. Many fought to the last man, while others surrendered when they ran out of ammunition. Heavy Canadian artillery fire caused many German casualties that had to be evacuated on the backs of Panzer IVs. A Canadian counterattack now regained some of the lost ground, so Meyer ordered his two remaining panzergrenadier battalions into action. II Battalion with three companies of Panzer IVs led the way in a tight wedge formation. This restored the situation and the Canadians were soon in retreat.

The panzer battalion command group now stumbled into a troop of Shermans and was wiped out. I Battalion, with one Panzer IV company, pushed forward into a sector held by British troops of the Royal Ulster Rifles. The two forces soon became intermingled in the village of Cambes. British Sherman tanks shot up German gun positions before being knocked out by Panzerfaust teams, while Panzer IVs suffered heavy losses from Allied anti-tank guns. Both sides now pulled back to defensive positions on either side of Cambes.

Meyer was all set to push forward when he spotted another Canadian brigade moving south around his right flank. The 21st Panzer Division's attack had still not started and Meyer was afraid his flank would be turned.

His kampfgruppe was just not strong enough to take on all of the 3rd Canadian Division, so he reluctantly called a halt to his attack. As night fell, the 25th Regiment adopted defensive positions and easily saw off a series of night probes by the Canadians.

Two Canadian regiments – the North Nova Scotia Highlanders and Sherbrooke Fusiliers – lost more than 500 men killed, wounded or captured, as well as 28 tanks destroyed or damaged, during the day's engagement. Meyer lost 300 casualties and 9 tanks. At the time, many of Meyer's troops were despondent, as they had failed to reach their objective. Given the odds, however, they had achieved an amazing result, stopping the Canadian advance in its tracks and thereby thwarting General Sir Bernard Montgomery's plans to seize Caen.

The following day saw Meyer forced to consolidate his small force until the rest of the division was in a position to attack. Out on the left flank, the *Hitlerjugend*'s reconnaissance battalion tried to link up with any German units still putting up resistance, but Meyer's flank was effectively hanging in open air. The halftrack-mounted reconnaissance troops had a lively day, skirmishing with British troops and tanks of the Durham Light Infantry and 4th/7th Dragoon Guards, convincing them that the German front was far stronger than it really was.

Pushing westwards from Caen, small *Hitlerjugend* patrols in SdKfz 250 halftracks or SdKfz 234 eight-wheeled armoured cars were trying to find out the extent of the Allied advance southwards. Operating in small groups, the German vehicles soon started engaging Allied advance patrols. By the evening, the battalion was pulled back to form a firm defensive line to cover the deployment of the 26th Panzergrenadier Regiment.

On 8 June, SS-Obersturmbannführer Wilhelm Mohnke's 26th Regiment was to attack at first light. This was Mohnke's return to combat duty after almost three years recovering from the loss of a foot in Yugoslavia and serving in a number of administrative jobs. His comrades were watching closely to see if he held up under the pressure. The division's Panther tank battalion was still delayed by fuel shortages, so his three panzergrenadier battalions would go into the attack with no tank support.

Mohnke's task was to drive back the Allied units that had been detected by the reconnaissance battalion as they moved forward on the extreme left of the *Hitlerjugend* Division's flank. Mohnke's men proceeded forward on foot, supported only by SdKfz 251/22 armoured halftracks armed with 75mm guns.

First into action at dawn was the 26th Regiment's I Battalion. Its men were tasked with seizing the village of Norrey-en-Bessin. Without armour support, the attack soon found itself bogged down. When the lead panzergrenadier companies were caught in the open by Canadian machine-gun, mortar and artillery fire, the Germans had to admit defeat. After many of the company and platoon commanders had been killed or wounded, the Waffen-SS attack was eventually repulsed.

In the centre of the regiment's attack was the II Battalion, which had been assigned the village of Putot-en-Bessin as its objective. Due to strong artillery support, the II Battalion was able to reach the village and surround three companies of the Canadian Royal Winnipeg Rifles inside a few buildings. The Canadians tried to escape, but the Waffen-SS killed or captured most of them. The British 24th Lancers counterattacked in response to the success of the Germans, getting in among the panzergrenadiers. More than 40 Germans were captured in this foray before the III Battalion's self-propelled anti-tank company intervened with its Marders and drove the British off.

MAX WÜNSCHE

Max Wünsche was born in Kittlitz, Saxony, on 20 April 1914. In 1934 he joined the SS-Verfügungstruppe, being commissioned as an SS-Untersturmführer in 1936. During the early war years he served as Hitler's personal orderly. In 1940, though, he left Hitler's side and joined the campaign in the West with the *Leibstandarte* Division. Remarkably, he won both the Second and First Class Iron Crosses within five days of each other. Transferring into tanks with the SS Panzer Regiment I, he stayed with armoured units for the rest of his military career. He won the Knight's Cross in January 1943 before joining the newly created *Hitlerjugend* Division later that year. He was tasked with training the panzer arm of this division, and he did a very good job with his young charges, turning them from boys into soldiers who performed admirably in Normandy. Indeed, his men were vital in holding the so-called Falaise Gap open, allowing vast numbers of retreating German units to flee to safety. For this he was awarded the Oakleaves. Captured by the British in August 1944 (he had been wounded just days before), he remained a prisoner of war until 1948. He died in 1995 aged 81.

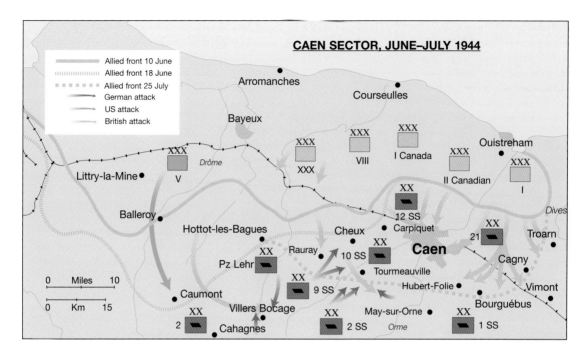

CAEN SECTOR, JUNE–JULY 1944

The fighting around Caen was part of Montgomery's plan to draw in as much German armour as possible to wear it down. This happened, but at a high cost to Allied armour.

As dusk was falling, the 7th Canadian Brigade launched a major counterattack, with heavy artillery and tank support. Under massive pressure, the II Battalion pulled out of Putot-en-Bessin, losing some 100 men in the action.

Meanwhile, Mohnke's armoured personnel carrier-mounted panzergrenadier unit, III Battalion, went into attack on the extreme left flank of his regiment. It rapidly relieved a badly shot-up panzergrenadier battalion of the Panzer Lehr Division in Brouay and then spent the day fending off one attack after another from British tanks.

Out on the *Hitlerjugend*'s extreme left flank, the reconnaissance battalion found itself outgunned by the British 8th Armoured Brigade. Pinpointed by British scouts, the battalion was now targeted by three artillery regiments and two battleships. The battalion's command post was wiped out in a single salvo, and its companies were also targeted, with total losses running to 80 men.

As the evening began, it was Meyer's 25th Regiment's turn to go forward on the attack. The offensive would enjoy the support of the *Hitlerjugend*'s Panther tank battalion. In a night attack, Meyer punched through the Canadian lines and surrounded a regimental headquar-

ters based inside the village of Bretteville d'Orgueilleuse. This attack, which was westward from his position, was intended to strike at the exposed flank of the Canadian brigade that was counterattacking Mohnke's regiment.

The 25th Regiment's reconnaissance company followed up on its motorcycles, close behind the two companies of tanks, and they were to storm Canadian trenches after the panzer assault. Panzergrenadiers were then to mop up the Canadian position. In characteristic fashion, Meyer went into battle riding in a motorcycle side car, his way of motivating his men to give their all, but showing how impetuous the 32-year-old leader could be in the heat of battle.

As they approached the village, the Panthers fanned out into attack formation and gathered speed. A wall of anti-tank gunfire hit them as they got to within 200m (656ft) of the village, knocking out several tanks. Spurred on by Meyer's presence, the tanks started to blast apart the village, with burning tanks and buildings turning night into day. The Canadians fired their salvos of parachute flares above the German tanks, silhouetting them, thereby providing excellent targets as well as temporarily blinding the Panther crews. Meyer now changed his tactics, sending groups of tanks and panzergrenadiers to penetrate the village from the north and south, thus avoiding the heavy anti-tank gunfire.

The Canadians retreated into a series of fortified strongpoints to try to hold off the attack. Meyer's

PANZER IV

The Panzer IV Ausf J model shown below was introduced into service in mid-1944, though Panzer IVs had been in service with German forces since 1939. The *Hitlerjugend* Division in the West in 1944 fielded a full battalion of 98 Panzer IV Ausf H and J tanks. The design of the Panzer IV meant it could be improved throughout the war, as its superstructure overhung the hull sides, thus enabling it to be up-gunned with relative ease. The Ausf J variant was armed with the 75mm KwK40 L/48 gun and carried 87 rounds for this weapon. An interesting feature of this model was the wire-mesh skirting on the hull sides which, combined with extra armour thickness, gave added protection.

Type:	medium tank
Length:	7m (23ft)
Width:	2.88m (9.5ft)
Height:	2.68m (8.9ft)
Crew:	5
Armament:	1 x 75mm, 2 x 7.92mm
Range:	210km (131 miles)
Speed:	38kmh (21mph)

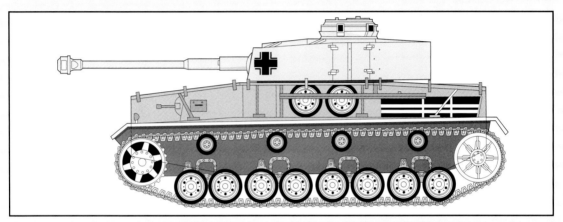

Panthers were able to get into the village, where they proceeded to shoot up Canadian bunkers and trucks.

In a night battle, some 22 Panthers circled the Canadian command post of the Regina Rifles Regiment, with Meyer darting in between them in his motorcycle! The I Battalion had not been able to penetrate the Canadian defences, leaving the Panthers unsupported. In the end Canadian PIAT bazookas and anti-tank guns firing new sabot rounds knocked out six of the Panthers, so Meyer reluctantly called off the attack as dawn was breaking.

Small groups of German motorcyclists had managed to get into the village, and were eventually able to make their escape back to German lines. Meyer's foray had been an expensive exercise, and had left 155 men dead, wounded or prisoners. The commander of the *Hitlerjugend*'s panzer regiment, Max Wünsche, had gone along for the ride on a borrowed tank, but for all his bravado had not been as lucky as Meyer and had ended up wounded.

Allied pressure on Mohnke's regiment continued during 9 June, with a series of attacks by both British and Canadian troops. The 8th Armoured Brigade continued to probe into the *Hitlerjugend*'s reconnaissance battalion, which now had been joined by a Panther company, attached to beef up its firepower. They traded fire with British Shermans all day, but were not able to hold back their advance. Only the arrival of elements of the Panzer Lehr Division could neutralize this threat to the *Hitlerjugend*'s flank.

Meyer tried again with another raid by the Panther battalion which took place early on in the afternoon, but lost seven tanks to Canadian anti-tank fire. He sent a company of 12 tanks forward without infantry and artillery, expecting the surprise and shock effect to unnerve the defenders who were now dug in in the village of Norrey-en-Bessin. The tanks formed a long line and headed out across open fields towards their objective when, one by one, the Panthers started to fall victim to Canadian tanks in ambush positions. Each Panther caught fire, and all the crews who escaped were badly burned. Canadian infantry then joined in, machine-gunning the survivors as they made their escape on foot. The whole episode was a dismal failure, with 15 men dead and 20 badly wounded.

The failure of the attack was a major problem for the *Hitlerjugend*, because it left a Canadian strongpoint jutting south into the line between the 25th and 26th Regiments. During the early hours of 10 June, the division's pioneer battalion was to go into action to neutralize the position.

A *Hitlerjugend* patrol returns to friendly lines under the watchful eye of a machine gunner, in the area northwest of Caen in early June 1944.

A heavily camouflaged *Hitlerjugend* SdKfz 251 armoured halftrack in one of the villages to the north of Caen. Good camouflage skills were essential for the SS soldiers.

German pioneers were considered élite infantry, specializing in assault operations and, as a result, great gains were expected to be made from their attack.

Under cover of darkness, the pioneers tried to approach the Canadian position in silence, but they were soon detected. Heavy mortar and artillery fire began raining down on the exposed pioneers. They managed to reach the edge of the village before the attack stalled. For most of the following day the men were pinned down, finding themselves unable either to advance or to retreat. By late afternoon, the pioneers managed to pull back, but they were forced to leave 80 dead or wounded behind. Allied naval gunfire support continued to pound the *Hitlerjugend* Division, and it was to have a devastating effect as 14in and 16in shells rained down on Caen. The use of altitude fuses meant the Allied shelling resulted in hot shrapnel raining down on German positions. When not actually fighting, Meyer had his men digging bunkers, trenches, artillery gun pits and panzer shelters. By digging large scrapes to drive their tanks into, the panzer crews protected their vehicles from the unrelenting barrages that smashed radio antennas, destroyed sighting optics or, in extreme cases, ripped off tank turrets.

Time and time again, Dietrich tried to muster his panzer divisions for a corps-level counterattack, but he was constantly having to reorganize his forces to plug holes in the front. The Panzer Lehr Division had still not arrived in strength, leaving the *Hitlerjugend* Division to hold the line to the west of Caen for another day. It was reinforced by the arrival of I SS Panzer Corps' artillery regiment, but this did little to even out the mismatch between German and Allied firepower in Normandy.

The Canadians were now joined by the British 50th Division for a major attack on the afternoon of 11 June. The reconnaissance battalion again proved its worth as a hard-hitting mobile strike force. A company of *Hitlerjugend* Panthers and the division's reconnaissance battalion raced to block their line of advance. Holding their fire until the British tanks had run ahead of their infantry, machine-gunners in the reconnaissance halftracks then raked the ranks of the Green Howards Regiment. Lying in ambush, the Panthers picked off the British Shermans of the 4th/7th Dragoon Guards from a hilltop firing line. The British attack faltered when one Sherman that had penetrated to within a few yards of the German battalion's command post was knocked out by a 75mm anti-tank gun. The arrival of the reserve Panther company sent the British reeling backwards. The British lost 250 men and 7 tanks in withering German fire.

At the same time, the Canadian 2nd Armoured Brigade had been launched against Mohnke's regiment.

The brunt of the attack fell on the divisional pioneer battalion, which was now holding the line south of Norrey-en-Bessin. A regiment of Shermans rolled forward, loaded with infantrymen on their rear decks. The pioneers were soon locked in fierce hand-to-hand combat. Shermans were stalked by German Panzerfaust teams through village streets and country lanes.

A Panzer IV company was moved forward from a reserve position to a hill that overlooked the Canadian line of advance. Hitting the Canadians in the flank, some 46 Shermans were soon burning fiercely in the Normandy fields. Not surprisingly, Shermans were soon nicknamed Ronsons, after the cigarette lighter, because of their alarming ability to burn.

The panzers now charged the confused mass of Canadians, sending them running back to their start-line. Almost 200 Germans were killed or wounded, along with 3 tanks destroyed.

As this desperate battle was taking place, the 40th Canadian Armoured Regiment, along with a commando unit, was launched against the village of Rots, which was at that point held by a composite kampfgruppe of divisional escort troops and a company of Panthers. Although more than 15 Shermans were knocked out, ultimately the attackers were far too strong for the defenders. They slowly fell back through the streets of the village, inflicting more than 100 casualties on the Allies as they went.

By nightfall, the Canadians were in complete control of the village. During the fighting, just under 70 Germans were killed or wounded, and 1 Panther tank was knocked out.

A *Hitlerjugend* Panther rolls through the ruins of Caen in June 1944. On the eve of D-Day the division had a total of 66 Panthers organized in a single battalion.

The fighting that took place in the fields and villages to the northwest of Caen was some of the most violent and brutal to be seen during the Normandy campaign. The *Hitlerjugend* Division lost more than 1000 dead, wounded or missing in these engagements, while the Canadians alone lost nearly 3000 of their men. Equipment losses were equally heavy on both sides. In those violent first engagements between the *Hitlerjugend* and Canadian troops, little quarter was ever given.

Meyer and a number of his officers were charged with war crimes after the conflict had ended. Meyer was charged with being responsible for five incidents on 7 and 8 June that involved the deaths of 41 Canadian prisoners. He was also charged with issuing orders to his division to give no quarter to prisoners. After long trials, Meyer and two others were found guilty of all or some of the charges and sentenced to death. Meyer later had his death sentence stayed, but his two comrades were not so lucky and they faced the hangman's noose in 1948. On his release, Meyer launched a campaign to clear his reputation as well as redeem that of his beloved *Hitlerjugend*.

On the German side, men of the *Hitlerjugend* claimed that they had executed three Canadians in reprisal for the deaths of ten German soldiers tied to a British armoured car and machine-gunned. Sadly, the truth of these events will never be known.

Villers-Bocage

In mid-June 1944, General Montgomery saw an opportunity to split the German front in Normandy and then take Caen from the rear. He committed his famed 7th Armoured Division to the offensive, codenamed Perch, and believed that victory would be quick and total. But he reckoned without the intervention of the Waffen-SS's leading tank ace, who would stop the British in their tracks.

Panzer ace Michael Wittmann poses for the cameras sitting on the barrel of his Tiger I, 1944. The tank has been coated with Zimmerit anti-magnetic paste, which had a grey tint.

With the Canadians and British stalemated in front of Caen by the stalwart defence of the *Hitlerjugend* Division, General Montgomery decided to exploit the gap in the German front. He resolved that this would best be done on the exposed Waffen-SS division's left flank. The Panzer Lehr Division was moving into place next to the *Hitlerjugend* after something of a long delay, but in turn its left flank was also exposed, and the Germans had not yet been able to establish a continuous front between the divisions shielding Caen and units fighting the Americans in the western part of Normandy.

Montgomery's answer was Operation Perch. The fresh British 7th Armoured Division was launched southwards around the open left flank of the Panzer Lehr Division on 12 June. Its mission was to outflank the Panzer Lehr, then swing around behind it and drive hell for leather through Villers-Bocage towards Caen, trapping both the *Hitlerjugend* and Panzer Lehr Divisions. On paper, the plan was very sound; indeed, it was straight out of the German Army's Blitzkrieg school of tactics. The execution was flawed, however, and the famous Desert Rats soon found their nemesis

in the shape of a single, determined Waffen-SS Tiger I tank commander.

The 57-tonne (56-ton) Tiger I tank had been in service with the Waffen-SS since late 1942. It had first seen action with devastating effect during the heavy fighting around Kharkov on the Eastern Front in February and March 1943. With its 88mm cannon, the Tiger could easily punch through the armour of Soviet T-34s and Allied Shermans at a range of more than 1500m (4921ft). At first the *Leibstandarte*, *Das Reich* and *Totenkopf* Divisions had each been assigned a Tiger I company of some 15 tanks, although the Tiger's notorious unreliability meant that often only half of a company's tanks were operational at any one time. These tanks had been used as spearhead units during the Battle of Kursk in July 1943.

As a result of the expansion of the Waffen-SS panzer corps in the summer of 1943, it was decided to remove the divisional Tiger companies and form two corps-level heavy tank battalions. These were nominally to have three Tiger I companies, each with 14 tanks apiece. The continued commitment of the *Leibstandarte*, *Das Reich* and *Totenkopf* Divisions on the Eastern Front through the winter of 1943 and into the spring of 1944 meant the two new battalions were not ready for action until just before the invasion of France in June 1944. The 101st SS Heavy Panzer Battalion itself was assigned to support I SS Panzer Corps, and the 102nd SS Heavy Panzer Battalion worked for the sister corps. They were to provide each of the Waffen-SS corps with a hard-hitting strike force, or a reserve counter-punch.

The 101st SS Battalion had been ordered to Normandy immediately after the Allied invasion, but persistent Allied air raids delayed the advance of its 37 operational tanks. It arrived in I SS Panzer Corps' sector west of Caen on 12 June, just as the Panzer Lehr Division was taking up position alongside the *Hitlerjugend* Division.

One of its companies, under the command of 30-year-old SS-Obersturmführer Michael Wittmann, was posted behind the army division and was to be used only as a reserve force. Wittmann was, by June 1944, one of the most highly decorated German tank commanders of the war, boasting the Knight's Cross with Oakleaves. He had received his first Tiger in early 1943, and by mid-1944 his kill tally ran to an astro-

nomical 119 tanks, almost all of which were claimed during a particularly successful year serving with the *Leibstandarte*'s Tiger company on the Eastern Front.

Operation Perch got under way during the afternoon of 12 June, with the 22nd Armoured Brigade leading the way. All went well until a single German anti-tank gun knocked out a British Stuart tank near the village of Livery. Rather than pressing on to exploit the open German flank during the light summer evening, the British commander, Major-General Bobby Erskine, chose to halt for the night. This was turning into no British Blitzkrieg.

WITTMANN ON THE RAMPAGE

Suitably rested, the 7th Armoured Division started out for Villers-Bocage at first light on 13 June. By 08:00 hours, its advance guard – the Cromwell tanks of the 4th City of London Yeomanry "Sharpshooters" (4 CLY) – was passing through the town. Another British tank unit, the 5th Royal Tank Regiment, a motorized infantry battalion from the Rifle Brigade, as well as assorted anti-tank and artillery units, were in or around the small Norman town under the command of the 22nd Armoured Brigade. 4 CLY's A Squadron halted on a

TIGER I

The awesome SdKfz 181, better known as the Tiger I, entered production in 1942. Armed with a massive 88mm long-barrelled gun, it could knock any tank the Allies could field at that time. It was the first tank to be fitted with overlapping wheels and suspension, which allowed for a very comfortable ride in a machine weighing 57,000kg (125,400lb). Crewed by five men, more than 1354 Tiger Is were produced during the war (production ceased in August 1944). The Tiger I saw action along the Eastern Front, and served with Waffen-SS panzer divisions, in the heavy tank companies. In 1944 the Tigers were withdrawn and formed into heavy tank battalions.

Type:	heavy tank
Length:	8.24m (27ft)
Width:	3.73m (12.25ft)
Height:	2.86m (9.5ft)
Crew:	5
Armament:	1 x 88mm, 2 x 7.92mm
Range:	100km (61 miles)
Speed:	38kmh (24mph)

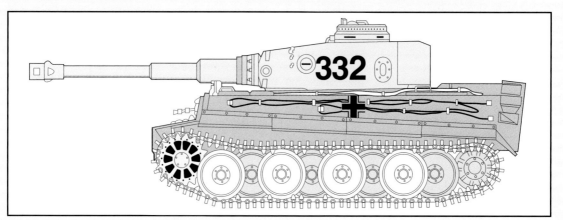

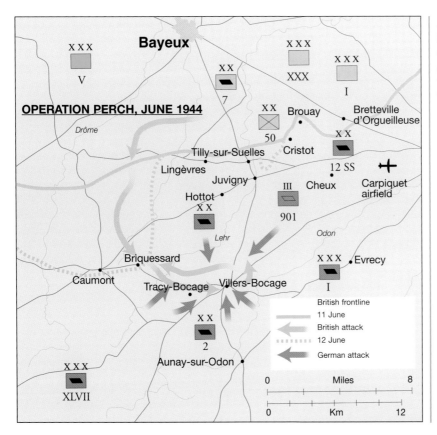

OPERATION PERCH, JUNE 1944

Bayeux

V

Drôme

7

XXX

XXX

XXX

I

50

Brouay

Cristot

Bretteville
d'Orgueilleuse

12 SS

Tilly-sur-Suelles

Lingèvres

Juvigny

Cheux

Carpiquet
airfield

Hottot

III

901

Odon

Lehr

Briquessard

Caumont

Tracy-Bocage

Villers-Bocage

Evrecy

I

2

Aunay-sur-Odon

XLVII

British frontline
11 June
British attack
12 June
German attack

0   Miles   8

0   Km   12

Left: The British Operation Perch was designed to allow the British 7th Armoured Division to break through to Villers-Bocage to trap the Panzer Lehr and *Hitlerjugend* Divisions.

Below: Tiger tanks of Wittmann's 2nd Company, 101st SS Battalion, on the road to the Normandy Front. These tanks would soon take part in the most famous Tiger action of the war, at Villers-Bocage.

prominent hill feature to the east of the town in order to have a rest and brew some tea!

Watching from a nearby wood was Michael Wittmann, who famously replied to his gunner Bobby Woll's comment, "they are acting as if they've won the war already", with: "We're going to prove them wrong."

Wittmann ordered his remaining operational Tigers and a Panzer IV from the Panzer Lehr Division to stay behind in their hide while he went on a quick reconnaissance mission into the town itself. He moved south of the British column which was strung out along the Caen road and, unobserved, was able to penetrate into the town. Four enemy Cromwell tanks of the 4 CLY headquarters troop were parked in the main street, with their crews dismounted, relaxing and making tea or carrying out minor repairs to their vehicles. Michael Wittmann caught them totally by surprise, and three of the British tanks were immediately destroyed as he rampaged along the street. One of the tanks was saved by a quick-thinking driver, though, who slammed his vehicle into reverse and backed into a garden.

Cruising down the main street of the town, Wittmann drove past this tank and soon found himself confronted by the whole of 4 CLY's B Squadron. After exchanging several shots with the British tanks, including a 17-pounder-armed Sherman Firefly, Wittmann backed off, reversing away and then turning around. His intention was to rejoin his other Tigers but, driving back down the main street, Wittmann found himself head-to-head with the surviving Cromwell tank that had come out to fight him. The two tanks traded rounds at almost point-blank range. Two British 75mm rounds bounced off the front of Wittmann's Tiger, until one of Woll's 88mm shells found its mark, destroying the British tank. Running short of ammunition, Wittmann pulled back and rejoined the rest of his company. After they had re-stocked on 88mm rounds, the company set upon the 4 CLY's A Squadron with a vengeance.

Unobserved by the British, Wittmann's Tigers were able to approach their unsuspecting prey from behind. First, they knocked out an M3 halftrack at the rear of the British column. This decisive action effectively trapped the British in a sunken road where, unable to move, their tanks and a range of other vehicles were little more than sitting ducks to their German attackers.

After first dealing with the Sherman Fireflys – which alone could threaten the Tigers – Wittmann's tank, helped by the Panzer IV, just drove along the column, picking off the enemy's vehicles one by one. By 10:30 hours, the 4 CLY battlegroup had virtually ceased to exist. The surviving troops on Point 213 surrendered at 13:00 hours.

Wittmann alone had accounted for 23 armoured vehicles, out of a total kill of 20 Cromwells, 4 Sherman Fireflys, 3 Stuarts, 3 artillery observer tanks, 16 Bren Gun carriers, 14 M3 halftracks and 2 6-pounder anti-tank guns. More than 100 British soldiers had been captured and some 62 had been killed. The commanding officer of the 4 CLY, the Viscount Cranley, was later found hiding in a wood when German infantry swept the area for prisoners – he, too, was captured.

As his tanks were finishing off A Squadron, Wittmann now decided to go after the remainder of the British force in Villers-Bocage itself. 4 CLY's remaining B Squadron had responded to calls for help from its comrades trapped on Point 213, but its men had found the route blocked by the knocked-out Cromwells and a steep railway embankment. A troop of four Cromwells and a Sherman Firefly were then sited in an ambush position in the main square in order to trap any German tanks that might try to push down the main street again for a second attack. A 6-pounder anti-tank gun was also positioned to fire into the side armour of any tanks that were seen to be driving past the square of the town.

THE BRITISH STRIKE BACK

Unaware of the "Tiger trap" that had been set for him, Wittmann set off into the town, with one of his Tigers and the Panzer IV in close support. The British tanks let Wittmann's Tiger pass by, then the 6-pounder opened up, striking the armoured monster in its vulnerable side armour. A Cromwell got the following Tiger with a similar shot and British infantry with PIAT bazookas opened up as well. The Panzer IV decided to beat a hasty retreat and, blasting at houses known to contain British infantry as it went, the tank turned and retreated at full speed down the main street of the town.

At this point the Sherman Firefly pulled out of the square and planted a 17-pounder shell in the engine of the escaping Panzer IV. The German crews bailed out of

MICHAEL WITTMANN

Michael Wittmann was born in Vogelthal on 2 April 1914. He joined the German Army in 1934 and was accepted into the *Leibstandarte* Division. He was commissioned as an officer in 1941, and later joined a new Tiger tank unit. His fame grew in correspondence with the increasing number of knocked-out enemy tanks. In one day at the Battle of Kursk, he personally destroyed eight tanks and seven artillery pieces, eventually reaching a tally of thirty tanks and twenty-eight artillery pieces by the battle's end. In 1944 he was awarded the Knight's Cross, adding the Oakleaves shortly after. It was in Normandy that Wittmann sealed his reputation and place in history. At the village of Villers-Bocage he single-handedly destroyed an entire Allied tank column at point blank-range with his Tiger, and was only stopped when his vehicle was disabled. He was awarded the Swords for this extraordinary feat of bravery and skill. He was killed in battle on 8 August 1944, outnumbered and outgunned by a squadron of Canadian M4 Sherman Fireflys. He died the most successful tank ace ever. His tally was more than 138 enemy tanks and 132 artillery pieces, plus many other vehicles.

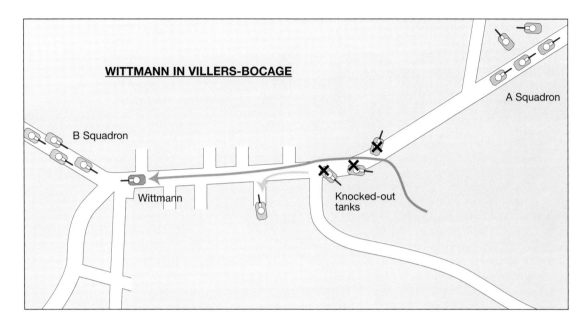

WITTMANN IN VILLERS-BOCAGE

A Squadron

B Squadron

Wittmann

Knocked-out
tanks

their tanks and took cover in the now ruined street. In the ensuing confusion, they were able to make good their escape. To prevent the Germans from recovering their damaged tanks in order to use them later on in the conflict, British troops stuffed petrol-soaked blankets in the tanks' vision ports and set them on fire.

Wittmann now walked more than 7km (4.3 miles) to the headquarters of the Panzer Lehr Division. There, he briefed the divisional operations officer on the action in Villers-Bocage. He was given command of a company of 15 Panzer IVs and ordered to clear the town of all British troops.

The remainder of Wittmann's tanks – as well as other Tigers from 101st Battalion's 1st Company – had already joined in the fight when he arrived back at the town at about 13:00 hours. The 1st Company Tigers led the attack into the main street of the town. In the meantime, a kampfgruppe of infantry from the Panzer Lehr Division joined the attack.

British infantry had now reinforced the town and, at the mercy of this strengthened force, the German tanks were met by a hail of PIAT bazooka rounds. Anti-tank grenades – which the British dropped from upper storeys – were to account for at least one of the four Tigers and one Panzer IV destroyed in the battle.

The Tigers that had survived the battle now pulled back, with this action leaving the remainder of the fighting to the Panzer Lehr infantry. By 17:00 hours, an exhausted General Erskine gave the order for the 22nd Brigade to pull out of Villers-Bocage. The battered

The route of Michael Wittmann's Tiger tank during the action in Villers-Bocage. At one point he traded shots with a British Cromwell at point-blank range.

remnants of this force were to take up their positions on a hill to the east. However, they were given no respite and were pressed closely during the night by the German troops. By the following morning, the Germans had severely dented the British force's morale and had managed to inflict more than 100 casualties.

The Germans continued to press forward, with the 101st SS Battalion's Tigers supporting elements of the 2nd Panzer Division. The men of these units were now arriving in accordance with orders, determined to give their full support to their battling comrades on the Normandy Front.

THE DESERT RATS WITHDRAW
A full-scale withdrawal of the 7th Armoured Division was now ordered by a panicked Montgomery. The commander was haunted by visions of his once élite division being cut off behind German lines where it would be left to an uncertain fate. Accordingly, at 14:00 hours, more than 300 RAF heavy bombers started raining 1727 tonnes (1700 tons) of bombs on Villers-Bocage to cover the withdrawal of the Desert Rats. A total count of one Waffen-SS Tiger was destroyed and three damaged in this massive airborne raid. The action would also leave 29 Tiger crew members as casualties.

Villers-Bocage following the action involving Wittmann's tanks and British armour. These are the remains of British vehicles after taking hits from 88mm German tank guns.

Still the Germans pressed the retreating British, and when the 2nd Panzer's reconnaissance battalion (comprising three motorized companies and one heavy motorized company) hit the 7th Armoured in the flank, Erskine called in fire from 160 British and American heavy guns to allow his men to break contact. One Tiger was knocked out in this fighting. By nightfall on 14 June, the 7th Armoured Division was back at its start-line of two days earlier. It would go down in the annals of history as the unit that suffered the first major Allied defeat of the entire Normandy campaign.

Instead of being a Blitzkrieg, Operation Perch had ended as a shambolic retreat. The materiel losses on the British side were not great and numbered fewer than 50 tanks. However, during the action, a whole divisional attack had first been thwarted and then decisively thrown back.

The military author Michael Reynolds, in his excellent book *Steel Inferno*, provides a succinct explanation of why the Germans were victorious at Villers-Bocage: "In the event, many of his [Montgomery's] commanders at

A Tiger in action in Normandy, possibly of the 101st SS Battalion, harrying the withdrawal of the British 7th Armoured Division from Villers-Bocage.

every level – company, battalion, brigade, division and corps – failed him, and more importantly failed their men. They displayed none of the panache, drive, imagination or willingness to take risks which this operation demanded. One can only guess what might have happened if the roles were reversed and men like Kurt Meyer, Joachim Peiper and Max Wünsche had been in command, with their tanks operating, like those of the British, under conditions of total air superiority."

Credit for this achievement must surely go to Wittmann, who saw the danger posed by the 22nd Armoured Brigade and was responsible for striking the decisive blow. It was his intervention that gave the Panzer Lehr Division's commander – the redoubtable Fritz Bayerlein – the time he needed to mobilize the counterattack force that was eventually strong enough to drive back the famous Desert Rats. In recognition of his efforts during Operation Perch, on the recommendation of Bayerlein, Wittmann was rewarded with

Swords to his Knight's Cross by a grateful Führer. The celebrated Waffen-SS officer was also promoted to the rank of SS-Hauptsturmführer. Smarting in his field headquarters, Montgomery was now preoccupied with devising his next offensive to prise Rommel's men out of Caen.

He came up with the idea of a corps-level attack. In this manoeuvre, three infantry divisions backed by enormous firepower would create a breach for the newly arrived 11th Armoured Division to exploit. More than 60,000 men, backed by more than 600 tanks and 900 guns, would be thrown into the attack. The objective would be the high ground to the west of Caen, just south of the River Odon. This would be the biggest Allied offensive in Normandy so far.

The Allied bridgehead in Normandy was now firmly secure, with thousands of ships delivering 35,000 men, 6000 vehicles and 25,401 tonnes (25,000 tons) of stores a day on to the French coast. By 17 June there were 557,000 Allied troops, with 81,000 vehicles – including 3200 tanks – ashore. The Germans were also racing to reinforce their armies in Normandy. By mid-June 1944, though, Rommel probably only had half as many men at the front as the Allies and some 859 armoured vehicles.

Hill 112

At the end of June 1944, General Montgomery was out-fought by the Waffen-SS in the course of his Operation Epsom. However, he was bleeding Hitler's élite panzer force white, and the likes of Rommel, Dietrich and Meyer were beginning to wonder how long their troops would be able to withstand such harsh punishment before they were annihilated.

A *Hitlerjugend* grenadier keeps watch from the slopes of Hill 112. The M1938 carrying case just above his right foot holds his gas mask. This item was issued to all German soldiers in the war.

With the blunting of the outflanking movement by the British 7th Armoured Division at Villers-Bocage, General Montgomery had to look again at how he was going to take Caen, and open a route for his armour to break out into the French countryside beyond. The arrival of the Panzer Lehr and 2nd Panzer Divisions in the German frontline to the west of Caen effectively closed down the option of any rapid movement by tank forces out of the Allied bridgehead. Any attack would have to punch straight through the German front.

Aware that the Allies were concentrating on pumping huge amounts of men and materiel ashore into their bridgehead, the German commanders, Rommel and Rundstedt, were constantly engaged in their efforts to muster a strong counterattack force to drive the British and Americans back into the sea.

Great hopes were now placed in the fresh divisions of Paul Hausser's II SS Panzer Corps. This unit was currently en route from the Russian Front, and was expected to be available in Normandy in the last week of June 1944.

At the same time, the *Leibstandarte* Division was also – at last – on its way to the front from Belgium, and *Das Reich* and the 17th SS Panzergrenadier Divisions were moving northwards from Toulouse and Bordeaux respectively. It was intended to launch Hausser's corps at the boundary between the British and American bridgeheads. This move would split the Allies apart and the Germans would then be able to crush each of them in turn.

The German plans, however, were constantly being thwarted by the late arrival of the armour necessary for this job. There was also a lack of infantry, which was needed to allow the panzer divisions already in the line to be pulled back and launched into the counterattack.

It was for these reasons that the few panzer divisions stationed in Normandy, such as the *Hitlerjugend*, were still holding the front west of Caen a week after being committed to action. Under a relentless bombardment by scores of guns, battleship broadsides and thousands of fighter-bombers, German combat power was being steadily eroded. The *Hitlerjugend*'s commander, Fritz Witt, succumbed to a naval gunfire barrage on 14 June when his command post was blasted by a huge salvo. Caught by shell splinters as he dived into a bunker, Witt was killed instantly. The 32-year-old Kurt Meyer was appointed in Witt's place, making him the youngest German divisional commander of the war.

Above: A light vehicle of the *Hitlerjugend* Division near Caen in late June (note the SS runes on the number plate). It is well camouflaged as a defence against Allied aircraft.

Above: *Hitlerjugend* grenadiers on the slopes of Hill 112. Note how exposed the side of the hill is, giving whoever controlled the summit excellent fields of fire.

Allied bombing of the French railway and bridge network played havoc with Rommel's attempts to bolster his battered front. The only safe way to move men and materiel by rail was under the cover of darkness, and the nearest railheads to the Normandy Front were a good day's drive away, in the western suburbs of Paris. This geographical constraint posed a particular problem for panzer units that had to make long road-marches to the front from railheads, since it put an immense strain on the sensitive tracks, engines and transmissions of their tanks. The damage caused by this rough ride forced many tanks to be left behind, from where they would be collected by their recovery parties.

These were losses that Rommel's small panzer force could ill afford. As the panzers approached the front, they started to receive attention from Allied fighter-bombers, the dreaded "Jabos". As an average, German units lost between 5 percent and 10 percent of their vehicle strength to Allied air attacks or mechanical breakdowns as they moved to Normandy. When the *Leibstandarte* arrived at the front in late June, its panzer battalions had only 75 percent of their tanks fit to fight.

Farther from the front, the activities of the French resistance – blowing up bridges and ambushing isolated German columns – were beginning to play a major part in delaying the arrival of Waffen-SS units. Forced by damage to the railway network to travel mainly by road, the *Das Reich* Division was plagued by resistance attacks. However, the division was hardened by years of fighting in Russia and its officers responded in the way they had in the East: brutally, and without any mercy.

SS RETRIBUTION

When the *Das Reich* reconnaissance battalion entered the town of Tulle, it allegedly found the remains of 62 German soldiers who had been mutilated, it was claimed, by some resistance fighters. This act of brutality was said to have taken place after the Germans had surrendered. In response, the *Das Reich* troopers rounded up 99 Frenchmen and hung them from lamp-posts.

If deterring others was the intention, it failed. Resistance attacks continued apace. Matters came to a head when a *Das Reich* convoy was fired upon near the town of Oradour, killing an SS-Hauptsturmführer. As revenge, the Waffen-SS men ringed the town, rounding up its entire population in the local church, before setting the church on fire. The blaze killed the 548 men, women and children inside the church. One German was killed when a slate fell off a roof and hit him on the head. In the hours that followed, every building in the town was either blown up or set on fire.

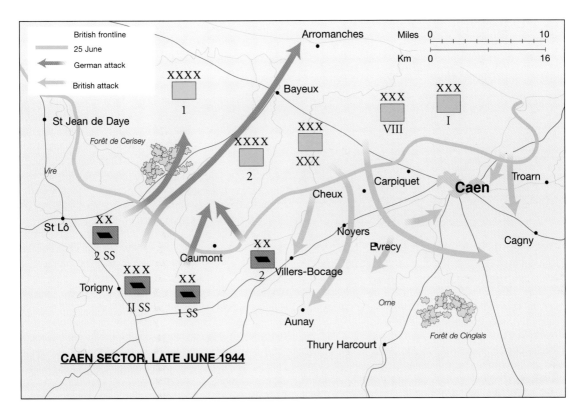

British frontline
25 June
German attack
British attack

Miles 0 ——————— 10
Km 0 ——————— 16

XXXX
1

XXXX
2

XXX

XXX
VIII

XXX
I

XX
2 SS

XXX
II SS

XX
1 SS

XX
2

Arromanches
Bayeux
St Jean de Daye
Forêt de Cerisey
Vire
St Lô
Caumont
Torigny
Carpiquet
Cheux
Noyers
Evrecy
Villers-Bocage
Aunay
Thury Harcourt
Caen
Troarn
Cagny
Orne
Forêt de Cinglais

CAEN SECTOR, LATE JUNE 1944

This massacre at Oradour was the worst incident of its type in the West to be committed by Waffen-SS troops. Rommel was outraged at the massacre, and during a conference with Hitler demanded that a number of *Das Reich* officers be punished. The main culprit during the massacre, SS-Sturmbannführer Otto Dickmann, was later killed in Normandy, and after his death the Waffen-SS leadership was able to hush up the incident.

Eventually 21 rank-and-file soldiers were put on trial by the French after the war, but it was soon revealed that these men had merely been conscripts from the French-speaking Alsace region, and consequently they were able to persuade the court that they were unwilling participants. After the war, the French did not rebuild the town, and it stands today as a monument to the suffering of the French victims who died there in 1944.

One week into the invasion, the Germans seemed to be losing the reinforcement race – until mother nature came to Rommel's assistance on 19 June. From that date, four days of storms raged in the Channel, with the result that two of the Allied prefabricated Mulberry harbours were smashed and some 700 ships were run ashore. The arrival of Allied reinforcements dropped to barely a trickle. Only some 9000 men a day were coming ashore, and 142,247

The German plan to drive a wedge between US and British forces in Normandy, and Montgomery's plan – codenamed Epsom – to capture Caen.

tonnes (140,000 tons) of supplies were stranded in various depots throughout England.

Montgomery's plan for Operation Epsom had to be put back until the last week of June. During Hitler's only visit to the Normandy front on 17 June, he ordered Rommel to prepare a massive counterattack. This would involve six panzer divisions, which would be tasked with smashing the Allied bridgehead. Until four of these divisions arrived in the last week of June, all the "Desert Fox" could do was hang on.

Montgomery was first off the mark, launching Operation Epsom on 25 June. This was aimed at punching through the forward positions of the *Hitlerjugend* Division. Lieutenant-General Sir Richard O'Connor's VIII Corps commanded the offensive, while the 49th, 15th and 43rd Infantry Divisions were responsible for taking the lead in the advance.

The 11th Armoured Division was held in reserve close behind the front, ready go into action once crossings

A *Hitlerjugend* Pak 40 during the fighting on Hill 112. Each of the division's 1st and 2nd SS Panzergrenadier Regiments had three of these potent anti-tank guns.

Shermans of the 24th Lancers and 4th/7th Dragoon Guards were also starting to roll forward into the attack from the eastern edge of the village. A fierce tank battle was developing in the fields south of the village when Meyer, who was watching from Rauray with Wünsche, started to receive reports that a major British attack was developing against the division's centre. He immediately called off the panzer attack and began moving troops to counter the new threat.

It was now the turn of the 15th Highland Division to attack. At exactly 07:30 hours, 700 guns started blasting the positions of the *Hitlerjugend* pioneer battalion around the village of St Manvieu. For 10 minutes this storm of destruction laid waste fields, villages and woods. Then the barrage started to move forward at a rate of 100m (328ft) every three minutes. Behind this torrent of fury came two brigades of British infantry, walking with fixed bayonets. This neatly scheduled attack soon broke down into chaos when nine British Shermans exploded in a minefield laid by the pioneers.

BLUNTING THE BRITISH ATTACK

By late morning the British had pushed 3km (1.8 miles) through the *Hitlerjugend* lines, and had captured Cheux. This success was far from easily won: the assaulting regiments had each lost more than 100 men. Several British tanks were victims of Panzerfaust fire in these actions, but nonetheless it seemed that the British armour had opened a way through to the Odon. Three armoured regiments were able to cruise on forward.

However, Meyer had not yet finished his work. He ordered all of his available tanks to move to cover the breach in the line. Panzer IVs were posted in ambush positions facing eastwards on the high ground at Rauray, and Panthers moved in from their reserve positions at Carpiquet airfield in order that they might hit the British from the other flank. Both sides were poised for battle.

Dietrich now released Tigers of the 101st SS Heavy Panzer Battalion and assault guns of the 21st Panzer Division. Numbers of 88mm Flak batteries were also mustered to form an anti-tank gun line ahead of the British tanks. All through the afternoon and into the evening, the German panzer crews and flak gunners duelled with the British tank crews.

As night fell, some 50 British tanks could be seen through the darkness, burning around Cheux. Meyer's

over the Odon River had been seized. Its objective was Hill 112, which dominated a swathe of the Norman countryside to the west of Caen. The gentle slopes of the hill were covered in open cornfields that provided superb fields of fire for the German gunners who were engaged in defending it. Meyer, Dietrich and Rommel correctly judged that whoever held the hill would control Caen, and with it Normandy, and they all resolved that no effort would be spared keeping it.

The British attack was sequenced, with the 146th and 147th Infantry Brigades hitting Wilhelm Mohnke's 26th Panzergrenadier Regiment at 05:00 hours. Heavy fog covered the battlefield, making it impossible for the German defenders to strike the British infantry before they were almost on top of their positions.

Heavy fighting surged around the village of Fontenay-le-Pesnel and the nearby Tessel woods. Two companies of Panzer IVs were called up to lead a counterattack, which stabilized the situation. However, the neighbouring 901st Panzergrenadier Regiment broke under the pressure, and had to be relieved by the panzers of the *Hitlerjugend* Division. By nightfall Fontenay village itself was still being fought over, with Waffen-SS men holding out in a string of strongpoints. The *Hitlerjugend* panzers, however, still managed to hold the high ground near the village of Rauray, and this vantage point was to play a crucial part in the forthcoming battle.

During the night, the commander of the *Hitlerjugend*'s Panzer Regiment, Max Wünsche, was ordered to form a kampfgruppe to throw back the 49th Division's penetration into Fontenay. Just as the *Hitlerjugend* Panzer IVs and Panthers were advancing into the dawn, British

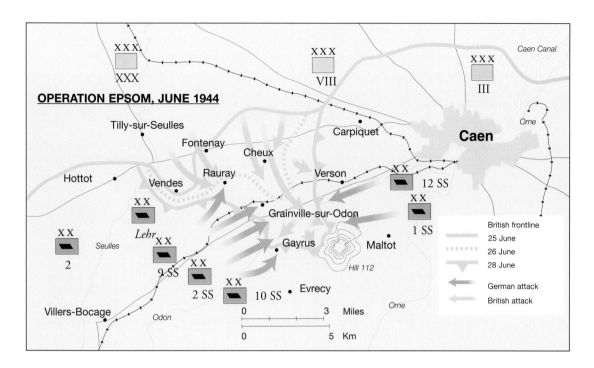

OPERATION EPSOM, JUNE 1944

Caen Canal

Tilly-sur-Seulles

Fontenay

Cheux

Carpiquet

Orne

Caen

Hottot

Vendes

Rauray

Verson

12 SS

Grainville-sur-Odon

1 SS

Lehr

Seulles

2

Gayrus

Maltot

Hill 112

9 SS

2 SS

10 SS

Evrecy

Orne

Villers-Bocage

Odon

British frontline

25 June

26 June

28 June

German attack

British attack

0   3   Miles

0   5   Km

desperate measure had just held the line. Some panzers had even managed to fight their way into St Manvieu and rescue groups of pioneers engaged in fighting behind the British lines. German losses were grievous, though. The *Hitlerjugend* Division lost more than 750 dead, wounded or missing, some 325 from the pioneer battalion.

Montgomery and O'Connor now made the decision to pile on the pressure even more and ordered that the 43rd Wessex Division be fed into the battle, allowing the 15th Division to push its 227th Highland Brigade forward through Cheux to make a dash for the Odon. The 4th Armoured Brigade was brought up to roll behind the infantry, and was to lead the breakout.

Blocking the British axis of advance between Grainville-sur-Odon and Marcelet was a kampfgruppe made up of 30 Panzer IVs and a number of StuG III assault guns. Based around Rauray were 17 Panthers of the *Hitlerjugend*'s 1st Panzer Battalion, backed by a dozen 101st Battalion Tigers. Holding the Odon were a number of 88mm batteries. A Panther company from the 2nd Panzer Division was also dispatched to help Meyer hold the line. Groups of pioneers and panzergrenadiers had turned many of the villages along the Odon into well-fortified strongpoints, but Meyer's defence plan relied on the long-range killing power of his panzer and flak guns.

The British attack got off to a slow start because Cheux was clogged with troops, tanks and supply vehi-

The British attempt to take Hill 112 during Operation Epsom was defeated thanks to the outstanding efforts of the Waffen-SS panzer divisions.

cles. This chaos was not helped by the fact that the 2nd Panzer Division's Panthers made an unauthorized attack and that its move was beaten back, with the loss of four out of its seventeen tanks.

A weak attack in the morning by one Scottish regiment was easily defeated by the panzers covering Rauray. Early in the afternoon, a strong force of Scottish infantry of the Argylls backed by the 23rd Hussars pushed south towards the Odon. Shermans duelled with Panthers, Tigers and Panzer IVs all through the day.

Just after 22:00 hours, the first tanks of the 23rd Hussars were across the Odon and fanning out towards Hill 112. Meyer heard that his vital ground was under threat when his radio interception unit picked up triumphant radio conversations from the British tanks as they advanced, apparently unopposed, from the Argylls' bridgehead at Mandrainville. Overnight the British 159th Brigade joined the Argylls, and elements of the 29th Armoured Brigade were also across the Odon, accompanied by more than 150 Sherman tanks.

During the night, Meyer had resorted to desperate measures to rush reinforcements to hold Hill 112. The

The Allies could bring down massive firepower on German units in Normandy, not only from artillery and aircraft, but also from warships lying offshore. This upturned Tiger was probably hit during an Allied bombing raid.

strongpoints at Rauray and Marcelet were abandoned to release a company of Panzer IVs and panzergrenadiers, as well as an 88mm battery from the Luftwaffe. They reached the summit during the night and were ready and waiting when the British tanks began moving forward at dawn on 28 June. British tanks were soon burning on the slopes of the hill. However, in response, RAF Typhoon strike aircraft were called in to rocket the German tanks, enabling the British infantry to start edging forward, gradually outflanking the outnumbered panzergrenadiers. By noon the Germans had been pushed off the exposed summit of the hill.

Wünsche was soon on the scene and set about mustering the remains of his panzer regiment to contain the British breakthrough. Panthers and Panzer IVs were positioned around three sides of the hill in order to pen in the British, who were threatening to overwhelm the thinly stretched defences. The presence of 30 *Hitlerjugend* panzers, backed by 88mm flak guns and Nebelwerfer rockets, was just enough to hold the line. Three times during the day Wünsche led his tanks forward into a storm of 17-pounder fire from the now dug-in British anti-tank guns in the woods along the banks of the Odon. The British were still determined to hold Hill 112 whatever the cost, feeding new armoured regiments into the battle until their point units ran out of ammunition or tanks. By the time the last of Wünsche's attacks went in at 17:00 hours, some 40 Shermans were smashed on the slopes of the vital ground. As darkness

fell over the battlefield, the British troops had retained their precarious foothold on Hill 112.

Meyer's division was now almost split in two by the huge British penetration. Mohnke's panzergrenadier regiment was just about holding out on the eastern edge of the British salient, and the remainder of the division was stopping O'Connor's tanks from driving directly into Caen from the east. The British were desperate to expand their breach and relentlessly attacked the *Hitlerjugend* positions during 28 June. The *Hitlerjugend* troops had been in action for almost 48 hours straight and were exhausted. Those who were not dead or wounded were falling asleep in their trenches and tank turrets. Help was now desperately needed if the division's front was not to collapse under the pressure.

Just in time, elements of the *Leibstandarte* and *Das Reich* Divisions were approaching the battlefield. They were to be launched in a coordinated attack to pinch off the top of the British salient. Kampfgruppe *Weidinger* from *Das Reich's Der Führer* Panzergrenadier Regiment was thrown in to bolster Mohnke's hard-pressed regiment around Grainville-sur-Odon. With only a handful of army Panthers in support, all Mohnke's Waffen-SS men could do was doggedly hold on to the string of villages along the north bank of the Odon through the day against attacks by a British infantry brigade with strong Churchill tank support.

On the other side of the salient, which had now been dubbed the "Scottish Corridor", two panzergrenadier battalions of the *Leibstandarte* entered the battle in a dawn attack from the village of Verson. Dietrich pulled together strong panzer support in the shape of 22 Panzer IVs from the 21st Panzer Division, a company of *Hitlerjugend* Panthers, and three Tigers of the 101st SS Battalion. At first the *Leibstandarte* kampfgruppe swept all before it, sending the Monmouthshire Regiment reeling back in disorder and destroying three British tanks. The advance continued for another 3km (1.9 miles) until the British defence solidified around Colleville. Then tanks of the British 4th Armoured Brigade were thrown in against the *Leibstandarte*'s flank. In the face of this onslaught and a massive supporting artillery barrage, the German attack faltered. Five Panthers were lost and several other tanks damaged. The *Leibstandarte* spearhead was less than 3km (1.9 miles) from the *Das Reich* troopers in Grainville-sur-Odon. Nevertheless, the Scottish Corridor remained open to Hill 112.

During the morning of 28 June, the German command in Normandy was thrown into crisis by the suicide of Colonel-General Friedrich Dollman, commander of the Seventh Army. Dollman was the senior German officer on the Normandy Front in the absence of Rommel and Rundstedt, who had been summoned to Berchtesgaden for a conference with the Führer.

DOLLMAN'S SUICIDE

The British seizure of the bridgehead over the Odon had thrown all the German plans for a counterattack against the British bridgehead into chaos. At 20:10 hours on 29 June, Dollman decided that the situation on the *Hitlerjugend*'s front was so precarious that Hausser's corps would have to be diverted for a immediate counterstroke against the western flank of the British salient. Hausser replied to Dollman that his troops would not be ready to take action for another day. Dollman was already in a precarious position. He had been placed under investigation for the loss of Cherbourg to the Americans two days before. Not wanting to face the wrath of the Führer for countermanding his attack orders, the colonel-general reached for his cyanide capsule.

The next most senior German officer in Normandy was Hausser, and within a few hours he had been ordered to replace Dollman. Fearing that it was not a good idea to change command just as his corps was about to attack, Hausser remained with his troops for one more day before handing over to SS-Gruppenführer Willi Bittrich, who was at that time the commander of the *Hohenstaufen* Division.

Throughout the night, Hausser's men were struggling to get into position for an attack at 06:00 hours. With a combined strength of more than 30,000 men, 79 Panthers, 79 Panzer IVs and 76 StuG IIIs, II Panzer Corps was the largest German armoured formation to enter battle en masse during the entire Normandy campaign. The corps' Tiger battalion had yet to arrive at the front, so it was unable to offer support for the attack on 29 June.

Alerted by their ULTRA code-breaking operation, the British were well aware of the impending counterattack. Montgomery, fearful of the 11th Armoured Division's tanks being cut off around Hill 112, decided that he would pull back the 4th and 29th Armoured Brigades from the bridgeheads south of the Odon and concentrate his tanks to beat back the German attack on the flanks of the Scottish Corridor.

THE WAFFEN-SS STANDS FIRM

Using his ULTRA intelligence, Montgomery now decided to unleash his artillery and airpower against II SS Panzer Corps. The *Hohenstaufen* and *Frundsberg* Divisions were caught in their assembly areas around Noyers by huge artillery barrages, then waves of RAF Typhoons swooped down to machine-gun and rocket their columns.

The *Hohenstaufen* was given the objective of Cheux, at the heart of the Scottish Corridor. An attack by 100 RAF Lancaster bombers played havoc with its attack and it did not roll forward until the early afternoon. With its two panzergrenadier regiments in the lead, the division quickly secured Grainville-sur-Odon. As the Waffen-SS Panzer IVs, Panthers and StuG IIIs took the lead for the advance on Cheux they ran into the British 4th Armoured Brigade. By the end of the day some 60 British tanks were burning in the fields. Around 30 panzers and assault guns were lost in this battle, which failed to produce the decisive breakthrough that its tacticians had anticipated.

At the same time, the *Leibstandarte* kampfgruppe tried to push westwards in order to effect a link-up with the *Hohenstaufen* Division. However, the *Leibstandarte*'s attack never got beyond its start-line: the Waffen-SS troopers had been hit hard by a British armoured regiment. Although the kampfgruppe did manage to destroy 12 tanks, later on it was forced to retreat and surrender 2 villages to the British 43rd Division.

South of the Odon River, the *Frundsberg* Division was ordered to clear the British from Hill 112. A barrage from 60 Nebelwerfers swept the hill prior to the assault and then *Frundsberg* pressed home its attacks, assisted by *Hitlerjugend* tanks firing from the southern and eastern slopes. Soon, *Frundsberg* and *Hitlerjugend* Panzer IVs were on the summit of Hill 112, and panzergrenadiers were then sent forward to mop up the last remaining British bridgeheads over the Odon.

Caen: Battle of Attrition

Montgomery's efforts to take the strategic Hill 112, outside Caen, during the second half of June 1944 came to naught. However, although the Waffen-SS divisions fought superbly to repel the numerous British attacks, they were slowly being ground down in a battle of attrition. The British had reserves of both men and tanks, whereas II SS Panzer Corps was woefully short of both.

Crossing a water obstacle with the aid of an MP40 submachine gun. Though the battles around Caen were fought during the summer months, violent thunderstorms turned the ground into a quagmire.

In front of Caen, Montgomery had not given up his ambitions to destroy the Waffen-SS panzer divisions and seize the Norman city. The *Hitlerjugend* Division was still the rock of the German defence, positioned in a semi-circle in its western suburbs. The arrival of II SS Panzer Corps had released Meyer's division from the responsibility of holding the western edge of the Scottish Corridor, and allowed him to concentrate it for the defence of Caen. The 25th Panzergrenadier Regiment was holding the villages to the northwest of the city, and Wilhelm Mohnke's regiment was holding to the west, centred on Carpiquet airfield. Meyer still had a kampfgruppe from the *Leibstandarte* under his command, and he posted it to the south of the airfield. Max Wünsche's panzers were holding the eastern edges of the Hill 112 feature. It would be mid-July before the *Hitlerjugend*'s sister division would be in Normandy in strength.

The *Frundsberg* Division was firmly entrenched on the summit of Hill 112 and the nearby Hill 113. It was now reinforced by the Tigers of the 102nd SS Heavy Panzer Battalion. Willi Bittrich's other division, the *Hohenstaufen*, was on the north bank of the Odon, linking his corps to the army panzer units to the west.

Dietrich and Bittrich could muster a combined total of 94 Panzer IVs, 45 Panthers, 48 StuG IIIs and just over 30 Tiger Is ready for battle.

It was now the turn of the Canadians to return to the fray, and they were given the objective of taking the northwestern corner of Caen in Operation Windsor. The attack opened on the evening of 3 July with a massive salvo from the British battleship HMS *Rodney*'s 16in guns. Then some 500 Canadian and British guns opened fire. Shells rained down on Carpiquet airfield throughout the night. At dawn the 8th Canadian Brigade was launched against the airfield. A forward panzergrenadier company held the attack briefly, while panzer reserves were mobilized. As the 17 tanks came up, a *Hitlerjugend* 88mm flak battery on high ground outside the airfield started to rip into the Canadian tanks. Throughout the day, the Canadians tried to push forward across the airfield's runway, but were rebuffed with heavy losses. RAF Typhoons were called in to blast a route through the defences. No panzers were hit and they kept up a furious resistance, hitting more than a dozen tanks and inflicting almost 400 casualties. To relieve pressure on the troops defending the airfield, a *Leibstandarte* panzergrenadier battalion was moved to

By early July the *Hitlerjugend* was suffering crippling losses trying to hold Caen. It had lost 50 percent of its tank strength, plus 28 percent of its manpower.

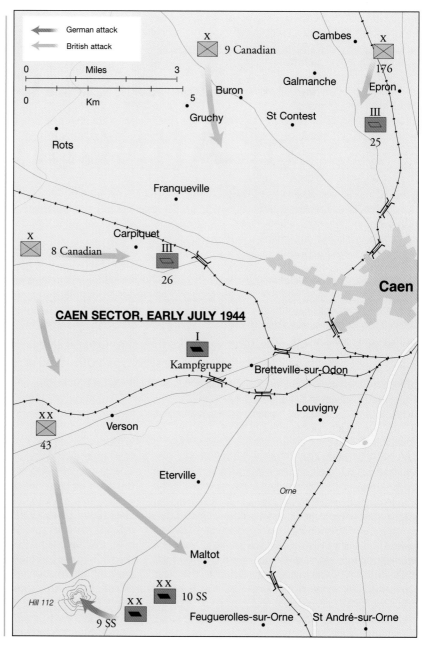

German attack

British attack

0 Miles 3

0 Km

X
9 Canadian

Cambes

X
176

Galmanche

Epron

Buron

5

III
25

Gruchy

St Contest

Rots

Franqueville

X
8 Canadian

Carpiquet

III
26

Caen

CAEN SECTOR, EARLY JULY 1944

I
Kampfgruppe

Bretteville-sur-Odon

Louvigny

X X
43

Verson

Eterville

Orne

Maltot

X X
10 SS

Hill 112

X X
9 SS

Feuguerolles-sur-Orne   St André-sur-Orne

its northern edge to launch a night attack. The assault was halted after German artillery fire mistakenly hit the Waffen-SS troopers.

Rebuffed with heavy losses at Carpiquet, Montgomery now decided to call up RAF Bomber Command to blast the *Hitlerjugend* out of Caen. During the evening of 7 July, some 467 Lancaster and Halifax heavy bombers dumped 2540 tonnes (2500 tons) of bombs on the city in a raid that turned much of it into rubble. To avoid any of his troops being accidentally hit, Montgomery held back the follow-up infantry assault until 08:00 hours on 8 July. Laudable though this was, it meant Meyer's men had time to recover from the shock of the raid in time to meet the inevitable attack.

First into the attack during Operation Charnwood was the British 176th Infantry Brigade, which was to seize the northern suburbs of Caen. Then the Canadian 9th Infantry Brigade would take the northwest corner of the city. Apart from a single company of *Hitlerjugend* Panthers, there were few reserves, and Meyer used them to rescue panzergrenadiers trapped by Canadian attacks. Almost 500 *Hitlerjugend* men were killed or wounded during the fighting. Meyer asked Dietrich for permission to withdraw, which was initially refused because it conflicted with a Führer order "to hold to the last bullet". By nightfall, Dietrich relented, and Meyer's battered division was starting to pull back into Caen and across the Orne River to a form a new defensive line, alongside the advance elements of the *Leibstandarte* which was finally arriving in strength. This was just in time. The *Hitlerjugend* Division had lost some 3300 men, or 28 percent of its manpower strength, and half its tanks had been knocked out since it was committed to battle on 6 June.

It was now the turn of the divisions of II SS Panzer Corps to feel Montgomery's wrath. The 43rd Wessex Division was given the objective of driving the Germans from Hill 112 once and for all, opening the way for the 4th Armoured Brigade to surge forward and seize crossings over the River Orne. Standing in their way was the *Frundsberg* Division of SS-Brigadeführer Heinz Harmel, reinforced by the pitiful remains of Max Wünsche's *Hitlerjugend* Panzer Regiment.

OPERATION JUPITER

Operation Jupiter kicked off with the usual heavy artillery barrage, after which two infantry brigades, supported by heavy Churchill infantry tanks, began frontal attacks on Hill 112 and the village of Maltot on its northern slope. When it looked as though 25 Churchills were going to take the summit of Hill 112, *Frundsberg*'s panzer battalion arrived from its reserve position and "brewed up" most of them. The commander of the 43rd Division eventually rescinded orders to commit the 4th Armoured Brigade's last tank regiment after its commander persuaded him they would suffer 75 percent losses.

Simultaneously, as the attack on Hill 112 was going in, the British 130th Brigade was assaulting Maltot. Three regiments of infantry backed by more Churchills had to attack across open ground to seize their objectives on the northern bank of the Orne River. After making good progress, the brigade was soon being raked by fire from three sides. Tigers of the 102nd SS Battalion on Hill 112 were firing into the British left flank, *Hitlerjugend* Panthers and Panzers IVs were to the attackers' front, and elements of the *Leibstandarte* kampfgruppe were on the right. The British were caught in a killing zone, which knocked out most of the attacking squadron of tanks. With close support from the Tigers, all the Dorset Regiment's anti-tank guns were knocked out and the British soldiers were soon streaming back to their start-line.

Back on Hill 112, the Duke of Cornwall's Light Infantry were launched forward into the attack as dusk was falling, and took the summit at last. A counterattack led by a handful of Tigers failed to dislodge the British from their newly won prize.

RETAKING HILL 112

With the key to the German position in central Normandy about to fall, Dietrich and Bittrich reshuffled their forces to strike back. SS-Standartenführer Sylvester Stadler's *Hohenstaufen* Division was released from west of the Odon to counterattack and retake Hill 112. By the middle of the afternoon on 11 July, the British infantry regiment was being ripped to pieces by machine-gun, tank, artillery, mortar and rocket fire. *Hohenstaufen*'s assault gun battalion led yet one more attack forward, and it swept away the Duke of Cornwall's, leaving 250 dead or wounded behind, including their commanding officer, on the summit of the hill. The Germans had regained control of Hill 112 and stayed on its summit for the rest of July.

On 15 July Montgomery launched Operation Greenline to expand the British front down the Odon valley. Its aim was to keep II SS Panzer Corps occupied while the British massed their armour for a major attack to the east of Caen. In this aim it succeeded. A break-through around Noyers forced Bittrich to move the *Hohenstaufen* to close the breach on 16 July. Only some 20 panzers could be mustered to form the assault kampfgruppe as it attacked from Hill 113 towards the Odon. The panzers ran into a British tank brigade and chased it off, knocking out 48 Shermans and capturing a dozen for the loss of five German tanks. The division was soon sucked into a meat-grinder battle. A day later its two panzergrenadier regiments had to be combined into a single kampfgruppe, while its panzer regiment could only muster 25 Panthers, 13 Panzer IVs and 15 StuG IIIs. The *Frundsberg* Division remained on Hill 112, fighting off a sustained series of attacks. In just over two weeks of fighting it had lost more than 2200 men. Its panzer regiment was reduced to 12 operational Panzer IVs and 6 StuG IIIs. Only with help from the 102nd SS Battalion's Tigers was the division able to hold the British at bay.

The bitter fighting to the west of Caen had bled II SS Panzer Corps dry, reducing the last panzer reserve to a shadow of its former self.

Operation Goodwood

Montgomery continued to pound the German lines defending Caen, and launched another offensive – codenamed Goodwood – in the second half of July 1944. Once again the SS panzer divisions fought off numerous armoured attacks and knocked out scores of tanks. But they suffered their own losses, and Waffen-SS commanders wondered how long they could contain the British.

A knocked-out Tiger I of the 101st SS Battalion during the fighting for Caen. This tank may have been disabled during the massive Allied bombing attack just prior to Operation Goodwood.

As British and Canadian troops inched slowly into the ruins of Caen, General Montgomery was putting the final touches to his next major offensive. He planned to throw in three armoured divisions – with 877 tanks which were to be backed by 10,000 assault infantry and 8000 vehicles – into the fray. The biggest preparatory bombardment so far in the campaign – involving some 712 guns, 942 British and 571 US heavy bombers – would deliver a massive 300,000 shells and some 7823 tonnes (7700 tons) of bombs on to the German defenders.

Operation Goodwood, as the offensive was codenamed, would be launched from the small bridgehead over the Orne River, to the east of Caen. The target for Operation Goodwood was the Bourguebus ridge above Caen. Standing in the way of the British was a defensive position laid out in considerable depth by the newly appointed German commander of the Caen sector, General of Panzer Troops Heinrich Eberbach. The front-line was held by the remnants of the 16th Luftwaffe Field Division. Behind it were the remnants of the 21st Panzer Division, supported by 88mm flak guns and Tiger tanks. In reserve on the Bourguebus ridge were the *Leibstandarte* and part of the *Hitlerjugend* Divisions, and

these units were to go into action under the command of the notorious Josef "Sepp" Dietrich.

This would be the first main test of the *Leibstandarte*'s panzer crews and many of its panzergrenadiers, who had only arrived at the front a week or so earlier. It is estimated that only some 14,000 men of the division were committed to the Normandy battle, because nearly 6000 trained recruits and logistic personnel were left behind at depots in Belgium. After more than a month's continuous fighting the *Hitlerjugend* Division was resting in reserve, except for a strong kampfgruppe under Max Wünsche, which Hitler ordered to the coast at the Orne estuary to counter a spurious invasion threat. Therefore the initial brunt of the coming fighting would fall on the *Leibstandarte*'s Panzer Regiment under the command of Joachim Peiper, with 59 Panzer IVs and 46 Panthers. The division's assault gun battalion had some 35 StuG IIIs ready for action and the 101st SS Battalion's 25 Tiger Is. The famous victor of Villers-Bocage, Michael Wittmann, was now in command of this unit.

In total, the Germans could scrape together some 4800 infantry, around 200 tanks and 50 assault guns. In addition to this unconvincing force, they had 36 75mm

At the end of the first day of Goodwood, the British 29th Armoured Brigade had lost 160 out of its 214 tanks, largely due to the efforts of the *Leibstandarte* Division.

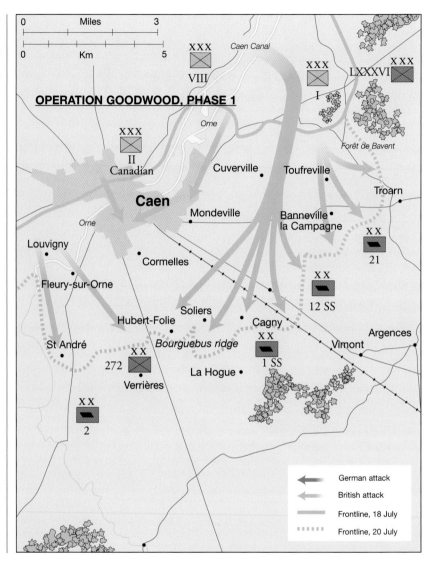

anti-tank guns, 72 88mm flak guns, 194 field guns and 17 Nebelwerfer rocket launchers. Their ability to blunt Operation Goodwood was doubtful.

The Allied artillery barrage began at 05:25 hours on 18 July, and 10 minutes later the RAF bombers appeared overhead and started to unload their deadly cargo on the positions of the 21st Panzer and 16th Luftwaffe Divisions. After nearly 1000 Lancasters had passed over the target zones southeast of Caen, two further waves of bombers, mainly US B-17s, added to the carnage. Hundreds of Germans were killed or wounded, and much equipment damaged or destroyed. Massive 57-tonne (56-ton) Tiger tanks were turned upside down, and

some German soldiers were driven insane by terror, but Montgomery's expectations for the bombardment soon proved to be very inaccurate. When the contrails of the last bombers disappeared just before 09:00 hours, the dazed defenders emerged from their bunkers, trenches or under their tanks to man their defences. While the Luftwaffe division was devastated by the air attack and did not offer serious resistance, the German reserve positions were not so badly hit. The Waffen-SS units were virtually untouched, and Dietrich immediately alerted them to be ready to counterattack.

Moving forward first was the British 11th Armoured Division, with some 214 tanks of the 29th Armoured

Brigade leading the way. These were arrayed in attack formation. The division's lead tank brigades moved out of the Orne bridgehead east of Caen with relative ease, covered by a rolling artillery barrage, then turned south before heading for Bourguebus ridge. In their wake there was chaos. There were not enough bridges for the follow-up artillery and supply units to cross the Orne River, and the 11th Armoured Infantry Brigade became bogged down in clearing two insignificant villages of a few isolated German defenders. The 7th Armoured Division was immobilized for the remainder of the day, not because of enemy gunfire, but because ahead of it were thick traffic jams that blocked the Orne River crossings.

The remnants of the 21st Panzer's assault gun battalion had already started to engage the 29th Brigade's lead regiment, the Fife and Forfar Yeomanry, destroying more than 20 Shermans. It was to conduct a fighting withdrawal towards the *Leibstandarte*'s "stop line" on Bourguebus ridge. By 10:00 hours Wittmann's Tigers had already moved up and were ripping into the Shermans of the 3rd Royal Tank Regiment (3 RTR).

The *Leibstandarte*'s commander, SS-Brigadeführer Teddy Wisch, forward on the ridge, was engaged in conducting a detailed reconnaissance. For once, the Allied fighter-bombers were unsuccessful in stopping the movement of the German panzers, and by noon Peiper's Panther battalion was lying in wait. It had moved up into hull-down ambush positions on the northern slopes of the Bourguebus ridge, where a series of sunken roads provided superb cover for the Waffen-SS tanks. While the Panthers held the British advance, Wisch intended to use his assault gun battalion in order to hit the British armoured phalanx in the flank.

PEIPER'S HIT-AND-RUN TACTICS

Peiper's Panthers fought a mobile battle. While his Panzer IVs and Tigers held ground, he led the Panthers forward four times on raids into the British tanks before withdrawing to cover in order to rearm and reorganize. At 12:45 hours the Panthers moved forward to the village of Soliers to engage the 29th Brigade for the first time. In the space of a few minutes, the Fife and Forfar Yeomanry lost 29 tanks. The regiment ceased to exist as a fighting formation. It took two hours for the British command to form a rescue column from the 23rd Hussars, who had been bogged down fighting the 88mm flak guns in Cagny. When they arrived below Bourguebus ridge they were greeted by the sight of dozens of Shermans burning across the hillside. Barely had the Hussars arrived when they started to take hits from the combined force of *Leibstandarte*'s Panthers, Wittmann's Tigers and the

21st Panzer's StuG IIIs. Four tanks exploded within minutes of entering the battle, and soon another 16 were out of action.

At this point the *Leibstandarte*'s StuG IIIs started to arrive, and Wisch fed them northwards to hit the right flank of 3 RTR. A further 20 British tanks were destroyed and the 29th Brigade began to waver; however, it did rally for just long enough to enable the Northamptonshire Yeomanry to attempt another move forward. But all of this was to no avail, and when 16 of its Cromwell tanks were knocked out, the regiment couldn't help but lose heart.

By nightfall panzer crews of the *Leibstandarte* were looking out on a tank graveyard. At least 160 of the 29th Brigade's 200 tanks were smouldering hulks. The Fife and Forfars and 3 RTR had each lost more than 40 tanks, while the Guards Armoured Division lost more than 60 tanks in its futile engagement with the 21st Panzer Division around Cagny.

THE SS LINE IS STRENGTHENED

During the night the British desperately tried to sort out the dreadful traffic jams in the Orne bridgehead and reorganize their battered armoured divisions for another attack, this time with three divisions attacking abreast. Just after first light, 3 RTR tried to push forward against the *Leibstandarte*'s Panthers, only to run into a wall of fire. Pinned down, the regiment lost 43 of its 60 tanks and the remaining Shermans pulled back behind a railway embankment for safety.

It would not be until late morning that General O'Connor, still commanding VIII Corps, managed to issue his orders to his shell-shocked and battered divisions for his coordinated attack. The assault could not be started until late afternoon, which gave Dietrich time to feed in the first elements of the *Hitlerjugend* Division, with two panzergrenadier battalions and some tanks, in between the right flank of the *Leibstandarte* and 21st Panzer. Wisch's remaining Panzer IVs were also brought into the "stop line" on Bourguebus ridge, and at last panzergrenadiers arrived in strength to give the *Leibstandarte*'s defensive line some depth. Later on that same afternoon, Kampfgruppe *Wünsche* also returned to the front. It had been caught up in an anti-invasion wild-goose chase, but now it was back it was tasked with providing the beleaguered Dietrich with another armoured reserve.

Lined up from west to east to take on the Waffen-SS was the battered 11th Armoured Division and the fresh 7th Armoured Division, while the Guards Armoured Division was tasked with taking on the *Hitlerjugend*. Wisch favoured the tactic of concentrating most of his tanks in the centre of the line on the Desert Rats' axis of advance. This decision would leave the left flank of the division held only by panzergrenadiers and a handful of StuG IIIs and 88mm Flak guns.

When the 11th Armoured began its attack at 16:00 hours, the German defence initially held. However, the now re-equipped 3 RTR pressed home the attack, and when it destroyed one of the two StuG IIIs holding the village of Bras, the other StuG withdrew. This was disastrous for the panzergrenadier battalion positioned in the village, as it now found itself without anti-tank protection. By 17:10 hours, 3 RTR and a British infantry battalion were mopping up in the village, and by the time they had finished they had 300 Waffen-SS prisoners.

The Northamptonshire Yeomanry was now launched forward again to exploit this success, only to run into Peiper's Panthers and more StuG IIIs in hull-down firing positions. In the space of a few minutes, 32 Shermans were ablaze and the British regiment ceased to exist as a fighting unit. As his tanks were dealing with this attack, the weight of the 7th Armoured hit Peiper's main "stop line" in the centre of the Bourguebus ridge. The rapid loss of eight Shermans stopped the Desert Rats in their tracks, and they made no attempt to close with the *Leibstandarte*'s hull-down tanks and 88mm flak guns.

On the *Leibstandarte*'s right flank, the *Hitlerjugend* found itself on the receiving end of the Guards Armoured's onslaught. Its defence was stiffened by the arrival of the first Panzerjäger IV self-propelled anti-tank guns, which boasted powerful L70 long-barrelled 75mm cannons. The day of 19 July had been a major defensive success for I SS Panzer Corps: it had knocked out 65 of the 11th Armoured's tanks and scores of others along its front.

The 7th Armoured Division tried its luck again against Peiper's tanks during the morning of 20 July and fared little better, with the County of London Yeomanry losing dozens more tanks to Panthers and Tigers. In the afternoon it was the turn of the Canadians to join Operation Goodwood from their bridgehead in southern Caen. With heavy fighter-bomber support, the Canadian 3rd Division hit the *Leibstandarte* panzergrenadiers and reconnaissance troops holding the division's extreme left flank. Typhoons weaved over the battlefield, strafing German tanks and gun positions with impunity. At first the air support proved decisive, and they drove back the Waffen-SS men from several villages. Then, at around 17:00 hours, a massive thunderstorm broke over the battlefield, at a stroke denying the Canadians their advantage. A *Leibstandarte* panzergrenadier battalion, backed by a company of StuG IIIs, was launched on a counterattack. The Saskatchewan Regiment was overrun and 208 men killed or captured. Then the kampfgruppe moved against the Essex Scottish Regiment, sending it back in considerable disorder. *Leibstandarte* panzergrenadiers fought on through the night, pushing the Canadians back, to restore the German line, despite the almost constant heavy rain.

By dawn on 21 July, I SS Panzer Corps was holding firm. Operation Goodwood had failed spectacularly to achieve its stated objective: to capture the Bourguebus ridge and break open the German front east of Caen. Montgomery did not give up his ambitions to destroy the German defenders southeast of Caen. He now planned a rolling series of offensives to keep Hausser and Bittrich's Waffen-SS panzer reserves occupied while the Americans launched their long-awaited decisive attack in the West.

A column of *Leibstandarte* vehicles in Normandy in July 1944 (note the divisional key symbol on the front of the halftrack). The front must be some way off, as the mood is relaxed and no effort has been made to camouflage the vehicles.

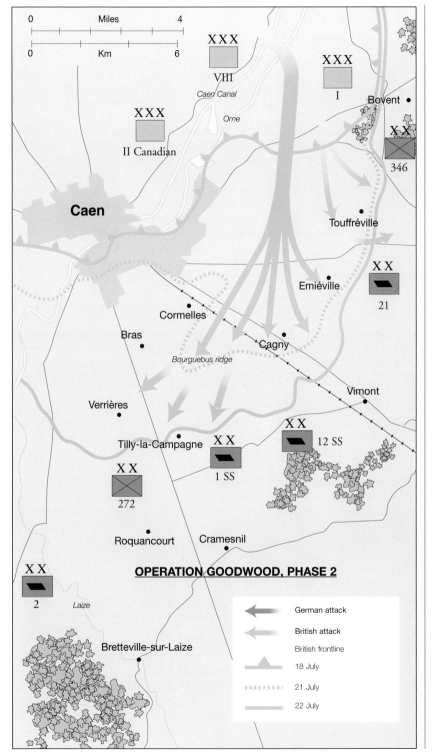

The British fed more units in to drive the Germans back, but Waffen-SS resistance only intensified. Montgomery's soldiers thus made only marginal gains.

OPERATION GOODWOOD, PHASE 2

German attack	
British attack	
British frontline	
	18 July
	21 July
	22 July

Soldiers of the *Leibstandarte* Division near the Bourguebus ridge in July 1944. The division had been in the German strategic reserve in early June, being committed in July.

The first of these offensives fell to the Canadians, and it would see them attacking the *Leibstandarte* on the Bourguebus ridge. They would be sent into attack over almost the same ground on which O'Connor's VIII Corps had been butchered six days before.

Operation Spring started with a night attack early in the morning of 25 July, after an air strike by 60 medium bombers. Then the Canadian infantry regiment of the 3rd Canadian Division advanced straight into the guns of the *Leibstandarte*. At 400m (1312ft) in front of their lines, the Waffen-SS tanks and panzergrenadiers opened fire. The North Nova Scotias were pinned down for more than 16 hours. By the time the regiment pulled back under cover of dusk, only 100 men returned. The 3rd Division's attacked was stopped dead.

The 2nd Canadian Division simultaneously attacked the left flank of the *Leibstandarte*. They benefited from the presence of a 17-pounder anti-tank gun battery that neutralized the Waffen-SS panzers and StuG IIIs, knocking out four tanks. Without panzer support, the *Leibstandarte* panzergrenadiers had to pull back, and by dawn the Royal Highland Light Infantry (RHLI) had captured the village of Verrières. British tanks of the 1st Royal Tank Regiment (1 RTR) were now sent forward to exploit this success. They ran into dug-in *Leibstandarte* StuG IIIs, and soon British tanks were burning across the hillside. Later in the morning, it was the turn of the Black Watch of Canada to attack. They were enfiladed by panzer fire from high ground to the west, and their

supporting tanks were decimated, so by the time they reached the crest of the Bourguebus ridge there were only 60 men left. More than 300 dead and wounded were littering the battlefield by 17:00 hours. Now the *Leibstandarte* launched a panzergrenadier counter-attack, led by 10 Panzer IVs. They were closing in on the RHLI in Verrières when two squadrons of RAF Typhoons swooped down, rocketing three German tanks.

When the full casualty returns started to arrive at II Canadian Corps' headquarters during the evening, senior commanders were horrified. More than 450 men were dead and some 1000 wounded, yet the frontline had only moved a few hundred metres farther south.

It took the British and Canadians six days to recover from the shock of Operation Spring. The 2nd Canadian Division was ordered to seize part of the summit of the Bourguebus ridge centred around Tilly-la-Campagne. After initial skirmishing on the night of 29/30 July, the main attack went in at 02:30 hours on 31 July led by the Calgary Highlanders. The attack failed, and for the next three days the Canadians resorted to pounding the village with artillery and air strikes, in between daily attempts to storm it. Each time, they were driven off with heavy losses. For the *Leibstandarte* men holding out in the ruins of Tilly-la-Campagne, this period entered their division's folklore as the most intense bombardment it had endured in six years of war.

As the *Leibstandarte* held firm south of Caen, the *Hitlerjugend* was withdrawn from the front to act as reserve for Dietrich's I SS Panzer Corps. Almost two months into the Normandy campaign, Kurt Meyer's division had suffered 3500 casualties. Its operational tank strength stood at 61 Panthers, 39 Panzer IVs and 27 Panzerjäger IVs on 30 July, as well as 19 Tigers of the attached 101st SS Battalion. The *Leibstandarte* was in better shape, and had 61 Panzer IVs, 40 Panthers and 23 StuG IIIs ready for action.

OPERATION EXPRESS

To the east of Dietrich's corps, Bittrich's *Frundsberg* Division had been holding firm on Hill 112 for more than two weeks, after the 43rd Division's failed attempt to take the strategic high ground. Montgomery kept feeding in units to keep up the pressure on the *Frundsberg* and 272nd Infantry Divisions. Thanks to the presence of the Tigers of the 102nd SS Battalion, most of these attempts failed with heavy losses. One Tiger was always kept on the hill's summit while the rest of the battalion's 19 tanks were held in reserve. Operation Express on 22 July saw two battalions of the Wiltshire Regiment, backed by the Churchills of the 9th Royal Tank Regiment (9 RTR), try to sweep up the eastern slope of the hill after they had taken the village of Maltot. The Tigers and Churchills clashed head on and the British tanks were getting the worst of the engagement, losing six tanks, when a forward air controller called down a squadron of Typhoons. The Tigers withdrew into cover, leaving the village in British hands along with 400 Wehrmacht prisoners. Hill 112 remained firmly in German hands for yet another week.

The *Hohenstaufen* Division was called back from the left flank of *Frundsberg* at the height of the Operation Goodwood battle and positioned in the Orne valley, guarding the southern suburbs of Caen. It helped the *Leibstandarte* defeat Montgomery's armoured offensive, forming a kampfgruppe to take back three villages captured by Canadian troops. Early in the morning on 22 July, two of the division's Panthers led forward a panzer-grenadier battalion which ran into heavy anti-tank gunfire. By the end of the day, nine of the division's twenty-four Panthers were out of action, but the key villages were secured. As Operation Spring got under way against the *Leibstandarte* on 25 July, the *Hohenstaufen* was also hit hard by Canadian troops. To restore the line, the division's panzer regiment and 102nd SS Battalion Tigers rolled forward, inflicting heavy losses on the attacking tanks.

Halted to the east, south and west of Caen by Hausser and Bittrich's panzer corps, Montgomery now switched the focus of his attack to the far west of the British sector. On 30 July, he launched Operation Bluecoat southwards towards Vire and Mount Pincon, with the 7th, 11th and Guards Armoured Divisions in the lead. II SS Panzer Corps was now diverted to block this move that punched a hole in the thinly held sector of the German line. RAF Typhoons soon located the Waffen-SS tank columns in the afternoon on 2 August. They launched 923 sorties, destroying 13 tanks and 76 trucks, holding up the deployment of the German tanks for most of the day. British armour was advancing through open countryside and French villagers came out to greet their liberators with some long-hidden bottles of Champagne.

The advance *Hohenstaufen* panzer kampfgruppe engaged the 11th Armoured Division near le Beny-Bocage on the afternoon of 2 August, knocking out five Cromwells in the process. The Tigers went into action against the 23rd Hussars near Chenedolle, turning a squadron's worth of Shermans into burning pyres.

The 102nd SS Battalion's Tigers were in the forefront of the action around Vire, and conducted an ambush against the regimental headquarters of the Northamptonshire Yeomanry. Then, *Frundsberg*'s panzer kampfgruppe – with seven Panzer IVs and eighteen Panthers – entered the fray and was responsible for destroying 20 British tanks. This

Above: Heavily camouflaged *Hitlerjugend* Panther tanks in July 1944. The division sent a battlegroup of Panthers to aid the *Hohenstaufen* defeat Operation Bluecoat in August.

Top: Panzergrenadiers of the *Hitlerjugend* Division south of Cagny in mid-July 1944. During this period the division successfully fought off the British Guards Armoured Division.

and other SS attacks brought British tank losses since the start of Operation Bluecoat to a massive 200 vehicles.

Then Bittrich launched a counterattack against the British at Chenedolle. *Hohenstaufen*'s Panthers were to account for 39 British tanks, and they also cut British supply lines. Panzergrenadiers stalked British tanks in the woods during the night, knocking out scores with Panzerfausts. Bittrich's tired troops kept pressing forward until the battle reached a climax on 6 August. Bittrich had brought Operation Bluecoat to a halt, and he established a strong defensive line around Vire. However, the German front in Normandy was beginning to crack.

Defeat in Western Normandy

As Montgomery's armoured divisions were feeling the power of I SS Panzer Corps' Panthers and Tigers east of Caen, the US Army was in the process of launching an offensive that would eventually destroy the German armies in Normandy. An ill-conceived Waffen-SS counterattack at Mortain would only add to the Germans' problems as their front in northern France collapsed.

Two Waffen-SS soldiers enjoy a rare moment of peace during the fighting in Normandy. Despite heavy combat and Allied materiel superiority, this photograph shows that morale among the SS units was still high.

The fighting in western Normandy was very different in nature from the open fields and villages around Caen. The constricted bocage terrain consisted of small fields lined with thick hedges and earthworks, as well as large areas of marshland that were impassable to tanks. It was a defender's paradise, so Rommel mainly deployed infantry divisions to contain the Americans.

A plethora of sunken roads, small woods and villages meant there was no room to manoeuvre large formations of tanks. The US Army quickly became bogged down in a series of small-scale engagements against dogged and expert German resistance. The so-called "Battle of the Hedgerows" would cost the Americans tens of thousands of casualties for little ground gained.

During June and into July 1944, the German defenders of the Seventh Army under Paul Hausser managed to inflict a steady stream of casualties on the "green" US Army units sent against them. Hausser's veteran units, such as II Parachute Corps and the 352nd Infantry Division, made Lieutenant-General Omar Bradley's First US Army pay for every inch of terrain it captured. In a series of disjointed divisional offensives, the Americans suffered some 50,000 casualties and hardly dented the German front. The two US Army divisions that took the town of St Lô in mid-July lost a combined total of 5000 casualties in bitter, house-to-house fighting. One division lost an incredible 150 percent of its officers and 100 percent of its soldiers in six weeks of action. US divisions maintained their combat power by constant infusions of so-called "battlefield replacements", which did nothing for their unit cohesion or the overall quality of their fighting expertise.

It took the Americans a long time to master the terrain and their enemy. Their equipment, such as the Sherman tank, proved under-gunned and under-armoured compared with German Panthers and Tigers. One thing the Americans possessed in overwhelming quantities was firepower in the shape of heavy artillery and airpower. They unleashed it regularly against Hausser's troops, and eventually the cunning Waffen-SS general was unable to compensate for the overwhelming materiel superiority enjoyed by the Americans. By 24 July, the veteran Panzer Lehr Division, for example, could only put some 3000 men in the field and a few dozen tanks. Since the end of June, only a trickle of German reinforcements had reached Normandy to

replace the 100,000 casualties sustained by Rommel's armies in the month after D-Day. The German front was approaching breaking point, and Hausser was running out of reserves to plug the gaps.

The threat to Caen meant that the front facing the British attracted the bulk of Rommel's panzer reserves, and Hausser could not call on his beloved I or II SS Panzer Corps to help him in the West. In mid-June only one Waffen-SS division could be spared to counter the US Army's attempt to link its two bridgeheads, Omaha and Utah. Delayed by air attack, the 17th SS Panzergrenadier Division *Götz von Berlichingen* arrived at the Normandy front just as the US Army was about to link up its bridgeheads at Carentan. In a furious counterattack against the US 101st Airborne Division, led by the 42 StuG IIIs of its panzer battalion, the 17th SS Division lost some 450 casualties. The panzergrenadiers came to within 500m (1640ft) of the town until a counterattack drove them back. The division then joined forces with the veteran 6th Parachute

Regiment to block the advance of two US corps for nearly a month in vicious, close-quarter combat. Relations between the two units were strained at first, after Waffen-SS officers attempted to try the commander of the parachute unit for treason at a field court martial. His "crime" was that he had ordered a retreat.

To provide a panzer reserve for the German front facing the Americans, Rommel ordered the *Das Reich* Panzer Division to the Periers region. Its panzer regiment boasted almost 26 Panthers, 50 Panzer IVs and 36 StuG IIIs ready for action. It was in position in early July and was called forward into action on 3 July to counter a possible breakthrough by the US 30th Infantry and 3rd Armored Divisions. The terrain prevented the large-scale employment of tanks, and the battle soon broke down into a series of small dogfights between individual German and American tanks. For two weeks the *Das Reich* troopers were locked in combat with the American GIs. Their greater battle experience and superior equipment meant they were more often than not able to get the better of the Americans, but in its first week of action the division lost just over 1200 men and some 30 tanks or assault guns, losses it could ill afford.

After a frustrating time fighting up the Cherbourg peninsula to capture the port city on 27 June, Bradley was able to turn his attention southwards during July, and began to plan for the breakout from Normandy. The idea was to open a breach and drive southwards to Avranches. Then Lieutenant-General George Patton's Third Army would carry on the advance, swinging west to encircle and destroy the German forces.

Chastized by his experiences to date, Bradley was determined to concentrate American firepower in a

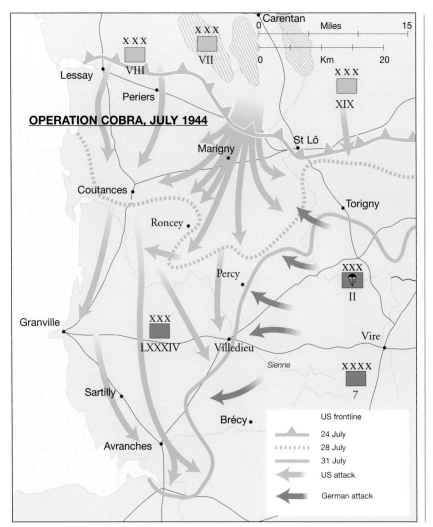

OPERATION COBRA, JULY 1944

Carentan

Miles

Km

Lessay

VHI

Periers

Marigny

St Lô

Coutances

Torigny

Roncey

Percy

Granville

Vire

LXXXIV

Villedieu

Sienne

Sartilly

Brécy

Avranches

US frontline

24 July

28 July

31 July

US attack

German attack

Once through the hedgerows of western Normandy, US armoured forces made good progress.

narrow sector to overwhelm the defenders. A 7000m (23,000ft) section of front to the west of St Lô was selected as the target for Lieutenant-General J. Lawton Collins' VII Corps in the appropriately named Operation Cobra. The plan called for 1500 heavy bombers, 380 medium bombers and 550 fighter-bombers to drop more than 4064 tonnes (4000 tons) of explosives on a target box that stretched 2500m (8202ft) behind the front. More than 1000 guns would join the barrage. Four fresh American divisions would then be unleashed. On paper, the plan looked unstoppable.

The offensive got off to an inauspicious start on 25 July when cloud obscured part of the target. Elements of the bomber force dropped their deadly cargo on US troops waiting to go into the attack, killing more than 100

and wounding almost 500. The effect on the Panzer Lehr Division, positioned in the centre of the target box, was even worse, though. Almost 1000 men died, and a regiment and a whole kampfgruppe were put out of action, along with all the division's tanks and guns. Despite this onslaught, the survivors came out of their trenches and bunkers fighting, holding up the offensive for 48 hours. Then Bradley committed the 2nd "Hell on Wheels" Armored Division en masse. Unlike Dietrich east of Caen, Hausser had no reserves to plug the breach in his line because Bradley had ordered all his troops to stage diversionary attacks to tie down German forces along the whole of the Normandy Front. Disaster threatened.

Hausser had tried to pull *Das Reich*'s Panther battalion out of the line to the west to throw against the

The German counterattack at Mortain was an ill-conceived affair. The Germans were able to muster a paltry 185 tanks to defeat US forces, which were gaining strength by the day. In addition, the sky was filled with hundreds of Allied aircraft.

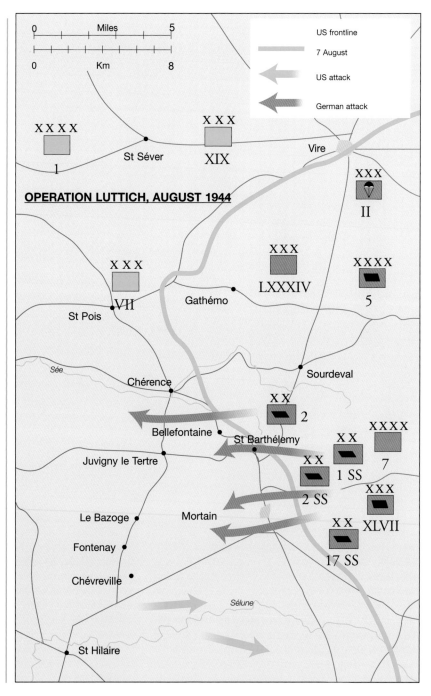

OPERATION LUTTICH, AUGUST 1944

American breakthrough, but it could not disengage in time. In the end only five Panthers made it to help the Panzer Lehr, and they were soon put out of action. The breakthrough broke the cohesion of the German front. By 27 July, huge columns led by 600 American tanks were streaming south towards Avranches with nothing to stop them. German units started to crack under the strain of constant American attacks and almost six weeks of fighting without relief. The *Das Reich* and 17th SS Divisions managed to pull back and form a line north of Coutances on 27 July, which held the Americans at bay for a day. Then the front behind them collapsed, and the two Waffen-SS divisions and the army's 353rd Infantry Division were soon trapped in a pocket south of Roncey. Fuel was running short and scores of tanks had to be abandoned. In the chaos, *Das Reich*'s commander, SS-Brigadeführer Heinz Lammerding, was wounded and then his replacement, the division's panzer regiment commander, SS-Obersturmbannführer Christian Tychsen, was killed in action. On the night of 28/29 July, the trapped troops made a bid for freedom, cutting through a loose cordon of US troops. Dodging past most of the Americans, the column clashed with a US armoured regiment.

The American tanks came off worst in the encounter, and by dawn on 30 July the three units were free. In their wake they had left roads littered with abandoned tanks, trucks, guns and other debris of war. US troops rounded up 4000 prisoners in the aftermath of the German escape bid. By the end of the month, some 20,000 Germans would be in American prison camps and Patton's tanks would be in Avranches.

In his headquarters in East Prussia, Hitler at first forbade any retreat in the face of the American onslaught. Then the Führer demanded a counterattack. Looking at the map table in Rastenburg, the solution looked simple. Eight of the nine panzer divisions in Normandy were to strike into the flank of the American incursion to cut off Patton's tanks.

To the likes of Hausser and the commanders of the divisions given the dubious honour of participating in Operation Luttich, the whole thing was total madness. All their units were seriously understrength, short of ammunition and fuel. For example, most of the panzer units would be disengaged from the Caen Front, where Montgomery's troops were also pressing forward strongly. Then they were expected to move almost 100km (62 miles) under constant Allied air attack to their concentration area, before massing for the assault.

The aftermath of the 20 July Bomb Plot against Hitler was still being felt in the ranks of the German forces in Normandy. When scores of army officers in France were arrested and executed for their part in the plot, rumours spread that they had been sabotaging the war effort. Mistrust grew between ardent Nazis and anyone who did not seem to show the necessary level of enthusiasm for continuing the struggle. So when senior officers, including Waffen-SS veterans such as Hausser, Dietrich and Bittrich, heard of the Führer's attack plans they were dismayed, but had to be careful about public criticism of

Panzergrenadiers of the *Götz von Berlichingen* Division during the Mortain attack. Throughout the offensive Waffen-SS soldiers were attacked by enemy ground-attack aircraft.

them. They went along with the arrangement because there was no alternative. Hitler was determined that the attack would go ahead, and he even took the planning out of the hands of his now mistrusted field commanders. A senior officer was dispatched from the Führer's headquarters with the detailed plan for Operation Luttich, even down to routes of march and artillery fire plans.

The balance of forces looked terrible. In total the Germans could muster only 750 operational tanks left in Normandy at the end of July, out of a total of 2200 sent to the front during June and July. The combined British and American armies had landed more than 6000 tanks in France since D-Day.

General of Panzer Troops Hans von Funck's XLVII Panzer Corps' headquarters was given command of the attack, which Hitler said was only to begin when all the eight panzer divisions were in place. By 6 August the size of the American breach was getting totally out of control. Thousands of American tanks and vehicles were pushing through Avranches. British tanks continued to push through their breach at Vire, tying down II SS Panzer Corps and preventing it from joining Operation Luttich. Even through he had only been able to gather together four of his expected eight panzer divisions, and hardly any of the promised Luftwaffe fighters were ready, Hausser ordered Operation Luttich to go ahead on 7 August.

At hand were the 2nd, 116th and Panzer Lehr Divisions, as well as part of the *Leibstandarte* and *Das*

Reich, which were reinforced with the remnants of the 17th SS Division. All told, Funck had a paltry 185 tanks to turn the tide of the war in Germany's favour.

Allied air supremacy was now such a problem for the Germans that Hausser ordered the attack to begin under cover of darkness at 02:00 hours on 7 August. Surprise was to be of the essence; accordingly, there was no preparatory bombardment. Hitler's micro-management of the planning for the attack meant all the key documents had been delivered by hand to the German commanders in France. This had the unintentional spin-off of ensuring that the British ULTRA code-breaking operation was not able to pick up any German radio traffic about the impending attack. Unaware of the coming onslaught, Bradley had only stationed the tired and understrength US 30th Infantry Division to guard the town of Mortain, which was the first objective of Operation Luttich. It had no warning of the impending attack.

OPERATION LUTTICH IS LAUNCHED

Waffen-SS participation in the Mortain counterattack, as Operation Luttich is now known, centred around three main units. SS-Standartenführer Otto Baum commanded a kampfgruppe made up from the *Das Reich* and 17th SS Divisions. Its objective was Mortain itself. The *Leibstandarte* was thrown into the battle piecemeal because of delays in moving the division from the Caen Front along congested roads and under incessant Allied air attack. Only a single panzer battalion with 43 Panthers and 7 Panzer IVs, along with the *Leibstandarte*'s reconnaissance unit and an armoured halftrack-mounted panzergrenadier battalion, arrived in time to go with the first attack wave. The rest of the division was several hours' march behind.

At first the German attack went well. *Das Reich* stormed into Mortain, scattering surprised American units out of its path. Its panzer regiment pushed past the town and headed 5km (3.1 miles) westwards. The division's reconnaissance battalion secured its left flank, moving 4km (2.5 miles) south of the town, which was soon the scene of fierce fighting between American infantry and Waffen-SS panzergrenadiers. The 17th SS Division's reconnaissance battalion hit the town from the front, and *Das Reich*'s *Der Führer* Panzergrenadier Regiment swept in from the north. A battalion of American infantry was surrounded on the crucial Hill 317 on the eastern edge of the town. To the west of Mortain, the US 120th Infantry Regiment fought desperate rearguard actions.

North of Mortain, the advance units of the *Leibstandarte* were assigned to the 2nd Panzer Division.

SS-Sturmbannführer Gustav Knittel's reconnaissance troops raced ahead of the tank force, spreading confusion in the American ranks. They surprised a US column near le Mesnil-Tôve and captured a large quantity of trucks and anti-tank guns, before pressing on a further 3km (1.8 miles) against little opposition. By late morning, however, strong American road-blocks were in place and Knittel's men had to pull back to defend le Mesnil-Tôve.

Just before dawn, the *Leibstandarte*'s tanks and panzergrenadier battalion began their attack on the strongly held village of St Barthélemy, after a 45-minute artillery barrage. While 30 Panzer IVs and infantry of the 2nd Panzer were tasked with taking the northern half of the village, the *Leibstandarte* was to take the southern section.

SLAUGHTER

Heavy fog hung over the battlefield, making it impossible for the German tanks to engage the defenders in the village at long range, so a combined tank-infantry assault was ordered to storm the American positions. By 11:30 hours the German tanks were on the far side of the village, but small groups of Americans were still holding out in cellars and bunkers. It was early afternoon before the Germans had cleared the village, and they captured almost 400 Americans in the process. The delay gave Bradley time to regroup and bring up reserves to contain the German attack. The US general still needed another day before he could be in a position to counterattack, so he turned to the Allied air forces to contain the German tank columns. By early afternoon the fog that had covered the Mortain region was finally lifting, at last exposing Funck's troops to devastating aerial attack.

Just after 12:15 hours on 7 August, the first of 271 RAF Typhoon fighters took off from forward airstrips in Normandy, their target the huge German tank and vehicle columns around Mortain. The Luftwaffe was nowhere to be seen. It took the RAF fighters 45 minutes to appear over the battlefield and they started to circle, looking for targets. For the next nine hours, the RAF squadrons maintained a constant presence over the battlefield. At any one time, there were never fewer than 22 aircraft overhead.

The German attack stalled as the Typhoons swooped to rocket and machine-gun any tanks or trucks they could find. Waffen-SS men dived for shelter and tried to drive their vehicles under cover, but it was to no avail. All afternoon the German columns were attacked from the air relentlessly. There was no prospect of any kind of advance. Columns of *Leibstandarte* tanks and trucks heading towards the battlefield were also caught in the air onslaught, further blunting the momentum of the German attack. One column was held up for several hours when an Allied fighter crashed on the lead German tank, blocking the road ahead. The RAF pilots claimed 84 tanks destroyed, 35 probably destroyed and 21 damaged, with another 112 vehicles hit. This was perhaps an exaggeration, but when the Germans pulled out of the sector a few days later, they left behind 43 Panthers, 10 Panzer IVs, 23 armoured halftracks, 8 armoured cars and 46 other vehicles. This was the first time ever in the history of warfare that airpower by itself had halted a ground force.

As darkness fell, the Germans tried to reorganize their battered forces and bring up more reserves. The continued resistance of the trapped Americans on Hill 317 outside Mortain thwarted *Das Reich*'s attempt to advance forward throughout the night and the following day.

More fog in the morning of 8 August provided the reinforced *Leibstandarte* with the opportunity to move forward in strength towards Juvigny and Bellefontaine. Now Bradley's reserves were in place and the *Leibstandarte*'s panzers ran into sustained anti-tank gunfire and were stopped in their tracks. American tanks went on the offensive against the 2nd Panzer, forcing Knittel's depleted reconnaissance troops out of le Mesnil-Tôve by the evening.

Not all the *Leibstandarte* Division was able to get through to join the attack, and a strong kampfgruppe had to be diverted northwards to seal an American incursion south of Vire which threatened the right flank of the attacking units.

American air and artillery fire now began to rain down on the German units around Mortain, again stalling any idea of pressing home the attack towards Avranches. It was no longer a case of pushing forward, but holding out against overwhelming odds. Throughout 9 and 10 August, increasing numbers of American tanks were pressing forward against the Waffen-SS lines. The German Panthers destroyed many Shermans in this battle.

Just as it was becoming clear that Operation Luttich was running out of steam, Hitler insisted on ordering more units to reinforce the attack. II SS Panzer Corps was ordered to pull out of the line southwest of Caen, where it was fighting Montgomery's Operation Bluecoat to a halt, in spite of protests from its commander, Willi Bittrich, to be sent westwards to reinforce Funck's doomed enterprise. The *Frundsberg* Division eventually managed to break free from the front near Vire and moved into position on the left of *Das Reich* during the night of 7/8 August. Heavy air attacks prevented it attacking towards Berenton until the morning of 9 August, when a grand total of 12 panzers were launched forward and 4 were quickly knocked out. Further British tank attacks north of Vire meant that the

The failure of the Mortain attack signalled the end of the German war effort in Normandy. And by early August, large numbers of Germans were giving themselves up.

Hohenstaufen Division had to remain there to contain this breakthrough and could not be sent to join the Mortain offensive.

Hausser had ordered that all attempts to continue the attack on Avranches should stop on the afternoon of 11 August, and soon afterwards began preparing plans for a withdrawal to a more defensible line to the east. Now the Waffen-SS units were desperately short of fuel because of the incessant air attacks, and many tanks and other vehicles had to be abandoned. Two days later, the *Leibstandarte* reported having only 14 Panzer IVs, 7 Panthers and 8 StuG IIIs operational. *Das Reich* was in an even worse condition, with only five Panzer IVs, three Panthers and eight StuG IIIs in the line.

In his eastern Prussian bunker, the Führer was furious at the failure of the attack and wanted a scapegoat. He ordered Funck sacked on 11 August. The following day, US tanks broke through *Das Reich*'s lines and relieved the trapped GIs on Hill 317. Of the 700 who had been surrounded five days earlier, only 400 were still fit for action. The US Army, backed by RAF Typhoons, had taken on the élite of the Waffen-SS and stopped it in its tracks. The failure of the offensive set the stage for the next and even greater disaster to befall German arms in France: the Battle of the Falaise Pocket.

August Storm for the Hitlerjugend

In early August 1944, Montgomery launched his final offensive at Caen, codenamed Totalize. The Hitlerjugend Division, commanded by Meyer, fought superbly to blunt this new Allied assault. In a series of savage battles, he stopped the Canadian and Polish tanks in their tracks, but his losses were high and Germany lost her top tank ace – Michael Wittmann.

A *Hitlerjugend* Panther knocked out during Operation Totalize. The division had 59 Panthers on 7 August 1944; three days later this had been reduced to 15 trying to hold back more than 700 Allied tanks.

After blunting Operation Luttich, the Allied High Command saw that it had the opportunity to trap the German armies in Normandy in a giant pocket. General Patton's Third Army was fanning out virtually unopposed into Brittany, heading towards the Seine River crossings. All that was needed was for the noose to be tightened around the 400,000 Germans still fighting in Normandy. Montgomery decided that now was the time to link up with Patton's spearhead. Operation Totalize was to begin on 8 August 1944.

Two infantry divisions, each led by an armoured brigade, were to advance due south along the main road out of Caen towards Falaise, on Route Nationale 158. This would be a very different style of attack to those previously attempted by the British or Canadians. Seven separate armoured columns would be formed, with as many infantry as possible loaded on armoured personnel carriers which had been created by converting self-propelled artillery pieces. This Allied force also had one major advantage over previous units that had attempted to seize the Bourguebus ridge. This time there were no Waffen-SS tanks and 88mm Flak guns waiting for them. The *Leibstandarte* had been pulled out to lead the attack

on Mortain, II SS Panzer Corps was fighting Operation Bluecoat to a halt near Vire, and the *Hitlerjugend* was in reserve. "Sepp" Dietrich was still in command of the sector, although his I SS Panzer Corps headquarters had only one Waffen-SS division, *Hitlerjugend*, with 59 Panthers, 39 Panzer IVs, 27 Jagdpanzer IVs and the 8 Tigers of the 101st SS Battalion under its command. They faced more than 700 British, Canadian and Polish tanks.

At 23:00 hours on 7 August, 1020 RAF bombers began the preparatory bombardment. As the 3517 tonnes (3462 tons) of bombs were exploding, the armoured columns started their engines and moved forward into the attack. For the next six hours, the columns pushed nearly 5km (3.1 miles) into the stunned German 89th Infantry Division. Resistance was patchy, but in terms of the previous attempts to take the Bourguebus ridge, the assault troops suffered relatively low casualties: in the region of 300 men. As dawn was breaking, the Allied troops had to all intents and purposes blasted open the German front. Shell-shocked survivors were streaming away from the fighting. For a few hours only one man stood between the Allies and victory: the *Hitlerjugend*'s commander, Kurt Meyer.

A Panzer IV of the 2nd Panzer Battalion, 12th SS Panzer Regiment, *Hitlerjugend* Division, in northern France.

He had rushed to the threatened sector to carry out a reconnaissance, and early in the morning stood on Route 158 as hordes of fleeing German infantry rushed past. Armed only with a carbine, he shamed the soldiers into standing firm with a couple of *Hitlerjugend* Panzerjäger IVs that had just arrived in the village of Cintheaux.

By midday, Meyer had brought up his battalion of Panzer IVs, some Panzerjäger IVs, and Michael Wittmann's Tigers to his improvised "stop line". Not content with just holding the onslaught, Meyer was going to attack. His mind was made up when he saw an American B-17 flying overhead dropping flares to mark targets for follow-up waves of bombers. The panzers would be safer from the American bombs if they mixed with the British, Canadian and Polish tanks. Wittmann's Tigers led the Panzerkeil (or wedge) forward. Meyer climbed on to the Waffen-SS ace's Tiger tank to wish him luck, not knowing that this would be Wittmann's last battle.

Meyer's unconventional tactics paid off. The panzer charge escaped the B-17s and drove headlong into the Polish armoured regiment and the British 33rd Armoured Brigade. The terrain was open and the Allied tanks had little cover from the German 75mm and 88mm high-velocity cannons. Wittmann's Tigers swung off Route 158 and hit the Canadian 4th Armoured Division. It was stopped dead, losing scores of tanks, but two Tigers were knocked out. Undeterred, Wittmann pressed on eastwards against the flank of the British Northamptonshire Yeomanry, blasting another 20 Shermans as he went. Hopelessly outnumbered, Wittmann pressed on towards St Aignan-de-Cramesnil.

British Sherman Firefly tanks, armed with the powerful 17-pounder gun firing tungsten sabot rounds, were waiting in ambush for the Tigers. A squadron of the Yeomanry is credited with putting an end to Wittmann's career which, to his credit, took in 138 tank kills. Five tanks zeroed in on Wittmann's Tiger, and consequently the turret was seen to explode – there were no survivors.

More Panzer IVs now joined the battle from the south, intercepting the 1st Polish Armoured Division's lead regiment and putting 24 Shermans out of action. *Hitlerjugend* 88mm flak guns were also in action against the Poles, to great effect. Again, the intervention of the *Hitlerjugend* Division had thwarted the Allied plans. Scores of Shermans were burning and the Allied advance was brought to a halt. Meyer ordered his forward kampfgruppe to fall back to a new line centred on the high ground around Point 140, 5km (3.1 miles) to the south, where the bulk of Max Wünsche's panzer regiment was now gathering.

In the confusion, the Canadian 28th Armoured Regiment and the Algonquin Infantry Battalion slipped through their lines to occupy Point 140. The result was a massacre. In a three-day battle, the Canadians lost 80 tanks and the Poles admitted to the destruction of 66 of their tanks. The battle had not been all one-sided, with Meyer suffering 414 casualties. His tank strength was now reduced to 20 Panzer IVs and 15 Panthers. Thanks to the arrival of additional tanks from the 102nd SS Battalion, he now boasted 15 Tigers. This was the last notable defensive success for Meyer's division. The great Allied jaws were now closing around the German armies in Normandy.

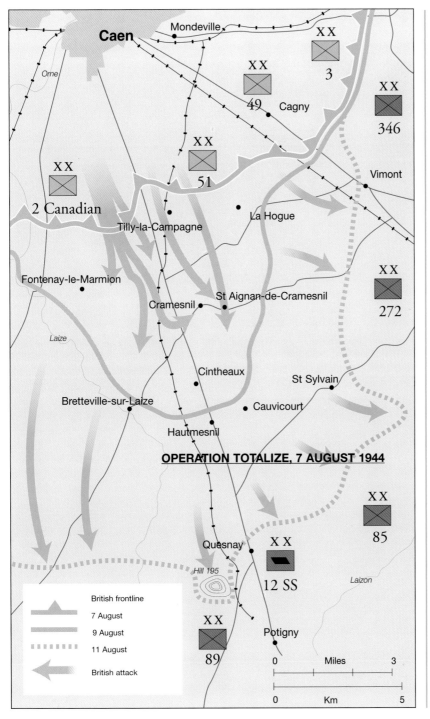

Caen

Mondeville

Orne

XX
3

XX
49

Cagny

XX
346

XX
51

Vimont

2 Canadian

La Hogue

Tilly-la-Campagne

Fontenay-le-Marmion

Cramesnil

St Aignan-de-Cramesnil

XX
272

Laize

Cintheaux

St Sylvain

Bretteville-sur-Laize

Cauvicourt

Hautmesnil

OPERATION TOTALIZE, 7 AUGUST 1944

XX
85

Quesnay

XX
12 SS

Laizon

Hill 195

XX
89

Potigny

British frontline

7 August

9 August

11 August

British attack

0   Miles   3

0   Km   5

Montgomery's offensive essentially destroyed the German front south of Caen, and decimated the *Hitlerjugend* Division.

The Falaise Pocket

The Waffen-SS panzer divisions had inflicted fearsome losses on Allied units in Normandy between June and August 1944. However, by mid-August German forces were threatened with encirclement and destruction. The SS units managed to keep open the Allied jaws before they finally snapped shut at Falaise, and what was left of the once mighty Wehrmacht in France retreated east.

German vehicles destroyed by Allied aircraft in the Falaise Pocket. Losses in tanks, artillery and armoured vehicles were a catastrophe for the Germans, and sealed their defeat in France.

While Kurt Meyer's panzer crews were duelling with Montgomery's tanks on the road out of Caen, the German front in Normandy was in the process of collapsing. Hans von Kluge, the commander of Army Group B, was pleading with Hitler to allow a withdrawal of the 400,000 troops that were now threatened with encirclement. The Führer ordered Kluge to stand and fight. The German armies were now being pressed into an ever-smaller area between Falaise and Argentan, and relentlessly pounded with artillery and air strikes. Kluge drove to visit Dietrich's headquarters on 15 August, and got stuck in the maelstrom for several hours after his convoy was strafed by Allied fighters and his radio truck destroyed. Suspicious that Kluge had been trying to negotiate a surrender, Hitler ordered him back to Berlin. Kluge bit on a cyanide capsule instead and was dead in seconds. The next most senior general in Normandy was Hausser, so he was appointed to command all the troops trapped in the Falaise Kessel (or kettle).

Kluge's replacement, Field Marshal Walther Model, reluctantly agreed to order a withdrawal on the 16th to set up a new line on the Dives River, but the senior Waffen-SS officers, who now held all the important commands in the kessel, had been pulling back for five days – they had realized that the battle was lost.

The *Leibstandarte*, *Das Reich* and 17th SS Divisions east of Mortain had been the first to fall back. Threatened by encirclement by American tanks to the south and British armour from the north, they staged a brief rearguard action on the Orne River at Putanges on the night of 17/18 August. After its sister divisions had safely crossed at midnight, the *Leibstandarte* blew up the last bridge and slipped away. II SS Panzer Corps was next to go, ordered to fall back through Argentan to form a counterattack force.

The *Hitlerjugend* was still holding off the Canadians and Poles on the northern shoulder of the kessel. Behind it, chaos reigned, with huge truck convoys trying to move eastwards under relentless Allied air attack and causing massive traffic jams. The Waffen-SS divisions fared better than most, and the vast majority of their support elements managed to escape eastwards before the pocket was sealed on 20 August. Elements of 23 German divisions were in the kessel. Command and control was breaking down; the frontline was being held only by small determined groups of men formed into ad

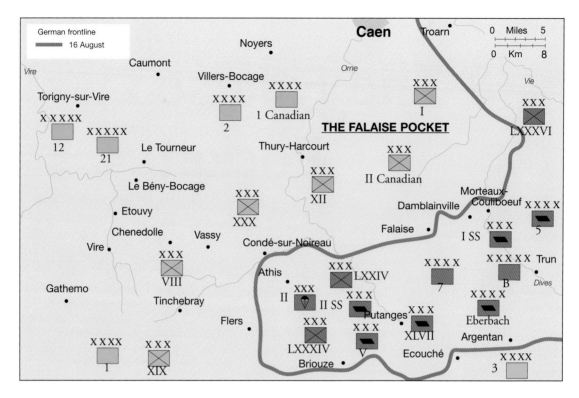

German formations were vastly understrength by the time they were caught at Falaise. Many of the Waffen-SS panzer divisions, for example, were reduced to 10 tanks apiece.

hoc kampfgruppen. The Allied pincers were closing in, and late on 18 August a corridor only a few kilometres wide remained open. Hitler now tried to pretend that a new front should be established on the Seine. All that the German commanders in the pocket were worried about was getting out alive.

Hausser ordered II SS Panzer Corps and *Das Reich*, which were now outside the kessel, to hold open a corridor for the remainder of the troops trapped inside. During the afternoon of 19 August, escape orders were issued at an impromptu conference in a quarry. Hausser, Meyer, Teddy Wisch of the *Leibstandarte* and the three senior army officers left in the kessel worked out the plan.

The last remaining tanks were put at the head of columns and the breakout began. The now wounded Meyer himself led one column, riding in the turret of a Panzer IV, accompanied by his chief of staff, SS-Sturmbannführer Hubert Meyer. Eventually, the *Hitlerjugend* command group was forced to make its way on foot through the night until it reached German lines.

During the early hours of 20 August, *Das Reich* scraped together its last 20 tanks to launch a final attack to keep the escape route open. All day the Waffen-SS men battled to keep the Polish 1st Armoured Division at bay, thereby allowing the trapped *Hitlerjugend* and *Leibstandarte* kampfgruppen to reach safety. Inside one of their armoured halftracks was the badly wounded Hausser, who had lost an eye during an artillery strike. It took the Allies two days to clean up the remnants of resistance inside the Kessel, taking 50,000 prisoners and finding 10,000 dead Germans in the carnage. More than 3000 vehicles had been left behind, including 187 tanks, 252 artillery pieces, 157 light armoured vehicles, 1778 trucks and 669 staff cars.

All the Waffen-SS panzer regiments were crippled during the Falaise battles. Few got away with more than 20 tanks, and Bittrich's corps reported on 21 August that it had no operational tanks at all. More importantly, many vehicles under repair had to be abandoned in the pocket, meaning no replacement tanks could be returned to action. Far more damage was done during the retreat across France to the German border in the last week of August and first two weeks of September. Allied air attacks and ambushes by French and Belgian resistance fighters inflicted more losses on the German convoys.

Hitler's idea of forming a new line on the Seine was a non-starter. Paris fell on 25 August following an uprising by the French resistance. Dietrich tried to form another line on the Somme with the *Leibstandarte*, *Das Reich* and *Hitlerjugend* Divisions a couple of days later, but it was soon outflanked and the divisions retreated to Germany through the Ardennes region of Belgium.

Resistance fighters ambushed a number of their convoys, including one carrying Kurt Meyer on 6 September. The *Hitlerjugend*'s famous commander was captured and, realizing the value of their prize, the Belgians kept him alive and handed him over to the Allies.

II SS Panzer Corps fought a stiff rearguard action against the Americans near Cambrai on 2 September. The *Hohenstaufen*'s remaining 88mm guns were deployed to blunt a tank attack and allow the rest of the corps to break free. The division's 32-year-old commander, SS-Obersturmbannführer Walther Harzer, remained behind to control the battle from his command halftrack. Harzer had taken over from the wounded Sylvester Stadler a few days earlier, and he was determined to make the Americans pay a heavy price for getting past his small kampfgruppe. More than 200 Shermans appeared later on in the morning. Harzer's gunners engaged them at their maximum range of

One of the StuG IIIs of II SS Panzer Corps that escaped from the Falaise Pocket. The corps was able to offer some resistance to the Allies as German forces retreated east.

3000m (9842ft) in order to inflict the maximum delay on the American pursuit. It worked.

The battered and tired remnants of the Waffen-SS panzers divisions were not welcomed back to Germany as heroes and given a well-earned rest. They were immediately told to get their units ready for action. Hitler was determined to continue fighting. Ad hoc kampfgruppen were formed and sent to bolster the defences along the Third Reich's western frontier. The front was barely held together at all by the 24 infantry and 11 panzer "divisions" that Model had under his command on 29 August.

The Wehrmacht stationed in the West was now a shadow of the force Rommel had used in his attempt to beat back the Allied invasion in June. During the 10 weeks of fighting since the Allies had landed in Normandy, the German forces had lost 23,109 dead, 67,240 wounded and 198,616 missing or taken prisoner. Almost 1500 of the 2248 tanks sent to Normandy had been destroyed, damaged or captured by the Allies.

Arnhem

The battles in and around Arnhem in the autumn of 1944 were clashes between élites. On one side were the highly motivated Allied airborne formations; on the other were masters of mechanized warfare – two panzer divisions of the Waffen-SS, albeit weakened by the fighting in France. The result was an epic battle that has since entered military folklore.

A StuG III of the *Hohenstaufen* Division in Arnhem during the final battle to liquidate the British paratroopers in the town. StuGs made up a high percentage of the division's inventory.

In the first week of September 1944, Willi Bittrich's II SS Panzer Corps was ordered to move to a reorganizing and refitting area north of the Dutch town of Arnhem. The unit had been in action continuously for just over two months, and was now desperately in need of a quiet period to get itself ready for battle again.

Plans were already in train to bring Bittrich's two divisions, the *Hohenstaufen* and *Frundsberg*, back up to strength, and Arnhem seemed like a good place to begin this time-consuming task. No longer worthy of the title "division", the *Hohenstaufen* and *Frundsberg* were dubbed divisional kampfgruppen. It was doubtful if the whole of the corps would be able to put more than 30 tanks or assault guns into the field.

Walther Harzer's *Hohenstaufen* was then ordered to move to Germany to be rebuilt there. Before it left, it was to hand over its remaining operational vehicles and heavy weapons to Heinz Harmel's *Frundsberg*, which was to remain in Holland. At the same time as this reorganization process was under way, contingency orders were issued stating that the two units were to be prepared to dispatch "alarm" kampfgruppen to crisis zones. Not believing intelligence reports that the Allied advance had run out of steam, Harzer decided to keep hold of many of his precious remaining tanks and heavy weapons until the very last minute, in case he had to send his men into battle. He simply ordered their tracks to be removed so they would be classed as non-operational and therefore exempt from the transfer instructions.

What new equipment had arrived – mainly 15 Panzerjäger IV self-propelled guns – had been dispatched to the Dutch-Belgian border, under the command of Kampfgruppe *Hienke*. This was formed around one of *Frundsberg*'s panzergrenadier battalions, an engineer and reconnaissance company. *Hohenstaufen* was ordered to provide an additional panzergrenadier battalion for this force, which was helping to build up the front south of the Dutch city of Eindhoven. It was increasingly involved in a series of inconclusive engagements along the border, and was sent into action in a futile attack against the Neerpelt bridgehead on 15 September, in which three of the Panzerjäger IVs were knocked out.

Harzer, although preoccupied with preparing to move his division by train to Germany, ordered his troops to form 19 company sized, quick-reaction infantry kampfgruppen. Much of his divisional equipment was being

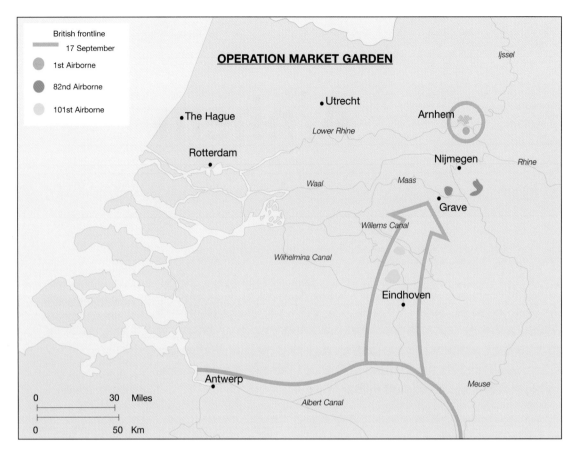

OPERATION MARKET GARDEN

British frontline
17 September

1st Airborne

82nd Airborne

101st Airborne

Ijssel

Utrecht

Arnhem

The Hague

Lower Rhine

Rotterdam

Nijmegen

Rhine

Waal

Maas

Grave

Willems Canal

Wilhelmina Canal

Eindhoven

Antwerp

Meuse

Albert Canal

0   30   Miles

0   50   Km

Market Garden was Montgomery's plan to end the war by the close of 1944. The shaded areas are the drop zones of the airborne divisions; the pink circle the main objective.

loaded on trains when the first Allied airborne landings occurred. His division was the closest to Arnhem itself, with the *Frundsberg* Division garrisoned farther to the north and west near Apeldoorn. Also in the Arnhem area were two other Waffen-SS units, which were not under II SS Panzer Corps' command. Major Sepp Krafft commanded a Waffen-SS noncommissioned training depot to the west of Arnhem, and in the outskirts there was also a 600-strong battalion of Dutch SS infantry.

Bittrich had his headquarters in a small village nearly 10km (6.2 miles) to the east of Arnhem. In Arnhem's Tafelberg Hotel, Field Marshal Walther Model was trying to patch together his hopelessly undermanned and under-equipped army group to defend the northwest border of Germany. He had a reputation for being a great improviser and, after his successes on the Eastern Front,

was nicknamed the "Führer's Fireman". Even at this point of the war, he was still ultra-loyal to Hitler and could be counted on to follow the Führer's orders to the letter. He was sitting down to lunch on 17 September with his staff when hundreds of aircraft were heard flying overhead. Operation Market Garden had begun.

By the beginning of September, the Allied armies in France and Belgium had largely outrun their supply lines. With only a fraction of the needed supplies coming ashore, they could no longer advance into Germany on a wide front. The recently promoted Field Marshal Montgomery successfully lobbied the Allied supreme commander, Eisenhower, to allow him to drive into Holland to seize bridges over the Rhine, and then advance into Germany's industrial heartland of the Ruhr.

The normally cautious Montgomery now came up with a very ambitious and daring plan to capture the strategic bridge across the Rhine at Arnhem with a parachute drop by the British 1st Airborne Division. The US 82nd and 101st Airborne Divisions would also be dropped to seize the bridges across the Waal and Maas

Left: Waffen-SS soldiers in Arnhem. The British troops of 2 Para fought off a series of attacks from their position at Arnhem bridge. However, they began to run desperately short of ammunition, and by 19 September their position was perilous.

Below: Arnhem bridge. This is a German photograph taken after an abortive attack on the British paratroopers on the other side. After fighting heroically without reinforcements or resupply, 2 Para surrendered on 21 September.

rivers, as well as the Willems and Wilhelmina canals, to allow the tanks of the British XXX Corps to motor 103km (64 miles) up from Belgium to relieve the troops on Arnhem bridge. In total some 35,000 Allied paratroopers and glider-borne troops would be dropped in the largest airborne operation in military history. Lieutenant-General Brian Horrocks would predict that his XXX Corps would be in Arnhem in 60 hours.

When RAF reconnaissance Spitfires photographed German tanks near Arnhem, the deputy commander of the First Airborne Army, Lieutenant-General Frederick "Boy" Browning, ignored the intelligence. Other Allied intelligence officers discounted the idea that the remnants of II SS Panzer Corps could put up serious resistance. The party was on, and nothing was going to spoil the show – except Bittrich's panzer troops.

Allied bombers and fighter-bombers hit targets all over southern Holland during the morning of 17 September. After 13:00 hours, when the first British paratroopers started to land to the west of Arnhem, Bittrich swung into action, alerting his troops with a warning order that was issued at 13:40 hours. With these brief orders he set in train the German counteroffensive that was to defeat Operation Market Garden. Harzer was ordered to assemble his kampfgruppen and move with "absolute speed" to contain and defeat the British airborne Oosterbeek landing. Meanwhile, the *Frundsberg* Division was to race south and hold the Nijmegen bridge across the Waal to stop reinforcements reaching Arnhem.

Harzer's men began moving into the town by whatever means they found: trucks, tanks, halftracks, cars, trams, even bicycles. SS-Obersturmbannführer Ludwig Spindler, commander of the division's artillery regiment, was given command of the kampfgruppe that would hold the western edge of Arnhem. At the same time its tank, artillery and reconnaissance units began putting into working order the vehicles that had been deliberately disabled to stop them being transferred to the *Frundsberg* Division. In two hours, his 400 men and 40 vehicles were rolling out of their camp towards Arnhem

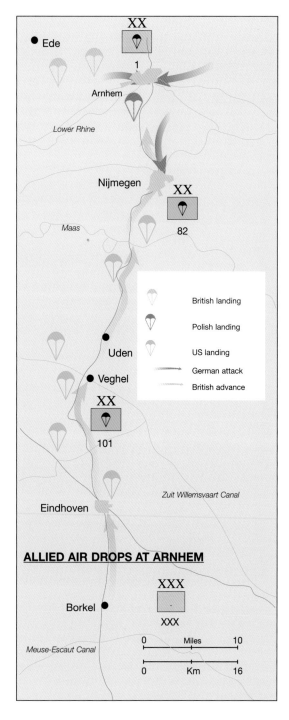

Ede

XX

1

Arnhem

Lower Rhine

Nijmegen

XX

Maas

82

Uden

British landing

Polish landing

US landing

German attack

British advance

Veghel

XX

101

Zuit Willemsvaart Canal

Eindhoven

ALLIED AIR DROPS AT ARNHEM

XXX

Borkel

XXX

Meuse-Escaut Canal

0	Miles	10
0	Km	16

The quick reactions of Field Marshal Model and Bittrich meant that within a day Waffen-SS battlegroups had the British penned into their drop zones.

town centre. They had orders to move ahead of the *Frundsberg* and secure Nijmegen bridge.

On the drop zones west of Arnhem, 8000 British troops were forming up and preparing to move off to their objectives. Within minutes, Krafft's trainee noncommissioned officers were in action, fighting in the forests around the British drop zones, delaying their advance for vital hours. One British airborne unit, the 2nd Battalion, the Parachute Regiment (2 Para), slipped past Krafft's men and was soon marching into the town centre. Minutes before 2 Para reached Arnhem bridge, Graebner's column raced across the huge structure and within an hour the men were in Nijmegen. An improvised Luftwaffe and police kampf-gruppe had already secured the strategic bridge, and Graebner had little to do. The *Frundsberg* Division was equally quick off the mark, and its reconnaissance battalion, under SS-Sturmbannführer Brinkmann, was on its way to Nijmegen. As the column of armoured halftracks approached Arnhem bridge, it came under fire from British paratroopers. 2 Para now held the northern edge of the bridge and several blocks of buildings nearby.

Far to the south, Kampfgruppe *Heinke* was soon in action against XXX Corps' Guards Armoured Division as it pushed up the main road towards Eindhoven. Artillery barrages and air strikes smashed the German para-troopers defending the road, and when the Waffen-SS Panzerjäger IVs tried to help, several were knocked out. British Shermans were soon streaming northwards.

Heavy fighting now raged all around Arnhem as Harzer threw more and more troops into action to stop the British establishing a firm base. Speed of response was more important than strength or coordination. It was imperative that the British be denied the chance to establish them-selves in firm positions. The battle for Arnhem bridge burst into life on the morning of the 18th, when the British para-troopers heard a column of tracked armoured vehicles approaching. Waffen-SS armoured halftracks, Puma armoured cars, Volkswagen jeeps and Graebner's captured British Humber scout car raced over Arnhem bridge at 48kmh (30mph), with Waffen-SS troopers train-ing their machine guns and rifles on the high buildings overlooking the elevated highway. Two vehicles got across the bridge unscathed and then the British Paras opened fire. Machine guns, mortars, PIAT bazookas, Sten guns and rifles raked the column. One halftrack took a direct hit and veered out of control before turning over. Other vehicles crashed into each other, effectively blocking the road. Two vehicles tumbled over the side of the elevated road. A handful of Waffen-SS men in the tangled wreckage tried to return fire. For almost two hours the carnage continued, until at last the remnants of Graebner's force pulled back to safety at the southern edge of the bridge, leaving 12 wrecked vehicles behind.

Army panzers were brought up to reinforce Brinkmann's kampfgruppe, and a determined effort was launched to blast out the British. As the battle was raging at Arnhem bridge, Spindler was continuing his effort to hold the 1st Airborne Division. His force had grown to 1000 men in several independent kampfgruppen, backed by 30 tanks. An ad hoc division of army and Waffen-SS units was also trying to build a front to block the British move westwards and to seal them in a kessel. The Germans were closing in.

During the morning of 18 September, Harmel returned to Arnhem and quickly received his orders from Bittrich, who declared: "Schwerpunkt [main effort] is south." No effort was to be spared to hold Nijmegen bridge and prevent a link-up between the British tanks and their airborne troops. Waffen-SS engineers on trucks and riding bicycles at last reached Nijmegen bridge. They immediately began preparing it for demolition. At midday, SS-Hauptsturmführer Karl Heinz Euling arrived to take command of the bridge defence kampfgruppe. Soon, armoured halftracks, mortars and four Panzerjäger IVs were rumbling over Nijmegen bridge. Artillery batteries were established on the north bank of the Waal to provide support.

LAYING THE TRAP
When American paratroopers edged into Nijmegen they were met with a heavy barrage of German artillery and mortar fire, sending them scurrying back to seek cover. More *Frundsberg* reinforcements arrived during the day, and Harmel set up his command post on the north bank of the Waal, from where he could observe the key bridge. Model relayed to him the Führer's orders that the bridge was not to be blown, but held to allow a German counterattack to restore the front along the Dutch-Belgian border. Harmel was having none of this nonsense, though, and was determined to order the bridge to be blown if British tanks attempted to cross.

Throughout the afternoon and into the night of 18/19 September, fighting raged in Arnhem. Tigers were brought up to blast the paras on Arnhem bridge, and the army's 280th Assault Gun Brigade arrived to support Spindler's drive against the main British force. Slowly, the Germans were becoming more organized and effective. Losses were heavy on both sides, with most German kampfgruppen suffering 50 percent casualties. The German armour was decisive, allowing the outnumbered Waffen-SS kampfgruppen to blast the British out of their positions.

The date 20 September signified the decisive phase in the battle. The Guards Armoured Division had linked up with the 82nd Airborne Division and planned to seize the Nijmegen bridge during the day. Harmel had some 500 Waffen-SS troopers in the town fighting alongside a similar number of Luftwaffe, army and police troops. 88mm and 37mm flak guns were emplaced in order to protect the large road ramps leading up to the bridge, and the Panzerjäger IVs were also in the town.

ALL-DAY BOMBARDMENT
British guns bombarded the German positions throughout the day, and American paratroopers and British Grenadier Guards edged into the suburbs of Nijmegen. The bombardment knocked out the key 88mm flak guns that provided the main defence of the bridge approach routes. In the afternoon a battalion of US paratroopers raced forward with canvas assault boats and set course for the northern bank of the Waal. German mortars and 20mm flak guns raked the boats, killing or wounding half the Americans, but they kept going through the maelstrom. Once ashore, they scattered the few old men and boy soldiers holding the rear end of the bridge. As the river assault was under way, a squadron of British tanks rushed the southern edge of the bridge. Several tanks fell to Panzerfaust fire from the Waffen-SS men. The tanks just kept moving and, within minutes, were up on the bridge, machine-gunning the *Frundsberg* engineers who were still placing demolition charges. Harmel immediately ordered the bridge to be blown. The engineer officer kept pressing the detonation switch. Nothing happened. Artillery fire had damaged the initiation cable; Nijmegen bridge was in British hands.

On Arnhem bridge itself, meanwhile, 2 Para was on its last legs, and Lieutenant-Colonel Johnny Frost surrendered during the morning of 21 September. They had no idea XXX Corps tanks were only 17km (10.5 miles) away. Thus ended an epic battle.

Harzer's troops continued to press back the eastern flank of the British force east of Arnhem. He ordered his kampfgruppe to form small penetration teams, each led by a couple of StuG IIIs, to push forward into the British lines. In addition, more guns were brought up to blast the British. South of the Rhine, a brigade of Polish paratroopers was dropped just behind the *Frundsberg*'s "stop line". With customary promptness, Harmel reorganized his small kampfgruppen to contain the new landing. A battalion of sailors was thrown in to hold the Poles, and 16 88mm flak guns were positioned to cover the road from Nijmegen. Batteries of Nebelwerfers were brought up to stop the Poles massing for infantry

Once the Waffen-SS had halted the British Guards Armoured Division, the position of the 1st Airborne Division farther north became hopeless.

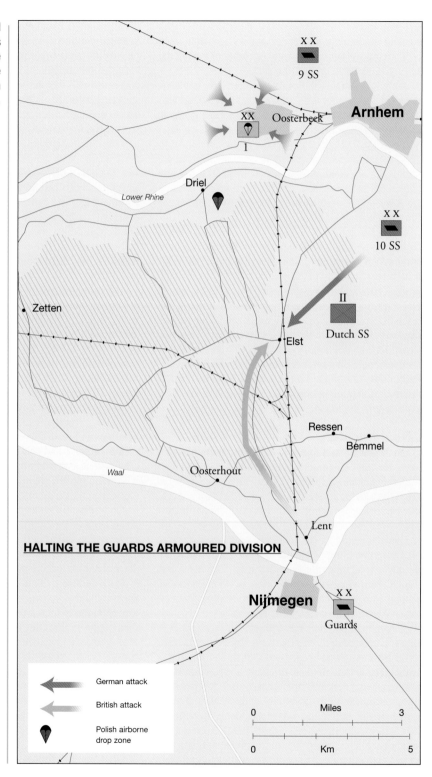

HALTING THE GUARDS ARMOURED DIVISION

German attack

British attack

Polish airborne drop zone

WILHELM BITTRICH

Wilhelm Bittrich was born in Wernigerode on 26 February 1894. He served during World War I as a fighter pilot, before joining the fledgling SS Fliegerstaffel *Ost* (SS Flying Echelon East). When Himmler announced the creation of the *Germania* Regiment, Bittrich was named as 2nd Company commander. He transferred in 1936 to the *Deutschland* Regiment, and then moved to the *Der Führer* Regiment in 1938 as commander of 1/*Der Führer*. He moved yet again, in June 1939, to the *Leibstandarte* Division, where he remained throughout the Polish campaign as Dietrich's adjutant. Later in the war he was awarded the Knight's Cross for his actions during the Western campaign in 1940. He served as commanding officer of the 2nd SS Panzer Division *Das Reich*, before he took command of the 9th SS Panzer Division *Hohenstaufen* in February 1942. When Hausser took command of the Seventh Army, Bittrich replaced him as commander of II SS Panzer Corps. He gained fame for his units' actions in defeating Allied forces at Arnhem. For this he was awarded the Oakleaves. He received the Swords in May 1945. He died on 19 April 1979 in Germany.

attacks. Every attempt to break through his line was rebuffed with heavy losses.

The 1st Airborne Division continued to hold out in the face of continuous German attacks. During the night of 23/24 September, 45 army King Tiger tanks arrived to help Bittrich. He sent 30 south to help Harmel stop the Guards Armoured Division, and the rest turned westwards towards the Oosterbeek Kessel. By 25 September, some 110 German guns were ringing Oosterbeek, bombarding the British trenches.

A "final attack" was ordered by Bittrich for 25 September. Four *Hohenstaufen* kampfgruppen made good progress, thanks to heavy King Tiger support, and one unit broke through the now depleted defences and overran a British artillery battery. Realizing that his 1st Airborne Division was on its last legs, Montgomery authorized its withdrawal during the night. After swimming across the Rhine to a precarious bridgehead held by the Poles, by dawn just under 2500 men had escaped. Bittrich's men rounded up some 6000 prisoners, the majority of whom were wounded, and buried more than 1000 dead British soldiers. The Americans lost another 3000 men, and XXX Corps lost 1500 men as well as 70 tanks. Bittrich's men were in awe of the fighting qualities of their British opponents, and the formalities of the Geneva Convention were generally observed during the battle. There were no accusations of the premeditated killing of prisoners that had sullied the reputation of Waffen-SS units in Normandy and later in the Ardennes.

German losses were equally heavy. Some 8000 German casualties were recorded for all the units engaged during Market Garden, from Eindhoven to Arnhem. In the Arnhem area, German units suffered more than 3000 casualties; and 1725 of these were killed. The majority of these casualties were incurred by Bittrich's units.

Bittrich's men, however, had defeated Montgomery's daring bid to end the war by Christmas 1944. The prompt reaction of the Waffen-SS panzer corps had ensured the key bridge at Nijmegen was defended and then the road to Arnhem blocked. This was the vital ground of Market Garden. Bittrich had spotted this in his orders, which were issued within minutes of the first Allied paratroopers landing. For the next week, he ensured his schwerpunkt remained firmly in German hands. No matter how bravely the British paratroopers fought in Arnhem, they were doomed as soon as Harmel's kampfgruppe took up defensive positions on Nijmegen bridge on 18 September.

Senior British intelligence officer Brian Urquhart had this to say of Arnhem: "My job as chief intelligence officer was to try to evaluate what the enemy reactions were going to be and how our troops ought to deal with them. The British airborne troops were going to be dropped at the far end of the operation at Arnhem – it was across the third bridge, so there were three bridges that had to be captured before you got to the British airborne troops. I became increasingly alarmed, first of all at the German preparations, because there were intelligence reports that there were two SS panzer divisions right next to where the British troops were to be dropped. These were the star troops of the German Army, the 10th and the 9th SS Panzer Divisions. They had been very badly mauled in Normandy and were refitting in this area. These were the best fighting troops in the German Army and they had heavy tanks. Airborne troops in those days had absolutely nothing. They had limited supplies of ammunition, and they could not fight heavy armour because they didn't have the weapons to do it."

The Sixth Panzer Army

The élite Waffen-SS panzer divisions were rebuilt at the end of 1944 in preparation for Hitler's new offensive in the West. Under the command of "Sepp" Dietrich, the Sixth Panzer Army was intended to deliver victory against the Western Allies. And as new tanks, halftracks and artillery were delivered to Dietrich's formations, morale among the SS divisions soared.

Hitler was already thinking about how he could regain the initiative in the war even before the last remnants of his battered armies had retreated across the German and Dutch borders in September 1944. The 20 July Bomb Plot had destroyed for good Hitler's trust in the army's generals. He wanted his favourite Waffen-SS general, "Sepp" Dietrich, to command the most powerful armoured force Nazi Germany had ever put in the field – the Sixth Panzer Army. Although nominally an army formation – rebuilt from the remnants of XII Corps that had been badly mauled in Russia during the summer – almost all of Dietrich's key staff officers were old hands from either his *Leibstandarte* or I SS Panzer Corps days.

To fill out his new army, Dietrich was given the two premier Waffen-SS corps headquarters, I SS and II SS Panzer Corps. I SS Panzer Corps boasted the *Leibstandarte* and *Hitlerjugend* Divisions, under the command of SS-Gruppenführer Hermann Priess, who had previously commanded the *Totenkopf* Panzer Division in Russia.

After his success commanding one of *Hitlerjugend*'s panzergrenadier regiments in Normandy, Wilhelm Mohnke, now an SS-Oberführer, was given the honour of commanding the *Leibstandarte*. Although Mohnke had fought well in Normandy, he was far from popular with his comrades. He lost a foot in the Yugoslav campaign, so missed fighting with Hausser's SS Panzer Corps in Russia, and he was still considered an "outsider" by many of the Waffen-SS officers who were now regimental and divisional commanders in Dietrich's army. Taking the place of Kurt Meyer, who had been captured in early September, was SS-Standartenführer Hugo Kraas, a highly decorated *Leibstandarte* Division veteran.

The victor of Arnhem, Willi Bittrich, remained in command of his beloved II SS Panzer Corps, and he had Walther Harzer at his side as chief of staff. He still had the *Hohenstaufen* Division, under the capable Sylvester Stadler, but the *Frundsberg* Division had been replaced by the *Das Reich* Division. Bittrich's corps, however, was now very strong and considered the most militarily professional in the Waffen-SS.

As befitted its status as one of the premier units of the Waffen-SS, the *Leibstandarte* boasted a formidable complement of tanks and armoured vehicles. Its panzer regiment was again commanded by Joachim Peiper, who had now recovered from wounds received in

Hitler's grandiose scheme for the Ardennes offensive involved an armoured thrust through the Ardennes to the port of Antwerp, at a stroke dividing the Allied armies in the West. It was to be 1940 all over again.

THE ARDENNES OFFENSIVE: THE PLAN

KING TIGER

The Tiger II, or King Tiger, was arguably the forefather of all modern main battle tanks. Weighing 70,000kg (154,00lb), it was as large as a modern M1 Abrams or Challenger II. Equipped with the extremely potent KwK 43 L/71 88mm gun, and fitted with 150mm (5.9in) frontal armour, the Tiger II was a true behemoth. Despite its weight, it was quick and smooth across country, and able to reach speeds of 38kmh (24mph). However, it suffered from serious mechanical problems, and many broke down during battle and were abandoned by their crews. When functioning, the King Tiger was a devastating weapon on the battlefield. In the Ardennes offensive, Tiger IIs were attached to the *Leibstandarte*.

Type:	heavy tank
Length:	10.26m (33.7ft)
Width:	3.75m (12.3ft)
Height:	7.26m (10.2ft)
Crew:	5
Armament:	1 x 88mm, 2 x 7.92mm
Range:	110km (68 miles)
Speed:	38kmh (24mph)

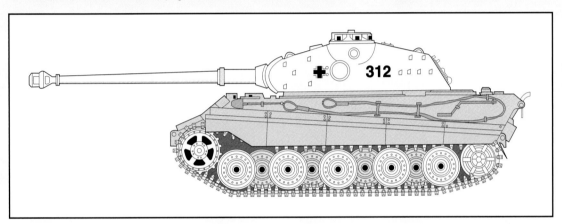

Normandy, and fielded 38 Panthers and 34 Panzer IVs in a single battalion. To beef up its firepower, the 501st SS Heavy Panzer Battalion – formed from the old 101st SS Battalion – was attached with 30 of the monster 70-tonne (69-ton) King Tiger tanks. The division's anti-tank battalion boasted 21 Panzerjäger IVs. The division had the pick of Germany's manpower, and veteran officers considered it to be on a par with previous intakes.

The *Hitlerjugend* Division was equally powerful, with 38 Panthers and 37 Panzer IVs in its panzer regiment, which were grouped in one battalion. It had a strong contingent of self-propelled anti-tank guns, including 22 Panzerjäger IVs, in its own anti-tank battalion. To add to its firepower, the army's 560th Anti-tank Battalion was attached to the panzer regiment, with 28 Panzerjäger IVs and 14 of the 88mm-armed Jagdpanthers. It continued to draw its recruits from the ranks of the Nazi Youth organization, which gave it its distinctive character. I SS Panzer Corps had four army Nebelwerfer and two army artillery regiments attached for fire support.

Bittrich's II SS Panzer Corps was next in line to receive men and equipment, and was not as strong as its sister formation. He only had two army corps-level artillery regiments attached.

The *Das Reich* Division had 80 percent of its designated manpower strength and a strong complement of armour. Its panzer regiment boasted two full battalions, with 58 Panthers, 28 Panzer IVs and 28 StuG IIIs. The division's anti-tank battalion had 20 Panzerjäger IVs.

The *Hohenstaufen* was the weakest Waffen-SS division, with only 75 percent of its allocated manpower under arms at the end of November 1944. Its panzer regiment had 35 Panthers and 28 StuG IIIs in one battalion, and 39 Panzer IVs and 28 StuG IIIs in a second battalion. Anti-tank firepower was provided by 21 Panzerjäger IVs.

Dietrich had an assortment of army artillery, assault gun, anti-tank gun and heavy tank battalions attached to his army, which, when added to the divisional equipment totals, gave him just under 400 Panzer IV, King Tiger and Panther tanks, 685 guns, 340 rocket launchers, 112 assault guns and 215 Jagdpanzers.

One of the most unusual units attached to Dietrich's army was the 150th Panzer Brigade led by SS-Sturmbannführer Otto Skorzeny. It was intended to infiltrate behind Allied lines, the men dressed in US Army uniforms, in order to spread chaos and confusion. Some 500 Waffen-SS men were attached to this 2800-strong unit.

The Ardennes Offensive

Hitler's last great offensive in the West, spearheaded by Dietrich's Sixth Panzer Army, commenced on 16 December 1944. At first it made good progress, aided by low cloud that denied the enemy air cover. But the road network in the Ardennes was not suitable for large-scale armoured advances, and soon the SS armoured columns were facing traffic jams and stiff American resistance.

Hitler's last great offensive in the West gets under way on 16 December 1944. A strong artillery barrage opened at 05:30 hours, and at 06:00 hours the infantry attacked. Enemy artillery replied two hours later.

At 05:30 hours on 16 December 1944, 1600 German guns and rocket launchers drenched the American frontline in deadly shrapnel. Then the first attack waves of infantry moved forward to clear a route for the panzer columns, which were to be unleashed to capture their first objective – the bridges across the Meuse – within 48 hours. The panzers would push on to Antwerp and victory.

"Sepp" Dietrich's Sixth Panzer Army was placed on the right flank of the assault and it would be the schwerpunkt, or main effort, for the attack. I SS Panzer Corps would lead the advance to the Meuse, with II SS Panzer Corps following close behind. Once the vital river crossings were secure, Bittrich's divisions would spearhead the advance on Antwerp. To help Dietrich reach the bridges before the Americans had time to destroy them, Otto Skorzeny's special forces brigade – with small teams wearing US uniforms taking the lead – was to race ahead of the Waffen-SS panzers and capture them in a coup de main operation. A regiment of Luftwaffe paratroopers was also to be dropped ahead of Dietrich's corps to capture a key road junction.

The sister *Leibstandarte* and *Hitlerjugend* Divisions would advance side by side towards the Meuse, after

army Volksgrenadier divisions had cleared a way through the string of weak American units holding the front along the Belgian-German border. Once unleashed, the two divisions would race through the narrow, forested valleys of the Ardennes until they reached the open countryside in the Meuse valley. The region's roads were winding and poorly maintained and, in most places, could barely take single-file traffic. The constricted road network in the Ardennes meant Dietrich's divisions had to be split up into self-contained columns, each of which was assigned its own specific route, or Rollbahn. All told, more than 6000 Waffen-SS vehicles had to be squeezed through the Ardennes road system. The speed of the Waffen-SS advance was determined as much by the commanders' traffic-control abilities as by their tactical skills.

The *Leibstandarte* Division was divided into three large kampfgruppen, centred on the panzer regiment and its two panzergrenadier regiments, and a "fast group" based on the division's reconnaissance battalion. *Hitlerjugend* was organized in the same way. The most powerful kampfgruppe was Joachim Peiper's, which had all the *Leibstandarte*'s tanks, its King Tigers, a panzergrenadier

By 20 December the Germans were having great difficulty repairing the roads in the rear in order to supply forward units. In addition, US resistance was hardening at St Vith and Bastogne.

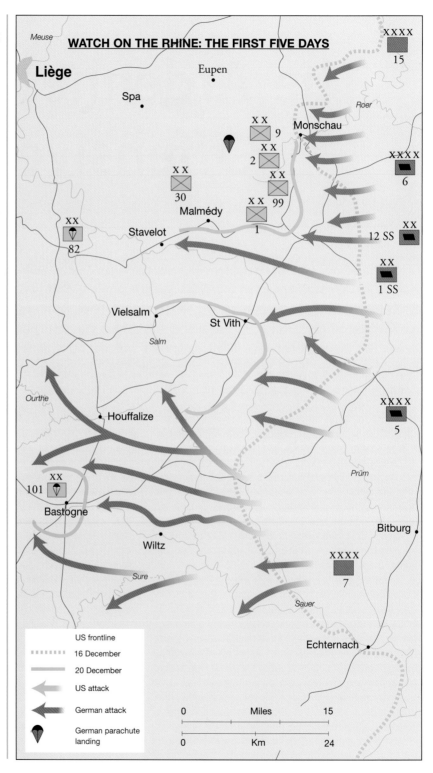

WATCH ON THE RHINE: THE FIRST FIVE DAYS

US frontline

.... 16 December

20 December

US attack

German attack

German parachute landing

0   Miles   15

0   Km   24

battalion carried in armoured halftracks, and a battalion of army howitzers. All told, he had more than 5000 men, 117 tanks, 149 halftracks, 24 artillery pieces, 40 anti–aircraft guns, and more than 500 other vehicles. It was the *Leibstandarte*'s lead unit, and the success of the offensive would depend on its progress.

The atrocious road network meant that each division was allocated no more than two Rollbahns each, so their kampfgruppen were lined up behind one another waiting for the lead troops to blast open a way forward. With little room for manoeuvre off-road, the lead kampfgruppe was effectively reduced to relying on the handful of tanks it could place at its head. Behind Peiper's kampfgruppe were nose-to-tail columns of tanks and trucks.

Although the Germans had amassed more than 17 million litres (3.73 million UK gallons) of fuel to support the offensive, the jammed road network meant the troops at the front of the convoys could not rely on refuelling tankers getting through to them. So Peiper and his colleagues in the lead kampfgruppe were ordered to seize US petrol dumps to maintain the pace of their advance.

The fog, rain and low cloud that shrouded the Ardennes provided cover from the Allied fighter-bombers that had paralyzed German panzer columns in Normandy in the summer. On the freezing night of 15 December, the *Leibstandarte* moved into its forward

Above: Waffen-SS armour and infantry during the early phase of the Ardennes offensive. The Germans were confident that rapid action could defeat superior Allied forces.

Below: Waffen-SS Panther tanks of the Sixth Panzer Army in the Ardennes. Despite many of the roads in the region being unsuitable for armour, panzer crews had undergone a great deal of driver training beforehand.

assembly areas behind the sector of front held by the 12th Volksgrenadier and 3rd Parachute Divisions. The *Hitlerjugend* was waiting a few kilometres to the north, behind the 277th Volksgrenadier Division.

The 12th and 3rd Divisions' attacks quickly stalled in the face of very determined, but poorly coordinated, American resistance. They were supposed to have captured the town of Losheim and its key road junction in a couple of hours, to allow Peiper's tanks to roar into action as dawn broke. Minefields held up the attack, and the two divisions were still fighting their way through American positions in the early afternoon. When a breach was opened, it was found a key bridge was blocked and a temporary one had to be built by army engineers. It was not until well after dark that his column got into Losheim, where Peiper was dismayed to find the commander of the lead parachute regiment had allowed his men to go to sleep. The determined Waffen-SS officer "took" the paratroopers under his command and they were soon loaded onto the back of his King Tigers, which pressed on into the night.

All night Peiper's men forged on, with two Panthers leading the way until they surprised an American scout company parked up in a village just before dawn. Running short of fuel, Peiper now made a diversion to raid a large US fuel dump. His tanks were soon being refuelled by sullen American prisoners. The Germans turned north towards the town of Malmédy.

When the lead Panzer IVs approached a crossroads in the hamlet of Baugnez they spotted a column of US soft-skinned vehicles ahead of them. They immediately started firing on the Americans, then raced at full speed towards them. Outgunned, the Americans offered no resistance, and in a few minutes, Waffen-SS men had herded almost 100 stunned Americans into a nearby field. Peiper then passed by in his armoured command halftrack and ordered the advance to continue, racing off westwards with his lead tanks. Back at Baugnez, the captured Americans were being machine-gunned by Peiper's men in an incident that would become notorious as the "Malmédy Massacre", even though it occurred several kilometres outside the town. Peiper and more than 70 other members of the *Leibstandarte* would later face war crimes charges for their involvement in this incident.

Behind Peiper's spearhead, the *Leibstandarte*'s other kampfgruppe, led by SS-Standartenführer Max Hansen, had already managed to break free and was advancing west. Containing the bulk of a panzergrenadier regiment and most of the division's Panzerjäger IVs, it was operating south of Peiper on a parallel Rollbahn.

The *Hitlerjugend* Division was not faring so well in its attempt to open up the northern Rollbahn and seize the strategic Eisenborn ridge. The US 99th Infantry Division put up stiff resistance and held off the attacks by the 326th Volksgrenadier Division. Rather than being used to exploit a breach in the American line, the division's two lead kampfgruppen had to be committed to the assault. Although the Waffen-SS Panthers inflicted heavy losses on the few American tanks barring their way, soon GIs with bazookas were picking off the German tanks at an alarming rate. This fierce fighting in a string of border villages allowed time for the Americans to form a firing line with their Shermans, M10 and M18 tank destroyers, and 105mm howitzers in the anti-tank role.

When the *Hitlerjugend*'s Panthers rolled forward on the morning of 18 December, they ran into a hail of well-aimed anti-tank fire. They made it to the American lines but soon 15 Panthers, 1 Panzer IV and 2 Panzerjäger IVs were ablaze. Kraas and Dietrich ordered a rethink, and the division's schwerpunkt was now shifted south in order to try

JOACHIM PEIPER

Joachim Peiper was undoubtedly one of the most talented and daring men to wear the uniform of the Waffen-SS. He was also one of the most controversial. He joined the *Leibstandarte SS Adolf Hitler* at the age of 19, and at the outbreak of war was serving as an adjutant on the staff of Heinrich Himmler. He fought on the Western Front in 1940, winning Second and First Class Iron Crosses. Personally very brave, on one occasion he led a lightly armed unit through enemy lines to rescue trapped comrades, bringing them back across the lines. For this he was awarded the Knight's Cross. His name became tarnished, however, during the Ardennes offensive in 1944. Though his tanks punched holes in the Allied lines in the Ardennes Forest, the lack of fuel blunted his thrust. However, during this action elements of his battlegroup killed an unarmed group of US prisoners at Malmédy. Peiper had nothing to do with the incident personally, but his name will be forever associated with the atrocity. Serving time in prison after the war for the Ardennes incident, he later retired to France. He was murdered at his house on 13 July 1976 by French communists.

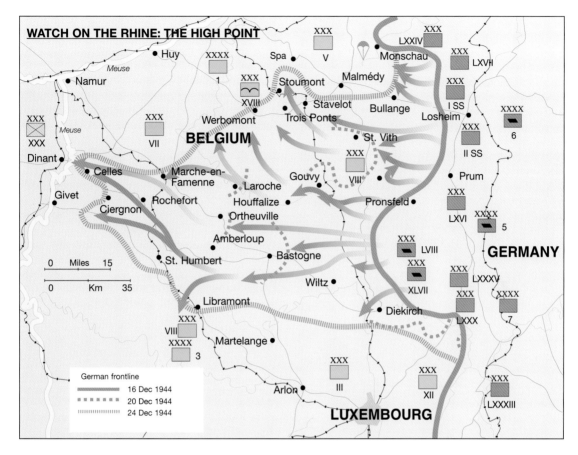

WATCH ON THE RHINE: THE HIGH POINT

Huy • Meuse • Namur • Spa • V • Monschau • LXXIV • LXVII • Stoumont • Malmédy • XXXX 1 • XVIII • Werbomont • Stavelot • Bullange • Losheim • I SS • Trois Ponts • BELGIUM • St. Vith • II SS • 6 • Dinant • Meuse • VII • Celles • Marche-en-Famenne • Gouvy • VIII • Prum • Givet • Laroche • Rochefort • Houffalize • Pronsfeld • LXVI • 5 • Ciergnon • Ortheuville • Amberloup • LVIII • GERMANY • St. Humbert • Bastogne • XLVII • LXXXV • Wiltz • LXXX • 7 • Libramont • Diekirch • VIII • 3 • Martelange • III • XII • LXXXIII • Arlon • LUXEMBOURG

0 Miles 15
0 Km 35

German frontline
━━━━ 16 Dec 1944
▪▪▪▪ 20 Dec 1944
⋯⋯⋯ 24 Dec 1944

to bypass the strong defence on Eisenborn ridge. Dietrich concentrated four corps artillery regiments to support a large attack on 21 December, but the Americans were fighting stubbornly and were not to be moved. When the panzer regiment attacked, it lost 11 more tanks. A further attack the following day met a similar fate, and the division was pulled out of the line to be re-assigned to push through behind the *Leibstandarte* Division.

The stalling of the *Hitlerjugend*'s attacks on the morning of 18 December meant that Peiper's kampfgruppe was now I SS Panzer Corps' schwerpunkt. Even so, he was still 30km (18.6 miles) from the Meuse, and 48 hours behind schedule. This was not a time to worry about his flanks. Peiper pushed all his tanks forward for one last, desperate lunge for victory.

At dawn that day, Peiper renewed his attack with added vigour. The Panthers rolled at full speed into Stavelot to seize its key bridge. With time critical, Peiper pressed on to seize his next objectives, the bridge over the River Amblève at Trois Ponts, and another bridge slightly farther south across the River Salm. The bulk of

By the end of the offensive the Germans had inflicted losses of 81,000 killed, wounded or captured. But then the panzers came to a halt 96km (60 miles) short of Antwerp.

the kampfgruppe headed for Trois Ponts, and a small contingent was sent to the Salm. American engineers were hard at work in Trois Ponts, laying demolition charges on the key bridge and mines on the roads as Peiper's lead Panthers rolled into town just before 11:00 hours. The vital bridge disappeared in a massive mushroom cloud. The same thing happened to the assault team sent to capture the Salm bridge, leaving Peiper's route on the main road westwards blocked. He therefore turned his troops around, and sent them northwards on a side road, which led through the village of La Gleize, in order to bypass the downed bridges.

Two hours later, his Panthers were through the village and heading westwards to the crossing at Cheneux. It was undefended and Peiper's tanks were soon across and heading westwards again. Allied fighter-bombers now swooped down, knocking out two Panthers and a dozen vehicles. The damage inflicted was minor, but the delay proved fatal to Operation Autumn Mist. It gave a group of American engineers just the time they needed to destroy Peiper's next target, the bridge at Habiemont. He now had to turn his column around and head back to La Gleize to rethink his options. He had only 31 operational tanks: 6 Tigers, 6 Panzer IVs and 19 Panthers. Once back there, he met up with Gustav Knittel's reconnaissance battalion which had made its way forward, along with a small convoy of fuel tankers. News also came in that American troops had recaptured Stavelot, so Knittel was ordered to retrace his steps and open up a supply route for Peiper.

After a night spent refuelling and reorganizing his tired troops, Peiper launched them into the attack again the following morning. This time he headed northwest towards Stoumont. One King Tiger and four Panzer IVs were hit before German infantry cleared the village. When the advance continued, the panzers ran into a battalion of Shermans emerging out of the afternoon gloom. His route blocked, Peiper ordered the panzers back to La Gleize. With American columns closing in from four sides, Peiper was effectively trapped. He held out until the evening of 23 December, when he was given permission to break out. The majority of his troops were left dead or wounded on the battlefield, along with more than 25 tanks, 50 armoured halftracks and other vehicles. Peiper's lunge for victory had failed.

THE EXPLOITS OF KAMPFGRUPPE HANSEN
The remainder of the *Leibstandarte* Division, led by Kampfgruppe *Hansen*, was making desperate efforts to catch up with Peiper, and this soon turned into a rescue mission when the commander of the division's panzer regiment found himself cut off by US reinforcements.

Hansen's advance had at first gone well, brushing aside a column of US reconnaissance troops near Recht on 18 December. Then it was ordered to push northwards towards Stavelot, but traffic chaos in the village prevented it moving until the morning of 19 December. Ten Tigers and Panzer IVs moved in on the village from the south, but their attack was literally stopped in its tracks when an American M-10 tank destroyer hit the lead King Tiger's side armour, penetrating the monster panzer and causing it to explode. Access to the bridge was blocked. Knittel's reconnaissance unit mounted its own attack on Stavelot from the west on that day, backed by two of Peiper's King Tigers. His men reached the centre of the village but they were too late to stop American engineers blowing the bridge.

The following day, *Hansen*'s panzergrenadiers renewed their attack on Stavelot but they now were ordered to bypass the village from the south and use forest tracks to find a route through to Peiper.

The move westwards was more successful and soon *Hansen* had troops situated overlooking the Salm River. US paratroopers from the 82nd Airborne Division had now arrived in strength, and were starting to build up a strong line blocking the route through to Peiper. The rescue effort eventually proved futile, and all *Hansen*'s men could do was hold open a bridgehead to receive their beleaguered colleagues. By the time Peiper's men had reached safety on Christmas Day, the *Leibstandarte* Division had shot its bolt. The destruction of Peiper's kampfgruppe had ripped the heart out of its offensive power.

Skorzeny's 150th Panzer Brigade fared little better than the other elements of I SS Panzer Corps. Only a handful of its sabotage teams were able to penetrate American lines, and none of them managed to seize the vital Meuse bridges. The psychological effect of their presence on the battlefield was far more important than their actual achievements.

THE ADVANCE TO ST VITH
Four days into Operation Autumn Mist, it was becoming clear that I SS Panzer Corps was stalled. Peiper's kampfgruppe was stuck at La Gleize, and the *Hitlerjugend* was getting nowhere on the Eisenborn ridge. The rapid advance of Peiper created one opportunity for Dietrich. The US 7th Armored Division and parts of three other divisions were still holding out in the town of St Vith, and Bittrich's mission was to push his two panzer divisions to the north and south of the St Vith salient, trapping the American force, before continuing westwards to the Meuse. It looked good on a map, but *Das Reich* and *Hohenstaufen*'s kampfgruppen had to contend with a road network that was hopelessly overloaded.

The *Hohenstaufen* led the northern pincer, pushing through Recht to attempt to seize Vielsalm. SS-Sturmbannführer Eberhard Telkamp led the *Hohenstaufen*'s panzer regiment into action on 21 December, and it soon ran into a strong 7th Armored Division Combat Command, with almost 80 Shermans and tank destroyers.

The battle came to a climax on Christmas Eve, when Telkamp ordered an all-out effort to break through to Vielsalm. Just as his panzer regiment was forming up to attack, USAAF P-47 fighter-bombers swooped down in waves and massacred his column. Now the *Hohenstaufen*'s northern pincer was well and truly blocked.

Das Reich had been ordered south of St Vith, but its column was halted when the division's tankers were

JAGDPANZER IV

The Jagdpanzer IV was developed in late 1943 from the Panzer IV medium tank. With the turret removed and the upper hull revised into a fixed superstructure, the low profile gave it an advantage on the battlefield. As with other Jagdpanzers, this five-man tank hunter was equipped with a Pak 38 75mm anti-tank cannon. It had an extended range of more than 220km (130 miles) on a tank of fuel, and was capable of firing a mix of ammunition including high-explosive and smoke. Though potent on paper, this vehicle was unreliable and produced in too few numbers (1139). It saw limited service with the Waffen-SS, though in March 1945 the *Wiking* Division still fielded a number of Jagdpanzer IVs.

Type:	tank destroyer
Length:	8.6m (28.1ft)
Width:	3.28m (10.5ft)
Height:	1.96m (6.5ft)
Crew:	5
Armament:	1 x 75mm, 1 x 7.92mm
Range:	220km (130 miles)
Speed:	45kmh (28mph)

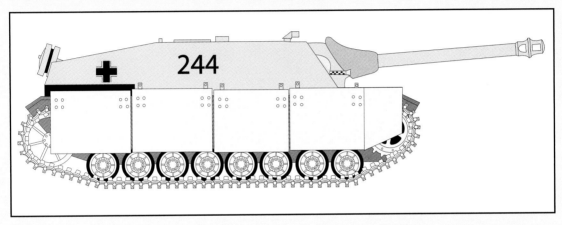

unable to get past road congestion and deliver the vital fuel to the vehicles. The commander of the reconnaissance battalion of *Das Reich*, SS-Sturmbannführer Ernst-August Krag, was allocated the bulk of his division's scarce fuel on 21 December for the vital task of infiltrating behind the St Vith salient to close the American escape route. The prize was to be the entrapment of 20,000 American troops. Krag's reconnaissance troopers were reinforced with a company of Panzerjäger IVs and a battalion of Wespe 105mm self-propelled guns.

Krag managed to slip through the American lines, and by the evening of 23 December he was in the village of Salmchâteau, only 3km (1.8 miles) from Vielsalm. Tanks of the 7th Armored Division were still holding the northern escape route open through that town, but Krag's appearance effectively blocked the southern route out of St Vith.

Denied his prize at St Vith, Bittrich was now determined to push *Das Reich* forward to exploit a gap in the American defences at Manhay, which offered a route westwards to the Meuse. SS-Obersturmbannführer Otto Weidinger's *Der Führer* Panzergrenadier Regiment at last received fuel on 22 December and was launched forward with a company of Panzer IVs and StuG IIIs in the lead. It ran into a battalion-sized force of 82nd Airborne para-

troopers, artillery batteries and a platoon of Sherman tanks during the early hours of 23 December at the key Barque de Fraiture crossroads.

When the initial attack was repulsed by the Americans, Weidinger pulled back and brought up his artillery battery to soften up the defenders who were fighting in the woods around the crossroads. With Panzer IVs and StuG IIIs leading the way, the Waffen-SS then closed in on the Americans. They were soon almost surrounded, then the German tanks started to pick off the Shermans and 105mm howitzers from long range. The three surviving American tanks pulled out through the last escape route, leaving the 100 paratroopers on their own amid 34 destroyed tanks and vehicles. They were soon being rounded up by the Waffen-SS men.

Setting off just after last light, the *Das Reich* columns got to within a few metres of the American positions to the southwest of Manhay, and then the Panthers opened fire. Within minutes, 17 Shermans were ablaze and the outlying defences of Manhay were breached. The American defenders of Manhay now realized the danger they were in and a retreat was ordered. Hundreds of Americans were streaming north out of the town, at the same time as the remainder of *Das Reich*'s Panthers

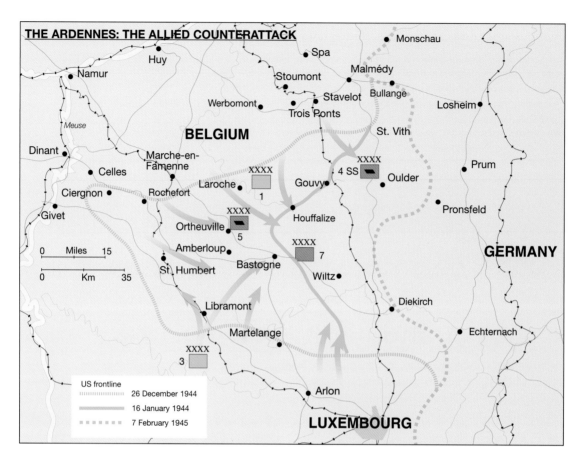

When the skies cleared, Allied aircraft were able to operate against the panzers. By early February 1945 the Germans were back on the start lines, having lost 800 tanks.

appeared from the south. Their appearance completed the American rout, and the equivalent of a brigade of troops was now in full flight.

The following day more American tanks arrived to seal the front around *Das Reich*, backed by 18 battalions of artillery. Ordered to press on westwards, Lammerding's men soon hit a rock-solid defence. Other American tank columns began to press in against its flanks, and two days later *Das Reich* had to give up Manhay or face complete encirclement.

Three Waffen-SS divisions were now in the line, next to each other, along the northern edge of the German salient or bulge in the US front. By 26 December, the *Hitlerjugend* Division had managed to battle its way through the grid-locked road systems, and it was positioned on *Das Reich*'s western flank, ready to kick-start

the stalled Sixth Panzer Army offensive. Most of the division's panzers and artillery were still stuck in jams many kilometres to the east, so the main responsibility for the attack fell on the 25th SS Panzergrenadier Regiment – helped by *Das Reich*'s Kampfgruppe *Krag* – by accident rather than design.

Starting out early in the evening, the heavily loaded panzergrenadiers had to march through deep snow. It took them five hours to close on their objectives. One battalion stormed into the village of Sadzot, completely surprising its American defenders there, many of whom were trying to keep warm in farmhouses rather than stand outside on sentry duty. The panzergrenadiers soon cleared the village and took many of the defenders prisoner. Surprise was not complete, though, and the Americans managed to get off a radio message calling for help before their command post was overrun. Another panzergrenadier unit pushed on past Sadzot and moved towards Erezee.

Kampfgruppe *Krag* had tried to advance along the main road to Erezee, via the village of Amonines. It ran

A battery of 150mm Panzerwerfer 42 Maultier rocket launchers during the Ardennes offensive. Tell-tale smoke trails made it essential for batteries to move quickly.

into a strong road-block and lost a number of armoured vehicles in the dark, so its commander decided that it should turn back.

The Americans now launched their reserve battalion to retake the lost village. They were backed by several M5 Stuart tanks, and for several hours the US paratroopers and Waffen-SS men fought it out in the streets and houses of Sadzot. By dawn 40 dead Germans were left in the village and the panzergrenadier battalion had pulled back to the woods on its outskirts.

The 75mm anti-tank guns were now duelling with the American tanks, but the heavy US artillery support kept the Germans pinned down. A stalemate reigned throughout the day, during which the *Hitlerjugend* began preparations to push forward again during the course of the coming night.

After leaving behind their vehicles, Kampfgruppe *Krag* was to push forward through the forests to the south of Sadzot, leading two battalions of the 26th SS Panzergrenadier Regiment that had moved up into the line earlier in the day. Their advance was unopposed until

they reached the far side of the forest, when heavy American small-arms fire stalled the attack. In terms of manpower during these clashes, more than 120 US paratroopers were lost, either killed or wounded. But such small successes were of little use.

The German High Command ordered the *Hitlerjugend* Division to halt its offensive operations during the afternoon, and the division was instructed to pull back. This was not so that it could rest and recuperate: it was now to concentrate for a new offensive elsewhere in the Ardennes.

This was the high-water mark of the Waffen-SS advance on the northern wing during Operation Autumn Mist. The tide had now turned irrevocably in favour of the Americans. Adolf Hitler's massive gamble in the West had failed miserably.

Defeat of the Sixth Panzer Army

By the end of December 1944, the German offensive in the Ardennes had ground to a halt and the Americans had relieved Bastogne. But Hitler insisted on a fresh attack by the Sixth Panzer Army. This resulted in a futile effort to retake Bastogne, which only served to wear down the armoured strength of the Waffen-SS panzer divisions fighting in Belgium.

A Nashorn heavy anti-tank gun in action during Operation Autumn Mist. Nashorns were usually grouped in heavy tank-hunter detachments. Their 88mm Pak 43 main guns were potent weapons.

A week after the start of Operation Autumn Mist, the German offensive had well and truly run out of steam. Dietrich's Sixth Panzer Army had been held in check along the Amblève River. To the south, the Fifth Panzer Army had advanced to within 15km (9.3 miles) of the Meuse at Dinant before being turned back by British tanks and Allied fighter-bombers. General of Panzer Troops Hasso von Manteuffel had managed to surround the American 101st Airborne Division in the town of Bastogne. However, a relief column from Lieutenant-General George Patton's Third Army punched through from Luxembourg to lift the siege on 26 December 1944.

Hitler wanted a renewed offensive to defeat the Americans, by cutting off Bastogne again to open a new route for further westward offensives. I SS Panzer Corps was to be sent south to close off the narrow 1km- (0.6-mile-) wide corridor linking Bastogne to Patton's army. The *Leibstandarte* did not reach its jumping-off position until late on 28 December, and was not ready to attack until late the following day.

The *Leibstandarte*'s westward attack was planned to coincide with an eastward push by the 3rd Panzer-grenadier Division and Führer Begleit Brigade, to cut the

Bastogne corridor. First to attack were some 30 of Poetsche's panzers, striking out just before dawn on 30 December. They headed out through morning gloom and, helped by panzergrenadiers, easily cleared out two frontline villages. American tank destroyers then made an appearance, hitting several of the panzers.

As the panzers approached the main road south out of Bastogne across open fields, the Americans mobilized two companies of Shermans to block their path. Now the clouds cleared to allow the intervention of Allied fighter-bombers. For more than two hours, the Thunder-bolts worked over the panzer column, claiming seven kills and delaying the advance as the tanks took cover in woods. The American tanks had now taken up ambush positions ahead of the panzers, and were waiting when Poetsche at last got his forces moving again.

For the next week the *Leibstandarte* soldiers held their hard-won ground against a series of strong US counterattacks. The Waffen-SS panzers found themselves "fire-fighting" small local incursions by American tanks on the fringes of the positions held by the panzer-grenadiers. Two precious King Tigers and several other panzers were lost in these scattered battles.

As the *Leibstandarte* was being brought to a halt south of Bastogne, I SS Panzer Corps was being mustered to the north of the town for a final push for victory. *Hitlerjugend* and *Hohenstaufen* had been pulled out of the northern shoulder and sent south, along with the 340th Volksgrenadier Division. Field Marshal Model visited the corps headquarters north of Bastogne on 2 January 1945 in order to put his seal of approval on the plans to smash open the American defences the following day. *Hohenstaufen* was to drive in from northwest of the town, and *Hitlerjugend* would attack from the northeast, as the Volksgrenadiers linked them together. Several Volks artillery brigades were mustered to provide fire support, which was fortunate, because the *Hitlerjugend*'s guns were stranded to the north due to lack of fuel.

At 09:00 hours on 3 January, the German attack was launched as planned. Led by 20 Panzer IVs, the *Hohenstaufen* advanced in the face of heavy American anti-tank fire. The attack stalled in the afternoon when the panzers were caught in open ground. Another attack was attempted in the early evening and suffered a similar fate. The division tried a surprise raid later in the night and penetrated some distance behind American lines before it was beaten back.

In the early afternoon the Volksgrenadiers and *Hitlerjugend* began to move forward. The Volksgrenadiers were soon bogged down in heavy fighting in large forests. *Hitlerjugend*'s panzer regiment led the division forward along the open ground to the left of the railway track, which headed south into the centre of Bastogne. It put 13 Panzer IVs, 7 Panthers and 15 Panzerjäger IVs into action, along with 28 Jagdpanzer IVs and 13 Jagdpanthers of

A StuG knocked out during Autumn Mist. It and many other precious armoured resouces were wasted by Hitler, who frittered away any chance of holding the Allies in the West.

the attached 560th Anti-Tank Battalion. Panzergrenadiers in armoured halftracks were close behind the German armour, and during the afternoon the armada made steady progress, advancing 3km (1.8 miles) despite heavy American artillery fire.

In a night attack, the *Hitlerjugend* made a further big advance, reaching the edges of the villages of Magaret and Bizory on the northern outskirts of Bastogne. Panzergrenadiers and Panzerjäger IVs now pressed into the large Azette wood in front of the town, cutting to pieces a US infantry battalion.

More attacks were now launched against Magaret and Bizory in the afternoon by the panzer regiment, but they couldn't dislodge the defenders. Wild rumours of German breakthroughs caused panic, and some GIs fled into Bastogne. Panzers penetrated the villages, only to be driven back by American Shermans and bazooka teams. The line held.

THE END OF AUTUMN MIST

An American breakthrough against the northern shoulder of the German front forced the withdrawal of the *Hohenstaufen* from Bastogne on 6 January. The *Hitlerjugend* Division was now totally exhausted by its exertions. On 9 January, Hitler finally realized that trying to take Bastogne was a lost cause, and authorized the withdrawal of the Waffen-SS divisions.

Operation Autumn Mist was officially over. Hitler's gamble had failed. The Germans lost 33,000 dead, 22,500 missing and 34,000 wounded. They also left behind more than 600 smashed tanks in the Ardennes. The Americans lost 8600 dead, 21,000 missing and 30,000 wounded, along with more than 733 destroyed tanks.

The Waffen-SS had spearheaded the operation and made some of the deepest penetrations into American lines. Many senior Waffen-SS officers, such as Dietrich, had been sceptical about its chances of success, but had given it their best shot. Figures for losses in the Waffen-SS divisions are hard to come by. Dietrich's Sixth Panzer Army lost some 10,000 dead in total. The armoured vehicle strength of the Waffen-SS divisions was soon restored to near establishment thanks to the smooth recovery of wrecked and damaged tanks from the early phases of the battle. Harder to replace were officer and noncommissioned officer casualties, which ran to nearly 50 percent in some Waffen-SS units.

Part VIII

Annihilation

1945

The Siege of Budapest

In October 1944 the Red Army crossed the Hungarian border and headed for the Danube, reaching the river to the south of Budapest and establishing a bridgehead on the west bank. Hitler, alarmed that Hungary was about to switch sides, had the SS take control of Budapest. But then the Red Army pushed west and laid siege to the Hungarian capital, which the SS desperately tried to hold.

The remains of Budapest's Royal Palace. Turned into a strongpoint by the Germans, it was gutted by the Red Army when the city fell. Some 20 percent of the city's buildings were destroyed in the siege.

In the twilight of the Third Reich, Hungary would be the theatre in which the final offensive of the élite Waffen-SS panzer divisions would play itself out. The first act began in March 1944, when the pro-German government in Budapest started to press for all Hungarian troops to be withdrawn from the Eastern Front. Alarmed that the Hungarian leader, Admiral Horthy, was about to defect, Hitler ordered German military occupation of the country. Horthy and other Hungarian leaders were briefly held hostage by Hitler to ensure Operation Margaretha went smoothly. Several German divisions, including the 16th SS Panzergrenadier Division *Reichsführer-SS*, were mobilized for the operation that met no resistance from the Hungarians. Fascists from the Hungarian Arrow Cross Movement rallied to the German cause and effectively took over key power positions in the Budapest government. In the wake of the occupation, a group of German officers led by Adolf Eichmann arrived in the Hungarian capital. His SS Commando Group was a successor of the old Einsatzgruppen from the early days in Russia, and its mission was to kill every Jew in Hungary. Over the next six months Eichmann's men would be responsible for killing or deporting more than 400,000 Jews.

As Soviet troops surged through the Balkans in the autumn of 1944, clearing Romania and Bulgaria of Axis forces, Hitler was increasingly worried that the Hungarians were intensifying their efforts to switch sides. This was just the situation that required the attention of the Führer's favourite Waffen-SS officer, Otto Skorzeny. Skorzeny served in the élite Waffen-SS *Das Reich* Division until being transferred to the SS commando organization. Skorzeny led some of the most daring missions of the war.

The Führer's suspicions proved correct, as the Hungarian leader Admiral Horthy had long been in negotiations with the Allies to switch sides. Skorzeny led an intelligence-gathering mission to Budapest, to find out exactly what was going on. Working largely in civilian clothes, he was able to infiltrate the heart of Horthy's regime.

Rival contingents of German and Hungarian troops were watching each other in Budapest with suspicion as Soviet troops closed on the country's borders. With the German garrison of Budapest called away to counter Soviet advances in October, this was the ideal moment for Horthy to make his move. Skorzeny struck first. A

team of SD men in civilian clothes lured Horthy's son into a trap. Soon he was heading for a concentration camp in Germany, as a way to ensure his father's loyalty.

Waffen-SS troops were massed around Budapest ready to strike against Horthy's regime, with the ruthless SS General Erich von dem Bach-Zelewski put in charge. He had just overseen the operation to crush the Polish revolt in Warsaw, and was keen to teach the treacherous Hungarians a lesson by blasting to rubble Budapest's Burgberg citadel with the giant railway-mounted 650mm (25.5in) "Karl" mortar. Fortunately, Skorzeny was able to convince Bach-Zelewski that more subtle methods could do the trick. On 15 October, Horthy made a radio announcement of his intention to negotiate an armistice with the Soviets to save Hungary from becoming a battleground. Later that evening Operation Panzerfaust was set in motion.

As the Waffen-SS *Maria Theresia* Cavalry Division moved to set up a cordon around the Burgberg to trap Horthy and his government, Skorzeny organized his assault column. He was able to muster several hundred men of the 500th SS Parachute Battalion, the Jagdverbande (Hunting Unit) Centre and four army Tiger

II tanks of the 503rd Heavy Panzer Battalion for his assault group. A detachment of Goliath robot demolition tanks were to tag along behind his column, ready to blast a path through any roadblocks.

At 06:00 hours on 16 October, Skorzeny led his column up the winding road towards the citadel. He was in the cab of the lead truck with two trusted comrades and the Tigers close behind. In the winter gloom, the first Hungarian checkpoints waved the column of German trucks and tanks past. Skorzeny coolly returned the sentries' salutes. When the SS men ran into a roadblock made of rubble at the gates to the Burgberg, Skorzeny pulled his truck to one side and let the Tigers roll forward. The barricade collapsed under the weight of a heavy tank, and as it emerged into the citadel courtyard the panzer commander swung his 88mm cannon towards a battery of anti-tank guns guarding the seat of the Hungarian Government. SS men stormed past the tank, pushing the surprised defenders to the ground and disarming them.

Meanwhile, Skorzeny put his pistol to the head of a Hungarian officer and demanded to be taken to the commandant of the citadel. A further dose of Skorzeny

Left: Otto Skorzeny in Budapest in October 1944, the scene of one of his great triumphs. With a small force of men Skorzeny had kidnapped the son of the regent, Admiral Horthy, and imprisoned his father. A pro-German government was then installed in Hungary.

Far left: The Hungarian leader Admiral Horthy (right), who tried to negotiate an armistice with the Soviets at the beginning of October 1944. This quickly led to his removal by SS special forces commanded by Otto Skorzeny.

bluster did the trick and the Hungarian officer surrendered his men in the interests of avoiding bloodshed. Several Hungarians failed to get the order to surrender and started firing at the SS men. Two Panzerfaust rockets soon silenced the unlucky Hungarians. Unfortunately for Skorzeny, he not did have the honour of seizing Horthy. The Hungarian leader's apartment was empty. He had already left the building to seek the protection of a senior SS officer, who was a relative of the German kaiser, thinking this would guarantee him better treatment than if he surrendered to a Nazi thug like Skorzeny.

The rest of Skorzeny's men were now moving to seize the other Hungarian ministries around the city and a brisk firefight broke out at the Ministry of War. Four Germans were killed in the action and three Hungarians died fighting off the SS attack before they received the surrender order. With the seat of government secure and Horthy in German custody, SS troops moved to occupy the remainder of the city. A puppet regime was installed. Skorzeny, however, had the privilege of escorting Horthy to his new home in a Bavarian castle.

A German counterattack at Debrecen during October by three panzer divisions knocked out 1000 Soviet tanks and momentarily halted the Red Army drive. This breathing space gave the Germans time to move up troops to form a defensive line outside Budapest. The dubious honour of defending the Hungarian capital fell to IX SS Mountain Corps, which had been pulled out of Yugoslavia during the autumn after being formed there for counter-partisan operations. The Waffen-SS corps was commanded by Karl Pfeffer-Wildenbruch, who had previously led the *Polizei* Division in France and Russia. Although experienced in counter-insurgency operations, he was no combat general and had little grasp of how to defeat Soviet tank attacks.

During late November, the Soviets opened a major offensive aimed at driving the Germans from Hungary. Red Army tanks advanced directly on Budapest, while to the north and south huge pincers swung around behind the city. By 1 December heavy fighting was taking place in the outer suburbs of Budapest.

Two Waffen-SS cavalry divisions formed the core of the defence of the city, along with the remnants of two army panzer divisions. The 8th SS Cavalry Division *Florian Geyer* boasted some 8000 men at the start of the siege, and the 22nd SS Cavalry Division *Maria Theresia*

Red Army soldiers in Budapest in February 1945. The Soviets massed 500,000 troops around the city during the siege, and subjected it to incessant artillery barrages.

was slightly better manned with just over 11,000 men. They each had some 30 field guns and around 20 assault guns or self-propelled Hetzer anti-tank guns. The army Feldhernhalle and 13th Panzer divisions together mustered fewer than 12,000 men and 40 tanks, including some of the monster Tiger II tanks. The remainder of the German garrison was made up of assorted logistical units, independent regiments and battlegroups, including the 1st SS Police Regiment. Some 50,000 Germans were defending Budapest, along with a smaller number of Hungarian troops. The Soviets threw more than 1000 tanks and 177,000 troops into their offensive.

As cavalry divisions, the two Waffen-SS units defending Budapest still had their horses, which were to prove something of a bonus when the Germans started running short of food during the siege. The two units were built around a cadre of veteran Waffen-SS men, but they had recruited a large number of Eastern Europeans in recent months who were starting to show signs of wavering now the war was almost lost. The 1st SS Police Regiment was recruited almost exclusively from Hungarians and was severely depleted by desertions, as were the regular Hungarian units. As the Soviet advance continued, the

most trusted SS men would be posted just behind the main defensive position to shoot any deserters.

The senior German Army officers recognized early on that the Soviets were trying to trap their troops in Budapest, and wanted to pull them back. Even the senior SS Higher and Police Leader in Hungary, Otto Winkelmann, was for abandoning the city. As usual, Hitler refused to allow any retreat and ordered that the city be turned into a fortress, in which the garrison was to fight to the last man and bullet.

As senior military commander in Budapest, Pfeffer-Wildenbruch could have ignored the Führer's orders, but he chose to follow them to the letter. He set up his command post in the tunnels under Budapest Castle Hill. From the safety of his bunker, Pfeffer-Wildenbruch rubber-stamped every mad order he received from Hitler. In the month it took the Soviets to encircle Budapest, the SS general did not even contemplate escaping with his men to safety.

The Soviet encirclement operation came to fruition on 24 December 1944 and trapped some 80,000 German and Hungarian troops in Budapest. The morale of the Hungarians had long collapsed and, except for hardline Arrow Cross supporters, most ordinary soldiers were just looking for a way to desert to the pro-Soviet Hungarian units or to find a way to go home. This placed an increasing burden on the hard-pressed Germans, who now had to rely on parachute drops by the Luftwaffe for supplies.

Parks and race courses were turned into improvised dropping zones with strong defences posted around them to stop the precious supplies falling into the wrong hands.

The two Waffen-SS divisions and the other SS police units were posted to hold the line in Buda, the district of the city to the west of the River Danube. Each unit was given a specific sector to defend, and local counter-attack groups were formed to drive off Soviet incursions. Some 120 German tanks and light armoured vehicles provided the core of these counterattack groups. These included a handful of monster Tiger IIs. Soviet anti-tank guns and air strikes took a growing toll on the German armour, but it was a lack of spare parts and fuel that eventually put most of the panzers out of action.

Conditions inside the city grew more desperate as the siege progressed into January. Apart from horse meat, the garrison had little fresh food and the winter tempera-tures dropped below -20°C (-4°F) at night. As the prospect of rescue diminished, morale collapsed. Even in the supposedly élite Waffen-SS units morale was at rock bottom. Only the fear of being captured by the

Soviets kept the Germans fighting. The commander of the German garrison did not help matters by constantly issuing unrealistic orders and parroting the promises from Hitler that the city would soon be rescued. Pfeffer-Wildenbruch was reported to be on the verge of a nervous breakdown and refused all offers of advice from his chief of staff, a talented young army officer. He also refused to pass on bad news to Hitler, and each day sent sycophantic reports of the garrison's glorious victories to the Führer's headquarters.

The Soviets were desperate to avoid a prolonged battle for Budapest because they wanted to save all their men, tanks and ammunition for the assault on Vienna. So when their offers to negotiate a surrender were turned down by Pfeffer-Wildenbruch, who was desperate to avoid being branded a "traitor" by Hitler, the Soviets

An 88mm flak gun of an unidentified Waffen-SS unit in Budapest during the Soviet siege. The "88" could penetrate 192mm (7.5in) of armour at a range of 1000m (3280ft). Note the ammunition cases stacked on the left.

From the northwest and west the units of IV SS Panzer Corps attempted to reach Budapest. They nearly succeeded, but were repulsed by strong Soviet counterattacks.

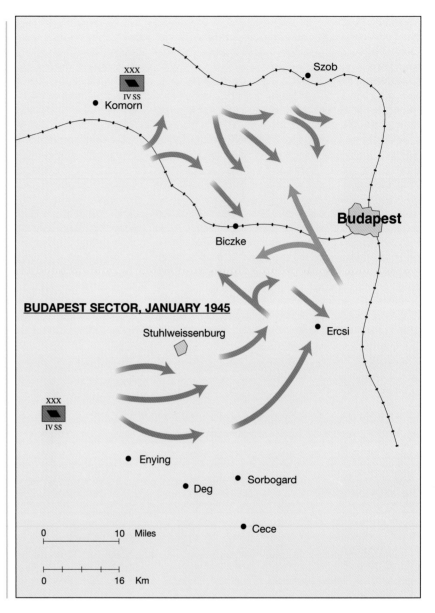

BUDAPEST SECTOR, JANUARY 1945

decided to step up their assault. Ordinary Soviet soldiers were no longer inclined to show mercy to the German defenders of Budapest, who had forced them to fight a needless battle in the dying days of the war.

In six weeks of systematic assaults, the Soviets bombed and dropped all the bridges across the Danube to split the German defence in two. They then overran Pest, the eastern district of the city, before turning their attention to the west. One by one the crucial parachute drop zones were overrun, further isolating the defenders.

For the Waffen-SS men in Budapest, this was a desperate time. All hope seemed lost and yet they kept on fighting. Some even had the time and energy to help the Arrow Cross stage several pogroms or massacres of remaining Jews in the ghetto district. Almost every building in the city had suffered some sort of battle damage, with almost one-fifth of the city rendered uninhabitable. Some 76,000 civilians were killed during the siege.

By the end of January 1945, the Germans were being relentlessly driven back to the Castle Hill district of

JAGDPANTHER

The Jagdpanther, like the Jagdpanzer before it, was the combination of an anti-tank gun placed on the chassis of an existing vehicle, in this case the Panther tank. Outfitted with the magnificent Pak 43 88mm gun and protected by thick, sloped Panther armour – 80mm (3.24in) on the upper front hull – the Jagdpanther was an excellent tank hunter. Crewed by five men, the Jagdpanther was put into production in January 1944, and in total 425 were built up to May 1945. Carrying 60 rounds of ammunition, the Jagdpanther was capable of destroying enemy tanks at ranges of up to 3000m (9842ft). The *Das Reich*, *Hohenstaufen* and *Frundsberg* Divisions had a company each in January 1945.

Type:	tank hunter
Length:	9.86m (32.34ft)
Width:	3.42m (11.2ft)
Height:	2.51m (8.23ft)
Crew:	5
Armament:	1 x 88mm, 1 x 7.92mm
Range:	210km (131 miles)
Speed:	46kmh (28.75mph)

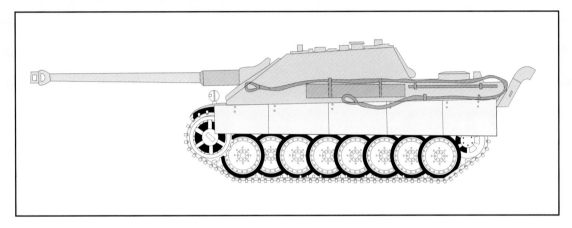

Tired and cold members of IV SS Panzer Corps during the Budapest relief operation. The SS got to within 24km (15 miles) of the city, but Hitler refused to order a breakout.

Budapest. Here was also the main hospital for the 10,000 German wounded, who were forced to endure pitiful conditions with only minimal medical supplies. Only some 23,000 Germans were now fit to fight, plus 20,000 Hungarians. The Germans could only muster 6 StuG III assault guns, 9 Hetzers, 12 Panthers and 10–15 other armoured vehicles, as well as 60 anti-tank or field guns.

In the first week of February, the Soviets closed in for the kill. Some 15,000 Germans and 10,000 Hungarians were now pushed back into a small perimeter around Castle Hill. The battle was lost and even Pfeffer-Wildenbruch now realized this. More than 30,000 German defenders of Budapest died during the siege. However, Pfeffer-Wildenbruch's fear about massacres of prisoners were unfounded. Some 10,000 Germans were captured and although there were several incidents of Waffen-SS being executed, the vast majority were treated relatively humanely by Soviet standards. When the siege of Budapest was over, everyone had had enough of killing.

Spring Awakening

The last major German offensive of World War II took place in Hungary. Codenamed Spring Awakening, the Third Reich's final reserves were gambled on a misconceived plan to seize Hungary's oil fields. The Sixth SS Panzer Army was earmarked to conduct the offensive, which commenced on 6 March 1945. However, after some initial gains the Red Army hit back with a vengeance.

A column of StuG IIIs of the Sixth SS Panzer Army in Hungary in February 1945. Note how wet the ground is. Adverse ground conditions seriously hampered the panzers' movement during Spring Awakening.

In his Berlin bunker in February 1945, an all-out offensive led by six Waffen-SS panzer divisions to secure Hungary's oil fields seemed very logical to Adolf Hitler. Almost to a man, however, the Führer's generals thought it was madness. Huge Soviet armies were at this time on the eastern bank of the River Oder, less than 160km (100 miles) from Berlin itself. The Third Reich's élite armoured forces were needed for the last-ditch battle to defend its capital from the Russians, or so it seemed to General Heinz Guderian, the penultimate chief of staff of the German Army.

The Waffen-SS panzer divisions started concentrating in Hungary in December 1944, after a Soviet offensive had pushed deep into the country and surrounded its capital, Budapest. By Christmas Day 1944, the city was surrounded. In response, Hitler ordered IV SS Panzer Corps to be moved from Poland to spearhead the rescue mission with the *Totenkopf* and *Wiking* Divisions. SS-Obergruppenführer Herbert Gille's men spent four days on freezing trains moving down to Komorno on the River Danube. They unloaded their 100 tanks and headed east to intercept Russian spearheads advancing westwards along the south bank of the Danube.

Operation Konrad got under way with a night attack on New Year's Day, which initially caught the Soviet XXXI Rifle Corps by surprise. The Waffen-SS Panthers and Panzer IVs crashed through the unprepared Russians and drove eastwards for almost 48km (30 miles), knocking out 200 enemy tanks as they did so.

The *Totenkopf* Division advanced directly eastwards on the left flank, along the banks of the Danube, while the *Wiking* Division moved southeastwards directly towards Budapest. When the *Totenkopf* hit a strong pak-front, it, too, turned southwards to join *Wiking's* push. Lacking the strength to batter his way past Soviet defences, Gille used his veteran troops to try to dodge past Soviet strongpoints and find a way through to Budapest. With the route south blocked, he sent *Wiking's Westland* Panzergrenadier Regiment on a march deep behind enemy lines after it found a route over the Vertes Mountains. With the Soviets now alerted to the German intentions, though, it was not long before they moved reinforcements up to close off the northern route into the Hungarian capital.

On 12 January 1945, the Waffen-SS troops pulled back from the front and disappeared into the forests

Tiger Is in Hungary, early 1945, possibly of the 509th Heavy Tank Battalion which was attached to IV SS Panzer Corps. The open hatches suggest the frontline is some way off.

along the Danube. The Soviets were convinced they had seen off the German attack. They had no idea that Gille's troops were in fact moving south to open a new front. Six days later they burst out of the morning mist to smash into the Russian CXXXV Rifle Corps, which without tank support was an easy target for the Waffen-SS units. The German tanks rolled over its frontline positions on 18 January, and then started to shoot up its supply convoys and artillery positions. By the evening they had covered 32km (20 miles), brushing aside a counterattack by the weak Soviet VII Mechanized Corps. More Russian tanks were sent into action the following day, and they received the same treatment. The *Totenkopf*'s anti-tank battalion, deployed with the advance guard of the division's *Totenkopf* Panzergrenadier Regiment, was instrumental in breaking up several counterattacks by the Soviet XVIII Tank and CXXXIII Rifle Corps. Its new Panzerjäger IV self-propelled guns were particularly effective. This heavily armoured version of the Panzer IV tank was equipped with the powerful L/70 75mm cannon, which was also used in the Panther tank.The Danube valley, with its open fields and small villages, was ideal tank country. By the morning of 20 January German armour was on the banks of the Danube. Gille's men now motored north-

wards, cutting into the rear lines of communications of the Soviet Fifty-Seventh Army. The Red Army was in a panic. The Soviet commanders on the west bank of the Danube were convinced they would soon be surrounded by IV SS Panzer Corps and the German Army's 1st Panzer Division. On 24 January, the *Wiking* and *Totenkopf* Divisions surged forward again, inflicting heavy losses on the Soviet V Guards Cavalry and I Guards Mechanized Corps. They got to within 24km (15 miles) of Budapest before the arrival of the last Soviet reserves, XXIII Tank Corps, stopped them in their tracks.

Three days later, 12 Soviet infantry divisions joined the tank corps in a major counterattack against the Waffen-SS divisions. The SS units held their ground, but Hitler now ordered IV SS Panzer Corps to fall back so it could regroup and join a major operation he was planning in order to defeat the entire Soviet army group in Hungary. Ignoring pleas from his generals that now was the moment to order a breakout from Budapest, Hitler refused to consider the idea. Budapest would be relieved by the Sixth SS Panzer Army. Therefore, there was no need for a breakout.

With Gille's men now falling back in the face of massive pressure, the Budapest garrison's position was becoming even more precarious. The Soviets were able to concentrate all their efforts on eliminating Pfeffer-Wildrenbruch's hapless command. The Waffen-SS general proved to be particularly inept, allowing his main supply dump to be overrun.

In January 1945, five Waffen-SS divisions were in the process of pulling out of Belgium after the failure of the Ardennes Offensive. Hitler wanted them concentrated to lead his offensive into Hungary, which he thought would turn the course of the war. A special order was issued by the head of the SS, Heinrich Himmler, for the divisions to be pulled back into Germany to be refitted for their new offensive. Almost the total production of Germany's shattered armaments industry was to be diverted to the SS divisions. The efforts to re-equip the Waffen-SS divisions stretched Germany's armaments industry to the limit. There were no more reserves left. The coming offensive would be the last throw of the dice for Hitler's Third Reich.

BUILDING THE SIXTH SS PANZER ARMY

Throughout January and into February 1945, new tanks, assault guns, halftracks, artillery and other equipment arrived by train at barracks and training grounds in central Germany. Thousands of raw recruits and drafted Luftwaffe and Kriegsmarine personnel, who no longer had aircraft or ships to serve in, found themselves pressed into the Waffen-SS. Crash training courses were organized to try to mould this raw material into an élite fighting force. The results were very mixed.

For the first time, six SS panzer divisions would be committed to an operation on the Eastern Front under the command of SS panzer corps, and two of those corps would be under the command of the Sixth SS Panzer Army. This army had been raised in September 1944 to lead the Waffen-SS panzer divisions in the Ardennes. SS-Oberstgruppenführer Josef "Sepp" Dietrich remained in command of this army. There was great rivalry between the two corps in the Sixth SS Panzer Army. The most favoured formation was I SS Panzer Corps *Leibstandarte Adolf Hitler* led by SS-Gruppenführer Hermann Priess, the former commander of the *Totenkopf* Division. It boasted the *Leibstandarte* and *Hitlerjugend* Divisions (the latter was to see action on the Eastern Front for the first time during the coming offensive). The *Leibstandarte* Division's panzer regiment was reinforced with a full battalion of 36 of the new super-heavy Tiger II, or King Tiger, tanks. These 71-tonne (70-ton) monsters boasted frontal armour 250mm (9.84in) thick that was impervious to almost all anti-tank weapons then in service. However, they were notoriously mechanically unreliable, and more would be abandoned on the battlefields of Hungary following breakdowns than were lost to enemy fire. The 501st SS Heavy Panzer Battalion was one of three such units created by the Waffen-SS in the final months of the war that used the Tiger II tank. These units grew out of the Tiger I compa-

nies that had served with the three original SS panzer divisions since 1943. The two other battalions, the 502nd and 503rd, were sent to the East Prussian and Berlin sectors in the final months of the war, and so missed the offensive in Hungary. The *Leibstandarte*'s other panzer battalion fielded 27 Panzer IV tanks, 41 Panthers and 8 anti-aircraft tanks.

The *Hitlerjugend* Division could only muster one battalion for its panzer regiment, with 40 Panzer IVs and 44 Panthers. The division also had 20 of the new Jagdpanzer IV anti-tank self-propelled guns, plus more than 150 armoured halftracks. Also attached to the division was the 560th Heavy Anti-Tank Battalion, which fielded 31 Jagdpanzer IVs and 16 Jagdpanthers. This latter vehicle combined a Panther chassis with a fixed 88mm cannon.

II SS PANZER CORPS

A heavy punch was also packed by II SS Panzer Corps, under the command of SS-Gruppenführer Willi Bittrich, which contained the *Das Reich* and *Hohenstaufen* Divisions. Like I SS Panzer Corps, Bittrich's command had a heavy artillery regiment equipped with towed 210mm howitzers, and a rocket launcher regiment with Nebelwerfers to provide heavy fire support during assault operations.

Bittrich's panzer regiments were short of tanks, but the shortfall was made up with Sturmgeschütz (StuG) assault guns. They were distributed to the panzer regiments' second battalions to augment their Panzer IVs. The *Das Reich* Division boasted 34 Panthers, 19 Panzer IVs and 28 StuG IIIs, while the *Hohenstaufen* Division had 31 Panthers, 26 Panzer IVs and 25 StuG IIIs. The *Hohenstaufen*'s sister division, *Frundsberg*, had served in II SS Panzer Corps all through the Normandy campaign, at Arnhem and during the Ardennes offensive, but in January 1945 it was detached and posted to the Vistula sector of the Eastern Front, taking with it its 38 Panzer IVs and 53 Panthers. It would not join the rest of the Sixth SS Panzer Army for the Hungary offensive.

Operation Spring Awakening was envisaged by Hitler as a knock-out blow against Soviet forces in the Balkans. The initial phase of the assault would be a three-pronged pincer attack to trap and destroy the Russian troops on the west bank of the River Danube. German forces would then turn eastwards and free the trapped garrison in Budapest. There was then talk of the offensive continuing southwards to drive the Red Army out of the Balkans altogether and regain control of Romania's oil wells. However, the whole scheme was based on fantasy. For one thing, Budapest was on the brink of falling even before Dietrich's troops had started their attack.

Hitler's attack in Hungary in March 1945 used up the last remaining panzer reserves, resources that were badly needed in Poland, where 6000 Red Army tanks were poised to strike for Berlin.

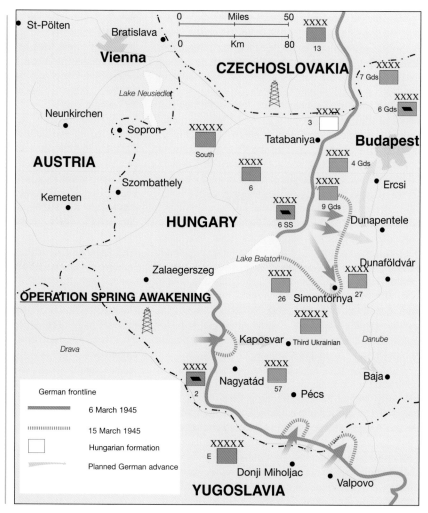

As the pitiful drama in Budapest was entering its final act, Dietrich's Sixth SS Panzer Army was at last arriving in Hungary in some strength. The German offensive would be conducted in two phases. It was to kick off with a preliminary operation, codenamed South Wind, by I SS Panzer Corps to destroy the Soviet bridgehead on the western bank of the River Gran, which threatened the German left flank along the banks of the Danube. The Soviet bridgehead, held by seven infantry divisions and a number of armoured units, was to be bludgeoned out of existence by a head-on attack by the *Leibstandarte* and *Hitlerjugend* Divisions.

SS-Obersturmbannführer Joachim Peiper, commanding the *Leibstandarte*'s panzer kampfgruppe, was to lead the attack, which was channelled by a series of wide water courses into a narrow 16km (10-mile) frontage. The battle-

field was criss-crossed by numerous canals, which were heavily defended by Russian anti-tank guns and dug-in T-34/85 tanks. The latter was the upgraded version of the T-34, which now boasted an 85mm high-velocity cannon as its main armament. Peiper commanded all the *Leibstandarte*'s tanks, including its Tiger IIs, a battalion of panzergrenadiers riding in armoured halftracks, and a battalion of self-propelled artillery.

Army infantry units were initially committed to the battle during the evening of 16/17 February, after a corps fire mission by all the German guns facing the bridgehead. The attack achieved surprise, and the infantrymen were at first able to advance 8km (5 miles) before they ran into the first enemy pak-front. Peiper ordered his King Tigers to motor to their assistance. When the heavy tanks rolled into the range of the Russian anti-tank guns, they started attracting heavy fire from the 76mm cannons. The shells just bounced off the front of the King Tigers, however, allowing the German tanks to destroy all the Soviet guns blocking the advance.

By evening, the *Leibstandarte* and *Hitlerjugend* Divisions were at Parizs Canal. Armoured kampfgruppen from both divisions advanced on 19 February, employing panzerkeil tactics. With the heavy King Tigers and Panthers in the lead, any Soviet tanks or anti-tank guns that tried to block the German advance were quickly silenced by the panzers' devastating firepower. By early afternoon the Waffen-SS tank crews were at the Danube, in the eastern bottom corner of the bridgehead.

The next day, the armoured spearhead was ordered to swing north to deal with the Soviet IV Guards Mechanized Corps that was still entrenched on the west bank of the Gran. Attacking southwards during the evening of 22/23 February, the combined panzer-infantry operation degenerated into confusion when German units failed to recognize each other in the darkness and started trading fire. This attracted Russian artillery fire, and the assault was stalled in no-man's land for several hours. Then the assault tanks got stuck in a minefield,

losing several vehicles. Only a daring flank attack by the division's armoured personnel carrier battalion saved the situation. After a day recovering from this carnage, I SS Panzer Corps spent 23 February preparing for the final assault on the Soviet bridgehead. The two Waffen-SS divisions staged a concentric night attack, with King Tigers and Panthers leading the way. The Russians eventually withdrew, blowing up the last bridge across the Gran at 08:30 hours on 24 February. They left a trail of destroyed and abandoned equipment behind them. More than 2000 Russians had been killed, a further 6000 wounded and 500 captured by I SS Panzer Corps. Some 71 tanks and 180 artillery pieces were also lost in the week-long battle. The Waffen-SS paid a heavy price for the victory, though, losing almost 3000 casualties and a dozen tanks destroyed. Scores more tanks were badly damaged, and had to be pulled back from the panzer regiments for urgent repairs.

Halftrack and wheeled vehicles of the Sixth SS Panzer Army during Spring Awakening. The ground was so waterlogged in places that even the halftracks were immobilized.

With the Gran bridgehead eliminated, Hitler was now able to order Operation Spring Awakening to roll forward to the south. Some 400,000 German troops, supported by 7000 artillery pieces, 965 Luftwaffe combat aircraft, and 400 tanks and self-propelled guns were to attack on 6 March. The schwerpunkt, or main effort, of the operation was between Lakes Balaton and Valencei, with the Sixth SS Panzer Army leading the way. It had the bulk of the German armour under its command. Gille's IV SS Panzer Corps was to support the operation on the left flank of Dietrich's army. For the first time ever, six Waffen-SS panzer divisions would roll forward into battle together. Not surprisingly, the Führer was very optimistic about Spring Awakening's prospects.

Unfortunately for the Führer, around 16 Russian rifle divisions were in the path of Dietrich's panzers, with two tank corps and two mechanized corps, with some 150 tanks, in direct support just behind the frontline south-west of Lake Balaton itself. Also, the Soviets were building up their armoured forces north of Budapest for their own offensive along the Danube valley – the Sixth SS Panzer Army would attack into the jaws of an over-whelming Soviet armada of more than 1000 tanks. The attack plan called for I SS Panzer Corps to advance southwards to link up with the Second Panzer Army advancing northwards. II SS Panzer Corps was to move directly eastwards towards the Danube, to protect the right flank of the Waffen-SS attack.

SPRING AWAKENING BEGINS

Operation Spring Awakening began officially at 04:30 hours on 6 March, with a massive barrage from the artillery of the Sixth SS Panzer Army. First to move forward were the panzergrenadiers of the *Leibstandarte*, whose first task was to open several lanes through a Russian mine-field before they could begin clearing an extensive system of trenches and strongpoints at bayonet point. This took all morning, and then the division's panzer kampfgruppe was able to race forward. But as its tanks and armoured halftracks tried to deploy off the roads to engage the enemy anti-tank guns, they started to get stuck in axle-deep mud. The panzergrenadiers had to press home their attacks without armoured support. Not surprisingly, the rate of advance was unimpressive.

Advancing on the *Leibstandarte*'s left, the *Hitler-jugend* Division found the going equally hard. II SS Panzer Corps' attack did not even reach its assembly area until well after dark. Thanks to their successful initial defence, the Russians were able to deploy an extra infantry corps, with limited tank support, across the path of I SS Panzer Corps. They did not move their main

armoured reserves, but kept them around Budapest in preparation for their own offensive.

On 7 March the German attack began to gather momentum, as both the *Leibstandarte* and *Hitlerjugend* Divisions at last broke through the Soviet defences and were able to launch their panzer kampfgruppen into action to exploit the breaches created by the panzergrenadiers. As dawn broke on 8 March, German fortunes looked as if they had changed. The *Hitlerjugend* surged 16km (10 miles) forward until it ran into a pak-front dug-in on ridge lines. The division's reconnaissance battalion was ordered to take the position in a night attack, to allow the advance to begin again at first light. A dozen Jagdpanthers and Jagdpanzer IVs formed a panzerkeil which charged up the hill and routed the defenders. The reconnaissance battalion's halftracks followed close behind, and the Waffen-SS troopers machine-gunned and grenaded the fleeing Russian troops as they drove among them.

Bittrich's men, spearheaded by *Das Reich*, now ran headlong into the Soviet XXX Corps and XVIII Tank Corps, which battled furiously to hold them back from the Danube. The Russians even resorted to using their heavy anti-aircraft artillery in the direct-fire mode against German tanks. The next day the *Hohenstaufen* and *Wiking* Divisions joined the attack, driving a wedge 24km (15 miles) into the Soviet line.

CARNAGE AT THE SIO CANAL

I SS Panzer Corps now caught up with the retreating Russians on the Sio Canal, with German Panthers and Jagdpanthers inflicting heavy losses on a number of Soviet truck convoys that had not yet crossed over the canal. The fighting along the Sio Canal reached a climax on 12 March with a major effort being mounted to push bridgeheads across the 30m- (98ft-) wide obstacle. The *Hitlerjugend*'s attack ended in a slaughter, when its fire-support panzers and Jagdpanzers were forced to fall back from the canal bank by a withering barrage of anti-tank gun fire. The panzergrenadiers pressed on, only to be machine-gunned in their rubber assault boats as they tried to row across the canal. A few of them made it across and established a precarious bridgehead. In the *Leibstandarte*'s sector, the attack fared better because the division was able to bring its troops forward through a town and protect them from enemy fire until the last moment, before they, too, rushed across the canal. Deadly 88mm flak guns were brought up to support the assault and, along with the King Tigers, they were able to neutralize many of the Soviet anti-tank guns and machine-gun bunkers. This firepower was enough to allow the establishment of a bridgehead during the night, and soon the division's combat engineers were at work erecting a tank bridge. A Jagdpanzer IV got over the structure, but the weight of a second vehicle was too much and it collapsed into the water. Constant repairs were needed to keep it open to allow reinforcements to cross. They were desperately needed to deal with a counterattack by a regiment of T-34/85 tanks.

I SS Panzer Corps managed to hold on to its bridgeheads for three more days in the face of incessant Soviet counterattacks. Battalions, then regiments, were fed into the battle by the Soviets to keep the Waffen-SS penned in. The Red Army was winning the battle of attrition.

With his route south effectively blocked, Dietrich decided on 15 March to switch the schwerpunkt of his army away from I SS Panzer Corps to Bittrich's front. The *Leibstandarte* and *Hitlerjugend* were ordered to disengage and move north, before joining the attack towards the River Danube.

The following day, however, the Soviets began their own offensive, which rendered Dietrich's orders irrelevant. More than 3000 vehicles, including 600 tanks, poured past Budapest and swept around both sides of Lake Valencei. Gille's IV SS Panzer Corps was engulfed in the storm, with the *Wiking* Division all but surrounded after a Hungarian division collapsed on its flank. Hitler issued orders that the division was to hold at all costs. The division's commander, SS-Oberführer Karl Ullrich, ignored the orders and pulled his troops back before they were trapped. The *Hohenstaufen* Division came to its rescue, also in defiance of the Führer's orders.

Bittrich and Gille now joined forces to hold open an escape route for I SS Panzer Corps, which was pulling back north as fast as it could to avoid encirclement. It managed to get out of the trap, but had to leave most of its damaged and bogged-in vehicles behind. By 20 March 1945, I SS Panzer Corps could only muster 80

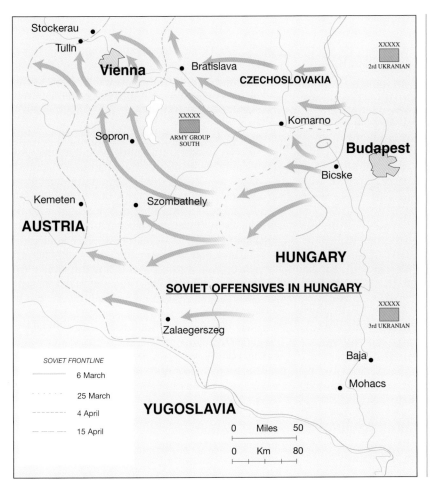

The Soviet counteroffensive in March 1945 shattered the German front on the Danube. What was left of the Waffen-SS panzer divisions in Hungary retreated to Austria.

Right: A tank-hunting team of the Sixth SS Panzer Army in Hungary. The soldier on the left is armed with a Panzerschreck anti-tank weapon. His comrade on the right carries a single-shot Panzerfaust.

Below: The strain begins to show for these panzer-grenadiers during Spring Awakening. By the middle of March 1945, German armoured forces had been halted west of the Danube, and the offensive had run out of steam.

tanks, assault guns and self-propelled guns fit for service. The remainder of Dietrich's army now mustered fewer than 100 tanks and assault guns. All the Waffen-SS divisions had suffered grievously during Spring Awakening, and most were below 50 percent strength without much prospect of any reinforcements to replace losses.

The German front in Hungary was shattered wide open by the Soviet offensive. It was never re-established. Dietrich's army started to fall back to Austria in the hope of defending the capital, Vienna. The Waffen-SS divisions were now constantly retreating, though every so often a handful of tanks and panzergrenadiers would turn to form a rearguard. However, they were soon outflanked and the retreat would begin again.

When news reached Hitler's bunker about the retreat of the Waffen-SS, the Führer flew into a rage. He sent a signal to Dietrich ordering the soldiers of the Sixth SS Panzer Army to remove their honorific Nazi armbands. In his eyes they were no longer fit to wear the Führer's name on their uniforms.

The effect on the morale of the Waffen-SS divisions in Austria was catastrophic. Senior commanders ripped off their medals in disgust and ordinary grenadiers started to desert in large numbers. The men of Dietrich's army could see that the war was lost. They tried to stage a rearguard action to defend Vienna, but it was futile. Soon they were heading westwards again. Once back on German soil, many of the conscripts now serving in the ranks of the Waffen-SS began to drift away. The hardcore officers

An image that sums up the state of Germany's armed forces in 1945. The Sixth SS Panzer Army may have been fully motorized on paper (as with the halftrack towing an anti-tank gun), but fuel and vehicle shortages meant horse-drawn transport was still relied upon (right).

started to concentrate on getting themselves and their remaining men away from the vengeful Soviets. Fighting the Führer's war was no longer their priority.

The Waffen-SS panzer divisions were all in Czechoslovakia or Austria in the first week of May. The *Leibstandarte* and *Das Reich* Divisions found themselves in central Czechoslovakia, amid an uprising against German rule. Their commanders negotiated a truce with the rebels and escorted several thousand German civilians out of Prague towards the advancing Americans. As they approached the American lines, the rump of the two divisions just melted away into small groups to try to find a way past the US Army outposts.

The *Frundsberg* Division was on the Czech-German border when the war ended and, rather than formally surrender, its officers and men split themselves up into small groups and headed for the American lines. A few made it, but most were trapped by Soviet patrols or killed by Czech partisans. Those captured by the Russians were shipped to Siberia, and only a handful returned home in 1955 when the Kremlin finally released its last batches of German prisoners.

In Austria, what was left of the *Hitlerjugend* Division surrendered en masse to the Americans under the watchful eye of a Russian tank column. At the last minute, the remaining 6000 *Hitlerjugend* troops stampeded past an American check-point rather than risk capture by the Russians. The *Hohenstaufen* Division was able to surrender peacefully to the Americans, while *Wiking* just broke up into small groups and disappeared into Austrian and Bavarian villages. Many of the staff officers of the various Waffen-SS panzer corps and the Sixth SS Panzer Army also took to the hills. American, British and French patrols soon arrested hundreds of Waffen-SS men as they tried to reach their home towns, or flee to Switzerland.

The *Totenkopf* Division suffered a tragic – or fitting, depending on one's point of view – fate after an epic journey to the American lines. In spite of managing to cross into the American sector, the 3000 *Totenkopf* men were then handed over to the Russians. The senior officers were separated from the bulk of the men and executed by NKVD secret policemen. Hundreds of others were also executed as the remnants of the division were shipped to Stalin's Gulag in Siberia.

Dietrich himself headed for Switzerland, dressed in traditional Bavarian costume, with his wife. Many of these fugitives, including Dietrich, were captured, although some were spirited away by the shadowy Odessa group to exile in Switzerland, Spain and South America. *Das Reich*'s Heinz Lammerding and the flamboyant Otto Skorzeny were among the lucky few.

As the remnants of Dietrich's army were being rounded up in a string of temporary prisoner-of-war camps spread throughout southern Germany, it began to dawn on the Waffen-SS that the victorious Western Allies were not going to treat them as honourable defeated opponents. The officers were soon separated from their men, and squads of investigators arrived to take statements about the deaths of Allied prisoners of war in a spate of incidents from Normandy to the Ardennes.

Last Stand in Berlin

It was supremely ironic that in the last days of the Third Reich, many of Hitler's Waffen-SS soldiers who fought in the rubble of Berlin were non-German nationals. The élite Aryan divisions of the Waffen-SS were in the process of saving themselves as their Führer faced his final days in his capital. And the greatest act of loyalty shown to him was by a group of French SS volunteers.

German troops in Berlin in April 1945. Prior to the battle for the city, every Red Army soldier, on orders from Moscow, had sworn an oath on the Soviet flag to fight with a special determination.

In January 1945 millions of Soviet troops, backed by several thousand tanks, guns and aircraft, stood poised to strike towards the German capital. During January and February, the Red Army smashed open the German defences in Poland and drove hundreds of miles westwards to the River Oder, some 56km (35 miles) to the east of Berlin. Amid this rout, SS chief Himmler had his chance at being an army group commander and suffered the indignity of being sacked by Hitler for incompetence. His brief tenure as commander of Army Group Vistula had seen thousands of German soldiers die in hopeless counteroffensives.

A key figure in the final battles around Berlin was the Waffen-SS general Felix Steiner, who still commanded what was left of his III SS Panzer Corps. During Himmler's brief command in Pomerania, Steiner's force had been grandly retitled the Eleventh SS Panzer Army, but in reality it consisted of little more than an oversized division. The core of Steiner's command was the *Nordland* and *Nederland* Divisions, which were still made up respectively of Scandinavian and Dutch Nazi sympathizers. They were both oversized regimental battlegroups with around 3000–4000 fighting troops each. His corps was later rein-

forced by the Flemish-speaking Belgians of the *Langemark* Division and French-speaking Belgians of the *Wallonien* Division, which were much smaller than the other two units of the corps. Steiner's men were a hard core of veterans from the Eastern Front, but were desperately short of tanks, artillery, trucks and other essential equipment. The *Nordland* Division's panzer battalion alone had heavy armoured vehicles in the shape of 26 StuG III assault guns and 2 Panther tanks, of which only half were operational at any time.

As the final deployment for the battle of Berlin was made during March 1945, Steiner's men were positioned to the north of the German capital behind the main defensive position on the Oder as a reserve counterattack force. Steiner's command was a shadow of its former self, and Hitler gave it an importance in his plans out of all proportion to its capabilities.

On the "Oder Line" under the German Ninth Army were two Waffen-SS corps headquarters, which had very few actual Waffen-SS units under their command. XI SS Panzer Corps was responsible for the key Seelow Heights sector just to the east of Berlin. Farther south, the V SS Mountain Corps headquarters controlled the

The battle for the Reichstag was the final drama of Hitler's Third Reich. The battle to take Berlin cost the lives of 100,000 German soldiers and a further 100,000 civilians. Hitler committed suicide on the evening of 30 April 1945.

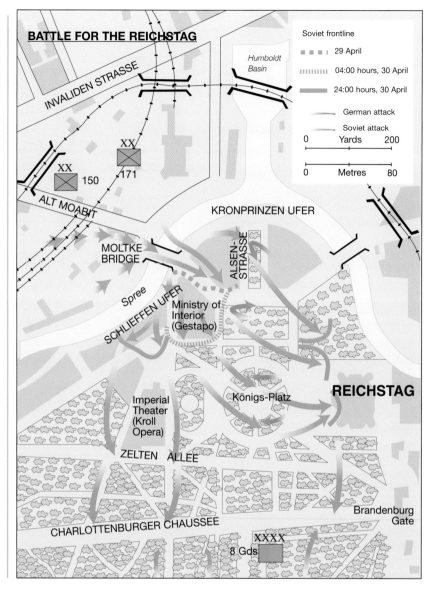

BATTLE FOR THE REICHSTAG

Soviet frontline	
▪ ▪ ▪	29 April
⫴⫴⫴⫴	04:00 hours, 30 April
▬▬▬	24:00 hours, 30 April
→	German attack
→	Soviet attack

Humboldt Basin

INVALIDEN STRASSE

XX 171

XX 150

ALT MOABIT

KRONPRINZEN UFER

MOLTKE BRIDGE

ALSEN-STRASSE

Spree

SCHLIEFFEN UFER

Ministry of Interior (Gestapo)

Imperial Theater (Kroll Opera)

Königs-Platz

REICHSTAG

ZELTEN ALLEE

CHARLOTTENBURGER CHAUSSEE

Brandenburg Gate

8 Gds XXXX

sector around the Frankfurt-am-Oder garrison. It had three Waffen-SS divisions, including the *30 Januar* Panzergrenadier Division, which had been formed earlier in the year out of instructors and administrative staff from the Waffen-SS training schools. The 35th and 36th SS Panzergrenadier divisions were also assigned to the corps, even though they were little more than squads of policemen, with little military experience or heavy equipment. The 36th Division was a particularly unsavoury unit of former criminals under the command of Dr Oskar Dirlewanger, who had led several massacre squads in Russia. This meant the corps commander, Jackeln, who had formed one of the early Einstazgruppen in Russia, was in like-minded company. The corps also had the 502nd SS Heavy Tank Battalion attached with 31 Tiger II heavy tanks.

Behind the lines Hitler ordered the mobilization of every able-bodied man, including pensioners and boys as young as 14 and 15. The old men were drafted into Volkssturm (People's Army) battalions, and the youngsters were assigned to *Hitlerjugend* (Hitler Youth) regiments. With German morale crumbling, the Führer

Waffen-SS soldiers in Berlin during the final days of Hitler's Reich. Many SS troops who fought in Berlin were non-German nationals, including Swedes and Frenchmen.

ordered draconian methods to be used to maintain discipline. Gestapo, SD, military police and Waffen-SS squads were deployed behind every army sector to stop desertions. These mobile squads had the power to execute any soldier or civilian deserting his post or expressing any sign of defeatism.

Within the Berlin "Defence Zone", the security of the central sector of the city, known as the Zitadelle sector, around the Reichstag and the Führer Bunker under the Reich Chancellery was the responsibility of the Berlin regiment of the *Leibstandarte* Division. It was under the command of one-legged Wilhelm Mohnke, who had the dubious honour of being the last Waffen-SS officer promoted to general by Hitler. This was an élite unit containing some 1200 veterans of the *Leibstandarte*, and it boasted a large quantity of weapons, including several Tiger II tanks of the 503rd SS Heavy Tank Battalion. Another 2000 hard-core Nazi militia men were drafted into the *Leibstandarte Adolf Hitler* Brigade to help man the defences of the Zitadelle.

The line-up for the battle for Berlin was awesome. Almost a million Germans, many of them old men and boys, equipped with some 850 tanks and 500 artillery pieces, mostly anti-aircraft or flak guns re-roled as anti-tank weapons, were confronted by 1.6 million hardened Red Army veterans, with 6300 tanks and 15,000 artillery pieces.

At 03:00 hours on the morning of 16 April, the Soviet assault began with a massive artillery barrage that smashed the German forward posts along the Oder River line. The defences on the Seelow Heights held out briefly before being overrun. Steiner was ordered to launch a counterattack with his corps to turn back the Soviet pincer movement, swinging around the north of the capital. The effort was futile and the two divisions were soon retreating. When the *Nordland* tried to fall back northwards, away from Berlin and to safety, the commander was removed from his post by the High Command in the Führer Bunker.

As the noose tightened around Berlin a week into the offensive, the *Nordland* Division was trapped in the city along with the Zitadelle garrison. It received last-minute reinforcements in the shape of 350 French Waffen-SS volunteers who had driven through Soviet lines to join the defence of Berlin. Their unit, the Waffen-SS *Charlemagne* Division, had only just been disbanded

after a spate of desertions. The hard-core members of the unit had nowhere else to go because the Free French government of Charles de Gaulle regarded them all as traitors. Their commander, Gustav Krukenberg, was sent to take over the *Nordland*, which occupied the southeastern sector of the Berlin perimeter. The scene when he arrived was apocalyptic. The divisional headquarters had just been bombed by Soviet aircraft. Dead and dying soldiers were littering the area. The surviving Waffen-SS men of the division were utterly exhausted and only 70 men were manning the front. The remainder were wounded or too exhausted to fight.

By 28 April, the German defenders were being driven back relentlessly and Soviet troops were fighting on the fringes of the Zitadelle defence sector. The *Leibstandarte* troops trapped inside put up fanatical resistance, launching counterattack after counterattack against Red Army troops battling through Berlin's city centre. Single Waffen-SS Tiger II tanks emerged from the ruins to take on columns of Josef Stalin II tanks, only to attract a hail of Soviet fire. It was heroic but futile.

The Berlin garrison was being steadily squeezed from all directions. Division affiliations broke down as units were chopped apart by the Soviets. Defenders coalesced around the few senior commanders still organizing resistance or who had communications with the Führer Bunker. The surviving foreign volunteers of the *Nordland* Division soon retreated into the Zitadelle sector and fell under Mohnke's command. Only some 600–700 men now remained in each of its two regiments, along with surviving French Nazis. The defence of the Zitadelle

OTTO KUMM

Otto Kumm was born on 1 October 1909 in Hamburg, and joined the SS before the war, being an SS-Obersturmführer in 1934. He served with the *Germania* Regiment before the outbreak of war in Europe. He was highly respected by both his superiors and subordinates, who considered him a brave and daring officer, as well as a resourceful character, able to beg, steal or borrow necessary pieces of equipment for his units. He served as regimental commander of the *Der Führer* Regiment during its campaign on the Eastern Front during Barbarossa, where he was awarded the Knight's Cross in 1942 for his leadership of the regiment. He was later awarded the Oakleaves by Hitler himself, and posted to the divisional staff of the 7th SS Gebirgs Division *Prinz Eugen*. His next promotion saw him take command of this division, and he fought extensively against Tito's partisans in Yugoslavia, his leadership of the division earning him the Swords to add to his Oakleaves. Otto Kumm became the last commander of what was left of the *Leibstandarte* Division on 6 February 1945, surrendering to the Americans on 8 May.

sector was also joined by a couple of hundred Latvian members of the Waffen-SS.

Street executions were now commonplace as Hitler loyalists tried to motivate the exhausted and demoralized defenders of Berlin. The Führer was still giving out medals in another attempt to keep his men fighting, personally awarding the commander of the 503rd SS Heavy Tank Battalion the Knight's Cross after his remaining two tanks destroyed an estimated 101 Soviet tanks and 26 anti-tank guns.

Inside the Führer Bunker, Hitler was increasingly deranged by the failure of his generals to rescue him. When he heard about Steiner's failure to attack, his faith in the Waffen-SS was shaken to the core. The hammer blow was repeated when reports started to emerge that Himmler was trying to negotiate with the Western Allies.

Hitler realized the game was up and there was no prospect of Berlin being rescued. SS troops and Soviet soldiers of LXXIX Corps were now fighting inside the Reichstag building a few hundred metres from the entrance to the Führer Bunker. On 30 April he dictated his last will and testament and married his mistress, Eva Braun. Then the pair committed suicide. His last act as commander of the remaining German forces in Berlin was to authorize them to break out. The army commander of the Berlin Defence Zone, Lieutenant-General Helmuth Weilding, was having none of this. He decided to enter into surrender negotiations with the Soviets early on the morning of 2 May to put an end to the slaughter. Senior Waffen-SS officers in the Führer Bunker had persuaded Weilding to delay his surrender for 24 hours to give them the chance to escape. Berlin was now on fire as fighting raged through the length and breadth of the city. Isolated German strongpoints in the city centre were still putting up resistance, and in the suburbs small groups of German

soldiers and refugees were already trying to find escape routes through the Soviet ring. The scene as Hitler's "Thousand Year" Reich came to its end was truly apocalyptic, with every aspect of civilization breaking down.

Surrender was not the Waffen-SS way. Mohnke and other senior Waffen-SS commanders resolved to break out of the city rather than give themselves up to the Soviets. Ten groups of Waffen-SS men from the Zitadelle defence force made their attempt to escape during the evening of 1 May, using Berlin's underground system to bypass Soviet positions. Several of these groups were ambushed and cut down by Soviet fire, including the group containing Hitler's close confidant, Martin Bormann. The 150-strong group led by Mohnke ended up in a brewery, and after a party they surrendered to the Soviets.

For the foreign Waffen-SS volunteers the surrender placed them in a very difficult position. They had good reason to fear that they would not get a good reception from the Soviets and readily decided to follow Mohnke's order to break out. The survivors of the *Nordland* Division gathered up five tanks and tried to drive out of the city, only to be ambushed by Soviet tanks. Only a handful of men made it to safety. The Latvian SS men decided to make their escape in small groups and disappeared into the night in civilian clothes. The French SS contingent, however, agreed to surrender with Weilding. Some 1500 defenders of the Zitadelle sector, including hundreds of Waffen-SS men, surrendered around the Reichstag at 13:00 hours on 2 May.

Moscow radio claimed the Red Army captured 134,000 German soldiers in the ruins of the city. Some individual Waffen-SS men were pulled from the columns and shot, but most were marched away. Those who survived in Stalin's Gulag prison system did not return home for more than a decade.

Part IX

Consequences
of an Ideology

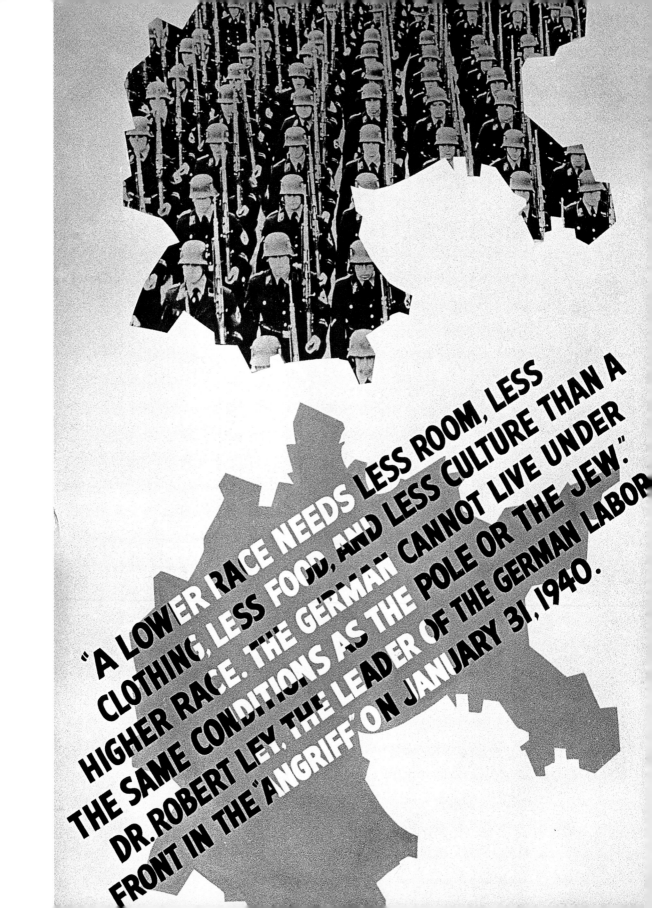

"A LOWER RACE NEEDS LESS ROOM, LESS CLOTHING, LESS FOOD, AND LESS CULTURE THAN A HIGHER RACE. THE GERMAN CANNOT LIVE UNDER THE SAME CONDITIONS AS THE POLE OR THE JEW."

DR. ROBERT LEY, THE LEADER OF THE GERMAN LABOR FRONT IN THE 'ANGRIFF' ON JANUARY 31, 1940.

Waffen-SS Atrocities

The soldiers of the Waffen-SS committed many atrocities during World War II, both on and off the battlefield. They were above all the racial warriors of the Third Reich, and they were contemptuous of all those that Nazi ideology classed as inferior races. As they held their own lives in low esteem, it was unlikely that they would accord the lives of their enemies greater value.

This was a poster printed by an anti-Nazi Jewish group during the war, but it sums up Nazi racial ideology. It was but a short step from feeding Jews and Poles less to shooting them outright.

The military prowess of the élite panzer divisions of the Waffen-SS is rarely called into question. They were undoubtedly formidable fighting forces that acquitted themselves with great distinction on the battlefields of World War II. However, the participation of Waffen-SS men in massacres across Europe during the war has cast a shadow over their military victories. Apologists for the Waffen-SS have tried to portray it as a separate and distinct military branch of the large SS organization, which had no role in the genocidal campaigns of murder against Jews and other racial groups considered subhumans by Hitler and his Nazi race-based ideology.

To try to draw a distinction between the "ordinary" soldiers of the Waffen-SS and SS "war criminals" is a mere semantic exercise. The Waffen-SS was an integral element of the SS, and even if its members were not specifically part of the Nazi murder machine that organized and conducted massacres and deportations, they certainly knew it was happening and helped ensure it did happen. A large number of Waffen-SS men and units, however, did undoubtedly participate in a series of massacres of civilians and prisoners of war across Europe between 1939 and 1945.

The collective guilt of the Waffen-SS stems first from the fact that the early leaders of the organization were the ringleaders and trigger-pullers during the infamous "Night of the Long Knives" in June 1934. "Old Guard" SS officers, such as "Sepp" Dietrich and Theodor Eicke, were the men who led the firing squads that killed off Hitler's enemies in the SA. Eicke even fired the first shots into the defenceless SA leader, Ernst Röhm. This was the first act of extra-judicial killing by Hitler, and effectively established his dictatorship.

It was the war in Russia that next showed up the Waffen-SS in its true light. It was the vanguard of Hitler's war of racial conquest. No mercy was shown to racial and political opponents of the Nazis by the Waffen-SS. According to Hitler and National Socialist ideology, the lives of Jews and Russians were totally worthless, except as forced labour to be exploited for the benefit of the German war effort. Russian civilians were treated with disdain, and their property, crops and houses were routinely looted or confiscated by Waffen-SS troops, even if this resulted in death or starvation in the country's harsh climate. Any Soviet commissar or political officer captured by the Waffen-SS was executed in accordance with Hitler's infamous "commissar order". The Geneva Convention was not applied to Soviet soldiers captured by the Waffen-SS, and they were routinely starved and denied medical treatment. Punishment killings of hundreds of Soviet prisoners were common occurrences in the Waffen-SS, with the *Leibstandarte* once killing 4000 prisoners in a four-day period. Revenge killings of thousands of civilians in response to partisan attacks were also a Waffen-SS speciality.

None of these actions in themselves were unique to the Waffen-SS. German police and army units, as well as locally recruited auxiliary forces, have also been implicated in atrocities on the Eastern Front. The SS, however, threw themselves into the war against the Soviet Union with a zeal that was unsurpassed in other branches of the German occupation forces. If there was a tough job that needed doing, the Waffen-SS would be there. The Waffen-SS clearly believed in its cause and did not flinch from carrying out its orders no matter how

murderous. The point was that the war in Russia was above all a racial struggle between the Aryan Germans and the "inferior" Slav races. The Waffen-SS was the racial vanguard of the National Socialist movement, staffed with pure Aryan recruits. Prior to Operation Barbarossa, Waffen-SS commanders went to great lengths to indoctrinate their men with Hitler's racial ideology to prepare them for the coming struggle. It was not surprising that when they were unleashed into battle, the Waffen-SS carried out its orders to kill and murder Hitler's "race enemies" with ruthless efficiency.

After the war, several former Waffen-SS officers tried to distance themselves from the SS mass-murder campaigns in occupied Russia, saying that they were only "simple soldiers who just fought at the front". This defence does not really hold water, given that few Wehrmacht or Waffen-SS units did not participate in some sort of rear-area security duty (which inevitably involved the routine mistreatment of civilians) at some time during their service in the East. Even if they did not participate in the murders of civilians themselves, cross-posting of Waffen-SS men between the various divisions and units of the SS organization meant its members were all aware of the true nature of German rule in occupied Russia.

Troops of the *Totenkopf* Division on the Eastern Front. Superb soldiers on the battlefield, the men of this formation were indoctrinated with a deep loathing of the "sub-human" Slavs.

A member of the Waffen-SS Feldgendarmerie, the military police, with a partisan suspect in Russia. The suspect is right to look worried – he is likely to be shot.

No Waffen-SS officer would ever contemplate refusing to serve in Russia out of moral scruples, and only one SS officer is documented as ever refusing to participate in a mass killing in the East. Several senior Waffen-SS officers and ordinary soldiers did suffer mental breakdowns as a result of their service in murder squads in the East, but that was after they had participated in the slaughter. It is hard to feel sorry for these butchers. Towards the end of the war, as defeat began to loom ominously over them, an increasing number of Waffen-SS officers and men tried to get out of serving in the East for fear of being captured by the Soviets. In the light of the brutal behaviour of the SS in Russia, captured Waffen-SS soldiers could expect little mercy. The attempts by senior Waffen-SS officers to escape Berlin in May 1945, after they had forced the city's citizens to endure its destruction at the barrel of the gun, were particularly distasteful.

Some Waffen-SS apologists try to lay the blame for the atrocities in the East at the door of rogue elements, such as locally recruited militia troops in the Baltic states and the Ukraine. Although it is true that these units at first were not part of the Waffen-SS, officers of the Waffen-SS did play a key role in recruiting these units because there were not enough SS men of German origin to man all the murder squads needed by the Einsatzgruppen. Then the Waffen-SS officially sanctioned many of these units by incorporating them into the organization from 1943 onwards. In any case, Waffen-SS units were committing atrocities almost from the start of Barbarossa, well before local units had been raised. For example, only two weeks after the start of the Russian campaign, the *Wiking* Division massacred 600 Galician Jews in "reprisal for Soviet cruelties".

It has also been claimed that the Waffen-SS played no part in the Holocaust and the industrialized killing of Jews. The concentration camp system was set up in the 1930s by Theodor Eicke of the SS-Totenkopfverbände that was incorporated into the Waffen-SS in 1940. Thousands of Waffen-SS men were also drafted to help the Einsatzgruppen's murderous campaign to exterminate the Jews of Eastern Europe, participating in mass killings or guarding ghetto districts where Jews from the west were concentrated before being sent to death camps. Waffen-SS units played a major role in the liquidation of the Warsaw Ghetto in 1943, which was little more than a exercise in mass murder.

Jewish women and their children about to be executed by an Einsatzgruppe murder squad in Russia. The Waffen-SS aided Einsatzgruppen atrocities in the East.

Even the supposed Waffen-SS combat units participated in the mass killing and deportation of Jews as part of the infamous "Final Solution". Jews were routinely executed or maltreated in areas controlled by Waffen-SS units. The *Totenkopf*, *Das Reich* and *Wiking* Divisions were all documented joining in the mass killings of Jews in Poland and Russia. Albanian Waffen-SS troops were also involved in loading Jews onto rail cars bound for the death camps.

The *Totenkopf* Division was particularly implicated in the concentration camp system. Even though it became part of the Waffen-SS in 1940, when its official administrative link to the camps was broken, the division continued to draw personnel from the camp system and wounded personnel from the front spent time recuperating on "light duties" in the camps. The 36th Waffen-SS Division also spent many months guarding ghettos in Poland and Russia. This was the infamous *Dirlewanger* Brigade, which became a volunteer unit of the Waffen-SS in January 1942. Recruited from convicted criminals, by the beginning of 1943 its 700 men comprised 50 percent non-Germans. As the war dragged on the unit pressed members of the SD, court-martialled Waffen-SS soldiers, army prisoners and even political prisoners from concentration camps into its ranks. The brigade's most notorious episode was during the 1944 Warsaw uprising, when Dirlewanger's men went on an orgy of killing and looting.

It has been estimated that at the height of the war, some 10,000 Waffen-SS men were serving away from their combat divisions on "special duties", supporting SS murder campaigns in the occupied East. The Waffen-SS also benefited from the huge SS slave labour empire, with weapons, uniforms, supplies and other equipment being provided direct from SS-controlled factories and warehouses in the main concentration camps.

Senior Waffen-SS officers had a hard time trying to deny they knew anything about the Final Solution. The ultimate Waffen-SS combat soldier, Joachim Peiper, served as Himmler's adjutant for a time, organizing meetings between the SS chief and heads of the concentration camp system. At least six Waffen-SS generals also at one time or another in the war held command appointments in the concentration camps, overseeing the mass murder of Jews and the use of millions of other prisoners for slave labour. One Waffen-SS general, Karl Wolff, boasted, "special joy now that 5000 members of the Chosen People [the Jews] are going to Treblinka [a death camp] every day". After the war Wolff was sentenced to four years in prison by a de-Nazification court in Germany. He served one week of his sentence before being released.

Waffen-SS crimes in the Balkans were of the same order as those in Russia, but had an added element because of the large number of local troops recruited into Waffen-SS ranks. Croat, Albanian and Bosnian Muslim units of the Waffen-SS treated the anti-partisan campaign in Yugoslavia as an extension of their age-old ethnic feuds, and were responsible for a series of horrendous massacres that the German High Command tried to pass off as battles. German Waffen-SS commanders

LAGER DACHAU

Originalphoto der SS von Dachau 1933

Above: Jews in the Warsaw ghetto are loaded into cattle wagons by SS guards for transport to Treblinka concentration camp and extermination. The ghetto was set up with the assistance of the Waffen-SS.

Left: A postcard "celebrating" the establishment of the first concentration camp in Germany, at Dachau. The camps were an integral part of the SS organization, not only for the incarceration of state enemies but as a vast manpower and revenue pool for Himmler's empire.

let their acolytes do their worst because it suited their purposes of keeping the ethnic communities in Yugoslavia fighting each other, and reducing the number of German troops required for occupation duties. In one incident in Greece, the Waffen-SS *Polizei* Division achieved the dubious distinction of being condemned by the Red Cross, a very rare occurrence. The condemnation followed an anti-partisan sweep and an ambush in which Waffen-SS troops were killed. The *Polizei* Division troops then staged a reprisal in the nearby village of Distrimo, which involved mass rape, looting and the summary execution of partisan suspects. Some 300 civilians were killed, and this outraged even the pro-German puppet government in Athens and the Wehrmacht. They invited the Red Cross to visit the village and several days after the event found corpses hanging from trees. The Waffen-SS tried to wash its hands of the incident by convicting an Watten-SS captain of falsifying a report, even though the reprisal was deemed "justified" for "military reasons".

In the West, the crimes of the Waffen-SS are generally better documented than in the East. The survivors were often able to make accounts of their experiences public, whereas in the East the Soviet Government and their satellite allies in the Warsaw Pact were less willing to allow independent scrutiny of wartime events, including Nazi war crimes. The Cold War stand-off that developed after 1945 also meant that some elements in Western governments did not want to give "visibility" to war

crimes conducted by people who were now key allies against the Soviets. This was particularly so in the case of refugees from the Baltic states and the Ukraine, who were leading lights in anti-communist movements. The fact that many of these people had been wartime collaborators with the Nazis and members of the SS was swept under the carpet. This policy came back to haunt the British and US governments in the 1990s, when evidence emerged after the collapse of the Iron Curtain that they had given refuge to former SS members who had participated in war crimes in Eastern Europe, even through their crimes were known to Western intelligence agencies.

Waffen-SS war crimes in the West fall into two distinct categories: the cold-blooded murder of prisoners of war and the massacre of civilians in anti-resistance reprisals. The massacre of US Army prisoners at Malmédy, Belgium, by the *Leibstandarte* Division in December 1944 is perhaps the most famous, but it is one of several. In 1940, *Leibstandarte* and *Totenkopf* troops participated in the murder of captured British soldiers in two incidents. The *Hitlerjugend* Division was also implicated in the killing of captured Canadian soldiers in Normandy in the summer of 1944.

These have been portrayed by Waffen-SS apologists as "heat of battle" crimes by tired and stressed soldiers, with the Normandy killings being excused because "both sides were doing it". Survivors of the massacres, however, have recounted how their Waffen-SS guards calmly gathered them up and machine-gunned them in cold blood after they had surrendered. In all these cases senior Waffen-SS officers were aware of what had happened and chose not to punish those involved. Most participants were promoted afterwards.

Piles of spectacles (left) and hair combs (right) taken from prisoners in concentration camps. Denials by Waffen-SS soldiers that they knew nothing of the camps are false.

Waffen-SS units rarely participated in anti-partisan operations in Western Europe, but when they did the results were very similar to those experienced in the East. In September 1943, after two *Leibstandarte* officers were captured by Italian partisans, Peiper ordered a town full of civilians to be shelled in reprisal, killing 34 people. The most famous Waffen-SS reprisal operation was in June 1944, when the *Das Reich* Division was attacked by French resistance fighters as it moved towards the Normandy battlefield. Some 99 French civilians were hung in reprisal in the town of Tulle; the following day, 642 civilians, including 207 children, were killed when the village of Oradour was razed to the ground in a further reprisal.

The *Reichsführer-SS* Waffen-SS division was involved in a series of three reprisal operations in northern Italy during August and September 1944, in which more than 1000 Italian civilians were killed. A Waffen-SS man from the division later commented, "personally I am of the opinion that the majority of partisans killed were women and children".

These reprisal operations cannot be whitewashed as battlefield incidents. They were all cold, calculated acts, carried out on the orders of senior Waffen-SS officers who knew what they were doing. Brutal reprisals for partisan attacks on German troops were the norm in the

Polizei Division troops on the Eastern Front. During its time in Italy the division committed many atrocities during anti-partisan sweeps. It was condemned by the Red Cross.

East, and the Waffen-SS was just bringing its tried and tested tactics to the West. The people of Western Europe must be thankful that Allied armies swept rapidly to the German border in the summer of 1944. The Waffen-SS divisions in France at this time were pre-occupied at the front, and had little time to turn their attention to dealing with the growing resistance problem behind their lines.

Ironically, when American, British and Soviet forces were inside Germany itself in early 1945, Waffen-SS soldiers turned on their own people. With his world crumbling around him, Hitler saw treachery and cowardice everywhere. He therefore ordered those still loyal to him to show no mercy to those who displayed "cowardice in the face of the enemy". Roving SS squads shot or hanged thousands of Germans for not fighting with fanatical determination. SS officers convened so-called emergency courts that dispensed instant justice to those brought before them, which usually meant death. Victims included an aged farmer who had disarmed a group of Hitler Youth who had planned to attack an American armoured column on bicycles. Even in Berlin during the last days of the war, fanatical Waffen-SS officers trawled the city searching for those guilty of cowardice, desertion or "resisting the war effort". German civilians suffered disproportionately as, when the Red Army approached, the citizens living in streets about to be attacked would hang white blankets from their windows as a sign of surrender (and in the hope that the Soviets would not blast their buildings with tank and artillery fire). However, German forces launched counterattacks and often recaptured said streets. The residents who had displayed the white blankets would then be hauled before the SS courts, to be either shot or hanged from lamp posts as a warning to others. Even after the fall of Berlin and the suicide of Hitler, SS officers still at large continued to shoot at Germans giving themselves up to the Red Army!

Despite the excuses of their apologists, the Waffen-SS was thoroughly tainted by its participation in Hitler's murderous policies of racial supremacy. Not only were Waffen-SS soldiers willing believers of this ideology, but they were also willing participants in the actual execution of Hitler's attempts to exterminate Jews and other people he considered *untermenschen*.

Individually, Waffen-SS officers and men were soon hardened to killing on behalf of their Führer and put a low value on human life, particularly on the lives of Germany's enemies. Civilians and enemy prisoners were regarded as a nuisance, and Waffen-SS officers had little compunction about ordering executions or reprisals. Although the Waffen-SS was embarrassed when some of its excesses were exposed during the war by the German Army High Command or the Red Cross, the perpetrators were invariably protected by Himmler. He had no time for such squeamishness.

The Malmédy massacre – the murder of US prisoners. If Waffen-SS soldiers considered their own lives cheap, what value could they place on the lives of their enemies?

Conclusion

The élite Waffen-SS divisions were resourceful battlefield opponents, who staved off total German defeat on a number of occasions. Their reputation was forged on the Eastern Front from early 1943, and in the West in 1944–45 the SS divisions performed similarly heroic feats. However, in the final analysis the Waffen-SS served one of the most infamous regimes in history.

The members of the élite Waffen-SS divisions were almost all volunteers and fanatical Nazis. They all believed in the justice of their cause and fought the war with a degree of zeal rarely found on the Allied side. This zeal was not confined to the élite SS divisions, however. Of the million or so men who served in the Waffen-SS, for example, over one-third died in battle. This was an unprecedented level of casualties that few other fighting formations, save the Imperial Japanese Army, could equal.

In the final analysis, the military professionalism, fighting spirit and élan of the Waffen-SS was not able to compensate for the overwhelming military supremacy of the Soviet Union, Britain and the United States. The war on the Eastern Front was the crucial battle for the Waffen-SS. It was in Russia that Nazi Germany's élite force fought its toughest and most important battles. It faced overwhelming odds and in the end was overrun by the Red Army. With Soviet tank production running at three times that of Germany, it was only a matter of time before the Eastern Front cracked. But it was not just a question of numbers (which has always been a convenient excuse for German failure). Stalin was also blessed with far more imaginative generals than Hitler. At several

key points, the Russians clearly out-commanded the Germans, allowing them, for example, to defeat Operation Citadel (the Battle of Kursk) and divert the Waffen-SS panzer divisions from the Kharkov front prior to the August 1943 Soviet offensive.

The war in the East moulded the Waffen-SS into the élite fighting force that caused the Western Allies so much trouble in Normandy in the summer of 1944, and later at Arnhem and in the Ardennes. The tactics and procedures pioneered on the Eastern Front by the Führer's "Fire Brigade" proved a major shock to the British and American armies when they landed on mainland Europe and faced the Waffen-SS panzers for the first time. The Western Allies were so impressed by these tactics that many were adopted after the war, and became the basis of NATO's battle plans to hold back any Soviet invasion of Western Europe.

Judged by the outcome of the war, the Waffen-SS failed in its mission. Its forays onto the battlefields of the Eastern Front, however, undoubtedly staved off a decisive defeat on more than one occasion. The intervention at Kharkov in February 1943 saved the Eastern Front, and probably extended the war by at least six months.

The further desperate battles around Kharkov in the autumn of 1943 also prevented a major Soviet breakthrough that would have shortened the war considerably. Similarly, the counterattack at Zhitomir cemented the German lines for another four months.

On the battlefields of Northwest Europe in the last year of the war, Hitler's Waffen-SS fought superbly. In Normandy it thwarted all of General Montgomery's attempts to break out of his bridgeheads and, after the American breakout, Waffen-SS generals took charge of the situation, leading trapped German Army units to safety out of the Falaise Pocket. At Arnhem, the lightning reaction of II SS Panzer Corps put paid to Montgomery's ambitious plan to end the war by Christmas 1944. Two months later the Waffen-SS was in the forefront of the Ardennes attack, making some of the deepest penetrations into American lines. The fact that SS troops advanced so far, given the terrible weather and road conditions, was a remarkable feat of arms. Even though Hitler's plan was fundamentally flawed and over-ambitious, Waffen-SS commanders gave it their best efforts. Five years into the war, despite their overriding losses, they still believed Germany could win.

In the end, the Waffen-SS troops were unable to turn back the Allied tide. Less than a year after D-Day, Hitler's Reich was in ruins. Their tactical prowess and fanatical fighting spirit could not compensate for Allied numerical and material superiority. For every Sherman tank the Waffen-SS knocked out in Normandy, there were 10 to take its place. At the same time, thousands of Allied fighter-bombers swarmed over the German Army in Normandy, denying it the freedom of manoeuvre.

On top of this must be added the effect of the Führer's ludicrous orders to hold to the last man in every situation. While the fanatical resistance of the Waffen-SS undoubtedly lengthened the war, in 1944 Hitler's insistence on holding Caen, his mad Mortain counterattack and his demands that the Ardennes offensive be continued into January 1945, all doomed the Waffen-SS to suffer horrendous and irreplaceable losses. Without the Führer's interference, the Waffen-SS panzers *might* have held out even longer.

For the opponents of the Waffen-SS panzer divisions, the experience was traumatic. For the British and Canadian armies in Normandy, fighting the Waffen-SS resulted in casualty levels on a par with those experienced in World War I. The British Army ended the war in total awe of its German opponents, and began to recast its armoured doctrine and tactics along the lines of those used by the Waffen-SS. The all-arms battlegroup became the normal tactical formation, and the mission command procedure was adopted instead of the rigid directed command method used in Normandy. The main post-war British tank, the Chieftain, was designed along the lines of the German Tiger. It was designed with armoured protection and firepower as the overriding priority, rather than the vehicle's mobility.

The Americans, who never had to face large numbers of Tigers in Normandy, stuck to their concept of having lightly armoured medium tanks along the lines of the Sherman. It was not until the 1970s that the Americans followed the lead of the British, and opted to field a heavily armoured tank, the M1 Abrams. This was part of a major effort by the US Army to recast its doctrine and equipment to counter the Soviets on NATO's central front. Suddenly, the Americans looked to the experiences of the Waffen-SS armoured units in their defensive battles and began to draw lessons from the tactics of their former enemies. Coming right up to date, the Americans used a version of the Panzerkeil, an armoured wedge, to batter through Iraqi defences during the 1991 Gulf War against Iraq. German Blitzkrieg strategy was also copied by American commanders during their drive on Baghdad during the Second Gulf War in 2003.

Fortunately for the peoples of occupied Europe, the attempt by Hitler's Waffen-SS divisions to hold back the Allies failed. In the autumn of 1944, France and Belgium were freed from Nazi tyranny and the final defeat of Germany in May 1945 completed the liberation of Europe.

Hitler's élite Waffen-SS force was designed and built to protect his murderous regime. Behind its black shield, millions of innocents were slaughtered and others oppressed. Evil certainly reigned in the shadow of the Waffen-SS.

Appendix 1: The SS and the army

The relationship between the SS and the German Army was complex and often antagonistic. As the war progressed and Germany was forced on to the defensive, a major split started to develop between the senior officers of the Waffen-SS and the higher echelons of Himmler's Allgemeine-SS (General SS), the main SS political and administrative branch.

By early 1944, veteran Waffen-SS combat generals, such as Paul Hausser, "Sepp" Dietrich, Willi Bittrich and Felix Steiner, were all disillusioned with Hitler's war strategy. They had lost thousands of men in brutal battles in Russia and all believed that Hitler's "no retreat – fight to the last man" strategy was bound to lead to Germany's early defeat. Hausser's retreat from Kharkov in early 1943 was the first symptom of this disillusionment, as the founder of the Waffen-SS was clearly not going to sacrifice the cream of the organization in a senseless battle to hold a strategically worthless city. The cauldron battles of the winter of 1943–44, when tens of thousands of German soldiers, including many Waffen-SS units, only escaped destruction from Soviet encirclement because Field Marshal Erich von Manstein organized breakouts against Hitler's expressed orders, further added to the alienation from the Führer.

Senior Waffen-SS commanders began to see that they had more in common with higher army commanders, such as Manstein, than with the fawning men who surrounded Hitler or the SS bureaucrats who worked for Himmler. The army and the Waffen-SS had been intense rivals in the 1930s, but by the middle of the war much of the tension had gone out of the relationship, particularly among field commanders of the élite Waffen-SS panzer units. The Waffen-SS and army panzer commanders fought side by side in some of the bloodiest battles on the Eastern Front, and soon a mutual respect developed. For a time Hitler would indulge the indiscretions of his favourite SS commanders, such as Dietrich, but by 1944 he was clearly also growing suspicious of them to a degree. Himmler also was not happy with the likes of Dietrich and Hausser openly siding with army commanders against him in policy arguments.

When most of the élite Waffen-SS panzer divisions were posted to France in the spring of 1944 as part of the build-up to counter the expected Allied invasion, their commanders came into contact with a very senior army officer who was involved in a new plot to kill Hitler – Field Marshal Erwin Rommel.

June 1944 was a black month for the Wehrmacht. US and British troops landed in strength in Normandy and Soviet troops smashed Army Group Centre. Around one million German soldiers were either killed or wounded in the space of a few weeks. Germany was now fighting a war on two fronts. In Normandy, the *Leibstandarte*, *Das Reich*, *Frundsberg* and *Hohenstaufen* Divisions were thrown into battle to try to stem the advance of the British and Americans. Their losses were horrendous and, although they at first checked the Allied advance, senior army and Waffen-SS commanders openly conceded that they could only delay, not defeat, the relentless drive of the Allies in Normandy.

Since he had been forced by Hitler to abandon his beloved Afrika Korps in Tunisia in the spring of 1943, Rommel had been transformed from a zealous pro-Nazi officer into a cynical and dispirited opponent of Hitler's regime. He opened secret contacts with anti-Hitler civilians and military officers, and also began sounding out senior officers in France about the possibility of launching a coup d'etat to depose Hitler and seek a negotiated peace with the Allies.

Rommel's loyal chief of staff, Lieutenant-General Hans Speidel, was at the centre of the field marshal's efforts to form a solid group of anti-Hitler officers in France. Although the details are confusing, it seems that Rommel approached several senior Waffen-SS officers in France who reacted favourably to his overtures. These included Dietrich and several senior *Leibstandarte* commanders. Rommel convinced them that Hitler had to be removed to allow a more rational leader to take over Germany. From the frontline in Normandy, Waffen-SS commanders immediately agreed that the orders arriving from the Führer's headquarters telling them not to retreat an inch were far from "rational".

Rommel's plan called for units of the army and Waffen-SS to occupy Paris and other cities to prevent ultra-loyal SS, SD or Gestapo men trying to rally support for Hitler. He and Speidel devised a system of coded messages to allow their allies to be alerted to developments, while keeping Hitler's faithful entourage guessing about what was going on.

When Colonel Count Claus von Stauffenberg planted a bomb in Hitler's Wolf's Lair headquarters in East Prussia on 20 July 1944, the whole plot unravelled. Hitler survived, and in Berlin the plotters were quickly rounded up by pro-Hitler army units. Rommel had also been badly injured in a British air strike a few days earlier, and was not able to coordinate the response of the senior army and Waffen-SS commanders in France. The July Bomb Plot turned into bloody farce, as Gestapo and SS squads hunted down anyone remotely connected with the plot and delivered them to torture chambers for interrogation.

Several thousand civilians and army officers were arrested and hundreds executed after show trials. The senior Waffen-SS officers escaped being tainted by involvement in the plot thanks to quick thinking by Dietrich, who pulled in some old favours and ensured that Speidel was released before he could be interrogated by the Gestapo squads.

The post-plot bloodletting did little to reassure veteran Waffen-SS field commanders of Hitler's rationality. The rank and file SS men were still fanatically loyal to their Führer, and several SS organizations participated in the purge with great zeal. This drove a further wedge between the Waffen-SS commanders and the rear-echelon SS men who were still parroting Hitler's claims that ultimate victory was only just around the corner.

After the 1944 July Bomb Plot, the power of the SS organization grew dramatically as Himmler took his revenge on the army High Command for its previous resistance to his schemes. Admiral Wilhelm Canaris' military intelligence organization, the Abwehr, was placed under the control of Himmler's RSHA security apparatus. The Abwehr's special operations unit, the Brandenburg Division, was also disbanded and replaced by Waffen-SS units.

The SS already had strong influence over the German war effort because it controlled the supply of forced labour to German industry, giving it huge financial resources and control over the country's economy. After the Bomb Plot this influence grew and Himmler ordered that the Waffen-SS be accorded a higher priority for receiving weapons and equipment.

The army and the Luftwaffe were also stripped of responsibility for the V-rocket programmes. Even before the first V-1s and V-2s were fired in anger, their potential as possible war-winning weapons was recognized by Himmler. He was determined that the SS would control and take the glory for these weapons. In February 1944, Himmler began to pressure the army's top missile scientist, Werner von Braun, to transfer from the army to the SS. When this failed, he had Braun and several other key scientists working at the Peenemünde missile research centre arrested on the charge that they were wasting valuable resources. General Walter Dornberger, who was the army's commissioner for special duties in charge of the development, training and operation of V-2 units, was able to secure the scientists' release after claiming the rocket programme was falling behind without their irreplaceable expertise.

The SS, however, moved fast to secure control of the V-weapons. Himmler appointed Hans Kammler, head of the SS construction office, to lead the SS V-weapon division, with Dornberger reduced to the status of his deputy. In January 1945, Kammler had managed to expand his empire to include full control of the Luftwaffe's V-1 programme. Kammler played a key role in controlling the V-2 operations in Holland, with a special SS unit operating missile-launch sites around The Hague. The strength of SS-Werfer Abteilung 500 was eight officers and about four hundred men, with about one hundred vehicles and missile launchers. When the rocket units were forced out of Holland in April 1945, Kammler regrouped them around the Nordhausen factory to stage a last stand as infantry.

Meanwhile, in the summer of 1944 Himmler was able to get himself appointed as commander of the Replacement Army, which was responsible for the recruitment, training and allocation to units of all German conscripts. The SS now had total control of the stream of manpower into its ranks. More than half of the Waffen-SS divisions were formed during this period,. The last nine months of the war, however, were characterized by a virtual collapse of the army and Waffen-SS training units as they were plundered ruthlessly by Himmler to form new Waffen-SS and army units with grand titles. Himmler put a premium on forming new units rather than rebuilding old ones. This meant he was eventually forced to draft in the instructors and other key staff from training schools and depots to form the command staff of the new units. Not only did this starve existing units of new recruits, but it meant there was no training infrastructure left to generate new replacements. Himmler did not allow the new units time to train properly before sending them to the front. When they were committed to battle they were quickly decimated. This was a double disaster, because there was no one left to train the next generation of Waffen-SS men.

As commander of the Replacement Army, Himmler was in charge of preparing for the defence of German territory. He placed local district Nazi chiefs, or Gauleiters, in charge of the defence of their regions rather than the army. So incompetent political hacks were given the job of organizing Germany's defences. Few supplies and little equipment were available for the hundreds of thousands of Volkssturm local militia forces that were mobilized to bolster the regular Wehrmacht and Waffen-SS. The only thing that Himmler seemed to organize properly were the execution squads from the SS, SD and Gestapo that were set up to roam behind the front and prevent desertions. They left a terrible legacy of butchery in the final days of Hitler's Reich.

Appendix 2: Waffen-SS Divisions

	Final Title	Formed as Division	Recruitment Zone	Main Combat Zones
1.	SS Panzer Division *Leibstandarte Adolf Hitler*	1942	Germany	Poland, Belgium, Balkans, Russia, France, Hungary
2.	SS Panzer Division *Das Reich*	1939	Germany	Poland, France, Balkans, Russia, France, Hungary
3.	SS Panzer Division *Totenkopf*	1939	Germany	Poland, France, Russia, Hungary
4.	SS Panzergrenadier Division *Polizei*	1939	Germany	France, Russia
5.	SS Panzer Division *Wiking*	1940	Western Europe, Scandinavia	Russia, Hungary
6.	SS Gebirgs Division *Nord*	1940	Germany	Norway
7.	SS Freiwilligen Gebirgs Division *Prinz Eugen*	1942	Southeastern Europe	Yugoslavia, Hungary
8.	SS Cavalry Division *Florian Geyer*	1942	Germany	Yugoslavia, Hungary
9.	SS Panzer Division *Hohenstaufen*	1943	Germany	Russia, Western Europe, Hungary
10.	SS Panzer Division *Frundsberg*	1943	Germany	Russia, Western Europe, Hungary
11.	SS Freiwilligen Panzergrenadier Division *Nordland*	1943	Western Europe, Scandinavia	Russia, Poland
12.	SS Panzer Division *Hitlerjugend*	1943	Germany	France, Hungary
13.	Waffen Gebirgs Division der SS *Handschar* (kroatische Nr 1)	1943	Yugoslavia (Muslims)	Yugoslavia
14.	Waffen Grenadier Division der SS *Galicia* (ukrainische Nr 1)	1943	Ukraine	Ukraine
15.	Waffen Grenadier Division der SS (lettische Nr 1)	1943	Latvia	Russia, Poland, Germany
16.	SS Panzergrenadier Division *Reichsführer-SS*	1943	Germany	Italy, Yugoslavia
17.	SS Panzergrenadier Division *Götz von Berlichingen*	1943	Germany	France
18.	SS Freiwilligen Panzergrenadier Division *Horst Wessel*	1944	Hungary	Poland, Czechoslovakia
19.	Waffen Grenadier Division der SS (lettische Nr 2)	1944	Latvia	Russia
20.	Waffen Grenadier Division der SS (estnische Nr 1)	1944	Estonia	Russia, Germany, Czechoslovakia
21.	Waffen Gebirgs Division der SS *Skanderberg* (albanische Nr 1)	1944	Albania	Albania
22.	SS Freiwilligen Cavalry Division *Maria Theresia*	1944	Hungary	Hungary
23.	SS-Freiwilligen Panzergrenadier Division *Nederland* (niederlandische Nr 1)	1944	Netherlands	Hungary
23.	Waffen-Gebirgs-Division der SS *Kama* (kroatische Nr 2)	1944	Croatia	Yugoslavia
24.	Waffen Gebirgs Division der SS *Karstjäger*	1944	Italy	Italy
25.	Waffen Grenadier Divison der SS *Hunyadi* (ungarnische Nr 1)	1944	Hungary	Hungary
26.	Waffen Grenadier Division der SS *Gombos* (ungarnische Nr 2)	1945	Hungary	Hungary
27.	SS Freiwilligen Grenadier Division *Langemarck*	1945	Flemish regions of Belgium	Russia, Poland, Germany
28.	SS Freiwilligen Panzergrenadier Division *Wallonien*	1945	French regions of Belgium	Russia, Poland, Germany
29.	Waffen Grenadier Division der SS RONA (russische Nr. 1)	1945	Russia	Czechoslovakia
29.	Waffen Grenadier Division der SS (italienische Nr 1)	1945	Italy	Italy
30.	Waffen Grenadier Division der SS (russische Nr 2)	1945	Russia	France, Czechoslovakia
31.	SS Freiwilligen Grenadier Division *Bohmen-Mahren*	1945	Czechoslovakia	Czechoslovakia
32.	SS Freiwilligen Grenadier Division *30 Januar*	1945	Germany	Germany
33.	Waffen Grenadier Division der SS (ungarnische Nr 4)	1945	Hungary	Hungary
33.	Waffen Grenadier Division der SS *Charlemagne* (französische Nr 1)	1945	France	Russia, Germany
34.	SS Freiwilligen Grenadier Division *Landstorm Nederland*	1945	Netherlands	Russia
35.	SS und Polizei Grenadier Division	1945	Germany	Czechoslovakia
36.	Waffen Grenadier Division der SS	1945	Germany/Eastern Europe	Russia, Poland, Germany
37.	SS Freiwilligen Cavalry Division *Lutzow*	1945	Hungary	Hungary
38.	SS Grenadier Division *Nibelungen*	1945	Germany	Germany

Appendix 3: Waffen-SS Officer Ranks

Waffen-SS/German Army	British Army	US Army
SS-Oberstgruppenführer/Generaloberst	General	General (5 stars)
SS-Obergruppenführer	General	General (4 stars)
SS-Gruppenführer/Generalleutnant	Lieutenant-General	Lieutenant-General (3 stars)
SS-Brigadeführer/Generalmajor	Major-General	Major-General (2 stars)
SS-Oberführer	Brigadier	Brigadier-General (1 star)
SS-Standartenführer/Oberst	Colonel	Colonel
SS-Obersturmbannführer/Oberstleutnant	Lieutenant-Colonel	Lieutenant-Colonel
SS-Sturmbannführer/Major	Major	Major
SS-Hauptsturmführer/Hauptmann	Captain	Captain
SS-Obersturmführer/Oberleutnant	Lieutenant	First Lieutenant
SS-Untersturmführer/Leutnant	2nd Lieutenant	Second Lieutenant

Appendix 4: Kharkov, February 1943

Waffen-SS order of battle

I SS Panzer Corps Headquarters (later II SS Panzer Corps)

SS-Panzer Abteilung 102/schw. (SS Tank Battalion 102/heavy)

SS-Panzer Abteilung 502

    (Tiger tanks from 1944)

Arko II. SS Panzer Corps/SS-Arko 102

    (artillery command)

SS-Artillerie-Abteilung 102

1. u. 2. SS-Gr. Werfer. Kompanie 102 (rocket)

SS-Flak Kompanie 102

SS-Werfer Abteilung. Generalkommando II (II Corps HQ)

SS-Panzer Corps/SS-Werfer Abteilung 102 (rockets)

Corps-Nachr. Abteilung 400 (mot.) (signals)

Leibstandarte Division Order of Battle (37 tanks, including 3 Tiger Is)

SS-Musik Corps

SS-Panzergrenadier Regiment 1

SS-Panzergrenadier Regiment 2

SS-Panzer Regiment 1

SS-Panzerjäger Abteilung (anti-tank)

SS-Sturmgeschütz Abteilung 1 (assault gun)

SS-Panzer Artillerie Regiment 1

SS-Flak Abteilung 1 (anti-aircraft)

SS-Werfer Abteilung 1 (rocket)

SS-Panzer Nachrichten Abteilung 1 (radio)

SS-Panzer Aufklärungs Abteilung 1 (reconnaissance)

SS-Panzer Pioneer Battalion 1 (combat engineer)

SS-Wachbattalion (mot.) (often detached in Berlin for security work)

Das Reich Division Order of Battle (66 tanks, including 7 Tigers Is)

SS-Panzergrenadier Regiment 3 *Deutschland*

SS-Panzergrenadier Regiment *Der Führer*

SS-Infantry Regiment *Langemarck*

SS-Panzer Regiment 2

SS-Panzerjäger Abteilung 2 (anti-tank)

SS-Sturmgeschütz Abteilung 2 (assault gun)

SS-Panzer Artillerie Regiment 2

SS-Flak Abteilung 2 (anti-aircraft)

SS-Werfer Abteilung 2 (rocket)

SS-Panzer Nachrichten Abteilung 2 (radio)

SS-Panzer Aufklärungs Abteilung 2 (reconnaissance)

SS-Panzer Pioneer Battalion 2 (combat engineer)

Totenkopf Division Order of Battle (95 tanks, including 9 Tiger Is)

SS-Panzergrenadier Regiment 5 *Thule* (later titled *Totenkopf*)

SS-Panzergrenadier Regiment 6 *Theodor Eicke*

SS-Panzer Regiment 3

SS-Panzerjäger Abteilung 3 (anti-tank)

SS-Sturmgeschütz Abteilung 3 (assault gun)

SS-Panzer Artillerie Regiment 3

SS-Flak Abteilung 3

SS-Werfer Abteilung 3 (rocket)

SS-Panzer Nachrichten Abteilung 3 (radio)

SS-Panzer Aufklärungs Abteilung 3 (reconnaissance)

SS-Panzer Pioneer Abteilung 3 (combat engineer)

Wiking Division Order of Battle (10 tanks)

SS-Panzergrenadier Regiment 9 *Germania*

SS-Panzergrenadier Regiment 10 *Westland*

SS-Panzergrenadier Regiment *Nordland* (left the division on 22 March 1943)

Estnisches SS-Freiwilligen Panzergrenadier Battalion *Narwa*

SS-Sturmbrigade *Wallonien* (temporarily attached in 1943–44)

SS-Panzer Regiment 5

SS-Panzerjäger Abteilung 5 (anti-tank)

SS-Sturmgeschütz Abteilung 5 (assault gun)

SS-Panzer Artillerie Regiment 5

SS-Flak Abteilung 5 (anti-aircraft)

SS-Werfer Abteilung 5 (rocket)

SS-Panzer Nachrichten Abteilung 5 (radio)

SS-Panzer Aufklärungs Abteilung 5 (reconnaissance)

SS-Panzer Pioneer Battalion 5 (combat engineer)

SS-Panzer Abteilung *Wiking* (1942–43)

Appendix 5: The Ukraine, 1943–44

German Sixth Army Order of Battle, July 1943

IV CORPS

    335th Infantry Division

    3rd Mountain Division

    304th Infantry Division

    209th Assault Gun Brigade

XXIV PANZER CORPS

    23rd Panzer Division

    3rd Panzer Division

    16th Panzergrenadier Division

    236th Assault Gun Brigade

II SS PANZER CORPS

    SS *Das Reich* Division

    SS *Totenkopf* Division

    1st Demonstration Rocket Regiment

    52nd Rocket Regiment

    6 x army artillery battalions

XVII CORPS

    302nd Infantry Division

    306th Infantry Division

    177th Infantry Division

    294th Infantry Division

XXIX CORPS

    336th Infantry Division

    17th Infantry Division

    25th Luftwaffe Division

    111th Infantry Division

    243 Assault Gun Brigade

German IX Corps Order of Battle, Defence of Kharkov, August 1943

    3rd Panzer Division

    168th Infantry Division

    SS *Das Reich* Division

    198th Infantry Division

    106th Infantry Division

    320th Infantry Division

    248th Infantry Division

    6th Panzer Division

German XXXXVIII Panzer Corps Order of Battle, November 1943

    SS *Leibstandarte* Division

    1st Panzer Division

    7th Panzer Division

    19th Panzer Division

    25th Panzer Division

    68th Infantry Division

    SS *Das Reich* Division kampfgruppe

Appendix 6: The Cherkassy Pocket

German order of battle, February 1944

The Rescue Force

III Panzer Corps

- SS *Leibstandarte* Division
- 1st Panzer Division
- 6th Panzer Division
- 16th Panzer Division
- 17th Panzer Division
- Heavy Panzer Regiment "Bake"
- 249th Assault Gun Brigade
- 54th Rocket Regiment

Operating in support of Rescue Force

XLVII Panzer Corps

- 3rd Panzer Division
- 11th Panzer Division
- 13th Panzer Division
- 14th Panzer Division
- 106th Infantry Division
- 282nd Infantry Division
- 320th Infantry Division
- 911st Assault Gun Brigade

In the Cherkassy Pocket

XLII Corps

- 88th Infantry Division
- 417th Infantry Regiment
- Kampfgruppe B (elements of the 112th 332nd and 255th Infantry Divisions)
- 805 Assault Gun Brigade

XI Corps

- SS *Wiking* Division
- SS Walloon Assault Brigade
- 57th Infantry Division
- 72nd Infantry Division
- 389th Infantry Division
- 202 Assault Gun Brigade
- GHQ Light Artillery Battalion

Hohenstaufen **Division Order of Battle**

- SS-Panzergrenadier Regiment 19
- SS-Panzergrenadier Regiment 20
- SS-Panzer Regiment 9
- SS-Panzerjäger Abteilung 9 (anti-tank)
- SS-Sturmgeschütz Abteilung 9 (assault gun)
- SS-Panzer Artillerie Regiment 9
- SS-Flak Abteilung 9 (anti-aircraft)
- SS-Flak Kompanie (anti-aircraft)
- SS-Panzer Nachrichten Abteilung 9 (radio)
- SS-Panzer Aufklärungs Abteilung 9 (reconnaissance)
- SS-Panzer Pioneer Abteilung 9 (combat engineer)

Frundsberg **Division Order of Battle**

- SS-Panzergrenadier Regiment 21
- SS-Panzergrenadier Regiment 22
- SS-Panzer Regiment 10
- SS-Panzerjäger Abteilung 10 (anti-tank)
- SS-Sturmgeschütz Abteilung 10 (assault gun)
- SS-Panzer Artillerie Regiment 10
- SS-Flak Abteilung 10 (anti-aircraft)
- SS-Panzer Nachrichten Abteilung 10 (radio)
- SS-Panzer Aufklärungs Abteilung 10 (reconnaissance)
- SS-Panzer Pionier Abteilung 10 (combat engineer)

Appendix 7: Waffen-SS Panzer Strengths

Normandy, 1 June to 13 August 1944

	1 June	1 July	18 July	25 July	5 August	13 August
Panther tanks						
Leibstandarte Division	38	25	46	34	46	7
Das Reich Division	25	26	?	41	1	3
Hohenstaufen Division	30	19	25	23	11	15
Hitlerjugend Division	48	24	21	37	9	7
Panzer IV tanks						
Leibstandarte Division	42	30	61	45	57	14
Das Reich Division	44	50	?	37	4	5
Hohenstaufen Division	41	10	20	21	8	11
Frundsberg Division	34	20	12	14	10	11
Hitlerjugend Division	91	32	16	21	37	17
StuG III assault guns						
Leibstandarte Division	44	31	35	32	27	8
Das Reich Division	33	36	?	25	6	8
Hohenstaufen Division	38	22	15	14	8	14
Frundsberg Division	32	25	6	11	7	5
17th SS Division	42	18	unknown	10	unknown	unknown
Tiger I tanks						
101st SS Battalion	37	11	6	13	20	8
102ns SS Battalion	28	14	19	30	20	7
Panzerjäger IV						
Hitlerjugend Division					10	5
17th SS Division					31	unknown

Appendix 8: The Normandy Campaign

Note: dates indicate when the division reached the frontline in June 1944.

I SS Panzer Corps *Leibstandarte Adolf Hitler* (7 June)

(Obergruppenführer Josef "Sepp" Dietrich)

    schw. SS-Panzer Abteilung 101 – 37 x Tiger I

    SS-Arko I (artillery command)

    SS-Artillerie Abteilung 101 – 4 x 21mm,
      6 x 170mm

    SS-Corps Nachrichten Abteilung 101/501

1 SS Panzer Division *Leibstandarte Adolf Hitler* (25 June to 6 July)

(SS-Brigadeführer Teddy Wisch)

19,618 men

SS-Panzergrenadier Regiment 1 – I & II Battalions only, 36 x SPW

SS-Panzergrenadier Regiment 2

SS-Panzer Regiment – 103 x Panzer IV, 72 x Panther

SS-Sturmgeschütz Abteilung 1 – 45 x StuG III

SS-Panzer Artillerie Regiment 1 – I & II Battalions, 8 x 105mm, 6 x 150mm, 4 x 100mm, 8 x Wespe, 5 x Hummel

SS-Flak Abteilung 1– 12 x 88mm, 9 x 37mm

SS-Werfer Abteilung 1 (rocket) – one battery, 5 x Nebelwerfer

SS-Panzer Nachrichten Abteilung 1 (radio)

SS-Panzer Aufklärungs Abteilung 1 (reconnaissance) – less one company

SS-Panzer Pioneer Battalion 1

12 SS Panzer Division *Hitlerjugend* (7 June)

(SS-Oberführer Fritz Witt until 14 June 44, then SS-Standartenführer Kurt Meyer)

17,000 men, 306 x SPW

SS-Panzergrenadier Regiment 25 – III Battalion with SPW, 12 x Pak 40, 12 x 75mm IG, 6 x 150mm IG, 2 x 20mm flak

SS-Panzergrenadier Regiment 26 – 12 x Pak 40, 22 x 75mm IG, 6 x 150mm IG, 2 x 20mm flak

SS-Panzer Regiment 12 – 66 x Panther, 98 x Panzer IV

SS-Panzerjäger Abteilung 12 – one company with 10 x PzJgr IV

SS-Panzer-Artillerie-Regiment 12 – 12 x Wespe, 6 x Hummel, 18 x 105mm, 4 x 150mm, 4 x 100mm

SS-Flak Abteilung 12 – 12 x 88mm, 9 x 37mm

SS-Werfer Abteilung 12 – one battery arrived

12 June, balance in July

SS-Panzer Nachrichten Abteilung 12

SS-Panzer Aufklärungs Abteilung 12

SS-Pioneer Battalion 12/SS-Panzer Pioneer Battalion 12

SS Ersatz Battalion 12 (in Arnhem with 2000 men)

II SS Panzer Corps Headquarters (28 June)

(SS-Obergruppenführer Paul Hausser, then Willi Bittrich from 28 June 44)

schw. SS-Panzer Abteilung 102 – 28 x Tiger I

Arko II SS-Panzer Corps/SS Arko 102 (artillery command)

Corps Nachr. Abteilung 400 (mot.)

9 SS Panzer Division *Hohenstaufen* (28 June)

(SS-Gruppenführer Willi Bittrich until 28 June 1944, SS-Standartenführer Thomas Müller until 14 July 1944, then SS-Standartenführer Sylvester Stadler)

15,898 men, 345 trucks

SS-Panzergrenadier Regiment 19 – 9 x Pak 40, 12 x 75mm IG, 6 x 150mm IG, 11 x 20mm flak

SS-Panzergrenadier Regiment 20 – 9 x Pak 40, 14 x 75mm IG, 6 x 150mm IG, 12 x 20mm flak

SS-Panzer Regiment 9 – I Battalion 79 x Panther, II Battalion – 48 x Panzer IV and 40 x StuG III

SS-Panzerjäger Abteilung 9 – one company with 12 x Pak 40

SS-Panzer Artillerie Regiment 9 – 12 x Wespe, 2 x Hummel, 12 x 105m, 12 x 150mm, 4 x 100mm

SS-Flak Abteilung 9 – 12 x 88mm, 9 x 37mm

SS-Panzer Nachrichten Abteilung 9 (radio)

SS-Panzer Aufklärungs Abteilung 9 (reconnaissance)

SS-Panzer Pioneer Battalion 9 (combat engineer)

10 SS Panzer Division *Frundsberg* (28 June)

(SS-Oberführer Heinz Harmel)

15,800 men

SS-Panzergrenadier Regiment 21

SS-Panzergrenadier Regiment 22

SS-Panzer Regiment 10 – II Battalion only with 39 x Panzer IV, 38 x StuG III

SS-Panzer Artillerie Regiment 10 – 11 x Wespe, 6 x Hummel, 12 x 105mm, 12 x 150mm, 4 x 100mm

SS-Flak Abteilung 10 – 12 x 88mm, 9 x 37mm

SS-Panzer Nachrichten Abteilung 10

SS-Panzer Aufklärungs Abteilung 10

SS-Panzer Pionier Abteilung 10

SS Ersatz Battalion 9 – 1000 men

2 SS Panzer Division *Das Reich* (1 July)

(SS-Brigadeführer Heinz Lammerding)

11,175 men, 227x SPW, 768 trucks

SS-Panzergrenadier Regiment 3 *Deutschland* – I & III Battalions only

SS-Panzergrenadier Regiment *Der Führer* – I & III Battalions only

SS-Panzer Regiment 2 – 50 x Panzer IV, 26 x Panther

SS-Sturmgeschütz Abteilung 2 – 41 x StuG III

SS-Panzer Artillerie Regiment 2 – 12 x 105mm, 4 x 100mm, 4 x 15mm, 6 x Wespe, 5 x Hummel

SS-Flak Abteilung 2 – 12 x 88mm, 9 x 37mm

SS-Panzer Nachrichten Abteilung 2

SS-Panzer Aufklärungs Abteilung 2 – four companies

SS-Panzer Pioneer Battalion 2 – three companies only attached

SS-Werfer Abteilung 102 – 18 x Nebelwerfer

II/Artillery Regiment 275 – 4 x 105mm, 4 x 100mm

II/Artillery Regiment 191 – 9 x 75mm, 2 x 150mm

Panzerjäger Abteilung 1041 – 15 x 88mm

17 SS Panzergrenadier-Division *Götz von Berlichingen* (10th June)

(SS-Standartenführer Otto Baum)

17,321 men

SS-Panzergrenadier Regiment 37

SS-Panzergrenadier Regiment 38

SS-Panzerjäger Abteilung 1 – 12 x Marder, 22 x Pak 40 (arrived later in month)

SS-Panzer Abteilung 17 – 42 x StuG III

SS-Panzer Artillerie Regiment 17 – 25 x 105mm, 12 x 150mm, 4 x 100mm

SS-Flak Abteilung 17 – 8 x 88mm, 9 x 37mm (arrived later in month)

SS-Panzer Nachrichten Abteilung 17

SS-Panzer Aufklärungs Abteilung 17

SS-Panzer Pioneer Battalion 17 (arrived later in the month)

Appendix 9: The Ardennes Campaign

SIXTH PANZER ARMY

(SS-Oberstgruppenführer Josef "Sepp" Dietrich)

I SS PANZER CORPS LEIBSTANDARTE ADOLF HITLER

(SS-Gruppenführer Hermann Priess)

    SS-Arko I (artillery command)

    SS-Corps Nachrichten Abteilung 101/501

1 SS Panzer Division *Leibstandarte Adolf Hitler*

(SS-Oberführer Wilhelm Mohnke)

22,000 men

SS-Panzer Nachrichten Abteilung LSSAH 1

Kampfgruppe *Peiper*

(SS-Obersturmbannführer Joachim Peiper)

SS-Panzer-Regiment LSSAH 1 – 38 x Panther,
    34 x Panzer IV

SS Panzer Abteilung 501 – 30 x Tiger II

SS-Panzer Artillerie Regiment LSSAH 1/II Battalion

SS-Panzergrenadier Regiment 2 LSSAH/III Battalion
    (SPW)

Kampfgruppe *Hansen*

(SS-Standartenführer Max Hansen)

SS-Panzergrenadier Regiment 1 LSSAH –
    6 x 150mm IG, 12 x 20mm

SS-Panzerjäger Abteilung LSSAH 1 – 21 x PzJgr IV,
    11 x Pak 40

SS-Panzer Artillerie Regiment LSSAH 1/I Battalion

Kampfgruppe *Sandig*

(SS-Standartenführer Rudolf Sandig)

SS-Panzergrenadier Regiment 2 LSSAH –
    6 x150mm IG, 12 x 20mm

SS-Flak Abteilung LSSAH 1 – 18 x 88mm,
    18 x 37mm

SS-Werfer Abteilung LSSAH 1 – 18 x 150mm,
    6 x 210mm

SS-Panzer Pioneer Battalion LSSAH 1

SS-Panzer Artillerie Regiment LSSAH 1/III Battalion

Kampfgruppe *Knittel*

(SS-Sturmbannführer Gustav Knittel)

SS-Panzer Aufklärungs Abteilung LSSAH 1

12 SS Panzer Division *Hitlerjugend*

(SS-Standartenführer Hugo Kraas)

22,000 men

SS-Panzer Nachrichten Abteilung 12

Kampfgruppe *Kuhlmann*

(SS-Obersturmbannführer Herbert Kuhlmann)

SS-Panzer Regiment 12 – 14 x Panther,
    37 x Panzer IV

506 Panzerjäger Abteilung (Army) – 28 x JgPz IV,
    14 x Jagdpanther

SS-Panzer Artillerie Regiment 12/I Battalion

SS-Panzergrenadier Regiment 26/III Battalion

Kampfgruppe *Muller*

(SS-Sturmbannführer Siegfried Muller)

SS-Panzergrenadier Regiment 25

SS-Panzerjäger Abteilung 12 – 22 x Jagdpanzer IV

SS-Panzer Artillerie Regiment 12/II Battalion

Kampfgruppe *Krause*

(SS-Obersturmbannführer Bernaard Krause)

SS-Panzergrenadier Regiment 26

SS-Flak Abteilung 12

SS-Werfer Abteilung 12

SS-Panzer Pioneer Battalion 12

SS-Panzer Artillerie Regiment 12/III Battalion

Kampfgruppe *Bremer*

(SS-Sturmbannführer Gerhardt Bremer)

SS-Panzer Aufklärungs Abteilung 12

II SS PANZER CORPS HEADQUARTERS

(SS-Obergruppenführer Willi Bittrich)

    Arko II SS Panzer Corps/SS-Arko 102
    (artillery command)

    Corps Nachr. Abteilung 400 (mot.)

2 SS Panzer Division *Das Reich*

18,000 men

(SS-Brigadeführer Heinz Lammerding)

SS-Panzergrenadier Regiment 3 *Deutschland*

SS-Panzergrenadier Regiment *Der Führer*

SS-Infantry Regiment *Langemarck*

SS-Panzer Regiment 2 – 58 x Panther,
    28 x Panzer IV, 28 x StuG III

SS-Panzerjäger Abteilung 2 – 20 x Jagdpanzer IV

SS-Panzer Artillerie Regiment 2

SS-Flak Abteilung 2

SS-Panzer Nachrichten Abteilung 2

S-Panzer Aufklärungs Abteilung 2

SS-Panzer Pioneer Battalion 2

Kampfgruppe *Krag*

(SS-Sturmbannführer Ernst-August Krag)

SS-Panzer Aufklärungs Abteilung 2

9 SS-Panzer Division *Hohenstaufen*

16,000 men

(SS-Oberführer Sylvester Stadler)

SS-Panzergrenadier Regiment 19

SS-Panzergrenadier Regiment 20

SS-Panzer Regiment 9

    I Battalion – 35 x Panther,
    II Battalion – 28 x StuG III, 39 x Panzer IV

SS-Panzerjäger Abteilung 9 – 21 x Jagdpanzer IV

SS-Panzer Artillerie Regiment 9

SS-Flak Abteilung 9

Bibliography

Addington, Larry. *The Blitzkrieg Era and the German General Staff, 1865–1941*. New Brunswick, NJ: Rutgers University Press, 1971.

Barker, A.J. *Hitler's Forces – Panzers at War*. London: Ian Allan Publishing, 1998.

Bartov, Omer. *Hitler's Army: Soldiers, Nazis and War in the Third Reich*. Oxford: Oxford University Press, 1992.

Bauer, Lt Col E. *The History of the Second World War*, London: Orbis, 1979.

Bethell, Nigel. *The War Hitler Won: The Fall of Poland 1939*. New York: Holt, Rinehart & Winston, 1972.

Bloch, Marc. *Strange Defeat*. New York: Norton Library, 1968.

Bond, Brian. *Britain, France, and Belgium, 1939–40*. New York: Brassey's, 1990.

Boog, Horst *et al*. (eds.). *Germany and the Second World War, Vol. IV: The Attack on the Soviet Union*. Oxford: Clarendon, 1998.

Brett-Smith, Richard. *Hitler's Generals*. London: Osprey, 1976.

Carell, Paul. *Hitler Moves East, 1941–1943*. Boston: Little, Brown & Co., 1964.

Carell, Paul. *Scorched Earth*. New York: Ballantine, 1971.

Chamberlain, Peter, and Doyle, Hilary. *Encyclopedia of German Tanks of World War Two*. London: Arms & Armour, 1999.

Clark, Alan. *Barbarrossa*. New York: William Morrow, 1965.

Cooper, Matthew, *The German Army, 1933–1945: Its Political and Military Failure*. New York: Random House, 1978.

Cooper, Matthew, and Lucas, James. *Panzer: The Armoured Force of the Third Reich*. New York: St Martin's Press, 1976.

Cooper, Matthew, and Lucas, James. *Panzer*. London: Macdonald, 1976.

Cooper, Matthew, and Lucas, James. *Panzergrenadier*. London: Macdonald and Jane's, 1977.

Cooper, Matthew, and Lucas, James. *Hitler's Elite*, London: Grafton, 1990.

Corum, James S. *The Roots of Blitzkrieg: Hans von Seeckt and German Military Reform*. Lawrence, KS: Kansas University Press, 1992.

Cross, Robin. *Citadel: The Battle of Kursk*, London: Michael O'Mara, 1993.

Davies, W.J.K. *German Army Handbook 1939–1945*. London: Military Book Society, 1973.

Davis, Brian L. *German Ground Forces: Poland and France, 1939–40*. London: Almark, 1976.

Davis, Norman. *Rising 1944*. London: MacMillan, 2004.

Deighton, Len. *Blitzkrieg: From the Rise of Hitler to the Fall of Dunkirk*. London: BCA, 1979.

Deist, Wilhelm *et al*. (eds.). *Germany and the Second World War, Vol. 1: The Build-up of German Aggression*. Oxford: Clarendon, 1998.

Department of the Army CMH Pub 104-18. *The German Campaigns in the Balkans (Spring 1941)*. November 1953.

Dinardo, R.L. *Germany's Panzer Arm: (Contributions in Military Studies)*. Westport, Connecticut: Greenwood Publishing Group, 1997.

Dinardo, R.L. "German Armour Doctrine: Correcting the Myths." *War in History 3, No. 4* (November 1996): pp.384–98.

Downing, David. *The Devil's Virtuosos*. London: New English Library, 1976.

Doyle, Hilary. *Panther Variants 1942–1945*. Oxford: Osprey, 2001.

Doyle, Hilary. *Panzerkampfwagen IV Ausf. G, H and J 1942–45*. Oxford: Osprey Publishing, 2001.

Dunnigan, James. *The Russian Front*. London: Arms and Armour, 1978.

Dupuy, Trevor N. *A Genius for War: The German Army & General Staff, 1807–1945*. London: Macdonald and Jane's, 1977.

Edwards, Roger. *Panzer: A Revolution in Warfare, 1939–45*. London: Arms & Armour, 1989.

Bibliography

Ellis, Chris, and Chamberlian, Peter. *The 88mm*. London: Parkgate Books, 1998.

Erickson, John. *The Road to Stalingrad*. New York: Harper & Row, 1976.

Erickson, John. *The Road to Berlin*. London: Weidenfeld & Nicolson, 1983.

Forty, George. *German Tanks of World War Two*. London: Blandford Press, 1987.

Forty, George. *The Armies of Rommel*. London: Arms & Armour, 1997.

Fugate, Bryan I. *Operation Barbarossa: Strategy and Tactics on the Eastern Front, 1941*. Novato, CA: Presidio, 1984.

Glantz, David M. *Zhukov's Greatest Defeat: The Red Army's Epic Disaster in Operation Mars, 1942*. Lawrence, KS: University of Kansas Press, 1999.

Glantz, David M. *Kharkov 1942*. Shepperton: Ian Allan, 1998.

Glantz, David M. *Barbarossa*. Stroud: Tempus, 2001.

Glantz, David M. *The Initial Period of War on Eastern Front*. London: Frank Cass, 1993.

Glantz, David M. *The Siege of Leningrad 1941–1944*. London: Brown Partworks, 2001.

Glantz, David M. *From the Don to the Dnieper*, Frank Cass, London, 1991.

Glantz, David M., and House, Jonathan. *When Titans Clashed: How the Red Army Stopped Hitler*. Lawrence, KS: University of Kansas Press, 1995.

Glantz, David M., and House, Jonathan. *The Battle of Kursk*. London: Ian Allan Publishing, 1999.

Guderian, Heinz (transl. Christopher Duffy). *Achtung-Panzer!* London: Arms & Armour, 1992.

Guderian, Heinz. *Panzer Leader*. London: Joseph, 1952.

Gunter, Georg. *Last Laurels*. Solihul: Helion & Company, 2002.

Gunzberg, Jeffery A. *Divided and Conquered: The French High Command and the Defeat in the West, 1940*. Westport, CT: Greenwood, 1979.

Haupt, Werner. *Assault on Moscow 1941*. Atglen, PA: Schiffer, 1996.

Haupt, Werner. *Army Group Center*. Atglen, PA:, Schiffer, 1998.

Hitler, Adolf. *Hitler's Table Talk*, London: Weidenfeld & Nicolson, 1953.

Hogg, Ian V. *German Artillery of World War Two*. London: Greenhill Books, 1997.

Jars, Robert. *La Campagne de Pologne (Septembre 1939)*. Paris: Payot, 1949.

Jentz, Thomas L. *Panzertruppen: The Complete Guide to the Creation and Combat Employment of Germany's Tank Force 1937–1942*. Atglen, PA: Schiffer, 1996.

Jentz, Thomas L. *Panzertruppen: The Complete Guide to the Creation and Combat Employment of Germany's Tank Force 1943–1945*. Atglen, PA: Schiffer, 2000.

Jentz, Thomas L. *Germany's Tiger Tanks: Tiger I & II: Combat Tactics*. Atglen, PA: Schiffer, 1997.

Jentz, Thomas, Doyle, Hilary, and Sarson, Peter. *Tiger I*, London: Osprey, 1993.

Keegan, John. *Waffen SS: the asphalt soldiers*. London: McDonald & Co, 1970.

Kennedy, Robert M. *The German Campaign in Poland 1939*. Washington, D.C.: Office of the Chief of Military History, 1956.

Kleine, Egon, and Kuhn, Volkmar. *Tiger*. Stuttgart: Motorbuch Verlag, 1990.

Knappe, Siegfried. *Soldat: Reflections of a German Soldier, 1936–1949*. New York: Dell Publishing Co., 1993.

Kurowski, Franz (transl. Joseph G. Walsh). *Deadlock Before Moscow: Army Group Center, 1942–43*. Atglen, PA: Schiffer, 1992.

Lehman, Rudolf. *The Leibstandarte*. Manitoba: JJ Fedorowicz, 1990.

Lucas, James. *Grossdeutschland*. London: MacDonald and Jane's, 1978.

Lucas, James. *Kommando: German Special Forces of World War Two*. London: Arms and Armour, 1985.

Lucas, James. *German Army Handbook 1939–1945*. Stroud: Sutton Publishing Limited, 1998.

Lucas, James. *War on the Eastern Front: The German Soldier in Russia 1941–45*. London: Greenhill Books, 1979.

Luck, Colonel Hans von. *Panzer Commander: The Memoirs of Hans von Luck*. Westport, CT: Praeger, 1989.

Lumsden, Robin. *Collectors Guide to the Allgemeine-SS*. Hersham: Ian Allan, 1992.

MacDonald, Charles. *The Battle of the Bulge*. London: Weidenfeld & Nicolson, 1984.

Macksey, Major K.J. *Panzer Division: The mailed fist*. New York: Ballantine Books, 1968.

Manstein, Erich von. *Lost Victories*. Chicago: H. Regency Co., 1958.

Mellenthin, F.W. von. *Panzer Battles 1939–45: A Study in the Employment of Armour*. London: Cassell, 1955.

Mitcham Jr., Samuel W. *The Panzer Legions: A Guide to the German Army Tank Divisions of World War II and Their Commanders*. Westport, CT: Greenwood Press, 2001.

Mitchell, Samuel. *Hitler's Legions*. London: Leo Cooper, 1985.

Mosley, Leonard. *The Reich Marshal*. London: Weidenfeld & Nicolson, 1974.

Müller, Rolf-Dieter, and Ueberschär, Gerd R. *Hitler's War in the East 1941–45: A Critical Assessment*. Oxford: Berghahn, 1997.

Müller, Rolf-Dieter, and Volkmann, Hans-Erich. *Die Wehrmacht: Mythos und Realität*. München: Oldenbourg, 1999.

Murray, Williamsom. *The Luftwaffe, 1933–1945*. Royston: Eagle Editions, 2000.

Nafziger, George F. *The German Order of Battle: Panzers and Artillery in World War II*. London: Greenhill Books, 1999.

Nafziger, George F. *The German Order of Battle: Infantry in World War II*. London: Greenhill Books, 2000.

Nafziger, George F. *The German Order of Battle: Waffen-SS and other units in World War II*. Pennsylvania: Combined Publishing, 2001.

Newton, Steven H. *German Battle Tactics on the Russian Front 1941–45*. Atglen, PA: Schiffer, 1994.

Nipe, George. *Decision in the Ukraine*. Manitoba: JJ Fedorowicz, 1996.

O'Neill, Robert J. *The German Army and the Nazi Party 1933–39*. London: Cassell, 1966.

Pallud, John Paul. *France 1940: Blitzkrieg in Action*. London: Battle of Britain, 1991.

Pallud, Jean Paul. *Battle of the Bulge: Then and Now*. London: After the Battle, 1984.

Perret, Bryan. *Panzerkampfwagen III*. Oxford: Osprey Publishing, 2001.

Pierik, Perry. *Hungary 1944–1945*. The Netherlands: Aspekt b.v., 1996.

Pimlott, John. *The Historical Atlas of World War II*. New York: Henry Holt and Company, 1995.

Reynolds, Michael. *Steel Inferno*. Staplehurst: Spellmount, 1997.

Reynolds, Michael. *Men of Steel*. Staplehurst: Spellmount, 1999.

Reynolds, Michael. *Sons of the Reich: The History of II SS Panzer Corps*. Staplehurst: Spellmount, 2002.

Rhodes, Richard. *Masters of Death*. Oxford: Perseus Press, 2002.

Ripley, Tim. *Steel Storm*. Stroud: Sutton, 2000.

Ripley, Tim. *Steel Rain*, Brown Partworks, London, 2001

Ripley, Tim. *Elite Units of the Third Reich*. London: The Brown Reference Group, 2002.

Ripley, Tim. *The Wehrmacht*. London: Fitzroy Dearborn, 2003.

Ripley, Tim. *Patton Unleashed*. London: The Brown Reference Group, 2003.

Restayn, Jean. *Tiger 1 on Eastern Front*. Paris: Histoire and Collections, 2001.

Ryan, Cornelius. *A Bridge Too Far*. London: Hamish Hamiliton, 1974.

Ryan, Cornelius. *The Last Battle*. London: William Collins, 1966.

Sadarananda, Dana. *Beyond Stalingrad*. New York: Praeger, 1990.

Salisbury, Harrison. *The 900 Days: The Siege of Leningrad*. New York: Da Capo Press, 1985.

Seaton, Albert. *The Russo-German War, 1941–45*. New York: Praeger, 1970.

Seaton, Albert. *The German Army, 1933–1945*. London: Weidenfeld & Nicolson, 1982.

Senger und Etterlin, General Frido von. *Neither Fear Nor Hope*. London: Greenhill Books, 1989.

Snyder, Louis L. *Encyclopedia of the Third Reich*. Ware: Wordsworth Editions, 1976.

Soviet General Staff. *The Battle for Kursk 1943* (eds. David Glantz and Harold Orenstein). London: Frank Cass, 1999.

Spaeter, Helmuth. *Die Einsätze der Panzergrenadier-division Grossdeutschland*. Friedberg: Podzun-Pallas-Verlag, 1986.

Stadler, Silvester. *Die Offensive gegen Kursk 1943*. Osnabrück: Munin Verlag, 1980.

Stein, George. *Hitler's Elite Guard at War, 1939–1945*. Ithaca, NY: Cornell University Press, 1984.

Stolfi, R.H.S. *Hitler's Panzers East: World War II Reinterpreted*. Norman: University of Oklahoma Press, 1993.

Stroop, Juergen. *The Stroop Report*. London: Secker & Warburg, 1979.

Sydnor, Charles. *Soldiers of Destruction: The SS Death's Head Division, 1933–1945*. Princeton, NJ: Princeton University Press, 1977.

le Tisser, Tony. *Berlin: Then and Now*, London: After the Battle, 1992.

le Tisser, Tony. *The Battle of Berlin*. London: Jonathan Cape, 1988.

Ungvary, Krisztian. *Battle for Budapest*. London: I.B.Tauris, 2003.

Whiting, Charles. *Hunters from the Sky*. London: Purnell, 1975.

Wilmot, Chester. *Struggle for Europe*. London: Collins, 1952.

Young, Desmond. *Rommel: The Desert Fox*. New York: Harper & Row, 1950.

Ziemke, Earl F. *The German Northern Theater of Operations, 1940–1945*. Washington, D.C.: GPO, 1959; CMH, 1989.

Ziemke, Earl F. *Moscow to Stalingrad*. Washington, D.C, GPO, 1987.

Ziemke, Earl F. *Stalingrad to Berlin*. Washington, D.C., US Government Printing Office, 1968.

Index

Picture credits

AKG Images: 84, 85, 86.
History in the Making: 30, 42, 43, 44t, 47, 50, 52t, 52b, 56, 60, 61, 66, 70, 71, 72, 74, 76, 77t, 77b, 82, 92, 95, 96, 101, 104, 105, 106t, 106b, 107, 111t, 111b, 113t, 113b, 114, 115t, 115b, 116, 120, 121, 124c, 124b, 127, 129, 132, 134, 138, 139t, 139b, 142, 144, 146, 151, 152, 154, 160, 162, 164, 168, 170, 173, 175c, 175t, 176, 179, 180, 181, 184, 189, 191, 192, 208, 210t, 210b, 212, 215, 216, 220, 222b, 224b, 228l, 228r, 229, 233, 238, 240t, 240b, 242, 246, 250, 253, 254, 256, 257t, 257b, 273, 282, 289t, 295, 296, 305, 307, 308, 310, 313, 316t, 316b, 317, 318, 321, 327.
Robert Hunt Library: 12, 15, 16, 18t, 18b, 19, 21, 24, 25b, 26, 28, 34, 38, 44b, 62, 68, 88, 89, 90, 102, 122, 130, 131, 140t, 140b, 158, 188, 196, 198t, 198b, 199, 202, 203, 205, 206, 219, 224t, 230, 234, 236, 244, 258, 260t, 260c, 263, 265, 266, 268, 270, 277t, 277b, 286, 289b, 298, 300, 302, 303, 304, 324, 326, 328, 329t, 329b, 330, 331, 332.
TRH Pictures: 14, 22, 23, 25t, 27, 55, 59, 80,112, 137, 222t, 225, 281, 290, 322.